LIBRARY OF HEBREW BIBLE/
OLD TESTAMENT STUDIES

558

Formerly Journal for the Study of the Old Testament Supplement Series

PERSEPOLIS AND JERUSALEM

Iranian Influence
on the Apocalyptic Hermeneutic

Jason M. Silverman

t&t clark

Published by T & T Clark International
A Continuum imprint
80 Maiden Lane, New York, NY 10038
The Tower Building, 11 York Road, London SE1 7NX

www.continuumbooks.com

Visit the T & T Clark blog at www.tandtclarkblog.com

Library of Congress Cataloging-in-Publication Data
Silverman, Jason M.
  Persepolis and Jerusalem : Iranian influence on the apocalyptic hermeneutic / by Jason M. Silverman.
     p. cm. -- (The library of Hebrew Bible/Old Testament studies ; 558)
  Revision of the author's thesis (doctoral)--Trinity College Dublin, 2010.
  Includes bibliographical references (p.   ) and index.
  ISBN-13: 978-0-567-20551-3 (hardcover : alk. paper)
  ISBN-10: 0-567-20551-7 (hardcover : alk. paper) 1. Apocalyptic literature--History and criticism. 2. Hermeneutics. 3. Achaemenid dynasty, 559-330 B.C. 4. Iran--Civilization--To 640. 5. Bible. O.T. Ezekiel--Criticism, interpretation, etc. 6. Bible. O.T. Daniel--Criticism, interpretation, etc. 7. Ethiopic book of Enoch--Criticism, interpretation, etc. I. Title.

  BS1705.S55 2012
  221'.046--dc23

                                    2011038967

ISBN: HB: 978-0567-20551-3

Typeset by Forthcoming Publications Ltd (www.forthpub.com)
Printed and bound in the United States

Some say the world will end in fire,
Some say in ice.
From what I've tasted of desire
I hold with those who favor fire.
But if it had to perish twice,
I think I know enough of hate
To know that for destruction ice
Is also great
And would suffice.

–Robert Frost

VIII

Whether at Nishapur or Babylon,
Whether the Cup with sweet or bitter run,
The Wine of Life keeps oozing drop by drop,
The Leaves of Life keep falling one by one.

XVIII

They say the Lion and the Lizard keep
The courts where Jamshyd gloried and drank deep:
And Bahram, that great Hunter—the Wild Ass
Stamps o'er his Head, but cannot break his Sleep.

XXXI

Up from Earth's Center through the Seventh Gate
I rose, and on the Throne of Saturn sate,
And many a Knot unravel'd by the Road;
But not the Master-knot of Human Fate.

–Omar Kayyam
(From *Rubaiyat*, trans. and adapted Fitzgerald)

CONTENTS

LIST OF FIGURES

PREFACE

The writings known as apocalypses sit at the vortex of East and West, constituting a significant source of scholarly controversies in the study of emerging Judaism and Christianity. These works—which largely fall in the period between the books which would eventually make up the collections of the Hebrew Bible and the New Testament—are powerful and often obscure, dealing with many of the perennial issues which occupy the religious mind: the problems of suffering and of evil, the afterlife, and the appropriate source of religious authority. As such, they are extremely important not only in the history of Second Temple Judaism (ca. 597 B.C.E.–70 C.E.), but for the history of religions as well. The issues which come into play in the study of the apocalypses are questions which underlie many areas in the humanities: How do humans receive, understand, reformulate, and transmit traditions?

A major desideratum in the study of the Jewish apocalypses is whether or not they evince Iranian influence, from either of the two relevant Iranian empires with which the Judaeans came into contact—the Achaemenid Empire (ca. 550 B.C.E.–330 B.C.E.) or the Parthian Empire (ca. 250 B.C.E.–224 C.E.). Although some scholars considered the potential of Iranian influence as early as the eighteenth century, an adequate, comprehensive study of the question remains unwritten. A plethora of studies on the problem were conducted around the turn of the twentieth century, yet their excesses and racial biases discredited the topic. Recent advances in the fields of Biblical Studies and Iranian studies, however, mean the time is ripe for renewed, in-depth research of the question.

Acknowledgments

This monograph is a condensed version of my doctoral dissertation, submitted in February 2010 at Trinity College Dublin. No dissertation or book is written alone, and this work has benefited from the insight and encouragement of many scholars.

My early efforts at grappling with the new field of Iranian studies were aided by the generous assistance, bibliographic information, and comments of Professor Almut Hintze (SOAS) and Dr. Bryan Rennie (Westminster College). The former also kindly saved me from several errors in the final version. This study would not have even begun or continued very long without the tireless efforts to procure obscure materials by the Interlibrary Loan Officer at Trinity, Ms. Jane Moriarty.

I am grateful to several scholars who critiqued drafts of various sections of the dissertation. The textual analyses benefited from the insightful observations of Professor A. D. H. Mayes, Professor John J. Collins, and Dr. Benjamin Wold. Professor Susan Niditch cast her careful eye over the Orality chapter. Several sections have also been improved through the suggestions and critiques of conference audiences.

Special thanks go to my long-suffering advisor, Dr. Anne Fitzpatrick-McKinley, who persevered as my research took an unexpected Iranian turn. She constantly reminded me to rein my wanderings back towards Biblical Studies and to clarify my writing.

Far more than can be quantified, this research owes a debt to the constant discussions, companionship, and encouragement offered by my biblical compatriots in Dublin, Father Murray Watson, Lidia D. Matassa, Amy Daughton, Audrey Barnett, Jason Michael Reid McCann, Claire Carroll, Máire Byrne, and Killian McAleese. They endured patiently more rantings than they probably ever cared to hear during our periodic coffees in "Paris" and helped organize the conferences where material from this dissertation was first publicly aired. I am particularly in the debt of Murray, Máire, and Killian, who acquired sources unavailable at Trinity and proof-read various drafts for me. Beyond academic debts, I am grateful for the continual encouragement received by my friends and family over the course of my studies.

Two years of my research were made possible by a scholarship from the Mediterranean and Near Eastern Studies Seminar (MNES), TCD. Most helpfully, I was able to attend several annual and international Society of Biblical Literature conferences due to the support offered through the conference travel grants of the Trinity Trust.

Earlier versions of two sections included in this study have previously appeared in print. A modified form of the section entitled "Types of Influence and Transmission" in the Prolegomena is published as "On Cultural and Religious Influence."[1] An older version of the first section of Chapter 2, "The Achaemenid Context" appears as "Iranian–Judaean Interaction in the Achaemenid Period."[2]

The transition from dissertation to monograph was graciously aided by the critiques of Professor Almut Hintze, Professor A. D. H. Mayes, and Dr. Sarah Pearce. Dr. Tony McNamara brought helpful sheers to the bulky dissertation. The publication process was facilitated by the generous help of Dr. Andrew Mein, co-editor of the LHBOTS series. Any remaining errors are my own.

English translations of the Bible follow the NRSV, except where otherwise stated.

1. In Jason M. Silverman, ed., *A Land Like Your Own: Traditions of Israel and Their Reception* (Eugene, Ore.: Pickwick, 2010).

2. In Lidia D. Matassa and Jason M. Silverman, eds., *Text, Theology, and Trowel: Recent Research into the Hebrew Bible* (Eugene, Ore.: Pickwick, 2011).

ABBREVIATIONS

AB	Anchor Bible
ABD	*Anchor Bible Dictionary*. Edited by D. N. Freedman. 6 vols. New York, 1992
AFS	*Asian Folklore Studies*
AJA	*American Journal of Archaeology*
AJP	American Journal of Philology
AJSL	*American Journal of Semitic Languages and Literature*
AJT	*American Journal of Theology*
ANET	*Ancient Near Eastern Texts Relating to the Old Testament*. Edited by James B. Pritchard. 3d ed. Princeton, 1969
ANF	Ante-Nicene Fathers
BA	*Biblical Archaeologist*
BASOR	*Bulletin of the American Schools of Oriental Research*
BDB	Brown, Francis, S. R. Driver, and Charles A. Briggs. *A Hebrew and English Lexicon of the Old Testament*. Based on the Lexicon of William Gesenius as Translated by Edward Robinson. Oxford: Clarendon, 1966
BHS	*Biblia Hebraica Stuttgartensia*
BJRL	*Bulletin of the John Rylands Library*
BJS	Brown Judaic Studies
Boyce, *HZ I*	Boyce, Mary. *A History of Zoroastrianism: The Early Period*. Vol. I. HO VIII.1.2.2A.1. Leiden: Brill, 1975
Boyce, *HZ II*	Boyce, Mary. *A History of Zoroastrianism: Under the Achaemenians*. Vol. II. HO VIII.1.2.2A.2. Leiden: Brill, 1982
Boyce and Grenet, *HZ III*	Boyce, Mary, and Frantz Grenet. *A History of Zoroastrianism: Zoroastrianism Under Macedonian and Roman Rule*. Vol. III. HO VIII.1.2.2.3. Leiden: Brill, 1991
BRLJ	Brill Reference Library of Judaism
BSOAS	*Bulletin of the School of Oriental and African Studies*
CBQ	*Catholic Biblical Quarterly*

CBR	*Currents in Biblical Research*
CH	*Church History*
CHI	*Cambridge History of Iran*, vol. 3. Edited by E. Yarshater. 2 vols. Cambridge: Cambridge University Press, 1983.
CHJ I	*Cambridge History of Judaism*. Vol. I, *Introduction: The Persian Period*. Edited by W. D. Davies and L. Finkelstein. Cambridge, 2000
COS	*The Context of Scripture*. Edited by William W. Hallo. 3 vols. Leiden, 1997, 2000, 2002
CSHJ	Chicago Studies in the History of Judaism
DJD	Discoveries in the Judaean Desert
DSD	*Dead Sea Discoveries*
DSSSE	*The Dead Sea Scrolls Study Edition.* Edited by F. García Martínez and E. J. C. Tigchelaar. 2 vols. Leiden, 1998
EncIr	*Encyclopaedia Iranica*. Edited by Ehsan Yarshater. London, 1985–. Online: www.iranica.com
HAL	Koehler, Ludwig, and Walter Baumgartner. *The Hebrew and Aramaic Lexicon of the Old Testament.* Translated by M. E. J. Richardson. Study ed. 2 vols. Leiden: Brill, 2001
HO	Handbuch der Orientalistik
HR	*History of Religions*
HTR	*Harvard Theological Review*
HUCA	*Hebrew Union College Annual*
IEJ	*Israel Exploration Journal*
IOS	*Israel Oriental Studies*
JA	*Journal Asiatique*
JAAR	*Journal of the American Academy of Religion*
JAOS	*Journal of the American Oriental Society*
JBL	*Journal of Biblical Literature*
JBR	*Journal of Bible and Religion*
JCama	*Journal of the K. R. Cama Oriental Institute*
JEA	*Journal of Egyptian Archaeology*
JETS	*Journal of the Evangelical Theological Society*
JHS	*Journal of Hellenic Studies*
JIES	*Journal of Indo-European Studies*
JJS	*Journal of Jewish Studies*
JNES	*Journal of Near Eastern Studies*
JQR	*Jewish Quarterly Review*
JR	*Journal of Religion*
JRAS	*Journal of the Royal Asiatic Society*
JRS	*Journal of Roman Studies*
JSJ	*Journal for the Study of Judaism in the Persian, Hellenistic, and Roman Periods*

JSOT	*Journal for the Study of the Old Testament*
JSS	*Journal of Semitic Studies*
JTS	*Journal of Theological Studies*
LCL	Loeb Classical Library
LSJ	Liddell, Henry George, and Robert Scott. *A Greek–English Lexicon*. Edited by Sir Henry Stuart Jones and Roderick McKenzie. 9th ed. Oxford, 1996
NINO	Nederlands Institute voor het Nabije Oosten
NTS	*New Testament Studies*
OP	Old Persian
OTP	*The Old Testament Pseudepigrapha*. Edited by James H. Charlesworth. 2 vols. New York, 1983, 1985
Pahlavi Texts I	*The Bundahis, Bahman Yast, and Shāyast Lā-Shāyast*. Translated by E. W. West. *Pahlavi Texts, Part I: Sacred Books of the East*. Edited by F. Max Müller. Vol. 5. Delhi, 1987. First published 1880 by Oxford University Press
Pahlavi Texts II	*The Dādistān-ī Dīnik and the Epistles of Mānūskīhar*. Translated by E. W. West. *Pahlavi Texts, Part II*. Edited by F. Max Müller. SBE 18. Delhi, 1987. First published 1882 by Oxford University Press
Pahlavi Texts III	*Dīnā-ī Maīnög-ī Khirad Sikand-Gümānīk Vigār Sad Dar*. Translated by E. W. West. *Pahlavi Texts, Part III*. Edited by F. Max Müller. SBE 24. Delhi, 1987. First published 1885 by Oxford University Press
Pahlavi Texts IV	*Contents of the Nasks*. Translated by E. W. West. *Pahlavi Texts, Part IV*. Edited by F. Max Müller. SBE 37. Delhi, 1988. First published 1892 by Oxford University Press
Pahlavi Texts V	*Marvels of Zoroastrianism*. Translated by E. W. West. *Pahlavi Texts, Part V*. Edited by F. Max Müller. SBE 47. Delhi, 1987. First Published 1897 by Oxford University Press
PFT	Hallock, Richard T. *Persepolis Fortification Tablets*. Chicago, 1969
RB	*Revue biblique*
RRelRes	*Review of Religious Research*
SBAW	*Sitzungsberichte der kgl.bayerischen Akademie der Wissenschaften*
SBE	Sacred Books of the East
ST	*Studia Theologica*
TAPA	*Transactions of the American Philological Association*
TS	*Theological Studies*

TynBul	*Tyndale Bulletin*
VT	*Vetus Testamentum*
ZAW	*Zeitschrift für die alttestamentliche Wissenschaft*
Zend-Avesta I	*The Vendidad*. Translated by James Darmesteter. The Zend-Avesta, Part I. Edited by F. Max Müller. SBE 4. Delhi, 1992. First published 1895 by Clarendon.
Zend-Avesta II	*The Sīrōzahs, Yasts, and Nyāyis*. Translated by James Darmesteter. The Zend-Avesta, Part II. Edited by F. Max Müller. SBE 23. Delhi, 1988. First published 1882 by Oxford University Press
Zend-Avesta III	*The Yasna, Visparad, Āfrīnagān, Gāhs, and Miscellaneous Fragments*. Translated by Lawrence H. Mills. The Zend-Avesta, Part III. Edited by F. Max Müller. SBE 31. Delhi, 1988. First published 1887 by Oxford University Press

PROLEGOMENA

Introit

Although the concept of Iranian influence on Judaism has been periodically mooted by scholars for centuries, a thorough and adequate study has yet to appear. The present study redresses this by focusing on the formation of the apocalypses and related phenomena in Second Temple Judaism.[1] Towards this end it is necessary to situate the discussion within two broad fields: the history of the question of Persian influence on Judaism and of the study of apocalyptic.

Before proceeding, however, a brief explanation for the focus of this study largely upon apocalyptic rather than on Second Temple Judaism more broadly is merited. The first reason is disciplinary: the majority of research on Iranian influence has fallen on the apocalypses, therefore they represent a convenient place to begin engagement with scholarship. The working hypothesis of this study provides the second: that the predominance of Iranian influence is to be found within apocalyptic. A focus on apocalyptic does not exclude or minimize potential influence on other forms of Judaism. The apocalypses are related to Second Temple Judaism as a whole via a dialectical, hermeneutical relationship (see Chapter 5).

This study argues that one of the catalysts towards the development of the apocalypse and its cognate worldviews in Second Temple Judaism was the adoption of a new "apocalyptic hermeneutic" by some Judaeans. This new "apocalyptic hermeneutic" was one which incorporated ideas and methods which find their best explanation as inspired by an Iranian milieu. The development of this new hermeneutic was undertaken by scribes and thus heavily influenced by the increasing importance of written over oral modes of discourse. One of the reasons this hermeneutic has eluded scholarship is due to its "evanescent" nature as a new, literate *interpretation* of recently written texts, as opposed to an entirely

---

1. This study uses "Judaeans," "Jews," and "Yahwists" as convenient synonyms. The possibility of "Yahwists" descended from Israelites or converts is not excluded by this usage. For related issues, see Mason, "Jews, Judaeans, Judaizing, Judaism," 247–512.

new theological or philosophical system. It requires more than merely the identification of textual allusions in the manner of traditional text-critical methods. It is this kind of hermeneutic and the ideas it usually implies that links the phenomena of the apocalypse and the millenarian movements.

Brief History of Iranian Influence on Judaism

Scholars have long contemplated the question of Zoroastrian influence on Judaism and Christianity.[2] Although there was a period of intense interest in the subject during the nineteenth and early twentieth centuries, comparatively little research into the details of the issue has taken place in the past century. Once scholars were quite enamored of the idea, yet "parallelomania"[3] took the idea to extremes and helped to discredit it.[4] Additionally, faulty oral theories as advocated by Gunkel and others prejudiced biblical scholars against the Iranian material, some of which comes from late Zoroastrian texts. Beyond the textual question, however, a focus on Hellenistic history has disguised the relevance of the Achaemenid and Parthian eras.

Two scholars, Moulton and Mills, illustrate the unfruitful methods which have dominated previous studies. Moulton already suggested that where influence on Judaism can be found, it can be found in the apocalypses, but he primarily based this claim on ideas of the inferiority of apocalyptic religion and the superiority of the biblical tradition.[5] Far from an acceptable reason for positing or rejecting influence, this type of reasoning has played a significant role in discussions in the past. Mills, the opponent of Moulton,[6] saw sweeping parallels between Zoroastrianism and both Judaism and Christianity, to the point of identifying the Platonic and Philonic *Logos* with the *Aməša Spəntas* of the Avesta.[7] His studies are tendentious and totalizing, and therefore of little contemporary

---

2. Dresden, "Survey of the History of Iranian Studies," 171–73; Boyce, *HZ I*, ix–xii; Asmussen, "Die Verkündigung Zarathustras," 22–24; Duchesne-Guillemin, *The Western Response to Zoroaster*, 86–87.

3. Term from Sandmel, "Parallelomania," 1–13.

4. E.g. Barr, "The Question of Religious Influence," 204–8; Neusner, "Jews and Judaism under Iranian Rule," part I.

5. Moulton, "Zoroaster and Israel I," 401–8; idem, "Zoroaster and Israel—A Reply," 16–18; idem, "Zoroaster and Israel II," 308–15; idem, "Zoroaster and Israel III," 490–501; idem, "Zoroastrian Influences on Judaism," 352–58; idem, *Early Zoroastrianism*.

6. Mills, "Mr. Moulton's Zoroaster and Israel," 508–14.

7. Mills, *Zarathuštra, Philo, the Achaemenids, and Israel*, 12–17.

use other than as examples of how not to proceed. Together Moulton and Mills illustrate two common faults in this early discussion: the ideologically charged nature of influence and a sweeping "parallelomania."

Most investigations into Persian influence can be labeled along three lines: ideological, enumeration of parallels, or discrete, brief studies. A concise discussion of these will demonstrate the need for a new study.

Ideological
One of the more extensive investigations into the potential of Iranian influence is Sheftelowitz's 1920 study. Scheftelowitz concludes that the similarities between the two traditions are mostly parallel developments, with only relatively "cosmetic" borrowings such as eschatology.[8] The strength of the Judaic religion was so strong that it inoculated Judaism from the Achaemenid's influence until the Greco-Roman period.[9] Despite Judaism's apparent resilience towards influence, however, Sheftelowitz is willing to see Babylon wield its power upon both traditions.[10] This is a peculiarly selective "resilience" on the part of Judaism.

Maynard proceeded along contrary lines, arguing that religions can only be influenced through "externals" and not ideas.[11] On this basis he lists practices which Judaism and Zoroastrianism do not hold in common. He then further claims that since only (superficial) similarities are to be found in apocalyptic literature, which "remained very much on the margin of the main current of Jewish thought," the parallels are thus unimportant.[12] Despite the logical and methodological problems inherent in Maynard's approach, his main reservation is due to the assumption that the Israelites held religious genius, and therefore had no need to borrow ideas. This kind of argument fails to advance research in any meaningful direction.

It is apparent that a non-value-laden understanding of influence is necessary to better undergird the investigation of intercultural, interreligious influence.

Enumeration of Parallels
In the final chapter of his *Western Response to Zoroaster*, Duchesne-Guillemin appraises the thesis of Persian influence in light of the Dead Sea Scrolls and Zurvanism. His treatment dismisses a few general parallels

---

8. Scheftelowitz, *Die altpersiche Religion und das Judentum*, 228–29.
9. Ibid., 4, 6.
10. Ibid., 153, 224–25.
11. Maynard, "Judaism and Mazdayasna," 163–64.
12. Ibid., 168.

(Philo's *Logos*, the messiah) and lists a few he favors (two spirits in the *Manual of Discipline*). Similarly, in his respective study,[13] Carter attributes the appearance in Judaism of strict monotheism, a developed angelology, personal eschatology, and resurrection to a catalyzing effect of Zoroastrianism, even positing an absorption of Persian proselytes.[14] While Carter's investigation laudably distinguishes between the whole-sale importation of new ideas and the catalyzing potential of ideas, his short book is terse and uncritical in its use and appraisal of both the Jewish and Zoroastrian literatures. With the exception of the appearance of the demon Asmodeus in Tobit, he prefers to discuss general similari-ties or parallels over investigating problematic details in the Jewish texts which find better explanation in Iranian sources. In 1966 Winston attempted to establish the importance of Iranian ideas for Qumran.[15] Winston merely offers a variety of interesting parallels, since, due to the limited length of the article, he is unable to tease out further evidence or structural considerations.

Cohn fares little better in detail. He forcibly argues for the influence of Zoroastrianism on Jewish and Christian apocalypticism.[16] After investi-gating the cosmological and historical beliefs of the ancient Near East peoples and the Vedic Indians, Cohn finds no eschatological beliefs which parallel those in the Jewish apocalypses.[17] However, he notes analogous eschatological beliefs developing in Iran under the name of Zoroaster. He gives an admirable summary of Zoroastrian beliefs (Chapter 4), and identifies it with the royal religion.[18] Without denying the role of Canaanite myths or Mesopotamian influences, Cohn sees the development of eschatology as due to influence during the Hellenistic period, perhaps partly due to the descendants of Iranian colonists in Mesopotamia and Anatolia.[19] However, only the last chapter of his book is devoted to exploring the parallels and details which the Jewish and Zoroastrians texts share. While his overall thesis is important for this study, he leaves much room for a more detailed study, to shore up his argument with specifics.[20]

13. Carter, *Zoroastrianism and Judaism*.
14. Ibid., 106.
15. Winston, "The Iranian Component," 187.
16. Cohn, *Cosmos, Chaos*; idem, "How Time Acquired a Consummation," 21–37.
17. Cohn, *Cosmos, Chaos*, Part I.
18. Ibid., 145.
19. Ibid., 220–21.
20. E.g. Dimant, "Review: Cosmos, Chaos, and the World to Come," 79–81; Choksy, "Review: Cosmos, Chaos, and the World to Come," 183; Collins, "Review: Cosmos, Chaos, and the World to Come," 347–48.

Boyce is also a strong advocate of the relevance of Iranian studies to the history of Judaism.[21] She traces influence well before the advent of the apocalypse in Second and Third Isaiah and the careers of Ezra and Nehemiah, as well as in the Priestly Code. Her individual suggestions are thought-provoking and deserve deeper investigation; however, since she frequently presents general parallel situations, her account could easily be accused of "parallelomania." She does, however, attend to the possible historical contexts for interaction, primarily in the Parthian–Hellenistic struggles in Anatolia.[22]

While open to and positive about Zoroastrian influences on the apocalyptic literature, Russell never investigates them in any depth. For him, Persian angelology "facilitated" the monotheistic tendency to demote old gods to angels and influenced the development of demonology,[23] and he parallels chronological schemata to ones in both Babylon and the *Bundahišn*.[24] Russell's work clearly points to the role of native Jewish traditions in apocalypticism while allowing for foreign elements. However, since his discussion never deals with the problems inherent in the Iranian sources or with the possible loci of transmission, it is susceptible to a charge of overly abstract parallelism. His views still require a more thorough investigation into how and where, if any, Iranian influence may be found.

Sadly, Yamauchi's recent massive volume, *Persia and the Bible*, fares no better.[25]

Studies Pointing in a Better Direction
Widengren analyzes *1 Enoch*, in which he sees quite a variety of parallels with four major points: dualism, "apocalyptic pattern," eschatology and judgment, and visions.[26] In addition to *1 Enoch*, he has suggested Parthian influence on Early Christianity.[27] His discussion falls within the context of his earlier work on the Parthians, so his comments largely consist of highlighting the role of the Parthians in the West through various parallels. Since the parallels noted are rarely discussed in depth

21. Boyce, *HZ II*, 188–95; Boyce and Grenet, *HZ III*, 361–65.

22. Boyce, *Zoroastrianism: A Shadowy but Powerful Presence*, 11–15.

23. Russell, *Method and Message*, 235, 260–62.

24. Ibid., 228–29.

25. Cf. Skjærvø, "Review: *Persia and the Bible* by Edwin M. Yamauchi," 501–4; Russell, "Review of *Persia and the Bible* by Edwin M. Yamauchi," 260–61.

26. Widengren, "Iran and Israel in Parthian Times," 152.

27. E.g. Widengren, *Iranisch-semitische Kulturbegegnung in parthischer Zeit*, 36–37, 67–70; idem, "Stand und Aufgaben der iranischen Religionsgeschichte II," 108.

or with regards to their significance in the Jewish context, they have not received much acceptance among biblical scholars. Nevertheless, Widengren's attention to a specific historical context for influence represents a solid beginning for a renewed appraisal.

Shaked believes that the dilemma at hand is not whether there was Iranian influence on Judaism but its extent and importance.[28] In his *CHJ* article he approaches the issue from the perspective of a few "cognate parallels" which are more "organically" woven into the warp and woof of the Iranian system than in Israel, indicating a likelihood that they were adopted piecemeal from Iran as they aided the Judaic system rather than originating in the Jewish context.[29] He is not content with just a general approach and offers closer examinations of Esther[30] and the relationship of Aramaic to OP.[31] Shaked's in-depth knowledge of the Iranian material and sensitivity to the contexts of both traditions points forward to a better, more critical appraisal of the role and importance of Iranian ideas upon Jewish traditions, enabling a more nuanced answer to the common observation of "cognate parallels."

Call to Re-evaluation: Towards a Methodology

Barr is highly skeptical of attempts to appeal to Zoroastrian influence on Judaism,[32] critiquing what he sees as an overly tendentious approach to the problem which sees influence as *necessary* to explain the development of Judaism, and therefore seeks evidence of it.[33] However, as Hinnells notes, the real question is not whether it is *necessary* but whether it did in fact occur.[34] Barr concludes that the Jews were uninterested in Persian religion since the majority of loanwords pertain to administration rather than religion.[35] However, the force of this argument is undercut by two points: (1) his own observation that Nehemiah, who was most likely extremely familiar with Achaemenid religion, only uses the likely loanword פרדס, negating the evidential import of loanwords for potential contact;[36] (2) the limitation of the concept of influence to "religious" concerns *per se*. Be that as it may, Barr admirably demonstrates the methodological care which needs to be taken when evaluating

---

28. Shaked, "Iranian Influence on Judaism," 309.
29. Ibid., especially 321–23.
30. Shaked, "Two Judeo-Iranian Contributions," 292–303.
31. Shaked, "Between Iranian and Aramaic," 120–37.
32. Barr, "Question of Religious Influence," 201–35.
33. Ibid., 204.
34. Hinnells, "Zoroastrian Influence on the Judeo-Christian Tradition," 9.
35. Barr, "Question of Religious Influence," 212.
36. Ibid., 213.

the probability of Judaean interaction with Iranian traditions and avoids the temptation to equate general parallels with influence *per se*. Barr's concerns highlight the need for an examination of the bases posited for proposed parallels.

In a series of articles,[37] Hinnells calls for a more nuanced understanding of the concept of influence than sometimes employed, posits a historical setting in the Parthian era, and points to various details which he finds illustrative of the influence of Iranian ideas. Among the details, he notes that the development of demonology in Judaism and Christianity—often conceded to be a result of influence—has further implications in other theological areas, notably in the role of a savior figure.[38] Therefore, structural similarities make influence appear likely. He briefly notes details in various apocryphal and New Testament texts which he feels demonstrate knowledge of Iranian ideas, in particular positing influence in the books of Matthew and Revelation.[39] These methodological arguments and the parallels he briefly mentions deserve a more thorough investigation. Hinnells's discussions on the nature of inter-religious influence are taken up in a following section as an essential part of any methodology dealing with issues of religious influence.

The question of Iranian influence deserves a thorough re-analysis which takes into account the historical context as well as all the evidence available. Indeed, several scholars call for this.[40] Re-opening the question of Iranian influences neither implies an uncritical acceptance of late texts nor a rejection of the advances in sociological and literary understandings of the apocalypses and millenarian movements; rather, it adds a new piece into the overall puzzle of the emergence of the new phenomenon in the ancient Near East.

Iranian Influence. This study deliberately discusses "Iranian" influence rather than "Zoroastrianism." "Zoroastrianism" in its classic and most well-known form was formulated in the Sassanian Empire and was the basis of the official Empire-sponsored religion. This is primarily the religion that is found in the ninth-century texts. This tradition is the

---

37. Cf. Hinnells, "Zoroastrian Influence on the Judeo-Christian Tradition," 1–23 and idem, *Zoroastrian and Parsi Studies*, 27–92 ("Zoroastrian Saviour Imagery," 45–72; "Zoroastrian Influence on Judaism and Christianity," 73–92).

38. In particular, Hinnells, "Zoroastrian Saviour Imagery" (in Hinnells, *Zoroastrian and Parsi Studies*, 46, 61).

39. Hinnells, *Zoroastrian and Parsi Studies*, 81–84.

40. Collins, "Review: Cosmos, Chaos, and the World to Come," 348; Davies, "God of Cyrus, God of Israel," 224–25; Grabbe, "Introduction and Overview," 33–34.

culmination of nearly 2000 years of religious tradition and does not
exhaust the forms and ideas in Iran up to and including the Sassanian
period. Just as it is misleading to speak of Rabbinic Judaism as the sole
form of Judaism or to use it as a definitive model for Second Temple
Judaism, it is misleading to attempt to focus only on Sassanian Zoroastrianism. For this reason, this study expands the discourse to "Iranian
religion." "Iranian religion" includes a matrix of more or less organically
related religious ideas traditionally transmitted by Iranian peoples. The
words "Iran" and "Iranian" derive from the Old Iranian word "Arya" or
"Aryan," which appear, for example, in the inscriptions of Darius I, and
are used to refer, in the first instance, to a group of linguistically related
languages and, by extension, to the peoples who have spoken those
languages.[41] The use of "Iranian religion" broadens the discussion to all
varieties of Iranian religion, rather than to focus merely on the forms
which were (or were not) consonant with the Sassanian forms. This is not
to discount the importance or relevance of Zoroastrianism, but to shift
the focus away from discussion of the (non-)relationship of "Orthodox
Zoroastrianism" to the Achaemenids' "Mazdaism" and towards an evaluation of the traditions in the sources as a whole.

A proposed method for understanding "influence" and for pursuing the
question appears below. First, it is necessary to clarify what is meant by
"apocalyptic."

Apocalyptic Studies[42]

Definition of Apocalyptic

The term "apocalyptic" has generated fierce debate as to its appropriate
referent and suitability. The major problem with the term is its tendency
to denote simultaneously a genre, a worldview, and a sociological phenomenon. Hanson proposes to replace the term "apocalyptic" with the
terms "apocalypse," "apocalyptic eschatology," and "apocalypticism"
for the three respective referents,[43] but the term "apocalyptic" still

---

41. OP is the Iranian language of the Achaemenids. The Iranian linguistic family
includes the languages of Farsi, Pashto, and Ossetic, and the linguistic area covers
much more space than the modern Islamic Republic of Iran.

42. Cf. Murphy, "Apocalypses and Apocalypticism," 147–79; Sandy and
O'Hare, *Prophecy and Apocalyptic*; DiTommaso, "Apocalypses and Apocalypticism
in Antiquity Part I," 235–86; idem, "Apocalypses and Apocalypticism in Antiquity,
Part II," 367–432.

43. Hanson, "Apocalypticism," 29–31; VanderKam, "Recent Studies in 'Apocalyptic'," 70–77.

periodically re-emergences in discussions.[44] The reason for this is the apparent—but difficult to define—relation between the three. Few scholars would argue for a one-to-one correspondence between apocalypses and apocalyptic movements, yet a relationship of some sort does exist. While there is at least a basic consensus over the genre of apocalypse, there is little agreement on either the nature of related movements or worldviews or their relations to apocalypses.

The modern period of scholarship in apocalyptic is often traced to the work of Koch, who calls for an increased investigation into form-critical considerations of the apocalypses.[45] This spurred scholarship to devote attention to individual apocalypses, ultimately resulting in the formation of a group to define the genre apocalypse, the results of which are published in *Semeia* 14 and revisited in *Semeia* 36.

For the purposes of the present discussion, the said definition of "apocalypse" is considered to be sufficient:

> "Apocalypse" is a literary genre of revelatory literature with a narrative framework, in which a revelation is mediated by an otherworldly being to a human recipient, disclosing a transcendent reality which is both temporal, insofar as it envisages eschatological salvation, and spacial insofar as it involves another, supernatural world, intended to interpret present, earthly circumstances in light of the supernatural world and of the future, and to influence both the understanding and the behaviour of the audience by means of divine authority.[46]

While several scholars have critiqued this definition on a number of grounds,[47] no superior definition has yet emerged to replace it. As long as the genre definition is recognized to be a modern scholarly construct, the term is useful for clarifying discussion.

Rowland prefers a definition in terms of direct heavenly revelation.[48] However, one is left to wonder, if "apocalyptic" is merely a belief in revelation, what separates the apocalyptic literature from prophetic literature or indeed any other revelatory genre? Unless one wishes to

---

44. Grabbe, "Introduction and Overview," and idem, "Prophetic and Apocalyptic: Time for New Definitions—and New Thinking," 2–43, 107–33, respectively.

45. Koch, *The Rediscovery of Apocalyptic*, 23–27, 123.

46. As defined in Collins, ed., *Semeia* 14 (1979): 9, and amended by Yarbro Collins, ed., *Semeia* 36 (1986): 7.

47. Most notably Sacchi, *Jewish Apocalyptic*, 21 n. 19, 26; Hellholm, "The Problem of Apocalyptic Genre and the Apocalypse of John," 13–64; Himmelfarb, "The Experience of the Visionary and Genre," 97–112; Sanders, "The Genre of Palestinian Jewish Apocalypses," 447–59; Aune, *Apocalypticism*, 39–65.

48. Rowland, *The Open Heaven*, 13–14.

discard all distinction between the two,[49] Rowland's observations are insufficient criteria to define "apocalypse." He seems to ignore how deeply the eschatology shapes various characteristics of the genre; his emphasis on revelation occasionally leads him to miss how central eschatological concepts are to the very revelations he discusses. Collins and Yarbro Collins are right to insist on the generic import of eschatology,[50] and to insist on "apocalypse" as a *literary* genre with a scribal, exegetical locus.

Aune argues that Collins's definition of the genre is too "inductive and descriptive," as well as lacking in a description of function.[51] He therefore offers a new definition in terms of form, content, and function, largely with Revelation in mind.[52] His insistence on the need for a supplement of function to the definition is well-taken and reflected in the definition above, but his definition is problematic and fails to account for the other apocalypses.[53]

On the basis of her studies in the Christian apocalypses, particularly the phenomenon of "tours of hell,"[54] Himmelfarb objects to Collins's categories of the apocalypses[55] as they place two Christian apocalypses with different visionary experiences (*Ascension of Isaiah* and *Apocalypse of Paul*) in the same category. More importantly, she also sees an overemphasis on the importance of eschatology in his definition to flaw its usefulness.[56] From her perspective, the similarities between visionary experience (i.e. tours) is more important than the presence or lack of universal eschatology. However, she refrains from offering an alternative paradigm.

Perhaps no term in Biblical Studies has generated more confusion than the term "eschatology." As Collins points out, there is a "minimum" consensus that eschatology refers to "future expectation,"[57] but such a definition is too nebulous to be useful, requiring additional epithets to become so (as, indeed, Hanson is compelled to distinguish between

---

49. E.g. Grabbe, "Introduction and Overview," 22–24.

50. Collins, "Genre, Ideology, and Social Movements," 16; Yarbro Collins, "Introduction: Early Christian Apocalypticism," 5.

51. Aune, *Apocalypticism*, 43.

52. Ibid., 60.

53. Yarbro Collins, "Introduction: Early Christian Apocalypticism," 5; cf. Collins, "The Apocalyptic Technique," 108.

54. Himmelfarb, *Tours of Hell*.

55. Collins, "Introduction: Towards the Morphology of a Genre," 14–15.

56. Himmelfarb, "The Experience of the Visionary and Genre," 97–112.

57. Collins, "Apocalyptic Eschatology as the Transcendence of Death," 21–22.

"prophetic eschatology" and "apocalyptic eschatology').[58] Despite attempts to the contrary,[59] the variety of futures envisioned by texts such as Amos or Daniel questions the validity of calling both merely "future expectation." Since the term eschatology itself is based on ἔσχατος, "farthest," "uttermost," or "end,"[60] it is best to reserve the term for "terminus," both of human history and of human life ("universal" and "personal" eschatology respectively).[61] To use the term "eschatology" to merely refer to a mundane future expectation simply creates unnecessary confusion. This study agrees with Mowinckel, understanding the term "eschatology" to only apply to a variety of beliefs concerning a decisive ending or transformation of either the cosmos or the individual.[62] In this view, it is redundant to speak of an "apocalyptic eschatology," and "prophetic eschatology" is non-existent. Similarly, the attempt to bundle other issues into the definition of eschatology[63] also further obscures the issue. This ἔσχατος can (and does) come in a large variety of types and schemata and may be conceived of as imminent or remote. Indeed, many of the differences between various eschatological programs and the texts in which they appear can be understood as relative to the question of imminence. One would expect significant differences between an end expected tomorrow and one expected thousands of years hence.

Typically wrapped up with eschatology is some sort of teleology.[64] This is, strictly speaking, a separate idea from the logical positing of terminations, but in the Jewish apocalypses it is firmly wrapped up into their understandings of the *eschaton*. In the prophetic literature, however, teleology appears without being joined to an eschatology: YHWH has a purpose (*telos*) behind his dealings in history, but these dealings are not related to an ultimate *eschaton*. The prophets often speak of YHWH's goals and plans; however, these do not coincide with cessation.[65] Indeed, they are open to reversal based on the people's response.[66] In the apocalypses, on the other hand, *telos* and *eschaton* are bound together, as they

58. Hanson, *The Dawn of Apocalyptic*, 11–12.

59. E.g. Grabbe, "Introduction and Overview," 22–25.

60. LSJ, 699–700.

61. E.g. Collins, "Transcendence of Death," 21–43; Collins would object to this restriction, however.

62. Mowinckel, *He That Cometh*, 125, 261–66.

63. As does Hanson, *The Dawn of Apocalyptic*, 11–12.

64. Bull, "On Making Ends Meet," 1–30, particularly 2–3.

65. E.g. Eslinger, "Ezekiel 20 and the Metaphor of Historical Teleology," 93–120.

66. E.g. Amos 5:15; Jer 4:1–4.

are in Iranian traditions (see Chapter 1).[67] One crux of theodical debate (an important, albeit not sole, component of apocalypses) is the resolution of *telos*: one answer is eschatological, and this is an answer which is not found in the extant prophetic literature as it is in apocalyptic.

For the purposes of clarity, the present study attempts to be precise in the use of apocalyptic terminology (Figure 1).[68] The term "apocalyptic" is here either an adjective or a convenient collective noun to denote all related concepts. The term "apocalypse" refers strictly to a genre of revelatory literature as defined above. Apocalypses are the products of "apocalyptic traditions," or schools of thought (e.g. Enochic, Qumranic), which are more specific than the "apocalyptic worldview"/"apocalypticism,"[69] but less coherent or organized than an "apocalyptic movement." Such traditions emphasize different parts of the common apocalypticism and can naturally interact with other traditions, apocalyptic or not. An apocalyptic tradition may or may not result in the writing of apocalypses or the formation of a distinct movement; it may also be absorbed into the overall framework of a larger religious tradition. If a "school of thought" coalesces with "members," it may be called a movement. If an apocalyptic movement expects the imminent end of the world and assumes a more radical disposition towards society, it may be called "millenarianism"/ "millenarism."[70] Apocalypticism is a worldview which manifests itself in the apocalypses and apocalyptic traditions, but also influences the general religious tradition. This worldview and its antecedents and sources is still fraught with uncertainty. One of its sources, however, is an attitude which may be termed an "apocalyptic hermeneutic." This apocalyptic hermeneutic is the approach and method whereby a tradent engages his or her experiences and religious traditions, influencing how he or she reads, evaluates, and applies them to his or her overall world-view. This, as a hermeneutic, both comes out of and creates its worldview by interpreting and placing data. In the context of apocalyptic, the sources will largely be Jewish traditions and the Hebrew Bible. It is largely this last category ("apocalyptic hermeneutic") with which this study is concerned (see Chapter 5).

---

67. It may be pertinent to note that most of the parallel millenarian movements mentioned by Worsley had previously encountered either Christianity or Islam, both traditions with an eschatology. See Worsley, *The Trumpet Shall Sound*, 230–33.

68. Instead of abandoning them, like Sacchi, *Jewish Apocalyptic*, 13–26.

69. Collins, "Prophecy, Apocalypse and Eschatology," 46.

70. Talmon, "Millenarism," 349–62. This is the exact inverse of Landes, "Roosters Crow, Owls Hoot," 19–46. It is misleading to identify "apocalyptic" with "imminence" as he does.

Apocalyptic can be approached via a variety of perspectives and methodologies, leading to an equal variety of conclusions. Some of the approaches chosen can be classed broadly as sociological-historical or in relation to their perceived sources.

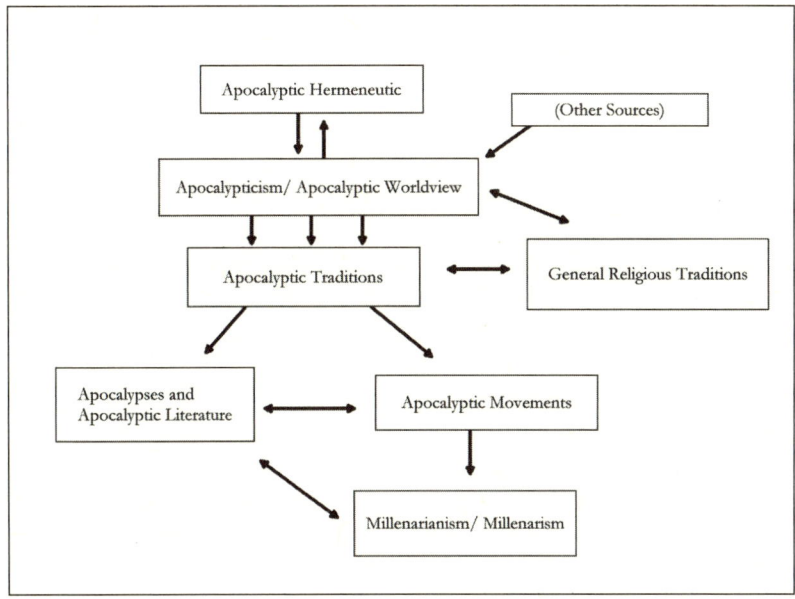

Figure 1. *Apocalyptic Terminology and Relationships*

Sociological-Historical

Plöger discusses apocalyptic against the background of Israel's transition from a nation-state to a religion.[71] For Plöger, two concepts are key: the usage of prophetic eschatology and the development of a "theocracy" or ruling priesthood. The seeds for later sectarianism were sown in the early Persian period; the restoration program assimilated prophetic eschatology as self-legitimation, while various dissenting "conventicles" maintained a more "dualistic" eschatology.[72] The essential difference between the two camps was the interpretation and use of the prophets: for the theocrats, the prophets were interpreters of the law, while for the conventicles, the eschatology still held living potential. The crises occasioned by the Seleucids catalyzed the latent schisms, more bringing to the forefront the pre-existing tensions in Jewish society than creating them.

71. Plöger, *Theocracy and Eschatology*, 29.
72. Ibid., 47–48.

Plöger's thesis has the benefit of emphasizing the importance of the interpretation of traditions to post-exilic Judaeans; indeed, he understands the difference between his two camps as largely one of the interpretation (and collation) of the prophets. However, his treatment too easily and without evidence creates defined parties and movements which may or may not have existed within Judaea and the diaspora. Additionally, a dichotomy between priests and prophets oversimplifies the overlap in interests which either role could have;[73] indeed, many of the apocalypses evince sincere interest in the workings of the cult, and the Pharisees were known for many "apocalyptic" beliefs. Further, the considerably pre-Maccabean dating of the earliest Enochic works questions the role of that crisis, even in terms of mere catalyst.

Hanson follows the lead of Plöger.[74] He traces the development of "apocalyptic eschatology" from "prophetic eschatology" in the later portions of Isaiah, Ezekiel, and Zechariah, seeing the "apocalyptic visionary" as merely an embattled prophet deprived of a king. While Hanson has deservedly come under criticism for his dichotomization of myth and history,[75] his emphasis on party politics and deprivation theory continues to be influential. However, the majority of Hanson's analyses in his book are dependent on the myth–history dichotomy—including his assignment of texts to various religio-political parties or their polemic—throwing doubt on his other results as well. Still, in light of the subsequent re-dating of the *Book of Watchers*, Hanson's appeal for a pre-Hellenistic dating for some of the origins of apocalyptic is a wise choice.

The sociology of deprivation is often applied to apocalyptic groups.[76] While there certainly is some merit to the observation that many millenarian groups are marginal and appear in times of crises, the appeal to deprivation is susceptible to four serious objections: many people experience hardship and deprivation without becoming apocalyptic;[77] the

---

73. E.g. the observations in Grabbe, "A Priest is Without Honor in His Own Prophet," 90–91.

74. Hanson, *The Dawn of Apocalyptic*; idem, "Prolegomena to the Study of Jewish Apocalyptic," 28–34.

75. Hanson, "Jewish Apocalyptic Against Its Near Eastern Environment," 58; for critiques, e.g., Roberts, "Myth versus History," 1–13; Collins, "Prophecy, Apocalypse and Eschatology," 75.

76. Aberle, "A Note on Relative Deprivation Theory," 7–12; Talmon, "Millenarism," 354; Hanson, *The Dawn of Apocalyptic*, 408–9; Berquist, *Judaism in Persia's Shadow*, 184–88; to a lesser extent, Nickelsburg, *1 Enoch 1*, 5.

77. Grabbe, "Prophetic and Apocalyptic: Time for New Definitions—and New Thinking," 111.

prophets can be analyzed as responding to deprivation;[78] groups in power may hold apocalyptic ideologies;[79] and the notion of relative deprivation is so nebulous as to be almost meaningless.[80] It is worth noting that apocalyptic-millenarian hopes are often fostered by those seeking a coherent worldview rather than merely in a socio-economic crisis.[81] One wonders, then, if instead of serving as cause, crises serve as intensifiers of pre-existing tensions.[82]

A better method is Cook's, who seeks to understand the Jewish and Christian texts through comparison with the apocalypticism or millenarianism of other cultures.[83] For Cook, the selection and emphasis upon certain traditional motifs in a new eschatological setting adequately describes the situation in Second Temple Judaism, as it does among the Native American Ghost Dancers.[84] His work offers glimpses into the actual functions of apocalyptic texts in real communities, beyond a simplistic reading of deprivation. Yet again, it is dangerous to automatically read a group or movement behind any given apocalypse *a priori*.[85] While there certainly are millenarian groups which created and nurtured texts, it is also possible some texts preceded the formation of "apocalyptic" communities (as appears to be the case at Qumran). Beyond the possibility of an individualistic origin to a given text, millenarian groups are not guaranteed to write in the genre of apocalypse: the correlation between the two phenomena is not one-to-one.

Relations to Previous Traditions

Prophecy. The understanding one has of the prophets undeniably impacts one's understanding of apocalyptic. The literature on prophets and prophecy and the relationship between these in the Hebrew Bible is vast.[86]

---

78. Blenkinsopp, *A History of Prophecy in Israel*, 37; Carroll, *When Prophecy Failed*, 8.

79. Cf. Cook, *Prophecy and Apocalypticism*, 2, 87.

80. Cf. Newman, *Proximity to Power*, 7–11.

81. Talmon, "Millenarian Movements," 29.

82. Note also the critiques of Tierney and Gurney, "Relative Deprivation and Social Movements," 33–47.

83. As, e.g., in Cook, *Prophecy and Apocalypticism*; idem, *The Apocalyptic Literature*; and idem, "Mythological Discourse," 85–106.

84. Cf. Cook, *The Apocalyptic Literature*, 36; idem, "Mythological Discourse," 94.

85. Grabbe, "Introduction and Overview," 25.

86. Cf. Petersen, "Defining Prophecy," 33–39; Blenkinsopp, *History of Prophecy*, 16–39.

Only the aspects deemed most relevant to the current issue can be discussed here.

Wellhausen understood the prophets as religious reformers who challenged the monarchy and the books which bore their names as belonging either to the prophets themselves or their followers.[87] While the uniqueness of some prophets' messages may indeed account for their remembrance, Wellhausen's view has long been noted to recreate the prophets in the mold of the Protestant reformers. Instead, for the purposes of the present study, a "prophet" is understood as a person who fulfills the role of speaking a message from YHWH to his or her contemporaries.[88] This is a fundamentally oral phenomenon, although reports could be written. Since a prophet could function as part of a prophetic group, alone, or as part of the cultic structure,[89] "prophet" should be understood as a *role* which one could perform once through a lifetime vocation.[90] By the time of the appearance of apocalyptic, however, the importance of this live intermediary was eclipsed; the rising importance of collections of prophetic literature played a part in this. "Prophetic literature" refers to the texts in the Hebrew Bible which were believed to be the records of the previously oral prophets, through whom YHWH spoke new message(s) to his people. The difference between the two is largely of medium and skill: the prophets required the skills of communication with YHWH and with their audience; the prophetic literature required the scholars' skills in interpretation and teaching.

Starting from the recognition that prophets were originally oral communicators, Doan and Giles explore the implications of presentation for the original prophetic event, the scribal record of it, and the presumed scribal re-enaction of it.[91] They make two important claims: (1) that the prophet himself had authority through his performance while the scribe had to "impersonate" the prophet to actualize the same authority;[92] and

87. Cf. Wellhausen, *Grundrisse zum alten Testament*, 57–64, 87–96.

88. As defined by Petersen, "Defining Prophecy," 37–38; cf. Carroll, "Ancient Israelite Prophecy and Dissonance Theory," 382; note, however, that Greene, *The Role of the Messenger*, 137–266, disagrees.

89. E.g. Lindblom, *Prophecy in Ancient Israel*, 206–7; Lang, *Monotheism and the Prophetic Minority*, 94; Blenkinsopp, *History of Prophecy*, 32–33.

90. 'Role" here is intended as "social role," as in Petersen, *The Roles of Israel's Prophets*, particularly Chapter 2; Kelle, "Ancient Israelite Prophets and Greek Political Orators," 69; van der Toorn, *Scribal Culture*, 69; rather than literary, as in Gross, "Lying Prophet and Disobedient Man of God," particularly 110–13.

91. Doan and Giles, *Prophets, Performance, and Power*, 19–48.

92. Ibid., 27.

(2) that a performance (e.g. a prophetic oracle) is judged by its impact.[93] These two claims have several implications on the rise of apocalyptic. First, while texts receive their power from the power of the performer, the power of subsequent performers is sub-ordinated to the text. In other words, the writing of prophecy simultaneously glorifies the recorded prophet while denying the possibility of encore performances. The scribe, therefore, cannot reclaim the same level of authority in his person, dependent as it is on a text. This not only confirms the implications of oral theory (Chapter 3), it perhaps helps explain the high incidence of pseudepigraphy in the apocalypses: a prophetically authored text carries more authority than a scribal re-performer.[94] Second, it reduces the importance of "prediction" for prophecy through a focus on the impact on the audience. A prophet's performance would be preserved and remembered if deemed "effective"—as the audience subjectively perceived it—whereas the scribal performance implies a "communal audience" which already accepted the prophet's performance as true, and thus more inclined to a predictive element.[95]

Perhaps the prophetic issue most relevant to the investigation of apocalyptic is the "end of prophecy." Although the end of prophecy is a misnomer, it is an impression which is given by the extant literature. This is partly a reflex of the disappearance of the prophetic literature genre, despite sporadically appearing self-proclaimed prophets.[96] The apparent occultation of prophecy is here understood as the upshot of three interrelated developments: the change in authority structure, the rise of textual authority, and the sociological dynamics sometimes called the "church–cult" dichotomy.[97]

Pre-exilic Judaean (and Israelite) society had a triad of authority sources: the king, the priests, and the prophets. The prophets largely functioned as mirrors of the *status quo*, both upholding and critiquing the institutions of cult and monarchy.[98] Scribes would have had a mostly

---

93. Ibid., 90.

94. For a more complex attempt to analyze pseudepigraphy, see Silverman, "Pseudepigraphy, Anonymity, and Auteur Theory."

95. Doan and Giles, *Prophets, Performance, and Power*, 101–2.

96. E.g. John the Baptist, Jesus, the Teacher of Righteousness. Cf. Josephus, *J.W.* VI.5.2 (*Josephus III*, 459).

97. E.g. Weber, *The Sociology of Religion*, 60–79, 104; Blenkinsopp, "The Social Roles of Prophets in Early Achaemenid Judah," 39–58; Schaper, "The Death of the Prophet," 63–79.

98. Cf. Carroll, *When Prophecy Failed*, 17. This contrasts with other oracles from the ancient Near East, where only oracles favorable to the king are preserved. See the collected oracles in Nissinen, *Prophets and Prophecy*.

administrative and relatively minor role. Following the restoration, Yehud's authority structure was altered from this paradigm. While executive power first devolved upon a local Persian governor, probably even the Davidic scion,[99] the ultimate authority was 850 miles away. This had the effect of increasing the authority of the Persian-supported priests (to the extent that the governor disappeared completely in a process still poorly understood)[100] as well as those with expertise in handling the imperial administration—scribes.[101] The loss of the Davidide both robbed prophets of their former patrons as well as problematized the critique of executive authority. A threat to Persian authority would have been a threat to the positions of both the priests and the scribes in a way which a critique of the Davidic monarchy does not appear to have been.[102] Simultaneously, the importance of writing—both generally and as a repository of authoritative traditions—was gradually increasing in Judaean circles. The codification and canonization of prophetic oracles would have reduced the authority of contemporary prophets: since the texts were already considered "validated" prophecies from true prophets, the insolvable question of validation was not an issue for them as it would have remained for the living prophets.[103] The pattern of revelation–codification–closing of canon/turn to exegesis can be seen repeatedly in the history of religions. Since the epistemology of new revelations is an intractable problem, communities will tend to curtail their recurrence after an initial period.[104]

Thus, prophecy in Judaean traditions was likely squeezed in a new political, sociological, and communicative setting. The continuing

99.   Grabbe, *Ezra–Nehemiah*, 135–36; Na'aman, "Royal Vassals or Governors?," 35–44; Boccaccini, *Roots of Rabbinic Judaism*, 47–50; Kratz, "Statthalter, Hohepriester und Schreiber im perserzeitlichen Juda," 93–119; a synthesis can be found in Albertz, *Israel in Exile*, 119–32.

100.   Cf. Na'aman, "Royal Vassals or Governors?," 44; Fishbane, *Biblical Interpretation in Ancient Israel*, 138; Barag, "Some Notes on a Silver Coin of Johanan the High Priest," 166–68; Avigad, *Bullae and Seals*; Stern, *Material Culture*, 200–209.

101.   Cf. Blenkinsopp, "The Sage, the Scribe, and Scribalism," 312; see Chapter 3.

102.   See the Achaemenid system of personal loyalty to the crown in Briant, *From Cyrus to Alexander*, 324–26.

103.   Lange, "Literary Prophecy and Oracle Collection," 259–60, fails to connect it to the dynamics of literacy.

104.   E.g. van der Toorn, *Scribal Culture*, 225–29; Blenkinsopp, "Social Roles," 21; idem, *Prophecy and Canon*, 124; Fishbane, "From Scribalism to Rabbinism," 440.

relevance of living prophets was probably confined to a more popular level.[105] In textual terms, the scribes appropriated the prophets' former role.

Grabbe problematizes the entire program of differentiating between prophecy and apocalyptic tradition, wishing to understand apocalypses as a subset of prophecy, and prophecy as a subset of divination.[106] The questions which Grabbe raises are important questions to keep in mind; the roles of myth and history, of scribality, of eschatology, and their relationship to the social situation are serious questions which have not yet found a satisfactory formulation. However, as Collins rightly critiques,[107] the denial of distinctions between prophetic literature and apocalypses hardly brings any clarity to the relevant issues, nor does it clarify the problems Grabbe identifies. A preferable method would be to understand how each category is used in the respective genres, rather than assimilating the two into a greater, vaguer genre.

Wisdom. In contrast to the prevailing scholarly consensus, von Rad argues that much of apocalyptic can better be seen as an outgrowth from sapiential traditions.[108] For him, the concept of history in the apocalyptic literature is too radically different from that in prophetic—in its scope, lack of reference to Israel's salvation history, and its determinism—to be connected with the prophets. Instead, the emphasis on the cultivation of knowledge fits better within a sapiential paradigm. In addition, he connects the two through prognostication and the development of deterministic ideas.[109] While his discussion of the idea is brief, it has provoked widespread discussion.[110] Ultimately, however, the parallel to be found between the apocalypses and the sapiential literature is a common originating milieu—that is, scribes and their scribal training in schools which utilized and contributed to sapiential writings—rather

---

105. Cf. Josephus, *J.W.* VI.5.2 (*Josephus III*, 459). cf. O'Connor, "'Take One, It's FREE!,'" 163–201; Ariel and Kark, "Messianism, Holiness, Charisma, and Community," 641–57; cf. Cohn, *The Pursuit of the Millennium.*

106. Particularly, his "Introduction" and "Prophetic and Apocalyptic: Time for New Definitions—and New Thinking," 2–43, 107–33. Cf. Grabbe, *Judaic Religion,* 232–36.

107. Collins, "Prophecy, Apocalypse and Eschatology," 44–52.

108. In von Rad, *Old Testament Theology,* 2:301–15; idem, *Wisdom in Israel,* 277–82.

109. On prognostication, see von Rad, *Wisdom in Israel,* 280; idem, *Old Testament Theology,* 2:307; for deterministic ideas, see idem, *Wisdom in Israel,* 262–70, 279.

110. E.g. Wright III and Wills, eds., *Conflicted Boundaries.*

than in a textual dependence. A strict delineation between prophetic and sapiential traditions is both misleading and unnecessary—it was most likely the same scribal circles ultimately responsible for preserving both corpora and thus heirs to both traditions.

Müller qualifies von Rad's position by linking it to "mantic wisdom,"[111] and in this he has been followed by most scholars.[112] Müller argues that the general context of חכם in the Hebrew Bible, *4QPrayer of Nabonidus*, and Dan'el at Ugarit demonstrates the "magisch-mantische" associations of the word.[113] He understands the resurgence of manticism in post-exilic texts as related to the resurgence of ancient myth in said texts.[114] Thus, for VanderKam, Enoch can best be understood as the Jewish version of Enmenduranki, seventh in the antediluvian sage lists.[115] Similarly, Mesopotamian traditions represented by the Akkadian predictive texts are very similar to some types of apocalypses (the historical-review type).[116] While in Müller's view this thesis offers answers to some of the long-standing questions in apocalyptic (pseudonymity, determinism, future-orientation),[117] the comparison between the apocalyptic sages and Mesopotamian mantic sages is too superficial for the weight placed upon it.

Recently, Bedenbender has rightly rejected the consensus on mantic wisdom.[118] Preferring the term "revealed wisdom" to "mantic wisdom," he notes that the very concept of the mantic sage—expert in knowledge of rituals and special "scientific" training—obviates the need for revelation.[119] Thus, Joseph and Daniel—the bases for Müller's thesis—do not act at all like mantic sages: they receive revelations rather than use mantic skills.[120] The authors of the Daniel and Joseph cycles are quite aware of this difference between their protagonists and the religious specialists of

111.   Müller, "Magisch-Mantische Weisheit," 79–94; idem, "Mantische Weisheit und Apokalyptik," 268–93.

112.   In particular, VanderKam, *Enoch and the Growth of an Apocalyptic Tradition*, and Collins, *Seers, Sybils* [*sic*] *and Sages*, 45, 340, 347; Davies, "Divination, 'Apocalyptic' and Sectarianism." The present author is grateful to Professor Davies for forwarding a copy of the latter to him. Collins discounts the importance of Ugartic Dan'el for the Book of Daniel; see Collins, *Daniel*, 1–2.

113.   Müller, "Magisch-Mantische Weisheit," 79–85, 87, 90–94.

114.   Ibid., 279.

115.   VanderKam, *Enoch and the Growth of an Apocalyptic Tradition*, 8.

116.   VanderKam, *From Revelation to Canon*, 274.

117.   Müller, "Mantische Weisheit und Apokalyptik," 281–92.

118.   See Bedenbender, "Jewish Apocalypticism," 189–96.

119.   Ibid., 191. See also Argall, *1 Enoch and Sirach*, 251.

120.   Bedenbender, "Jewish Apocalypticism," 191–92.

Egypt and Babylon, taking pains to draw attention to the *revealing* YHWH in place of the messengers' skill (cf. Gen 41:16; Dan 2:22, 27).

Bedenbender specifically notes a difficulty with the parallel of the *baru*: the *baru*'s skill was based on the technical inspection of sacrificial offal (extispicy) and oil-patterns on water (lecanomancy), not on dream interpretation (oneiromancy), let alone the writing of revelatory litera-ture.[121] The apocalyptic preoccupation with revelation contrasts highly with the technical interpretations of phenomena that appear in the Meso-potamian literature.[122] Indeed, at least at Mari, the mantic arts often functioned to verify messages received via prophetic means (i.e. "reve-lation").[123] When dreams are mentioned in Mesopotamian texts, their meaning is straightforward and clear, requiring only verification rather than explanation.[124] It is therefore hard to understand the role of dream-interpretation-through-revealed-exegesis as "mantic," and thus, the character of Daniel is no mantic.[125] There is little if any evidence of apocalyptic authors' interest in the interpretation of entrails; there is, however, much interest in the eschatological interpretation of the Torah and prophets. This points to another difficulty with Müller's thesis which Bedenbender's critique notices: the prediction of the near future and of the eschaton are two very different concepts that need not lead from one to the other.[126] While omen literature and the apocalypses do often deal with the future, the future, with which they deal are of qualitatively different kinds: it is the difference between predicting the outcome of the next presidential election and predicting the fall of the current world order. One does not lead to the other without some serious impetus and change of assumptions. More to the fore is the appearance of revealed interpretations rather than mantic interpretations.

Davies argues that Bedenbender has ignored the presence of two kinds of dreams in Mesopotamia, one of which did not require specialist inter-pretation.[127] He therefore argues that apocalyptic, prophetic, and wisdom

121.   VanderKam, *Enoch and the Growth of an Apocalyptic Tradition*, 56–62; Bedenbender, "Jewish Apocalypticism," 193. Bedenbender himself cites 61.

122.   Cf. the examples of omen interpretation in *ANET*, 495; Jastrow, *Babylo-nian–Assyrian Birth-Omens*. The dreams do not require any specialized interpretation (*ANET*, 451, 606).

123.   Cf. the documents in Nissinen, *Prophets and Prophecy*, nn. 8, 10, 14, 16, 17, 22, 25, 27, 29, 36, 38, 39, 44. Cf. Fleming, "Prophets and Temple Personnel in the Mari Archives," 55–56.

124.   Nissinen, *Prophets and Prophecy*, nn. 36 and 38.

125.   Cf. Bedenbender, "Jewish Apocalypticism," 191.

126.   Ibid., 194.

127.   Davies, "Divination, 'Apocalyptic' and Sectarianism," §2.2.

literature should be understood as forms of divination and "apocalyptic" as a term abandoned.[128] He is certainly correct insofar as a broad history of religions perspective is concerned; nevertheless, distinctions in form, method, and ideology do exist between the phenomena, and it is worth attempting to tease these out, at least as is applicable to the development of Second Temple Judaism. The Yahwistic written tradition certainly perceives a difference in any case. The apocalyptic literature evinces no interest in either technical dream interpretation or verification, thus is not "mantic" as the term is understood here. Still, Davies's caution against drawing overly sharp, *a priori* distinctions is a valuable warning.

The relationship between sapiential and apocalyptic literature has again occupied scholars of late. What emerges from a number of scholars' suggestions and observations—more implicitly than explicitly—is the importance of a common denominator for every book: scribal origins.[129] It is clear that both genres and styles are related by a shared social situation, if not necessarily shared ideologies or groups. Recognizing the scribal origin of all genres then also points to several issues which the student of apocalypticism must consider: the role and nature of education and the development of scribal hermeneutics.[130]

If one understands sapiential literature as related to the training of scribes, then one of the keys for understanding the relationship between the genres is epistemology, or more specifically, the issue of revelation. While all scribes would have been trained through the cultivation of traditional and Torah-based knowledge, they clearly did not hold uniform views on the role or importance of revelation, and thus on the interpretation and relative role of the traditional wisdom. A scribe who accepted a revelatory epistemology would be willing to write, read, and study apocalypses, while a scribe who rejected it would not. However, even if a scribe who accepted a revelatory epistemology did not write an apocalypse, that scribe's hermeneutic and literary production would still bear the hallmarks of such an approach to tradition. Goff's study of

128.   Ibid., esp. §3.

129.   Cf. Nickelsburg, "Wisdom and Apocalypticism in Early Judaism: Some Points for Discussion," 20, 34; Tanzer, "Response to George Nickelsburg," 48; Wright, "Putting the Puzzle Together," 108; and Horsley, "The Politics of Cultural Production," 124, 145, all of which are in Wright and Wills, eds., *Conflicted Boundaries*. A similar viewpoint may be discernable in Knibb, "Apocalyptic and Wisdom in *4 Ezra*," 63–65.

130.   Note in particular the contributions by Goff and Horsley: Goff, "Wisdom, Apocalypticism, and the Pedagogical Ethos of 4QInstruction," 57–68; Horsley, "Politics of Cultural Production," 123–48.

4QInstruction is in this regard illuminating.[131] He notes that *4QInstruction*, while sharing a pedagogical function with the sapiential literature, *presumes an already known revelation.* Whereas an apocalypse imparts or shares the experience of a new revelation and gives it authority, *4QInstruction* admonishes scribes to study a revelation which is already accepted as authoritative. To put this in more concrete terms, *Sirach* represents a scribe who rejects a revelatory epistemology, *1 Enoch* represents scribe(s) who wish to impart a new revelation, and *4QInstruction* represents scribes who have accepted a new revelation and continue in the scribal tradition of study and interpretation (including that revelation). One of the decisive factors in characterizing these works is their hermeneutical presuppositions, as well as their chronological relation towards the material from which they derive their wisdom.

From Prophecy–Wisdom Dichotomy to Interpretation. The above discussion of prophecy and wisdom highlights the importance of interpretation for apocalyptic. This emphasis is supported by Smith's comparative work in cults from the ancient Near East.[132] He understands apocalyptic movements and apocalypses to stem from an "apocalyptic situation"—in the ancient Near East, the scribes' loss of royal patronage—but more generally, in a situation in which traditions require "rectification."[133] This "rectification" is not a result of failed prophecy, but the need to fit a new situation into an older paradigm, to fit a previously unimaginable situation into a traditional framework. Smith's comments highlight the importance of reinterpretation and of scribes in the appearance of apocalypticism. This perspective is a helpful corrective to appeals to cognitive dissonance or relative deprivation for several reasons. First, cognitive dissonance depends too much on an idea of unfulfilled predictions: the sources and preoccupations of the apocalypses are much broader than the "correction" of failed prophecies.[134] Secondly, the concept of relative deprivation—encompassing any *perceived* deprivation—is too nebulous

---

131. Goff, "Pedagogical Ethos of *4QInstruction*," particularly 64–67. Cf. his elaboration in idem, "Discerning Trajectories," 657–59, 661–67.

132. Smith, "Wisdom and Apocalyptic," 131–56, reprinted in idem, *Map is Not Territory*, 67–87; idem, "Native Cults in the Hellenistic Period," 237.

133. Smith, "Wisdom and Apocalyptic," 137, 149; idem, "A Pearl of Great Price and a Cargo of Yams," 7–8, 16, 19. Also discussed in idem, *Imagining Religion*, Chapter 5.

134. Contra Wilson, *Prophecy and Society in Ancient Israel*, 307–8; cf. Nickelsburg, "Apocalyptic Judaism," 74, 81–83, which does not even mention failed prophecy.

to count as a meaningful analytical tool.[135] The intellectual aspect which these two ideas do invoke and have in common, however, is the reinterpretation of older traditions in the light of a new situation. This is, of course, a matter of hermeneutics.

Aune investigates the role of biblical interpretation which claimed revelatory status as "prophecy," also known as "charismatic exegesis." He understands this phenomenon as a "hermeneutical ideology" in a context of interpretive disputes.[136] This ideology presupposes a common sacred text as well as difficulty in its interpretation. While this phenomenon is not restricted to apocalypses, it is an important factor in them and their general setting. This idea places the apocalypses in a context which requires other previous and contemporary genres: based on generally accepted revelatory texts, they claim either an additional or an interpretive revelation which is counter to other contemporary interpretations of the same texts or traditions.[137] This points to a few important contexts for the apocalypses: the role of interpretation, the situation of interpretational conflict, and the presence of "authoritative" texts.

Tigchelaar emphasizes the importance of the interpretation and the systematization of prior traditions in both Zechariah and the *Book of Watchers*,[138] although he sees this as less true for the *Book of Watchers*.[139] He also briefly notes an apparent shift from prophets to scribes, probably in the context of the "accumulation of a corpus of religious texts."[140] While all living traditions receive continual (re)-interpretation, Tigchelaar's observations lead to further queries about the hermeneutics used and their sources. The importance of these questions is borne out further by his observation that the disparate and encyclopedic interests of the texts still serve to further a "comprehensive interpretation."[141]

For these reasons, the relationships between prophecy, wisdom, and apocalyptic should be viewed through the lens of an *Apocalyptic Hermeneutic*. The apocalyptic hermeneutic is primarily to be regarded as a *shared interpretive framework* which interrelates apocalypticism, the

---

135. Cf. the similar reservations of Newman, *Proximity to Power*, 7–11.

136. Aune, *Apocalypticism*, 298.

137. This raises the question of why the authors chose this form rather than other contemporary forms (such as *pešer*), an intriguing question which cannot be answered here.

138. Tigchelaar, *Prophets of Old*, 243–44, 253, 265.

139. Tigchelaar, "Some Remarks on the Book of the Watchers," 145; idem, *Prophets of Old*, 248.

140. Tigchelaar, *Prophets of Old*, 254, 263.

141. Ibid., 247.

apocalypses, and millenarianism. It is not a shared theology, nor is it a coherent, systematic philosophy. It is a method of receiving and reshaping traditions which shares identifiable aspects while producing noticeably divergent results. It is an intellectual paradigm through which many Judaeans of the Second Temple period channeled their concerns, queries, and teachings. By correlating apocalyptic to the Apocalyptic Hermeneutic and placing the primary locus of Iranian influence there, this study maintains that Persia's relevance to *apocalyptic* as a whole and not just individual *apocalypses* can be better understood and formulated.

Foreign Sources. In addition to Judaean precursors, apocalyptic has an international context. A common referent for Jewish apocalyptic is the matrix of Jewish nationalism in the face of an encroaching Hellenism.[142] There is no denying the importance of the Hellenistic context of many of the apocalypses, nor that nationalistic sentiment certainly factors heavily into many of their analogous texts. The term "Hellenism," however, should not be understood as the dichotomized opposite of Judaism, as sometimes understood.[143] A group's interaction with the *Zeitgeist* may be better understood as a complex dialectic than a confrontation. There is no denying the importance of renewed nationalistic interests in the Hellenistic world,[144] from traditional cultural motifs to desires for political independence, yet this resurgence also happened in the context of a remarkable, pan-ancient Near East admixing and borrowing of myths, religions, and laws.[145] However strong a nationalistic urge in any given movement is, this is rarely an effective barrier to the influence of foreign

142. Hengel, *Judaism and Hellenism*, 196; Collins, "Jewish Apocalyptic Against Its Hellenistic Near Eastern Environment," 27–36; Russell, *Method and Message*, 15; Müller, "Mantische Weisheit und Apokalyptik," 290–92.

143. E.g. especially, Hengel, *Judaism and Hellenism*, 196: "*Thus the picture of history in apocalyptic is above all a fruit of the Jewish struggle for spiritual and religious self-determination against the invasion of Jerusalem by the Hellenistic spirit*" (emphasis his); this has been critiqued by Aune, "Transformations of Apocalypticism in Early Christianity," 60; Collins, "Hellenistic Near Eastern Environment," 30–31; Gruen, "Hellenistic Judaism," 95–96. Note in particular the work of Gruen, *Heritage and Hellenism*, notably 1–40; Smith, *Palestinian Parties*, 57–61; Levine, *Judaism and Hellenism in Antiquity*, 3–15.

144. Collins, "Hellenistic Near Eastern Environment," 33; idem, "Cosmos and Salvation: Jewish Wisdom and Apocalyptic in the Hellenistic Age," 138, 142; idem, *The Apocalyptic Imagination*, 34–38.

145. E.g. *Prophecy of a Potter, Demotic Chronicle, Oracle of Hystaspes, Sibylline Oracles*; cf. Smith, *Palestinian Parties*, 60–61; Levine, *Judaism and Hellenism*, 18–19.

elements, even among so-called nativist/revivalist movements.[146] Further, the various regions which produced apocalypse-like literature shared not only the experience of Hellenistic rule but also shared Achaemenid rule and its end. It is worth noting that Alexander's empire was largely contiguous with the Achaemenid Empire. One may wonder, then, whether the Persian past or Hellenistic present was the more important aspect of the era's common *Zeitgeist*; the relative roles of Hellenism and the previous "Achaemenid *Koine*" have yet to be assessed. Although any discussion of the apocalypses by necessity must deal with their Hellenistic context, the significantly pre-Maccabaean appearance of the oldest known Jewish apocalypse (the *Book of Watchers*) raises the question whether Hellenism's role was in the origins or the evolution of the phenomena.

Few would dispute the influence of Egyptian, Assyrian, Babylonian, and Greek contexts. While the possible relevance of Persia is often alluded to, it has too long gone without a serious evaluation. If one accepts that the traditions of the Judaeans were affected by the other imperial powers with which they came into contact, one would *prima facie* assume the same must be true for the Persian Empire. Certainly, if Persia did not have an influence, there ought to be a significant reason for such an exceptional status.

Apocalyptic and the Nature of Religious Discourse

Types of Language. An important consideration in apocalyptic studies is the type of language used and form of discourse it represents. Sandy notes that with both prophecy and apocalyptic an emotional as well as an intellectual response appears to be what the authors desired.[147] He even suggests that the apocalypses depend on a sense of mystery for their effectiveness.[148] The poetic and artistic aspects of the literatures certainly should be kept in mind when attempting to understand them: the people responsible were poets, artists, and communicators, not necessarily systematic theologians or astute politicians. While they had urgent and deeply felt opinions on various matters, their ideology need not necessarily reduce to simple or propositional ideas. The nature and type of languages, as well as the forms employed, could hold meaning for the authors in less cerebral ways. When attempting to understand the texts it

---

146. Cf. Wallace, "Revitalization Movements," 276; Hinnells, "Zoroastrian Influence on the Judeo-Christian Tradition," 10; Smith, "Native Cults in the Hellenistic Period," 236–49.

147. Sandy, *Plowshares and Pruning Hooks*, 198.

148. Ibid., 127.

is important to consider categories of hyperbole, symbol, and metaphor as well as myth and theology. The use of symbolism often cannot be reduced merely to the supposed referent: other connotations and shades of meaning are carried by the use as well.[149]

Stone highlights the need to understand the texts as religious texts, not necessarily theological treatises,[150] and this opens up analyses in a few new directions and methodologies. In particular, this means an openness to the potential of the texts to transmit authentic religious experiences, and that traditional text-critical categories are therefore misleading in this respect.[151] Stone's approach underscores the importance of understanding the texts not merely in the context of ideological struggle, but in the context of real religious communities, with needs and experiences beyond analytical, disputational, or materialistic categories.[152] While culture forms the language and style of any textual creation, traditional language, tropes, or subjects need not eliminate either the genuineness of experience or the variety in potential interests.[153]

Nature of "Traditions." What is "tradition"? A pioneer in this regard, Boccaccini attempts to understand "Middle Judaism" by way of intellectual "traditions."[154] Noting that genres and even identical ideas can service very separate agendas or ideologies, Boccaccini seeks to trace "ideological traditions"—traditions which transcend genre and even party boundaries—behind the various extant literatures of Second Temple Judaism. He identifies three main traditions: a Zadokite tradition, a Sapiential tradition, and an Enochic tradition. In some ways, Boccaccini's discussion recalls Smith's discussion of parties and politics,[155] replacing the terminology of politics with "tradition." While it is nebulous and perhaps requires further elucidation, "tradition" is a better way to acknowledge both the continuity and changes visible in the texts as well as their independence from particular "parties." An individual is certainly capable of being influenced by several intellectual "traditions" regardless of social-economic status or "party" affiliation.

149. Bryan, *Cosmos, Chaos*, 27–31.
150. Stone, "On Reading an Apocalypse," 72.
151. Stone, "A Reconsideration of Apocalyptic Visions," 177–79; cf. Rowland, *Open Heaven*, 217–34.
152. Cf. Bruce, "Religion and Rational Choice," 193–205; Drønen, "Scientific Revolution and Religious Conversion," 241.
153. Stone, "A Reconsideration of Apocalyptic Visions," 179; cf. Stone, "Lists of Revealed Things," 420, 435–36.
154. Boccaccini, *Middle Judaism*, 25, 129.
155. Smith, *Palestinian Parties*.

Boccaccini's emphasis on the antagonistic stances possible within the genre and worldview of the apocalypses, as he illustrates between the *Book of Dreams* and Daniel, is apt and needs to be kept in mind when discussing the apocalyptic phenomenon. A cursory overview of sectarian and political strife will confirm that the bitterest debates can flourish between the closest of ideological allies. His reminder that similar positions can reappear in a variety of genres and among different parties must also be remembered in the discussion.

Martínez uses the term "apocalyptic" to refer to a tradition which is evident in, but not restricted to, the apocalypses. He defines this tradition as

> A current of thought that is born in the religious context and specific culture of post-exilic Judaism, that develops over a long period, reacting interactively with other currents of thought of the Jewish environment, such a [*sic*] prophetic tradition to the wisdom tradition, and is shaped in the various works that we call "apocalypses."[156]

For Martínez a tradition is able to contain contradictory positions within itself, as a tradition consists of both inheritance and development.[157] Nevertheless, there can be distinct heirs with significant enough discrete traits to speak of separate traditions (or sub-traditions). As he demonstrates, Qumran certainly inherited much from the Enochic tradition, but it is also characteristically different.[158] The interactions between various traditions are not thereby negated, but it helps to maintain a distinction between the preoccupations of the common (apocalypticism) and the unique (a specific apocalyptic tradition).

A recognition of the role of traditions refocuses attention on the importance of the history of ideas for the study of apocalyptic. While the sociological and comparative approaches serve as a necessary corrective to previous studies, they too often ignore the importance of ideas— specifically religious ideas—in the respective texts, and thus misunderstand one of the central purposes of the texts. A look at ideas and theology is necessary both to understand the texts in question fully, and to correlate the otherwise disjointed concepts of apocalypse, millenarianism, apocalypticism, and apocalyptic hermeneutics. The appearance of apocalyptic groups and apocalypses is often understood in matrices of materialistic machinations.[159] Yet material concerns and political ambition

---

156.   Martínez, "Is Jewish Apocalyptic the Mother of Christian Theology?," 147.
157.   Martínez, "Apocalypticism in the Dead Sea Scrolls," 200, 226.
158.   Ibid., 199–226.
159.   Daniels, "Charters of Righteousness," 3–18, particularly 4–6; Horsley, "Religion and Other Products of Empire," 13–44; idem, "Politics of Cultural

do not exhaust the realms of human interest and motivation.[160] In texts which purport to be "religious" in nature, it is also appropriate to seek more "religious" motivations as well.

To understand some of the streams which fed into the apocalypses, it is necessary to understand the period which preceded them as well as their contemporary contexts, both the Hellenistic period—which is often the focus of apocalyptic studies—as well as the Achaemenid period. Judaeans in this period did not all inhabit the same social location, and thus probably held divergent interests and tendencies. One factor was surely "foreign influence."

Types of Influence and Transmission

The positing of foreign influence has a long scholarly pedigree. Yet, researchers have often understood the ancient processes of tradition-creation and tradition-dissemination as if carried out through a cut-and-paste method appropriate to their modern world. The proper understanding of the ancient texts themselves and the methods of cultural influence in general require the recognition of several communicative contexts. First, it is important to note that the vast majority of the population was either completely or functionally illiterate. Except for the educated elites, all knowledge of traditions was acquired aurally. Second, while the textual creators were scribes, they did not have the luxury of vast and accessible deposits of texts; even their textual activities were in a more thoroughly oral environment than today. Because of this, it is necessary to investigate the role and effects of the introduction of new media upon a society in terms not only of the preservation, creation, and dissemination of tradition, but also in the interaction of traditions (see Chapter 3). Influence and parallels cannot be restricted to direct textual quotations or borrowings.

The study of influence demands clear terminology and a working methodology for assessing its presence and effects.[161] The term "influence" is here understood as one type of "interaction." "Interaction" includes all types of social intercourse, from superficial to significant—political and social structures as well as cultural and religious elements

---

Production," 123–48; idem, "The Origins of the Hebrew Scriptures in Imperial Relations," 107–35; Kelber, "Roman Imperialism and Early Christian Scribality," 135–54.

160. Cf. Anonymous, "Why Wars Happen," *The Economist*, 16 December 2008.

161. Barclay, *Jews in the Mediterranean Diaspora*, 82–102, analyzes Hellenization using the terms "assimilation," "acculturation," and "accommodation." He overlooks the unconscious aspects in his discussion, however.

are included in the concept. This is nigh on universal.[162] The scholarly use of the term for the intellectual side of interaction—"influence" or "dialogue"—is inconsistently used, however, with a variety of connotations attached. It is therefore important to note what is not meant by the word "influence" here: it does not mean a wholesale "cut-and-paste" of literate materials from one canon to another (e.g. from the *Bundahišn* to *1 Enoch*). Neither does it denote a religious conversion under another name, and nor does it indicate the "syncretism" or "assimilation" of anthropologists.[163] Of concern here is not the development of entirely new systems or traditions, but of change within a system due to external interaction; the question of how much change a system or tradition can undertake before becoming a new system is an interesting problem, but it cannot be broached here.[164] In the present study interaction and influence are understood as unavoidable aspects of the human condition, ones which have impacted and continue to impact all traditions and religions. In all cultures, influence is a subtle affair and requires much thought to tease out.

Hinnells offers a foundational discussion of the types of influence possible between communities.[165] He notes two basic types of influence, each with their own variations: (1) the conscious imitation or borrowing of elements from another tradition, which can be either positive (i.e. accepting ideas accepted in another tradition) or negative (i.e. rejecting ideas which are rejected in another tradition); (2) conscious rejection of another tradition. The rejection of a tradition, however, can still affect the rejector's own tradition in two ways: (a) by rejecting aspects of one's own traditions seen to conform too closely to the rejected one; (b) by utilizing the modes of discourse of the rejected tradition to combat or

---

162.   Lesser, "Social Fields and the Evolution of Society," 41; Light, "Ortho-syncretism," 185; Vroom, "Syncretism and Dialogue," 109; Boyd and Richerson, *The Origin and Evolution of Cultures*, 333, 421; Swadesh, "Diffusional Cumulation," 1–21.

163.   Some of the differences in terminology relate to focus: "syncretism" often implies either the wholesale merging of two (or more) independent traditions or the conscious "cherry-picking" of foreign elements (e.g. Stevens-Arroyo, "Syncretic Sociology," 217–36). The first is not the intention here; the second would only be one kind of influence.

"Assimilation" is sometimes used in ways amenable to the present study; cf. Abdi, "Notes on the Iranization of Bes," 133–62.

164.   For an interesting attempts, see Drønen, "Scientific Revolution," 232–53; Harrison, "Cultural Boundaries," 10–13.

165.   See Hinnells, "Zoroastrian Influence on the Judeo-Christian Tradition," 9–11.

argue with it. Hinnells notes that type 1 will often occur consciously while type 2 will often occur unconsciously, although either can simultaneously function consciously and unconsciously.[166] In addition to these forms of influence, a tradition can be influenced by using new ideas to re-interpret native ideas. This last type of influence is the most difficult to detect, because it will for the most part utilize native ideas and motifs and will claim to be an organic growth of the tradition. All of these types of influence are possible—even likely—even in situations *without* external coercion, simply due to general milieu. An officially supported "missionary" program is not necessary for influence to occur; it can quite simply happen when individuals interact on a personal level. This personal level includes administrative scenarios as well as scenarios from the course of everyday life. The potential role of home life and women in particular, in terms of intermarriage, should also be kept in mind, although it is not addressed in any detail here.[167]

Two studies from a slightly different scholarly debate highlight two important aspects of any religious tradition: within each system there is a continual presence of hermeneutics as well as a hierarchy of importance for each element within the tradition.[168] No human is static, and tradents will continually (re-)interpret their traditions. However, in this process, elements which are considered to be more peripheral are prone to more extensive reinterpretation than those which are central. Vroom, emphasizing the incorporation of "foreign" and "incompatible" elements within a tradition, argues that such incorporation involves the reinterpretation of old beliefs as well as a reconfiguration of the relative structural importance of elements within the receiving system.[169] Without limiting the discussion to traditions which are "incompatible" as Vroom does, his observations on the results of influence or borrowing on the receiving tradition are still useful for evaluating less radical influences. The reinterpretation of elements within a system and the importation and adaptation of elements into a system will necessitate the altering of the "ratios" and relations in that system. When analyzing potential instances of influence, then, it is necessary to consider: (1) areas in the receiving tradition which are most susceptible to reinterpretation (i.e. how central or peripheral it

166. Ibid., 10.
167. See Brosius, *Women in Ancient Persia*; Bakker, "The Lady and the Lotus," 207–20. For different social levels, see Steward, "Levels of Sociocultural Integration," 337–53, especially 352–53.
168. Vroom, "Syncretism and Dialogue," 103–12; Light, "Orthosyncretism," 162–85.
169. Vroom, "Syncretism and Dialogue," 109.

is); (2) the re-interpretation which would be needed or effected by the influence or borrowing; (3) the relative structural impact on the receiving system.

Light understands religions to consist of three "cognitive entities": symbols, categories into which symbols are arranged, and the organizational rules which govern the importance and interactions of symbols and categories.[170] The rules which govern the relative importance or types of acceptable change will vary drastically from tradition to tradition, so that rules which are valid for one tradition will not likely be the same for another. This means that a change (or influence) which one tradition may be able to accept as normal and unproblematic could very well be "*a drastic and traumatic alteration in foundational understanding from the viewpoint of the other tradition.*"[171] This relates to Vroom's understanding of the structural importance of a given element within a tradition, and Light's illustrations make the point amply clear: while the Chinese religions are easily able to assimilate a new deity, the same is not true of the monotheistic religions. Even though two religions may share an analogous category of "divinity," they need not have the same structural importance, thus qualifying any superficial parallel between them.[172] Thus, to a Christian scholar, the adoption of a new deity looks like a drastic change, while to a devotee of Chinese religion, it would not. As a result, Light posits "two principles of religious syncretism"—the principle of religious change and the principle of cognitive integrity[173]—which could interact suggestively with a metaphor of "recipe."[174] These are similar to the views of Vroom noted above. Light posits that change will most likely produce a re-arranging of the structure and a redefinition of symbols within that structure, although the tradents will understand the process as simply a normal part of the hermeneutical process. Further, it is to be expected that the elements most likely to be influenced or borrowed are of less structural importance to or fit within currently existing categories of the receiving tradition. In other words, interaction will appear completely natural and organic within the adapting system, even if, from another (outside) perspective, it will be understood as quite radical.

---

170. Light, "Orthosyncretism," 163.
171. Ibid., 178. Emphasis original.
172. Cf. Sandmel, "Parallelomania," 5, 7.
173. Light, "Orthosyncretism," 180.
174. Lyman and O'Brien, "Cultural Traits," 225–50.

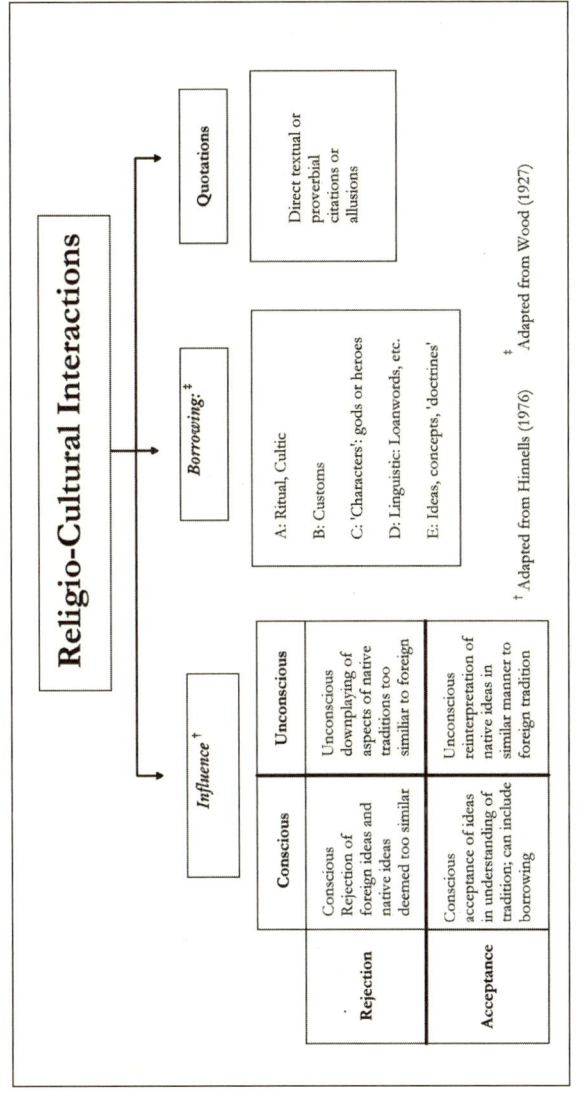

Figure 2. *Terms for Religio-Cultural Interaction*

The terms "interaction," "influence," and "borrowing" are distinguished and defined as follows. "Interaction" denotes the participation in social and intellectual intercourse with those of other religions and cultures which occurs in normal human society.[175] This interaction can have three types of result on a culture as it is visible in texts. "Borrowing" refers to the usage of a discrete element which is taken from another culture or religion. This is similar to, but here distinguished from, "quotation," which is reserved solely for the direct and intended reference to a text or saying. "Influence" designates the reshaping, selection, and/or interpretation of ideas, stories, characters, or doctrines from the native traditions due to interaction with another culture.[176] This can be conscious or unconscious, positive or negative. These three forms of interaction are not, in practice, so easily delimited; however, it is useful to make the distinction for purposes of clarity (see Figure 2). Immediately apparent from these definitions is the fact that two types of interaction—incidences of quotation and borrowing—are the easiest to identify.[177] All four forms of influence delineated are difficult to spot, with the negative forms perhaps impossible without the aid of additional, non-textual evidence.[178] A rather intimidating amount of data would probably be needed to demonstrate the unconscious rejection of internal traditions due to similarities with another tradition, and as such it is probably not often possible for Second Temple Judaism; nevertheless, the possibility ought to be kept in mind.

Given the subtleties involved in interaction, how can its presence and effects be detected in texts?

Barr delineates two basic approaches to comparative studies: general and specific.[179] He notes that general comparisons or lists of parallels do not constitute evidence of interactions; detailed, specific argument is needed to demonstrate that the general parallel is indeed not just the result of happenstance.[180] Specifically, he emphasizes the need for explanatory

---

175.   Thus, similar to "assimilation" in Barclay, *Jews in the Mediterranean Diaspora*, 92.

176.   Similar to "accommodation" in ibid., 96.

177.   For allusions, see Wold, *Women, Men, and Angels*, 49–78; for quotations, see Schultz, *The Search for Quotation*, 109–12, 214. Willey, *Remember the Former Things*, 82–83, presents seven dubious criteria for allusion.

178.   E.g. Clarke, ed., *Archaeological Perspectives*; Abdi, "Notes on the Iranization of Bes," 135.

179.   Barr, "Question of Religious Influence," 204; cf. Frye, "Iran and Israel in Antiquity," 71, "general" and "detailed."

180.   Barr, "Question of Religious Influence," 206.

circumstances and motivations which occasioned borrowing. This also needs to be undertaken with an understanding of the structural import of the proposed influence or borrowing in both source and new context. Although Barr only briefly alludes to the possibility of negative or unconscious influence,[181] his insistence that proposed parallels must be understood within the greater structural contexts is important. Rarely do people or groups adopt wholly different ideas to their own, nor do they adopt them without adaptation to their own worldview. The student must be careful to understand how a detail or concept could both be transformed by *and* transform the receiving tradition.

In broaching the question, Wood suggests five criteria which a proposed parallel must satisfy to be considered an instance of borrowing: (1) Did the receiving tradition have a need which the borrowed idea fulfilled? (2) Are there similar sources in the receiving tradition which could evolve in a similar manner? (3) Did similar ideas pre-exist in the receiving tradition? (4) Could the element come from elsewhere as well? (5) Can the source tradition be reliably dated earlier?[182] Wood's last criterion is certainly the most important; the source must predate the reception. The fourth question is also a valid concern; if similar ideas do appear in multiple contexts, one must decide whether there are enough details to justify the identification of a single source, or whether the idea is more the result of a general *Zeitgeist*. However, the first criterion is historically dubious, depending on the intent of the question: the proper historical question is not the *necessity* but the *probability* of what *did* happen in the past.[183] If Wood means that there must be a "space" or way in which the element can be utilized, then that is the same as the next two criteria. The second and third criteria appear to be the same criterion. For interaction to exist, there must be a "hanger" upon which the borrowed "coat" can hang in the receiving "wardrobe." People rarely adopt ideas which appear to them wholly alien.[184] Thus, Barr's concerns about the structural import in both traditions is necessary to understand the nature and likelihood of interaction.

In light of the above considerations, five general criteria and one additional criterion for "influence" are here proposed. The first two criteria are really preconditions: (1) the proposed source must predate the proposed incidence of interaction, and (2) there must be a plausible historical

---

181. Ibid., 208, 230.

182. Adapted from Wood, "Borrowing between Religions," 104–5.

183. Cf. the comment in Hinnells, "Zoroastrian Influence on the Judeo-Christian Tradition," 9.

184. The criteria for an element being "alien" rather than simply novel vary greatly between individuals and systems.

context for the interaction. The remaining criteria are more difficult to establish or demonstrate: (3) the foreign element must make more structural "sense" in the original context than in the new one; (4) there must be a "hook" or way in which the foreign element could be included in the receiving tradition; (5) there must be discrete, distinctive elements which betray the origin of the element. These must be more distinctive or specific than potential parallels from other sources. Any form of borrowing in a text is certainly evidence that interaction on some level has occurred, but on its own is insufficient to demonstrate the presence of influence. The accumulation of multiple, detailed borrowings certainly tilts the scales towards the possibility of influence,[185] yet a sixth criterion is needed to demonstrate influence as defined above: (6) there must be an interpretive or structural change in the receiving tradition on account of the influence. This is perhaps the most important (albeit evanescent) of the six criteria.

The first two criteria are straightforward and require no further justification. The others require more elucidation. The third criterion—the foreign element must make more structural sense in its original context—means that there should be indications that the element more "organically"[186] fits within the source tradition than in the receiving one, therefore making it more probable that its appearance in the receiving tradition is due to interaction rather than parallel internal developments. For example, the belief in the Davidic covenant in Jerusalem leads logically to the concept of the inviolability of Zion. If the same Zion doctrine were discovered in a text from a neighboring country without an analogous royal tradition, it could indicate borrowing or influence. The fourth criterion is the requirement for a "hook" or space for the new element in the receiving tradition. This is similar to Wood's insistence on the fulfilling of a need and Barr's insistence on a plausible motivation.[187] There must be a way in which the receiving tradition could have incorporated the element and still have perceived it as being consonant with said tradition (in line with Light's principle of cognitive integrity).[188] A potential example would be the adaptation of a dualism as a response to monotheistic theodicy. The fifth criterion—the need for discrete details—is the most commonly utilized. One must demonstrate why the proposed source tradition is more probable than another. Many societies have

---

185. Cf. Sandmel, "Parallelomania," 10.

186. Shaked's terminology, Shaked, "Iranian Influence on Judaism," 323.

187. Cf. Wood, "Borrowing between Religions," 104; Barr, "Question of Religious Influence," 206.

188. Light, "Orthosyncretism," 180.

analogous stories and traditions; for the parallel to be more than merely illustrative there must be discrete, distinct details betraying the original source. These could be linguistic terms or names, but could theoretically be anything. The last criterion, (6), relates to the overall structure of the receiving tradition as it can be reconstructed. This is perhaps the vaguest and most difficult of the criteria to be demonstrated adequately, but it is necessary for the attempt to be made. As both Vroom and Light note, the introduction of new elements into a system often necessitates either a reinterpretation or a reorganization of other elements in the receiving tradition (as well as the reinterpretation of the element itself). Thus, a polytheistic religion which adopts a new god will most likely correspondingly modify the functions of other, similar gods in the pantheon, perhaps even replacing some of them. It is within this criterion that Light's discussion of symbols, categories, and organizational rules becomes most helpful. Each tradition has symbols and categories which are more central and others which are more peripheral. Central elements will be more resistant to influence, while more peripheral ones will be less so. When analyzing the structure of a proposed receiving tradition, it is necessary to determine the radicalness of the proposed element within the perspective of that tradition: the "organizational rules" of the receiving tradition must be taken into account. For example, the structural importance of monotheism in Christianity would lead one to expect that either no foreign deities would be adopted or would be adopted in a drastically altered manner. This, of course, fits the assimilation of deities as saints and angels: open categories in the Christian tradition in a way the category "divinity" is not.

When seeking to understand the potential relevance of Iranian traditions, then, it is important to remember the various types of interaction which could occur, as well as to consider the six criteria noted above. Prior to analysis of particular texts or elements, however, must come at least a preliminary investigation of the structure of the two traditions in focus. The scholar must consider how the proposed interaction would have been perceived by contemporary tradents. Finally, the overall interpretative import must be considered.

This study, therefore, proceeds first to establish the historical priority of the Iranian traditions as well as their relative structures, then considers the historical, social, and communicative contexts for interaction, before attempting to directly investigate individual apocalyptic texts as sample test cases. The test cases are texts commonly associated with the origins of apocalyptic as well as texts which have been compared with Iranian traditions in the past—Ezek 37, Ezek 38–39, Dan 2, and sections from

1 Enoch. Sadly, constraints of space forbid any engagement with the "dualistic" texts found at Qumran and must be reserved for subsequent study. The final step is to build upon the test cases and to analyze the hermeneutical changes which Iranian influence would entail upon a receiving Judaism. The study concludes with suggested of implications and ideas for further research.

Chapter 1

THE IRANIAN SOURCES:
RELIGION AND ROYAL IDEOLOGY

Introduction to Iranian Religion in the Achaemenid Period

The question of Iranian influence on Judaism faces several methodological issues which must be addressed before discussing any suspected instances of influence. Grabbe[1] identifies five broad areas of consideration: the dating of Zarathuštra (Latinized Greek, Zoroaster) and his subsequent tradition; philological and textual problems; the dating of the literature; the mechanisms for influence; and the difficulty of demonstrating or disproving influence in general. The present chapter addresses the issues of the dating, nature, and content of Iranian traditions and texts; the subsequent chapter investigates the historical setting in view of establishing possible mechanisms and settings for influence. While all of the issues Grabbe identifies must be dealt with, the list itself unnecessarily limits the discussion to Zoroastrianism *per se*. Because the religious and ideological traditions in Iran most likely encompassed much more than what became known as orthodox Zoroastrianism, this chapter explores the question of Iranian religion as it can be reconstructed by the sources rather than getting caught up in the evaluation of Zoroastrianism(s).

For the purposes of influence, the date of Zarathuštra (or even his existence) is really a non-question; Zarathuštra's date, whether 1500 B.C.E. or 569 B.C.E., is still before the rise of Jewish apocalyptic literature—indeed, before the rise of the Achaemenid state. Knowledge of and influence by Iranian ideas can be demonstrated in various Greek writers; the information available from these sources allows one not only to date Iranian religious ideas but also to verify something of the nature and content of those ideas and their accessibility to non-Iranians.

---

1. Grabbe, *Yehud*, 362–63.

The important focus of investigation is the ideas which were current during the Achaemenid and Parthian empires, not necessarily those which dominated during the Sassanian Empire. Hence, ideas and symbols which may from a later perspective be considered "heterodox" or "non-Zoroastrian" are still relevant for exploration. Therefore, the question of Persian religion need not be limited to the Zoroastrian texts or even to the Zoroastrian tradition. One must be open to the possibility of influence by other Iranian religious traditions (perhaps "unorthodox" traditions), Imperial ideology and propaganda, and cultural influences of a more general nature, indeed even of general *Zeitgeist*.

Having expanded the discussion beyond so-called orthodox Zoroastrianism, the question remains as to the form of the religious beliefs which were present in the Achaemenid and Parthian Empires. The basic premise of the methodology used here is that at least some aspects of the contemporary religious beliefs and practices may be reconstructed by the careful and critical comparison of several sources: (1) the OP inscriptions and other contemporary written documents and archaeological remains, such as those found at Persepolis; (2) the reports of the classical authors as they pertain to the politics and religion of the Persians; and (3) the Zoroastrian writings.

Each of these three main sources has benefits and difficulties. The OP inscriptions have the advantage of being securely dated and contextualized, and thus offer very valuable checks for chronology. They are, however, unfortunately terse and focus on a rather narrow range of topics, largely dedicatory. In addition to the inscriptions, a variety of archaeological remains and administrative records (in Neo-Elamite and Aramaic) provide valuable sources. Like the OP inscriptions, the classical sources have the benefit of being more or less securely dated. They also tend to be much longer than the OP materials and offer a vast variety of reports, anecdotes, and opinions on the Persians and their traditions. However, the various classical writers vary in reliability and must be used with much caution. Some of the authors may indeed offer some of their material from personal observation; often, however, they (mis-)understand the Persians to fit their narratological or philosophical purposes (e.g. Xenophon's depiction of Cyrus as the ideal philosopher-king). The classical writers certainly provide valuable perspectives on the nature of Persian ideas available to other groups, even those outside of Iranian empires, but one has to be careful to separate the Iranian material from the Greek interpretation. The final primary sources of material are the Zoroastrian writings, mainly extant only in their ninth-century C.E. redaction. These writings are an extremely varied and complex conglomeration of writings from a vast variety of eras and locations—the late dating of the extant *manuscripts* is no more decisive for antiquity than the Qumran finds for the writing of the Hebrew Bible. The most important of these texts is the Avesta, the much earlier sacred scripture of the Zoroastrians.[2] The remaining texts are largely late compilations in Pahlavi (Middle Persian) which purport to translate, comment on, and/or systematize the teachings of the Avesta. The more famous of these compilations include the *Bundahišn*, which is a collection of cosmological and eschatological lore, the *Zand-ī Wahman Yašn*, which is an apocalypse supposedly written as a commentary to a lost Avestan *Yašt*,[3] and the *Mēnōg-ī Xrad*, which is a collection of a ninth century Zoroastrian priest's summary of Zoroastrian theology. The final compilations of all of these Pahlavi works can be dated due to references to events of (or the fall of) the Sassanian Empire. It is primarily these Pahlavi works which are vulnerable to the charge of anachronistic usage for comparative purposes, as they are manifestly late. However, even here the picture is not as simple as it may first appear. Much in these writings is classified as *zand*, or "interpretation": they often quote an Avestan text and then proceed to comment and expand on it. Since the *zand* sometimes quotes a passage which is not found in the extant Avesta, the Pahlavi sources can be quite useful for the reconstruction of lost Avestan texts and ideas.[4]

Zoroastrian tradition claims that there were originally 21 *Nasks* ("books") of the Avesta, although only one of those *Nasks* survives as fully extant.[5] While 21 may be a later, theologically based number, it is clear that much lore and theology has been lost (it is traditionally claimed that only one fourth of the original Avesta has survived). Because of this, the Pahlavi *zand* offers an invaluable source of otherwise lost Avestan material. The most famous example is the *Zand-ī Wahman Yašn*: while there is no known extant *Yašt* to *Vohu Manah* (the Avestan name for *Wahman*), it seems most likely that there was one which has been lost, and at least the quoted sections belonged to it.[6] This means that the late material cannot simply be ignored. Thus, even though the majority of

---

2. The Avesta is the Zoroastrians' scripture; the surviving portions consist mostly of hymns (*Yašts*) and liturgy (*Yasna*), including the *Gāthās*, the hymns attributed to Zoroaster.

3. *Yašts* are hymns devoted to a deity.

4. Cf. Hultgård, "Forms and Origins of Iranian Apocalypticism," 391–92; Widengren, "Leitende Ideen," 101–4.

5. In *Zend-Avesta I*, xxxi–xxxii, Darmesteter notes that 18 out of 30 supposed *Yašts* and only 1 *Nask* (book) out of 21 (The *Vidēvdāt*) is wholly extant. Cf. Humbach et al., *The Gāthās of Zarathushtra*, 1:4.

6. Hultgård, "Bahman Yasht: A Persian Apocalypse," 127–28.

written Iranian material is extant only in late sources, it can be useful with careful critical analysis.

As part of the effort to define the genre of apocalypse, Collins investigated the phenomenon in Iranian literature.[7] As is appropriate in a volume dedicated to the genre of apocalypse, Collins's discussion deals primarily with the Persian examples of that genre. He finds two (*Zand-ī Wahman Yasn* and the *Ardā Wirāz Nāmag*) which conform to his paradigm (Ia, IIc).[8] His analysis is admirable for dealing with the genre as extant in Iranian tradition, but it bypasses the question of the relevance of Iran for influence. Although he dates the generic apocalypses late, the influence of Iranian ideas need not be restricted by the limits of genre. Other texts which are not formally classed as apocalypses may nevertheless hold relevance.

Overview of Issues

Much debate over the possibility of Persian influence gets caught up on the date of Zarathuštra ("Zoroaster" in English, from the Greek Ζωροάσ-τρης), and thus on the antiquity of associated religious ideas. Iranian scholars have no real consensus on a date for his life; two schools give widely divergent dates—one based on a native tradition of 258 years before Alexander, and the other based largely on linguistics (usually ca. 1500–1000 B.C.E.).[9] The "traditional date" for Zarathuštra (ca. 569 B.C.E.) is unreliable—Skjærvø suggests that this date rests on "mythical" chronology, hardly a promising starting point for historical dating.[10]

---

7. Collins, "The Persian Apocalypses," 207–17.

8. Ibid., 208.

9. Rudolph, "Zarathuštra - Priester und Prophet," 84–88, chooses the ninth and eighth centuries. Boyce gives divergent dates for Zoroaster: 1000–900 B.C.E. in Boyce, *HZ I*, 3; 1500–1300 B.C.E. in idem, "Persian Religion in the Achaemenid Age," 280; 1400–1200 B.C.E. in idem, *Textual Sources for the Study of Zoroastrianism*, 11, idem, *Zoroastrians: Their Religious Beliefs and Practices*, 2, and idem, "On the Antiquity of the Zoroastrian Apocalyptic," 75. Olmstead, *History of the Persian Empire*, 102–3, accepts an equation of Darius's father Hystaspes with Zoroaster's patron *Vīštāspa* and thus a late date, as does Herzfeld, "The Traditional Date of Zoroaster," 136 (570 B.C.E.). It is much more likely that Hystaspes had been named in honor of the legendary Kavi, patron of Zarathuštra. The same opinion is held by Kent, "The Name of Hystaspes," 55. Kellens has analyzed nine of Darius's given genealogy as homonymic with the legendary figures of the Avesta (cited by de Jong, "The Contribution of the Magi," 88; the author could not access this work, however).

10. Skjærvø, "The Antiquity of Old Avestan," 16; Kingsley, "Greek Origin." The author is grateful to Dr. Almut Hintze for these references. For a suggestion that the date was based on political propaganda by Xerxes, see Kingsley, "Meetings with Magi," 193–94.

Further, there was no tradition of fixed dating until the Seleucids.[11] It is worth noting, however, that *both* chronologies place Zarathuštra *prior* to the Achaemenid Empire. Thus, the correctness of either school of thought little affects the antiquity relative to Jewish apocalyptic literature.

The oldest sections of the Avesta—the so-called Old Avestan sections of the *Yasna*, the *Gāthās* (the poems supposedly by Zarathuštra himself), and the "Yasna of the Seven Chapters" (the *Yasna Haptaŋhāiti*)—are usually dated by linguists around 1000 B.C.E. through comparison with Rig Vedic Sanskrit, and are possibly much older.[12] Skjærvø avers that various archaic features of Old Avestan compared with Young Avestan— the non-contraction of vowel sequences, the retention of *ii̯* and *uu̯* vowels, the regular use of aorist forms, and the unity of ablative and genitive endings[13]—require it to predate the Younger Avesta by at least 200 years.[14] The other parts of the Avesta are thus more recent—the "Young Avesta" dates from the pre-Achaemenid to the early Parthian Periods, and the *Vidēvdāt* ("Laws against the demons") to the late Achaemenid period.[15]

The evidence for these datings is linguistic. The end of the OP language is securely dated by the OP inscriptions and the appearance of the transition into Middle Persian (Pahlavi) in the fifth century B.C.E. evidenced therein (by loss of case endings, vowel shifts, etc.).[16] The appearance of four similar changes in both OP and Young Avestan indicates a common origin which must predate the historical emergence of OP (ca. ninth century B.C.E.).[17] The Persians appear to history in Western Iran in the ninth century, therefore the split between Young Avestan and OP must predate that time, as the Persians appear speaking OP.[18]

11. See Shahbazi, "The Traditional Date of Zoroaster Explained," 30–31. He explains 569 (32–33) as a confusion with Cyrus's conquest of Babylon; cf. Boyce, "Persian Religion in the Achaemenid Age," 279–80.

12. Fortson, *Indo-European Language*, 205; cf. Rudolph, "Zarathuštra," 87–88, 98; Boyce, *HZ I*, 3; Kellens, *Essays on Zarathustra and Zoroastrianism*, 1. See also Skjærvø, "The Antiquity of Old Avestan," 36–37, where he gives a tentative timetable which places the Old Avesta ca. 1700–1200 B.C.E. and the Young Avesta ca. 600–400 B.C.E.

13. Skjærvø, "The Antiquity of Old Avestan," 26–27.

14. Kellens, *Essays on Zarathustra and Zoroastrianism*, 35; Fortson, *Indo-European Language*, 205.

15. Skjærvø, "The Avesta as Source for the Early History of the Iranians," 63, implies a late Achaemenid date; Kellens, *Essays on Zarathustra and Zoroastrianism*, 35, however, considers it Sassanian.

16. Skjærvø, "The Antiquity of Old Avestan," 36.

17. Ibid., 33.

18. Ibid.

Since OP itself was turning into Pahlavi by the end of the Achaemenid Empire, its parallel dialect is unlikely to have lasted drastically longer as a spoken language.[19] Therefore, the language of the Younger Avesta is more or less contemporaneous with the OP inscriptions,[20] and on this basis alone the *Gāthās* and the *Haptaŋhaitī* must date at least to 700 B.C.E. Thus, the entirety of the extant Avesta—by linguistic evidence alone—must pre-date or be contemporaneous with the Achaemenid Empire. The lack of Iron Age references, references to the Western Iranian lands, or of an urban civilization or empire in the Avestan texts is consonant with the linguistic dating.[21] The linguistic development of the name of Ahura Mazda from a separable pair of epithets in the *Gāthās*, to a fixed name in the Young Avesta, to a single word (*Auramazdā*) in the inscriptions is also consistent with a dating which is prior to and contemporaneous with OP's use.[22] Widengren further avers that the Sassanian Zoroastrian scholar-priests' use of Pahlavi translations of the Avesta for their commentaries and epitomes demonstrates that the Avestan language was long dead, and that the texts preserved in Avestan are more likely to be preservations than late compositions.[23]

Beyond linguistic relationships, the close parallels between the Avesta and the *Rig Veda* and between Zoroastrian practice and Brahmanic practice demonstrate that some of the ideas, religion, and rituals evidenced in the writings go well back into Indo-Iranian prehistory.[24] It is agreed by most scholars, however, that these scriptures were oral and not written down until very late, perhaps not until the Sassanian period.[25]

---

19. Ibid., 36.

20. Fortson, *Indo-European Language*, 212.

21. Boyce, "On the Antiquity," 75; idem, *HZ II*, 1–3; Rudolph, "Zarathuštra," 92–93; Frye, *The Heritage of Persia*, 40. See also the opinion of Stausberg, who sees the city as an Achaemenid innovation. Stausberg, "Persepolis, Zoroastrianopolis, Metropolis," 14.

22. Hartman, "Datierung der junavestischen Apokalyptik," 69–72. See his very useful chart (Figure 2). Cf. Asmussen, "Die Verkündigung Zarathustras," 21.

23. Widengren, "Leitende Ideen," 153–55.

24. Indo-European Studies is based on the linguistic comparison of many modern and ancient languages, and posits a single common antecedent group for all of them. This group includes Old Irish, Norse, Latin, Hittite, Sanskrit, and the Iranian languages. "Indo-Iranian" is used of a branch of that family. For an overview, see Fortson, *Indo-European Language*; Ramat and Ramat, *The Indo-European Languages*; Mallory, "A Short History of the Indo-European Problem," 21–65.

25. Kellens, *Essays on Zarathustra and Zoroastrianism*, 33; cf. Zaehner, *The Dawn and Twilight of Zoroastrianism*, 25–26; Widengren, "Leitende Ideen," especially 92, 153–55.

Thus the discrepancy between the linguistic evidence for the "composition" and the date of the earliest manuscripts requires a very long period of oral transmission, of which some biblical scholars are understandably skeptical.[26] The antiquity of the traditions, however, can be investigated through several avenues: the linguistic evidence noted above, ritual and mythological parallels with the *Rig Veda*, parallels with Achaemenid texts and archaeology, and the evidence of Greek authors.

The religion of the *Rig Veda* corroborates the antiquity of many details, such as the ritual use of *Haoma* (Avestan)/*Soma* (Sanskrit), to which the large find of mortars and pestles at Persepolis is usually linked (see Figure 3).[27]

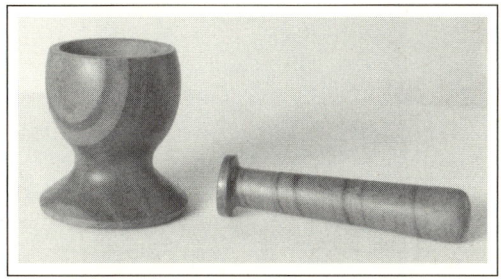

Figure 3. *Mortar and Pestle from Persepolis*
(Chicago Oriental Institute P-57934).
Courtesy of the Oriental Institute of the University of Chicago

Haoma was deified in both traditions, and it is characteristic of rites from very early on through to modern Zoroastrianism.[28] Scholars debate whether *Haoma* was stimulating, intoxicating, hallucinatory, or all three, with multiple suggestions for identification of the original plant (modern Zoroastrians use *Ephedra*).[29] The ritual respect of the hearth fire and the

26. E.g. Grabbe, *Judaism from Cyrus to Hadrian*, 101.

27. E.g. Bowman, *Aramaic Ritual Texts*, 7; Dandamaev and Lukonin, *Culture and Social Institutions*, 334; Cameron, *Persepolis Treasury Tablets*, 5.

28. The *Gāthās* only possibly allude to *Haoma* twice, in *Yasna* 32.14 and (possibly) 48.10 (Insler, *The Gathas of Zarathustra*, 49, 93); the Younger Avesta, however, makes much mention of *Haoma*, both as plant and as divinity—*Yasna* 9–11, also called the *Hom Yašt* (see *Zend-Avesta III*, 230–47).

29. Wasson, "The Soma of the Rig Veda: What Was It?," 169–87, identifies it with a hallucinogenic mushroom; Winfuhr, "Haoma/Soma: The Plant," 699–726, identifies it instead with ginseng. Boyce, *Zoroastrians: Their Religious Beliefs and Practices*, 5, 125, 173, describes the current use of Ephedra. For a fuller discussion, see Boyce, *HZ I*, 157–60; Gnoli, "Bang I: In Ancient Iran," 689. Falk, "Soma," argues for Ephedra. Thanks to Dr. Hintze for the latter reference.

use of grass or twigs (*barəsman*) are also common to both.[30] Bundles of twigs usually interpreted as the *barəsman* can frequently be seen on Achaemenid seals and engravings (see Figure 4). These details show that both Achaemenid archaeology and the Indian parallels conform to the general ritual pattern visible in the Avesta.

Figure 4. *Man with the* barəsman *(British Museum ANE 123949).*

Prior to their split, the Indo-Iranians had two groups of divinities, the *Ahuras/Asuras* and the *Daēuuas/Devas*, which Boyce characterizes as "ethical" and "amoral," respectively.[31] In India the *Asuras* became demons, and the *Devas* the gods, and the reverse in Iran. That these terms are Indo-Iranian can be seen by the correspondence of some of the names of the *Daēuuas* in the Young Avesta with the *Devas* of the *Rig Veda*—notably Indra and the Nasatyas (which also occur in the Mitanni treaties).[32] The Gathic innovation seems not to have been the "demonization"

30. Boyce, *Zoroastrians: Their Religious Beliefs and Practices*, 5; de Jong, *Traditions of the Magi*, 117; Kanga, "Barsom," 825–27.

31. Boyce, *HZ I*, 52–55; Zaehner, *The Dawn and Twilight*, 37, 39, 66, prefers remoteness and closeness.

32. Thieme, "The 'Aryan' Gods of the Mitanni Treaties," 301–17.

of the *Daēuuas* as such, but rather the rejection of their propitiation; the *Asuras* continue to receive sacrifice in the *Rig Veda*, even after their loss of status. The denial of the legitimacy of apotropaic rites, which are so amply attested in the Brahmanic literature and so central to the religious mindset of his time, easily explains at least some of the resistance experienced by the early Zoroastrian communities as evidenced in the *Gāthās*,[33] and perhaps also the persistence of some such rites, even after the adoption of some of Zoroaster's ideas.[34]

Central to the religious systems of both the *Rig Veda* and the Avesta is the concept of *aša* or *rta*—"cosmic right order," "truth"—although they developed in different ways. Whereas in India *rta* was usually contrasted with *anrta*, "disorder," in Iran *aša* came to be contrasted with *druj*, "falsehood," "deceit."[35] Whether or not Zarathuštra is the initiator of this alteration it is clearly integral to the thought of the *Gāthās* and can be seen in the inscriptions of Darius I, and to a lesser extent, Xerxes I.

Both traditions have hereditary priests who are considered *maθran-/ mantrín-*, "expert in *maθras* (the divine word)."[36] Boyce considers it likely that Zarathuštra himself was trained as a priest from the age of seven, as is evidenced among the Brahmans and the modern Zoroastrians;[37] however, the antiquity of the tradition is unaffected by Zarathuštra's historicity.[38] The memorization and recitation of the sacred word was one of the chief duties of the Indo-Iranian priests and appears to be characteristic of the profession in both traditions. Even in modern times, the verbatim recitation of hymns by Hindus by memory is reported.[39] The parallels noted above serve to demonstrate the antiquity of the religious milieu visible in the Avesta.

The Zoroastrian tradition contains much more material, however, than just the extant Avestan texts. A variety of epitomes, commentaries, and translations of Zoroastrian scriptures also survive in Pahlavi works of the ninth century C.E. (e.g. *Bundahišn*, the *Zand-ī Wahman Yašn*, and the *Dēnkart*). Much of the mythology and theology for which the Zoroastrians are known comes largely from these very late, post-Islamic redactions,

---

33. See in particular *Yasna* 46.1–4, 8 and 49.1–12. Cf. *Yasna* 28.6; 31.18; 32.13; 43.15; 51.12, 14 (Insler, *The Gathas of Zarathustra*, 81, 83, 95, 25, 41, 49, 65, 105, and 107, respectively).

34. Malandra, *An Introduction to Ancient Iranian Religion*, 18; Boyce, *HZ I*, 225, 251–52. Cf. the discussion of Plutarch's evidence below.

35. Kellens, *Essays on Zarathustra and Zoroastrianism*, 100. Cf. below.

36. Ibid., 88, 99; cf. Gonda, *Vedic Ritual*, 213–39; Boyce, *HZ I*, 8–11.

37. Boyce, *HZ I*, 7, 183.

38. See Skjærvø, "The State of Old Avestan Scholarship," 103–14.

39. See Müller as quoted in Lester, "Hinduism: Veda and Sacred Texts," 144.

though they contain much material that appears archaic. With careful methodology, even these works provide a valuable source of information on much earlier traditions; Widengren offers a number of criteria for determining quotations, translations, and paraphrases of Avestan material in Pahlavi works.[40] While these late texts can prove valuable, then, they are used here merely as supplementary material to the more surely archaic material of the OP sources, Greek authors, and the Avesta.

For these reasons, the usage of the Zoroastrian literature does not require an uncritical assumption of the antiquity of late texts. If a classical or Achaemenid text can be demonstrated to parallel a Pahlavi text, it is likely that at least a nucleus of that idea existed in the Achaemenid period, even if the final form as evidenced in the Pahlavi did not. Each text and passage will have to be assessed on its own. Despite their lateness, comparisons with the Pahlavi texts can help make better sense of the ideas in the earlier texts; the Avestan texts consist largely of allusive poetry and liturgy, while the Pahlavi works contain epitomes and systematic treatises.

On purely linguistic grounds, this study accepts that the extant Iranian texts can be roughly dated as follows (following Skjærvø): the Old Avestan texts—pre-Achaemenid; OP texts and the Young Avestan texts—Achaemenid (this includes the *Vidēvdāt* and the Avestan sections of the *Aogəmadaēca*); the *Zand-ī Wahman Yašn*—Early Hellenistic core with later accretions; the remainder of the Pahlavi texts—considered late, unless comparisons with Rig Vedic, Classical, and OP texts demonstrate a likely antiquity, or can be demonstrably shown to be quotations.[41] Thus, despite the heavy emphasis on the *Zand-ī Wahman Yašn* and the *Oracle of Hystaspes* in the literature, the method here focuses more the Avestan liturgies and hymns and the Greek reports of Iranian religion.

Evidence from Classical Authors

A useful place to begin investigating the religions of the Iranians is the more concretely datable classical authors. The following only selects a few significant points to illustrate the basic method and background utilized in this study.[42]

40. Widengren, "Leitende Ideen," 101–4.

41. For this timeline, see Skjærvø, "The Avesta as Source," 166–67; idem, "The Antiquity of Old Avestan," 39; cf. Widengren, "Leitende Ideen," 92, 153–55. Ichapora, "The Legendary History of Iran," 106–10, supports the Achaemenid dating for the *Yašts*.

42. Cf. Clemen, *Fontes Historiae Religionis Persicae*; Jong, *Traditions of the Magi*.

Plato

The first datable appearance of the name "Zoroaster" in Greek is in *Alcibiades* I.121–122. In this passage Plato discusses the training of the Persian royal heir. The "wisest" of the child's four teachers teaches him "the Magian lore of Zoroaster, son of Horomazes; that is the worship of the gods" (ὁ μὲν μαγείαν τε διδάσκει τὴν Ζωροάστρου τοῦ Ὡρομάζου ἔστι δὲ τοῦτο θεῶν θεραπεία).[43] This passage reveals knowledge of the name of Zoroaster as well as his association with the Magi ca. 390–374 B.C.E. It also shows the Greeks, however muddled their understanding, considered the royal religion to be associated with Zoroaster. According to *Lives of the Philosophers* III.6–7, Plato even planned a trip to visit the Magi.[44] If true, this would imply that the Magi were well known and had a reputation for learning. Seneca even claims that Magi were in Athens when Plato died and offered sacrifice to him at his death.[45] Plato also demonstrates the success of Darius's Behistun propaganda (*Laws* III.695B): he repeats the story of Bardiya's usurpation as given by Darius.[46] These brief passages seem to link—at least in nominal form—the Zoroastrian tradition and the royal cult, as well as imply that a combination of official propaganda and a modicum of non-official information was available to non-Iranians.

Aristotle

Two fragments from Aristotle's *On Philosophy* give relevant information.[47] According to Pliny, Aristotle states that Zoroaster lived 6,000 years before the death of Plato. Shahbazi considers the number 6,000 to be an interpolation for 600, and he uses this revised number as support for his dating of Zoroaster (ca. 1080 B.C.E.).[48] Although ingenious, this explanation implies that the Iranians had kept a more or less reliable chronology of the prophet's life, which seems unlikely. Kingsley notes that, according to Diogenes Laertius, Xanthus the Lydian—who was one of Aristotle's sources—recorded that Zoroaster had lived 6,000 years before Xerxes's crossing of the Hellespont.[49] Since the number 6,000 is

43. Plato, *Alcibiades I*, 167.

44. *Diogenes Laertius I*, 283; cf. Olmstead, *History of the Persian Empire*, 449.

45. Letter 58, line 31 (Seneca, *Ad Lucilium Epistulae Morales*, 404–7).

46. *The Laws, Books I–VI*, 228–29. However, Tuplin, "Darius' Accession in (the) Media," 237, emphasizes the differences in the accounts.

47. Ross, *Select Fragments*, 79–80.

48. Shahbazi, "The Traditional Date of Zoroaster Explained," 34–35; Humbach, et al., *Gāthās of Zarathushtra*, 26, also accept the 600 revision and uses it to place Zoroaster ca. 1080 B.C.E.

49. Kingsley, "Meetings with Magi," 190.

prominent in a variety of Iranian and Armenian eschatological schemata, Kingsley suggests this piece of information was royal propaganda portraying Xerxes as ushering in the eschatological renovation of the world, *Frašo.kərəti* ("making fruitful, renovation").[50] If this is true, then here is evidence of deliberate religio-political propaganda from the Achaemenids reaching Greek ears. This propaganda also presupposes an eschatology like the late *Bundahišn* and the *Dēnkart*. Besides this "official" propaganda, Diogenes Laertius credits Aristotle with describing the teaching of the Magi as an ontological dualism, with a good spirit named "Zeus and Oromasdes" and an evil god named "Hades and Areimanius." These names are very clearly those of Ahura Mazda/Ohrmazd and Angra Mainyu/Ahriman with their logical Greek counterparts; in the Greek writings and inscriptions Ahura Mazda is frequently identified with Zeus.[51] The depth of Aristotle's engagement with or investigation of the philosophical implications of this dualism cannot be determined from the length of the fragment, but it is possible other Greek philosophers did. These two fragments, then, seem to confirm a pre-Hellenistic antiquity for both eschatology and ontological dualism in the Iranian religious tradition, as well as at least nominal dissemination of the ideas outside "theological" Magian circles.

Herodotus

Herodotus, the most extensive written source for first half of the Achaemenid Period, records valuable information on Persian religious practice. In his *Persian Wars* (or *Histories*) I.131–132, Herodotus observes that the Persians do not "set up statues and temples and altars," considering such behavior incongruous with the non-anthropomorphic nature of the gods.[52] He claims they sacrifice on mountain tops, worshipping a list of naturalistic gods (sun, moon, earth, fire, water, winds), as well as the "whole circle of heaven" which he calls Zeus. Calling Ahura Mazda the "whole circle of heaven," is Avestan; the Avesta describes him as clothed in the sky (*Yasna* 30.5).[53] Boyce considers the list a "fair

---

50. Ibid., 191–94. Cf. Strouve, "Religion of the Achaemenids and Zoroastrianism," 534.

51. Classical renderings of Iranian deities are not necessarily so straightforward, however. Cf. Arrian, *Anabasis* VII.14.5 (*Arrian II*, 251), where he mentions a temple to "Asclepius" at Ecbatana; a number of problematic identifications could be proposed here: *Airiiaman, Θraētaona, Trita, Anāhitā, Haurvātat* and *Amərətat*. Cf. Carnoy, "The Iranian Gods of Healing," 294–307.

52. Herodotus, *Books I–II*, 170–73.

53. Boyce, *HZ I*, 193; idem, *HZ II*, 179–80; the phrase in question seems to refer strictly speaking to Spenta Mainyu. Cf. Malandra, *An Introduction to Ancient*

attempt" at rendering the *Aməša Spəntas* (a doctrine discussed below),[54] but this is an unnecessary identification: the list is congruent with the nature-worship and the worship of *Miθra* (with his frequent identification with the sun) attested in the Avesta and the Persepolis finds.[55] The issue of (fire-)temples in Achaemenid Persia is much more fraught.[56] Herodotus also claims they have a rather simple worship ceremony at which a Magus is required to sing "of the birth of the gods" (θεογονίην). Boyce considers this description as consonant with "orthodox Zoroastrian lay observance," although Benveniste and Zaehner dissent.[57] The issue of "orthodoxy" aside, it fits well with the evidence for Achaemenid practice in particular and Indo-Iranian practice generally, regardless of the identity of the θεογονίην.[58]

Also well known is Herodotus's claim that Persian boys are taught "riding, archery and truth-telling" (I.136), and that the Persians consider lying to be one of the greatest offences (I.138).[59] The importance of the idea of truth (Avestan *Aša*, OP *Arta*) can be seen positively in the *Gāthās* as well as negatively in the Bisitun (Behistun) inscription of Darius I. *Aša* is an extremely important concept in the *Gāthās*: one of the *Aməša Spəntas*, it appears both personified and as a common noun.[60] Those who choose *aša* are commonly contrasted with those who choose *druj* ("falsehood").[61] *Aša* occurs in the *Gāthās* over 80 times, quite remarkable

Iranian Religion, 40; Insler, *The Gathas of Zarathustra*, 33; Skjærvø, "Ahura Mazdā and Ārmaiti," 401–2.

54. Boyce, *HZ II*, 179. However, Jong, *Traditions of the Magi*, 102, rejects this, seeing a naturalistic explanation.

55. E.g. Hallock, *PFT*, 559 (PF 1955), 567–8 (PF 1960, line 4); the various natural gods in the *Yašts*. Herodotus's information on *Miθra* is, however, problematic. For one solution, see Edwards, "Herodotus and Mithras: Histories I.131," 4.

56. For discussions, see Keall, "Archaeology and the Fire Temple," 15–22; Stronach, "On the Evolution of the Early Iranian Fire Temple," 605–27; Boyce, "Ātašdān," 7–9; Stausberg, "Persepolis, Zoroastrianopolis, Metropolis," 48–49; Henkelman and Kleber, "Babylonian Workers in the Persian Heartland," 169.

57. Boyce, *HZ II*, 181; Benveniste, *The Persian Religion*, 29–30; Zaehner, *Dawn and Twilight*, 167.

58. Benveniste, *The Persian Religion*, 31, thinks that the "theogony" is the *Yašts*, but not the *Gāthās*, as the *Yašts* are explicitly liturgical; this position, however, ignores that the entirety of the *Yasna*, which includes the *Gāthās*, is a liturgical text. Russell, "Zoroastrian Notes," 6, suggests *Yasna* 30. Most commentators, however, favor a *Yašt*; cf. Gershevitch, "Old Iranian Literature," 2–3. It is also possible Herodotus refers to now-lost cosmogonic hymns or was mistaken.

59. Herodotus, *Wars I–II*, 176–79.

60. E.g. *Yasna* 28.3; 33.7, 12; 34.6; 44.9. Cf. Boyce, *HZ I*, 212–13; Narten, "Bahman I: In the Avesta," 487.

61. I.e. *Yasna* 30.10; 31.1; 46.6, 11; 49.11; 51.10, 14; 53.6.

given the length of the text. In the Bisitun inscription, Darius attributes the uprisings surrounding his accession and the authority of the "Pseudo-Bardiya" to *Drauga* ("Falsehood"), the OP equivalent of *Druj*. *Drauga* as an active force is mentioned four places,[62] while the act of insurrection is several times referred to as "he lied" (*adurujiya*).[63] In fact, Darius repeatedly declares that "Ahuramazda brought me aid" (*Auramazdāmai upastām abara*) and that this was so because he was "no follower of Falsehood" (*nai draujana āham*).[64] While the Behistun text clearly served a political purpose, the rhetoric of the text frequently utilizes religious language consonant with the religious tradition and the importance of the *Aša-Druj* dichotomy.[65] Indeed, Skjærvø notes "lexical correspondences" between DBb 6–13 and *Yasna* 60.5[66] and suggests that Darius saw himself as the ideal worshipper of Ahura Mazda, perhaps even portraying himself as a *Saošiiant*[67] in the Susa inscription (DSf 15–18).[68] Since in the *Rig Veda*, *Rta* (= *Aša*) is contrasted with *anrta* (= **anaša*, "disorder"), rather than the Sanskrit equivalent of *druj*, *druh*,[69] it seems that the opposition of Truth/Order (*Aša*) to Falsehood/the Lie (*druj*) is characteristic of Iranian religious thought, if not Zoroastrianism *per se*.[70] It is highly likely that Herodotus was accurate in pinpointing this area of royal ideology, which was also consonant with the thought of the Avesta.[71]

Herodotus also declares that the Persians consider the sun to afflict leprosy in recompense for sin (I.138). This must refer to *Miθra*, who was frequently identified with the sun and responsible for protecting the contract.[72] In the *Bahram Yašt* (14.48) one of *Miθra*'s associated deities,

62. Schmitt, *The Bisitun Inscription*, I §10, IV §54–56, IV §63, IV §64 (51, 54–56, 63, 64).

63. Ibid., I §16, III §49, IV §52 (54, 67, 68).

64. Ibid., IV §63 (71).

65. Skjærvø, "Avestan Quotations in Old Persian?," 10. Cf. Schwartz, "The Religion of Achaemenian Iran," 685–86; Benveniste, *Persian Religion*, 35–40, strongly disagrees.

66. Skjærvø, "Avestan Quotations," 50–51.

67. *Saošiiant* is a Gathic epithet meaning "victorious one, over-comer, savior" which becomes a technical term for the final eschatological savior.

68. Skjærvø, "Avestan Quotations," 57, 58.

69. Kellens, *Essays on Zarathustra and Zoroastrianism*, 101.

70. Boyce, *HZ II*, 120–21, thinks that Darius's use of *drauga* indicates his Zoroastrianism. Cf. Skjærvø, "Avestan Quotations," 55.

71. *Aša* also appears in the common Achaemenid throne name "Artaxerxes" (OP *Artaxšasa*, "ruling through truth"); cf. Boyce, *HZ II*, 178; Schmitt, "Artaxerxes," 654–55. See also pp. 149–71, below.

72. Boyce, *HZ I*, 24–25; Herodotus, *Wars I–II*, 179. Frye, "Mithra in Iranian History," 64, is happy to see Greek evidence as confirming *Miθra*'s role with oaths.

Vərəθragna, protects the faithful who do not lie to *Miθra* from leprosy,[73] and in Zoroastrianism *Miθra* was one of the deities who weighed the actions of the dead.[74] He also notes that the Magi practice exposure, while the Persians embalm their dead in wax before burial (I.140).[75] Both of these burial practices are attested in the archaeological record of Asia Minor.[76] In the midst of a somewhat legendary tale, Herodotus notes that King Darius (I) refused to pass under the remains of a dead body (I.187).[77] If this story has any historical reality, it seems to indicate some form of concern for ritual purity in regards to death. Some have thought the rock tombs of the Achaemenids, as well as the reference to embalming in wax, indicate a concern for the avoidance of contamination, but there is evidence that regular Persians were interred with no ritual barriers, only clay coffins, between the corpse and the earth.[78] It is certain that later Sassanian scruples over burial were not yet universally current in the Achaemenid period, but the Magi may have been beginning to think in that direction. Evolution in Iranian funeral practices is likely illustrated by the change in meaning of the word *daxma* from "grave" to "exposure area."[79] At least one clear concern for purity exists, however—the protection of fire from the contamination of bodies. Herodotus reports that fire was venerated as a god (III.16).[80] *Ātar*, "fire," appears often in the Avesta, and images of "fire altars" are common on Achaemenid seals.[81]

73. *Zend-Avesta II*, 244. The previous verse (47) explicitly links the protection to not-lying.

74. *Miθra* is described as being "debt-paying" and having 10,000 eyes in the *Mihr Yašt* (10).7, 18–19, 69, 82 (Gershevitch, *Hymn to Mithra*, 77, 83, 107, 113; *Zend-Avesta II*, 121, 124, 139–40); Boyce, *Textual Sources*, 28–29; cf. idem, *HZ I*, 31.

75. Herodotus, *Wars I–II*, 178–81. Strabo (XV.3.20) repeats this, but adds a detail of incestuous marriage (Strabo, *Geography VII*, 183–85).

76. Shahbazi, "The Irano-Lycian Monuments," 174–89.

77. Herodotus, *Wars I–II*, 235.

78. Schmidt, *Persepolis II*, 117–23; Stronach, *Pasargadae*, 40–43, does not mention any graves, but he suggests purity as a possible reason for the design of Cyrus's tomb. Cf. Frye, "Religion in Fars Under the Achaemenids," 175.

79. Grenet, "Burial II," 559.

80. Herodotus, *Wars III–IV*, 23.

81. Cf. *Yasna* 36.1, 3 (Narten, *Der Yasna Haptaŋhaiti*, 40–41); *Yašt* 19.46–49 (Hintze, *Zamyād-Yašt*, 241–66). For some seals, see Pope and Ackerman, eds., *A Survey of Persian Art*, vol. 4, plate 123, C and F; plate 126, J and H; drawings in Moorey, "The Persian Empire," 47; also the discussion in Houtkamp, "Some Remarks on Fire Altars of the Achaemenid Period," 23–48, and in Root, "From the Heart: Powerful Persianisms in the Art of the Western Empire," 118–22; Choksy,

In the course of the Greek campaign, Herodotus claims Xerxes buried alive nine boys and maidens at "Nine Ways," and that Xerxes's wife buried fourteen nobles' sons to the god of the netherworld (VII.114).[82] Such apotropaic rites are strictly forbidden in Zoroastrianism. This behavior contradicts the earlier information given by Herodotus that the Magi were concerned with the defiling aspects of the corpse, if indeed they practiced exposure for that reason, and if Darius's above scruple is historical. If the accounts of live burial are historical, there are two possible explanations: either the Magi had yet to develop a concern for the purity of the earth and the practice was some form of "black" Iranian practice, or the events were more political or judicial than religious. Considering the so-called *Daivās* (OP for *Daēuuas*) Inscription of Xerxes (XPh §4b.35–41), where Xerxes boasts of ending the worship of the *Daēuuas* in an unmentioned location (*daivadāna*)[83]—he even contrasts the worship of the *Daivās* with the worship of Ahura Mazda and *Arta*[84]— it is difficult to accept Xerxes assenting to a "black" ritual. If these events are compared with the stories Herodotus tells of Cambyses's treatment of a royal judge who accepted a bribe (V.25) and Astyages's treatment of Harpagus (I.119),[85] a political or judicial setting looks more probable. While the Harpagus incident is suspect due to Herodotus's largely legendary treatment of Median history and the Cambyses incident could fit into his portrait of the emperor as a madman, the Great King still was the final arbiter of justice and not beyond drastic punitive measures. Many of the Greek authors are intent on portraying moral lessons in their writings, with the decadence of the Persian kings a favorite topic.[86] Attributing these live burials to apotropaic rites or a queen's selfishness may be a "misunderstanding" that fits Herodotus's theory of Xerxes's *a priori* inferiority to his father and to Cyrus.

"Reassessing the Material Contexts of Ritual Fires in Ancient Iran," 229–26; also note the comments of Strabo XV.3.14, 16 on the purity of fire and water (Strabo, *Geography VII*, 175, 179).

82. Herodotus, *Wars V–VII*, 417; Boyce, *HZ II*, 167–69.

83. Kent, *Old Persian*, 150–52; Malandra, *An Introduction to Ancient Iranian Religion*, 51; Boyce, *Textual Sources*, 105; another translation can also be found in *ANET*, 316–17. Boyce, *HZ II*, 175–77; Briant, *From Cyrus to Alexander*, 550–53; Abdi, "The 'Daiva' Inscription Revisited," 46–50.

84. XPh §4b.40–41 (Kent, *Old Persian*, 150–52).

85. Cambyses is said to skin a judge who took a bribe, cover the judicial chair with his skin, and force his son to sit on and judge from that seat (Herodotus, *Wars V–VII*, 27); Astyages is said to feed Harpagus his own son (Herodotus, *Wars I–II*, 154–57).

86. Cf. Plato, *Laws I–VI*, 230–33 (III.695); Kuhrt, "The Achaemenid Persian Empire," 97–98.

Herodotus (I.140) also notes that the Magi kill every creature except dogs, something resonant with the later Zoroastrian practice of killing "*xrafstras*," obnoxious creatures considered to be the creation of Angra Mainyu.[87] Instruments for the destruction of such creatures can be found in the Avestan text, the *Vidēvdāt*.[88] This is quite a peculiar practice to Herodotus, and he remarks that the Magi consider it virtuous; something of the later theological justification for the practice must have existed in at least some form by this time. Indeed, it is perhaps related to Xerxes's habit of sponsoring the killing of scorpions north of Susa.[89] Despite some scholars' opinions that this habit was a Magian or Median innovation, the killing of *xrafstras* appears to be an Iranian practice, as it appears in such a role in Indian texts.[90] Further, Herodotus records Xerxes honoring a particularly beautiful tree (VII.31).[91] Boyce finds this to be typical of Iranian religious practice and possibly related to one of the *Aməša Spəntas*.[92] Whether or not there is any relation to an *Aməša Spənta*, this act fits with the nature-worship recorded earlier by Herodotus, as well as with the noted Persian predilection for paradises.[93]

Greeks quite commonly remarked on the Persians' veneration of rivers or water, but Herodotus records that Xerxes scourged the Hellespont with a hundred lashes, calling it a "bitter water" (πικρὸν ὕδωρ, VII.35).[94] Later Zoroastrian doctrine considered salt water to be fresh water corrupted by Angra Mainyu, which Boyce thinks explains this behavior.[95] While the source she quotes is quite late (*Bundahišn*), the account in Herodotus could be considered evidence for the antiquity of the belief. The first chapter of the *Vidēvdāt* contains an analogous system of Angra Mainyu's counter-creations, although salt water is not included in the

---

87. Herodotus, *Wars I–II*, 178–81; Boyce, *Zoroastrians: Their Religious Beliefs and Practices*, 44, 76, 179. On veneration of dogs, see Boyce, *HZ I*, 302–3.

88. *Vidēvdāt* 14.8 and 18.2 (*Zend-Avesta I*, 168, 189).

89. Aelian, *On the Characteristics of Animals* XV.26 (*On the Characteristics of Animals III*, 250–53); cf. Briant, *From Cyrus to Alexander*, 402.

90. Jong, *Traditions of the Magi*, 338–42.

91. Herodotus, *Wars V–VII*, 245.

92. Boyce, *HZ II*, 165.

93. Tuplin, *Achaemenid Studies*, 80–131; cf. Briant, *From Cyrus to Alexander*, 442–43. Trees do appear to have been deliberately cultivated by the administration. PFa 33 links ten types of trees with the location of several *partetaš* (Hallock translates these as including olive, apple, quince, mulberry, pear, and date). This must be relevant. See Hallock, "Selected Fortification Texts," 116, 135–36; cf. Stronach, "Čahārbāg," 624.

94. Herodotus, *Wars V–VII*, 346–49.

95. Boyce, *HZ II*, 166; cf. idem, *HZ I*, 232; Zaehner, *Dawn and Twilight*, 160.

pericope.[96] The earlier-noted occurrence of *xrafstras* in Herodotus, however, may indicate that theological speculation on such issues was already underway in Xerxes's time. In VII.191,[97] the Magi sacrificed to Thetis and the Nereids to make a storm cease. Shahbazi considers the Nereids to be a Hellenized form of the Ahuranis, consorts of Ahura Mazda. It is possible that Thetis is an attempt to translate *Arədvī Sūrā Anāhitā*, a water-goddess of Indo-Iranian origin who was later assimilated to Anaïtis, and whose cult is well-attested in Achaemenid times.[98]

Herodotus periodically associates the Magi with the interpretation of dreams (I.107, 120; VII.19).[99] This could be considered a Greek confusion with the Babylonians, long noted for astrology and oneiromancy. While the first mention is in a clearly legendary tale of Astyages, it is probable that the professional religious caste of the Achaemenids served their royal patrons in this manner, since it was a traditional priestly duty in many (if not all) of the conquered lands. On their own, these reports of oneiromancy are insufficient to ascertain the level and importance of such activity among the Magi. Despite their fame and obvious importance to Iranian religious life, the Magi remain unfortunately little known. Herodotus's general picture of the Magi as important priests in the empire is—at least on that point—consistent with the evidence from Persepolis, if not particularly illuminating.[100]

Xenophon

Xenophon is problematic for historical investigation. It is clear that much of his historiography is dependent on previous writers, particularly Herodotus, and that he has Hellenized, philosophized, or novelized much of his material.[101] Xenophon follows Herodotus in crediting the Persian education with truth-telling (*Cyr.* I.vi.33).[102] He has Cyrus offer libations after dinner (*Cyr.* II.iii.1);[103] a note in the LCL edition claims that this is a

---

96. *Zend-Avesta I*, 4–10; Anklesaria, *Pahlavi Vendidâd*, 1–14.

97. Herodotus, *Wars V–VII*, 509.

98. Shahbazi. "Monuments," 156; cf. Boyce, *HZ I*, 71–72; Zaehner, *Dawn and Twilight*, 160–61. Anāhitā's cult certainly predates Artaxerxes II, as she appears on seals. Moorey, "Aspects of Worship and Ritual on Achaemenid Seals," 225, suggests her iconography can be found among the Oxus Treasure finds.

99. Herodotus, *Wars I–II*, 139, 156–59; idem, *Wars V–VII*, 333.

100. The Magi do appear in various tablets, often associated with the mysterious *Lan* ceremony. The significance and meaning of this is still debated; cf. Handley-Schachler, "The *Lan* Ritual," 195–204; Razmjou, "The *Lan* Ceremony," 103–17.

101. See Sancisi-Weerdenburg, "The Death of Cyrus," 459–71.

102. Xenophon, *Cyropaedia Books I–IV*, 119.

103. Ibid., 177.

Greek interpolation, but libations are attested both in later Zoroastrian use and in the Persepolis tablets, including for the *Haoma*-ceremony.[104] Xenophon's descriptions of Cyrus's sacrifices are reminiscent of the phrases which appear in the OP inscriptions ("Ahuramazda and the other gods who are")—in *Cyr.* III.iii.21–22 Cyrus sacrifices to Zeus and every god brought to his attention; in VII.i.1 he has Cyrus offer sacrifice and libation to "ancestral Zeus"; in VIII.v.57 Cyrus sacrifices to Hestia, ancestral Zeus, and "any other god the Magi suggested." In VIII.vii.3, he offers to ancestral Zeus, Helius, and all the gods.[105] Zeus and Helius could easily be understood as Ahura Mazda and *Miθra* or *Huuar Xšaēta* (*yazata* of the sun) and Hestia is possibly linked to the cult of the hearth fire.[106] Xenophon claims Cyrus was devout, singing and sacrificing daily, and that he instituted a college of Magi (VIII.i.23–24).[107] The Magi do appear frequently in the Persepolis tablets, and it is likely that they were the official priests to the Achaemenid Dynasty from the beginning, perhaps holding pre-eminence in the Median Empire as well.[108] It is possible that Cyrus organized an official cult training apparatus, even though no Iranian "church" is known until the Sassanian period,[109] but Xenophon could also be simply projecting his image of the ideal ruler onto Cyrus.

Xenophon describes a procession of Cyrus as headed by four bulls for "Zeus and the other gods as the Magi directed." The procession also had horses to be sacrificed to the Sun and three chariots—a chariot for Zeus (with white horses), one for the Sun, and a third chariot (unassigned) with purple trappings, followed by a fire altar (VIII.iii.11–12).[110] Since by Artaxerxes II's reign (404–359), the court acknowledged Ahura Mazda, *Miθra*, and *Anāhitā* in its inscriptions,[111] and Xenophon's expedition was during Artaxerxes II's reign, it is reasonable to assign the

---

104.   Boyce, *HZ I*, 155–56; on the *Haoma* ceremony, see 157–62; Duchesne-Guillemin, "The Religion of Ancient Iran," 353–54. For the tablets, e.g., Cameron, *Persepolis Treasury Tablets*, on Tablet 11 (101) there appears a *Haoma*-priest; Hallock, *PFT*, 229 (PF771), is the receipt for a libation to Ahura Mazda.

105.   Xenophon, *Cyropaedia I–IV*, 279; Xenophon, *Cyropaedia Books V–VIII*, 203, 287, 361, 423.

106.   Boyce, *HZ I*, 154–55.

107.   Xenophon, *Cyropaedia Books V–VIII*, 317.

108.   Briant, *From Cyrus to Alexander*, 245–46, 267–68; Dandamaev and Lukonin, *Culture*, 331–32; cf. Bowman, *Aramaic Ritual Texts*, 6, 10, 31. For the tablets, e.g., Hallock, *PFT*, PF 757, 788, 769, 772 (226–27, 229).

109.   For a concise overview, see Duchesne-Guillemin, "The Religion of Ancient Iran," 323–76.

110.   Xenophon, *Cyropaedia V–VIII*, 355.

111.   Kent, *Old Persian*, 154.

three chariots to this triad; in any case, the chariot for Zeus is certainly for Ahura Mazda and that of the sun for *Miθra*. Perhaps one may wish to see the other member of the old Indo-Iranian triad, **Vouruna*, as here venerated,[112] but this is unlikely considering the lack of attestation for his worship. If Ahura Mazda is **Vouruna*, as Zaehner suggests,[113] then the third chariot cannot be his in any case. The one piece of evidence given of this god is the purple trappings. Shahbazi suggests that the chariot was in honor of Kavi Vīštāspa, the patron warrior-king of Zarathuštra (or more properly, his *frauuašī*).[114] If Arrian is to be believed, deceased kings were given sacrifical honors,[115] and some scholars argue that the kings' *daimon* in Plutarch's *Artaxerxes* is the royal *frauuašī*.[116] Additionally, Boyce claims that in Iran purple was the color of warriors[117] and Strabo mentions purple as one of the summer wardrobe choices of Persian warriors, though it is unclear why.[118] If this warrior association is correct, then Shahbazi's suggestion is possible, although the martial aspects of *Anāhitā* in her assimilation to Ištar may also explain the purple trappings. Since it is known that Artaxerxes II set up temples to *Anāhitā*[119] but references to Vīštāspa's *frauuašī* are lacking, *Anāhitā* seems a more likely candidate for the chariot.

The information derivable from Xenophon is largely consonant with the other sources, albeit within a Greek veneer. While useful as a check, it offers little that is completely novel, of major consequence, or not massively problematic for use.[120]

Plutarch

In his *Moralia, Isis and Osiris* (46–47), Plutarch gives a fairly lengthy description of Persian religion.[121] Although writing around 120 C.E., he

---

112.   Boyce, *HZ I*, 37. Boyce even argues that the formula "*Auramazdā utā Miθra baga*" in A²Pa 24–25 (Kent, *Old Persian*, 156) is the triad Mazda, *Miθra*, and **Vouruna*. See Boyce, "Apạm Napāt," 149. It should be noted, however, the numerous interpretations proposed for "*baga*." Cf. Sims-Williams, "Baga II: in Old and Middle Iranian," 405.

113.   Zaehner, *Dawn and Twilight*, 66–68, as does Jakobson, "The Slavic God Velesb," 42.

114.   Shahbazi, "Iranian notes 1–6," 500–502.

115.   *Anabasis* VI.29.7 (*Books V–VII; Indica*, 295).

116.   Plutarch, *Artaxerxes* XV.5 (*Plutarch Lives XI*, 163). Cf. Taylor, "The 'Proskynesis' and the Hellenistic Ruler Cult," 53–62, esp. 54, 57.

117.   Boyce, *HZ II*, 21, 147, 287.

118.   Strabo, *Geography* XV.3.19 (Strabo, *Geography VII*, 183).

119.   Berossus, *Babyloniaca* III.5.2 (Burstein, *The Babyloniaca of Berossus*, 29).

120.   See Tuplin, "Persian Garrisons in Xenophon," 67–70.

121.   Plutarch, *Isis and Osiris* (*Moralia V*, 111–15).

claims his information comes from Theopompus, who wrote in the fourth century B.C.E.[122] This passage is very significant for the dating of several concepts. He ascribes to Zoroaster (as well as "the great majority of the wisest of men") an ontological dualism. He also describes a good god "Oromazes" and an evil god "Areimanius," with Mithras in the middle, an apotropaic rite involving "omomi" ($\ddot{o}\mu\omega\mu\iota$), the killing of noxious animals, an eschatological battle between the two gods, the creation of six supportive- and counter-gods, and a cosmology. Putting aside the question of the orthodoxy of the Zoroastrianism described here, a few important ideas are unambiguously evidenced. A radical ontological dualism is linked with an eschatology which contains a period of war and a final victory for the forces of the good god, and these two antagonists are clearly identified as Ahura Mazda and Angra Mainyu. This is also accompanied by what could be called a proto-angel– and demonology, creatures which are clearly created by the respective gods to aid them in their battles against each other. Sundermann even argues that Plutarch's description of Angra Mainyu's demise as due to hunger parallels the myth of his swallowing by *Āz*, the demon of hunger.[123] The eschatological scenario described by Plutarch parallels many details in the *Bundahišn* (e.g. 1.17–18, 26–27; 2.5–7; 30.7–32).[124] These passages in the *Bundahišn* have a much more systematic and extensive eschatology than any other extant Iranian text; the appearance of the same themes in Plutarch, however, proves that the ideas long predate the *Bundahišn*'s ninth-century redaction.

It is frequently pointed out that the rites described in Plutarch's passage are not consonant with Zoroastrian teachings.[125] Indeed, the practice of apotropaic rites is generally considered to be one of the integral prohibitions of Zarathuštra. However, attempting to limit the discussion of Persian religious ideas to the "orthodox" Zoroastrian position is unnecessary. The information Plutarch gives here perhaps reveals religious ideas that may hint towards the origins of the religious movement known as Mithraism or may simply reflect "black" practices;[126] however, contra

---

122. Benveniste, *Persian Religion*, 69.

123. Sundermann, "The Zoroastrian and the Manichaean demon *Āz*," 333.

124. *Pahlavi Texts I*, 7, 9–10, 12, 123–29; Anklesaria, *Zand-Ākāsīh*, 7, 9, 33, 261–63. Cf. Hultgård, "The First Chapter of the Bundahišn," 167–90; idem, "Persian Apocalypticism," 70–74.

125. Benveniste, *Persian Religion*, 73–75; Boyce, *HZ I*, 171; cf. Boyce and Grenet, *HZ III*, 456–60; Zaehner, *Zurvan, a Zoroastrian Dilemma*, 13; Moulton, *Early Zoroastrianism*, 128–30; Griffiths, *Plutarch's De Iside et Osiride*, 474–75.

126. However, Jong, *Traditions of the Magi*, 179–80, sees the description as based on Zoroastrian polemic, and thus not reflective of any real sect at all.

Boyce, the role of *Miθra* as mediator is not necessarily so foreign to Iranian doctrine—the role of *Miθra* as judge could easily be interpreted or extended to mediation, as could his role as protector of the contract.[127] The role of *Miθra* as mediator does appear in the *Zand-ī Wahman Yašn*, and Shaked understands Plutarch as reflecting an older understanding which was lost by the Pahlavi redactions.[128] Further, the system of six good gods and six counter-gods seems to be identical to the doctrine of the *Aməša Spəntas* and their evil counterparts.[129] His subsequent mention of 24 deities can also be related to the Zoroastrian calendar dedications.[130] It is remarkable, then, how much of Plutarch's information is constant with the late Pahlavi writings. It is certain, anyway, that similar cosmological and systematic treatments of Iranian traditions were underway centuries before the Sassanians.

Strabo

Strabo, writing in the first century C.E., combines personal observation with the works of previous Greek authors. His *Geography* provides a few details on Persian religious customs which are congruent with the Zoroastrian tradition and the OP inscriptions. In XV.3.13, he restates Herodotus's information (I.131) that the Persians use neither statues nor altars.[131] However, two sections later he notes not only a large number of "temples to the Persian gods" in Cappadocia, but claims to have seen a procession of a statue of "Omanus" himself (XV.3.15);[132] he had previously noted Armenian temples to Anaïtis (XI.14.16).[133] This can be understood two ways: that there was a historical development in Persian religion from the time of Herodotus to Strabo in which "fire temples" (Πυραιθεῖα) became normative; or, that temples were used "selectively," either only for certain gods or rituals or by certain groups who existed simultaneously with "traditional," "exterior" worship. Boyce and Grenet suggest that "Omanus" is *Vohu Manah*, one of the *Aməša Spəntas*;[134] perhaps this points to either a prominence of the *Aməša Spəntas* by the first century, or to a link between adherence to the doctrine and temple-use.

127.   Boyce and Grenet, *HZ III*, 478–79; Benveniste, *Persian Religion*, 88.
128.   Shaked, "Mihr the Judge," 14–19 (Section V); cf. Kuiper, "Remarks on the Avestan Hymn to Mithra," 46.
129.   Humbach et al., *Gāthās of Zarathushtra*, 13 n. 17, understands a reference to the *Aməša Spəntas* in this passage.
130.   Jong, *Traditions of the Magi*, 195.
131.   Strabo, *Geography VII*, 175.
132.   Ibid., 177.
133.   Strabo, *Geography V*, 341.
134.   Boyce and Grenet, *HZ III*, 250, 270.

Strabo's depiction of the education of Persian boys (noble, presumably) is quite suggestive, particularly if it is more than an elaboration of the account in Plato. Beyond paralleling the particular disciplines of study, Strabo describes a course of oral training which sounds distinctly like a heroic-poetic tradition.[135] In a largely oral culture, the deliberate inculcation of cultural and religious traditions is to be expected, especially among the nobility.[136] An anecdote attributed to Dinon also places minstrels, at least, as early as the Median court.[137] Strabo's description, then, confirms the existence of at least one potential medium that made possible the transmission of the traditions which are extant only in later manuscripts.

Strabo also offers descriptions of the general Persian sacrificial rituals, all of which are similar to the pictures drawn from the Avesta and OP.[138] He describes sacred fires, prayers, blood sacrifice, libations, bundles of sacred twigs, and the presence of Magi. These descriptions require all of these elements—if based on personal observation—to date to the early Roman period at the latest, and—if based on previous Greek writers—to a much earlier period. The Persian archaeological record, however, confirms Strabo's description as accurate for the Achaemenid period as well: seals discovered at Persepolis depict a ritual with a man/two men with mouth(s) covered holding twigs before a table with mortar and pestle and a fire altar.[139]

Religious Situation in Iran

Before approaching the issue of Judaean–Iranian contacts, it is necessary to investigate the religious situation in Iran and the matrix of religious ideas likely to have been encountered in the Achaemenid Empire (and the later Parthian Empire). The details are heavily debated, but aspects relevant to the question of influence can be picked out from amid the melée without having to decide on all of the tricky questions in the history of Iranian religion.

It is common to distinguish between three forms or stages in the development of Iranian religion, namely: the early Indo-Iranian religion, the religion of the reformer (the so-called Zarathuštrianism), and later

135. Berossus, *Babyloniaca* XV.3.18 (*Geography VII*, 179).

136. Boyce, "The Parthian *gōsān* and Iranian Minstrel Tradition," 10–45; Skjærvø, "Royalty in Early Iranian Literature," 99–108.

137. Athenaeus, *The Deipnosophists* XIV.633 (*Athenaeus VI*, 417–19).

138. See XV.3.14, 15, 16 (*Geography VII*, 175–76, 177, 179).

139. See Schmidt, *Persepolis II*, 26, plate 7 (PT3 363); 9–10, plate 7.

Zoroastrianism.[140] Boyce, however, dissents from many in the evaluation of the difference between "Zarathuštrianism" and Zoroastrianism, seeing a greater continuity of thought between the *Gāthās* and the Avesta.[141] Many scholars also add a fourth "Zoroastrian heresy" commonly called Zurvanism.[142] Jong characterizes three basic approaches to the history of Zoroastrianism, which he calls the "fragmenting, harmonizing, and diversifying" approaches, and he criticizes what he sees as an overly Hegelian view of history in each.[143] Rather than trying to impose evolutionary or dialectical models on the evidence, it is important to allow a realistic picture—one which will often be messy and contradictory.

Shaked has rightly criticized the prevailing understanding of Zurvanism as a Zoroastrian heresy or independent religion,[144] such as dominates much discussion of Achaemenid period religion.[145] "Zurvanism" refers to the myth that both Ahura Mazda and Angra Mainyu were twins born of the god Zurvan ("Time") that some scholars take to be the defining belief of a separate "heresy" or faith. The question of the relationship between Zoroastrianism and Zurvanism is essentially the perennial question of whether the religion as taught by Zarathuštra was monotheistic or dualistic: Was the dualistic understanding a corruption or faithful continuation of the religion of the *Gāthās*? And, was the dualism "primary" or "secondary"? The debate essentially hinges on the interpretation of a single Gathic passage, *Yasna* 30.3–5. Insler translates this passage as the following:

> [3]Yes, there are two fundamental spirits, twins (*yəmā*) which are renowned to be in conflict. In thought and in word, in action, they are two: the good and the bad. And between these, the beneficent have correctly chosen, and not the maleficent. [4]Furthermore, when these two spirits first came

140.   Malandra, *An Introduction to Ancient Iranian Religion*, 4; cf. Schwartz, "The Religion of Achaemenian Iran," 664–97; Gershevitch added an additional term "Zarathuštricism," but it apparently was not taken up subsequently. See Gershevitch, "Zoroaster's Own Contribution," 12–38.

141.   E.g. Boyce, *HZ II*, 241–42.

142.   E.g. Boyce, "Some Reflections on Zurvanism," 304–16. A particular proponent was Zaehner, "Zurvanica I," 303–20; idem, "A Zervanite Apocalypse I," 337–98; idem, "A Zervanite Apocalypse II," 606–31; idem, *Zurvan*.

143.   Jong, *Traditions of the Magi*, 43–45.

144.   Shaked, *From Zoroastrian Iran to Islam*, Section V (220–40); previously published in Shaked, "The Myth of Zurvan," 219–36. Cf. Jong, *Traditions of the Magi*, 66, who agrees.

145.   In particular, see the work of Zaehner, *Dawn and Twilight*, 175–247, and, of course, Zaehner, *Zurvan*; cf. the work of Widengren; see, e.g., Widengren, "Leitende Ideen," 129–36.

together, they created life and death, and how, at the end, the worst existence shall be for the deceitful but the best thinking for the truthful person. [5]Of these two Spirits, the deceitful chose to bring to realization the worst things. (But) the very virtuous spirit, who is clothed in the hardest stones, chose the truth, and (so shall those) who shall satisfy the Wise Lord continuously with true actions.[146]

Particularly vital to the interpretation of this passage is the understanding of the term "twins" (*yəmā*). Some interpret it literally, and thus posit an original but derivative dualism;[147] others metaphorically. Of these latter, depending on whether or not Spenta Mainyu is equated with Ahura Mazda, some scholars conclude a dualism,[148] or a monotheism[149] (see Figure 5). In the midst of this hermeneutical melée, however, two things are certain: the interpretation of the verse is exceedingly difficult and ambiguous, and the force of Zarathuštra's teaching was primarily an *ethical* dualism. The implications of these two points are very significant, and often overlooked in the discussion.

	Ahura Mazda and Spenta Mainyu Not Identified	*Ahura Mazda and Spenta Mainyu Identified*
Monotheistic/ Monistic	Ahura Mazda ↙ ↘ Angra vs. Spenta Mainyu Mainyu	? ↙ ↘ Angra vs. Ahura Mazda = Mainyu Spenta Mainyu
Dualistic	Ahura Mazda Angra Mainyu vs. ↓ Spenta Mainyu	Angra vs. Ahura Mazda = Mainyu Spenta Mainyu

Figure 5. *Scholarly and Potential Readings of* Yasna *30*

That the interpretation of this passage is ambiguous can be clearly seen in the continual divide between scholars.[150] What is not appreciated

---

146. Insler, *The Gathas of Zarathustra*, 32–33.

147. Duchesne-Guillemin, "The Religion of Ancient Iran," 339; Fox, "Darkness and Light," 132–33; Eliade, *A History of Religious Ideas*, 1:310; cf. the Zurvanite interpretation.

148. Boyce, *HZ I*, 193–94; (as a protest against monotheism) Henning, *Zoroaster: Politician or Witch-Doctor?*, 46–49; Lommel, *Die Religion Zarathustras*, 20–25.

149. Haug, *Essays on the Sacred Language*, 149, 304–5; Kent, "The Name Ahuramazda," 207; Zaehner, *Dawn and Twilight*, 50–51.

150. Cf. Gignoux, "Monotheism or Polytheism?," 65–71, who refuses to make a decision on the matter.

is that this ambiguity most likely, if not definitely, *existed already in the adherents of the tradition* in the Achaemenid, Parthian, and Sassanian periods, just as it does today. It is in this light that the "Zurvanite" myth must be viewed: this teaching took the word "twin" literally and posited that Ahura Mazda and Angra Mainyu were twins born of the god Zurvan, "eternal time," an interpretation also followed by many modern commentators. Thus, a dualism grounded in a (remote) monotheism. Simultaneously, the Magi may have interpreted the word "twins" simply as an ontological co-eternity of the two deities. Some modern commentators attempt to describe Zarathuštra's teaching as monotheistic in tendency or actuality, and see this tendency also in the inscriptions of Darius I and Xerxes.[151] While a plethora of gods or entities are evident in the *Gāthās* and the *Yasna Haptaŋhāiti*, there is no doubt that Ahura Mazda always takes a place of prime importance, as he does in the OP inscriptions. Much scholarship considers the renewed presence of Indo-Iranian deities in the Younger Avesta and *Vidēvdāt* as a "backslide" or capitulation to the old Iranian polytheism, but this is far from clear.[152] The resolution of this issue brings up the second point above: the focus of Zarathuštra's message.

That the *Gāthās* teach an ethical dualism focused upon the person of Ahura Mazda is unquestionable, even if expressed with ritual terms.[153] All of the *Gāthās* can easily be seen to be drawn from this premise: that humanity is presented the choice between *aša* and *druj*, and that Ahura Mazda is the god exclusively of *aša*. This teaching had ontological implications; what is unclear is whether or not Zarathuštra himself drew these implications. The force of his teaching is, to borrow a term coined in the discussion of the monotheism of Israelite religion, *monolatrous*; whether or not other deities existed, Ahura Mazda alone was source of all which was worthy of worship. In this light, his teaching had a monotheistic-appearing tendency situated in an ethical dualism. However, in light of the subtlety of his verses, these two tendencies—monistic and dualistic—appear in constant flux, and have led modern commentators to

---

151. Zaehner, *Dawn and Twilight*, 155–61. Without commenting on monotheistic tendencies, Briant, *From Cyrus to Alexander*, 550–53, sees Xerxes's inscriptions as consonant with Zoroastrianism. Cf. Skjærvø, "Avestan Quotations," 3, who sees a "close genetic relationship" between the two religions.

152. Zaehner, *Dawn and Twilight*, 79–82; Benveniste, *Persian Religion*, 26–27.

153. Skjærvø, "The Antiquity of Old Avestan," 25; Kellens, *Essays on Zarathustra and Zoroastrianism*, 63–79, 91; Hintze, "The Rise of the Saviour in the Avesta," 86–88, in a slightly different context, questions the ritualistic interpretation of Gathic elements.

conflate the ethical with the ontological dualism.[154] The tradition is thus susceptible to simultaneous interpretations of dualism and monotheism, in a tension which refuses to be removed.

In an interesting article, Boyd and Crosby discuss the history of this problem and attempt a solution which is highly illuminating.[155] They place the question of dualism versus monotheism in the perspective of eschatology: while current reality is dualistic, the end of history will also be the end of Angra Mainyu, and thus of dualism, or, as they phrase it, "Zoroastrianism combines in a manner unique to itself among the major religions of the world a cosmogonic dualism and an eschatological monotheism."[156] Two of the arguments which Boyd and Crosby utilize are of much interest to the present study: they reveal the integral nature of time and the *eschaton* to the theological system, and the link of Ahura Mazda with wisdom. "Time plays an absolutely decisive role in the Zoroastrian religion, even to the point of altering in a fundamental manner the ontological status of Ahura Mazda."[157] It is this concept which unifies Zoroaster's monolatry and his ethical dualism, as well as explaining the myth of the subordination of Ahura Mazda and Angra Mainyu to Zurvan (the personification of the concept *zruuān akanārag*, "eternal time")—the fates of both are indeed dependent on time.

The basic translation of the name "Ahura Mazda" as either "The Wise Lord" or "Lord Wisdom" is well known;[158] the importance of this role as the god of wisdom is pointed out by Boyd and Crosby. It is this role, they argue, which enables Ahura Mazda to guarantee his ultimate victory over Angra Mainyu despite his ontological limitations and without compromising the role of the ethical human will.[159] This doctrine is highly sophisticated and balanced, and it is to be expected that a multiplicity of understandings and simplifications of it would quickly circulate. That neither the monotheistic or dualistic interpretations are wholly correct helps explain some of the confusion over the matter, both in modern research and in ancient observers.

154.   In fact, the use of "dualism" in scholarship often conflates all kinds of binary oppositions which may or may not be related. For a pertinent study to this effect (albeit with terminology which this author would not endorse), see Gammie, "Spatial and Ethical Dualism," 356–85.

155.   Boyd and Crosby, "Is Zoroastrianism Dualistic or Monotheistic?," 557–88.

156.   Ibid., 575.

157.   Ibid., 576.

158.   Kuiper, "Ahura Mazda 'Lord Wisdom'?," 25–42, rejects the meaning "Lord Wisdom"; Kent, "The Name Ahuramazda," 200–209, accepts either interpretation.

159.   Boyd and Crosby, "Is Zoroastrianism Dualistic or Monotheistic?," 578.

The second clear point is the ethical thrust of the above-quoted passage, as of the *Gāthās* as a whole. While unavoidably containing cosmological, ontological, and ritual referents, the *Gāthās* are prayers which emphasize the righteous choice made by the speaker (the original composer as well as the present reciter) before the god, and as an "added benefit" encourage the listener to make the same choice. The term "twins" emphasizes the duality of the choice more than making an ontological statement. As Boyce noted, Zarathuštra was not a modern systematic theologian nor philosopher[160]—indeed, Choksy prefers to call him a devotional poet.[161] This choice is available to every human, just as it was to the divine beings—both or all hundreds of them. On its own the teaching is able to adapt to a form of polytheism by subordinating all to the choice, and thus either to the realm of Ahura Mazda or Angra Mainyu. Whether this "adaptation" involved a fall from monotheism to polytheism or a reform from polytheism to monotheism is immaterial to present concerns.

Ethical dualism and ontological dualism are not the only important dualisms in the Zoroastrian texts; a dualism between material/tangible and immaterial/intangible (Avestan **mainiiauuaka-* and **gaēiθiiaka-*, Pahlavi *mēnōg* and *gētīg*) also plays an important role.[162] This concept is both similar to and very different from the dualism between spirit and matter found in Greek philosophy, but the importance of this has generally been overlooked in the debates over potential Iranian or Hellenistic influences on Jewish thought. The material and immaterial dualism cuts across *both* of the other dualisms in Iran (ethical and ontological); neither is valued nor disvalued compared to the other, unlike in Platonic or Gnostic systems.[163] In fact, the physical world is of immense value as it was created with the express purpose of defeating Angra Mainyu.[164] While the implications of the *mēnōg* and *gētīg* dichotomy certainly underwent significant elaboration, possibly even absorbing some Neo-Platonic influences in the Sassanian period,[165] the dualism appears

---

160.   Boyce, *HZ I*, 201. Cf. Oxtoby, "Interpretations of Iranian Dualism," 661.

161.   Choksy, "Hagiography and Monotheism in History," 407–21.

162.   On the issue of *mēnōg* and *gētīg*, see Lommel, *Die Religion Zarathustras*, 93–129; Boyce, *HZ I*, 229–36.

163.   Shaked, "The Notions *mēnog* and *gētīg*," 59–60; Hasenfratz, "Iran und der Dualismus," 37–38, 40.

164.   E.g. *Gr. Bund.* 3 (esp. vv. 23–24)//*Sh. Bund.* 2.9–11 (Anklesaria, *Zand-Ākāsīh*, 20–45; *Pahlavi Texts I*, 14). Cf. Shaked, "The Notions *mēnog* and *gētīg*," 70–73.

165.   Shaked, "The Notions *mēnog* and *gētīg*," 60.

already in the *Gāthās*.[166] As Shaked shows, this dualism is intimately entwined with the eschatological perspective of Zoroastrianism, and it makes sense of the apparent duplication of eschatological events: justice is served both in the spiritual (*mēnōg*) and physical (*gētīg*) planes.[167]

A Zoroastrian idea which has been alluded to several times is the doctrine of the *Aməša Spəntas*, or "Holy/Bountiful/Beneficent Immortals."[168] These are abstract entities which appear in the *Gāthās* and are standardized into a list of six or seven in the Young Avesta. They are difficult to classify, as they are personifications of abstract ideas[169] and alternate in use between the abstract concept and personification.[170] The most important are *Vohu Manah* ("Good Thought") and *Aša Vahišta* ("Best Truth/Order") in the *Gāthās*, and while the *Aməša Spəntas* were not systematized into a fixed list (or indeed even given that name) in the *Gāthās*, they clearly are important to its thought.[171] At some point, the *Aməša Spəntas* were associated with the seven elements of the creation, possibly under Greek influence.[172] It is impossible to know exactly how Zarathuštra envisioned these entities, but Boyce may be right to consider them as an attempt to "ethicize" the Indo-Iranian nature religion.[173] In the Bisitun Inscription and on his tomb, Darius is surrounded by six co-conspirators, and some have seen a conscious imitation of Ahura Mazda and the *Aməša Spəntas* here.[174] Spənta Ārmaiti does appear in

166.   E.g. *Yasna* 28.2; 31.11; 43.3 (Humbach et al., *Gāthās of Zarathushtra*, 1:117, 129, 152).

167.   Shaked, "The Notions *mēnog* and *gētīg*," 75, 83–84.

168.   Boyce, *HZ I*, 196–97, 264.

169.   They are standardized as *Vohu Manah* (Good Purpose or Thought), *Aša* (Truth, Order), *Amərətat* (Immortality), *Ārmaiti* (Devotion or Piety), *Haurvātat* (Health or Wholeness), *Xšaθra* (Dominion or Kingdom), and sometimes *Spənta Mainiiu* (the Holy Spirit). See Boyce, *HZ I*, 203; Kellens, *Essays on Zarathustra and Zoroastrianism*, 48.

170.   As essentially emanations of Ahura Mazda, cf. Zaehner, *The Dawn and Twilight*, 46; as independent beings, Boyce, *HZ I*, 201–4. Cf. Humbach et al., *The Gāthās of Zarathushtra*, 1:13–14, 16; Duchesne-Guillemin, *The Western Response to Zoroaster*, 39–41; Mills, *Zarathuštra, Philo, the Achaemenids, and Israel*, 12; Rudolph, "Zarathuštra - Priester und Prophet," 110.

171.   Kellens, *Essays on Zarathustra and Zoroastrianism*, 50–54.

172.   The seven elements are fire, water, earth, sky/metals, plants, animals/cattle, humanity. See Boyce, *HZ I*, 203–5.

173.   Boyce, *HZ I*, 204–9, 220–22; cf. Kellens, *Essays on Zarathustra and Zoroastrianism*, 18; on 62 he refutes this.

174.   Boyce, *HZ II*, 91–94; Shahbazi, "An Achaemenid Symbol II," 125; however, Jong, *Traditions of the Magi*, 56 n. 50, rejects this theory. The present author is exploring this elsewhere.

six unpublished Persepolis Fortification Tablets.[175] Beyond this, they only appear sporadically in more or less probable allusions during the Achaemenid period, including the passages noted above in Plutarch and Strabo. Given their highly ritual allusions, however, it is also possible their significance was confined to the priestly class.[176]

The Magi

The Greek authors and the Persepolis tablets make the importance of the Magi undeniable; if they did not hold a monopoly on religious specialization in the Achaemenid Empire, they certainly were the most important priests of the Iranian religion, at least in the western areas of the empire. What is decidedly uncertain is exactly what they were; Herodotus (I.101)[177] claims the Magi were one of the six tribes of the Medes, but they also consistently appear in his history as priests; they also receive rations for offerings in the Persepolis tablets, where they are linked to the mysterious *Lan* ceremony.[178] Strabo describes them as one of the three tribes of Persis, but he also labels the "Chaldaean" wise men both "tribes" and "sects."[179] Scholars variously understand them to be an ethnic tribe, a sociological caste, or professional class,[180] portraying them as converts to Zoroastrianism, opponents to Zoroastrianism, and mercenary ritualists willing to sacrifice regardless of the convictions of the client.[181] Several scholars make the Magi central to their understanding of the transformation of "Zarathuštrianism" into "Zoroastrianism" and/or Zurvanism.[182]

---

175.   Listed in Henkelman, *Other Gods Who Are*, 530–31; cf. 327–28.

176.   Jong, "The Contribution of the Magi," 94; idem, *Traditions of the Magi*, 186; Hintze, "On the Literary Structure of the Older Avesta," 50. Kellens, *Essays on Zarathustra and Zoroastrianism*, calls the *Gāthās* "speculative ritual," 112.

177.   Herodotus, *Wars I–II*, 133.

178.   E.g. Hallock, *PFT*, 226–27, 229 (PF757, 769, 772). For studies on the *Lan*, see Handley-Schachler, "The *Lan* Ritual," 195–204; Razmjou, "The *Lan* Ceremony," 103–17; Henkelman, *Other Gods Who Are*, 181–304.

179.   As a Persian tribe: XV.3.1 (Strabo, *Geography VII*, 157); on the Chaldaean sect-tribes: XVI.1.6 (203).

180.   As a tribe: Diakonoff, "Media," 141; as a caste: Moulton, *Early Zoroastrianism*, 187; as a hereditary class: Boyce, *HZ II*, 19–20, 84–85.

181.   Converts: Zaehner, *Dawn and Twilight*, 161–65; opponents: Boyce, *HZ II*, 21, 66–67; as due to royal influence: Schwartz, "The Religion of Achaemenian Iran," 696–97; as "mercenaries": Gershevitch, *Hymn to Mithra*, 16–17.

182.   Fontaine, *The Light and the Dark*, 5:27, 29, claims the Magi were Medians who corrupted Zoroastrianism into Zurvanism, echoing Moulton, *Early Zoroastrianism*, 198, 197, where the Magi are described as responsible for the Avesta's divergence from the *Gāthās*. Zaehner, *Dawn and Twilight*, describes a ping-pong-like

Much of the Greek and Latin evidence for the Magi is unusable, as the figure of the Magus gradually became assimilated with the image of the sorcerer (and thus the origin of the word *magic*).[183] The Greeks frequently credit the Magi with astrology, divination, and magic, traits scholars sometimes attribute to Babylonian influence.[184] While Babylonian influence on the Persians is undeniable, scholarly discussion of the influence upon the Magi is frequently in conjunction with the Magian "corruption" or misunderstanding of the Zoroastrian tradition.[185] Indeed, Zurvanism's supposed tendency towards fatalism is sometimes attributed to this influence.[186] Nevertheless, the sources allow no conclusions on their influence as differentiated from Iranian religion in general.[187] All that is certain is that they were important, commonly associated with the name of Zoroaster, supported by the Great Kings, and hereditary.

Although relatively unnoticed, the ambiguity of the Magi seems to parallel the status of another priestly tribe, the Levites.[188] The Torah's description of the role and position of the Levites is ambiguous, just like the descriptions of the Magi: sometimes the Levites are distinguished from priests, and sometimes they are not.[189] The Levites were hereditary, just like the Magi. If priests in these groups generally became priests because they were born into a priestly family, the image or analogy of a tribe is fairly apt, regardless of the origin of the group. Perhaps a better word to use than "tribe" is "caste." It is worth noting that just as Second Temple Judaism had several parties within the priestly group—there is no reason to assume that the Magi were a unified group.

---

alternation between the "Zurvanites" and the "Mazdeans," utilizing the terms "primitive," "catholic" and "reformed Zoroastrianism"; cf. Fox, "Darkness and Light," 133–34.

183. Colpe, "Development of Religious Thought," 826–28; Jong, *Traditions of the Magi*, 387, 393.

184. Cf. Boyce and Grenet, *HZ III*, 278, 368, 386–89; Colpe, "Development," 826–31.

185. E.g. Schwartz, "The Religion of Achaemenian Iran," 690, 696–97; Moulton, *Early Zoroastrianism*, 182–253 (Lectures VI and VII), finds the Magi responsible for the Avesta and its "Semitic overtones." Jong, "The Contribution of the Magi," 90–91, notes the unhelpfulness of this approach.

186. Zaehner, *Dawn and Twilight*, 236–44; Boyce, *HZ II*, 234–35.

187. Jong, "The Contribution of the Magi," 90–92, 95.

188. Neusner, "The Rabbi and the Magus," 81, would rather compare the Magi to the Rabbis.

189. For example, see the overview in Grabbe, *Priests, Prophets, Diviners, Sages*, 41–43, 52–53; cf. Levine, *Numbers 1–20*, 104–5; Tuell, *The Law of the Temple in Ezekiel 40–48*, 121–52.

Persian Archaeology and Royal Ideology[190]

While less specific than a particular cultus, the remains of Achaemenid imperial art reveal a consistent religio-political ideology of the Great King which differed from those of previous empires, some of which is consonant with Avestan ideas.[191] The art and archaeology of Iran deserves a much more thorough investigation in this regard.[192] Nylander points out subtle but significant alterations to Mesopotamian monumental traditions in the imperial reliefs that betray a specific and intentional royal ideology. This ideology glories in the extent and multiplicity of the empire and in its subjects' *voluntary* submission and subservience to the Great King.[193] The procession of peoples bearing gifts on the Apadana and at the "Gate of All Nations" at Persepolis, as well as Darius I's foundation tablet at Susa, reveal this (see Figure 6). In contrast to Egyptian and Assyrian iconography, where the king is depicted crushing the opponents of world order, the Achaemenid art portrays the king as welcoming the collaboration of peoples in the maintenance of the world.[194] Whereas the Assyrians graphically used violence in their aesthetic, the only visible violence in the Achaemenid repertoire is the hero slaying a monster and the lion killing a bull (see Figure 7). Yet, even in these scenes there is still an odd sense of serenity, of the proper order remaining upheld.[195] Both the lion and the bull are common symbols in the ancient Near East,

190. The present author is working on a fuller discussion of this elsewhere.

191. See the discussion in Nylander, "Achaemenid Imperial Art," 345–60.

192. For some studies in these areas, see Appendix I.

193. Root, *King and Kingship*, 262. On reusing tropes known in Elam, see Alvarex-Mon, "Imago Mundi," 203–37.

Much of the iconography is lost due to its perishable nature. See Cameron, "Persepolis Treasury Tablets Old and New," 166; Quintus Curtius Rufus, *History of Alexander* V.vii.5 (*Quintus Curtius I, Books I–V*, 387). Based on his excavations, Schmidt, *Persepolis I*, speculates that heat damage evinces extensive wall-hangings (78–79) and that monumental sculptures (81) graced Persepolis.

194. Nylander, "Achaemenid Imperial Art," 54–55.

195. The Lion-Bull symbol is itself highly debated. Root, *King and Kingship*, 236, sees it merely as a symbol of royal power. Bivar, "Document and Symbol in the Art of the Achaemenids," 49–67, sees it as a symbol of *Miθra* assimilated to Nergal; Stronach, "Icons of Dominion," 387, suggests it represents the Great Kings' total power over nature and man. Axworthy, *Empire of the Mind*, 8, suggests (without discussion) a far-fetched interpretation of image as a symbol of Angra Mainyu attacking *Vohu Manah*. Bizarre interpretations have a long pedigree, however. Perhaps the most lingering is an astrological/calendrical interpretation; cf. Hartner, "Old Iranian Calendars," 725–36; Marsh in Vesta Sarkhosh Curtis et al., eds., *The Art and Archaeology of Ancient Persia*, 87; and Alvarex-Mon, "Imago Mundi," 228, who calls it "elementary powers charged with the stability of the world."

but their ubiquity in Achaemenid art is one of its most conspicuous aspects. Bulls and lions, either singly or together, appear in carvings, on seal impressions, coins, plates, and as the capitals of magnificent pillars. The prevalence and stylization of the bulls and lions indicates a deliberate and particularly Persian ideology in their use.

Figure 6. *Detail from Apadana (Chicago Oriental Institute PS-73).*
Courtesy of the Oriental Institute of the University of Chicago

Figure 7. *Lion and Bull Relief (Chicago Oriental Institute P-468).*
Courtesy of the Oriental Institute of the University of Chicago

Far from implying a postmodern hero in the Great King, this ideology of diversity instead urges recognition of the yet poorly understood ideological and theological underpinnings of the Persian Empire. That this world order is explicitly or implicitly in the name of Ahura Mazda is visible in all of the kings' inscriptions from Darius I.[196] Skjærvø even suggests that Darius not only quotes the Avesta in OP translation, but saw himself as partially fulfilling the role of a *saošiiant* by making the world *fraša* an important eschatological term.[197] It seems, then, that at least aspects of the Avestan tradition were important to royal ideology, at least from Darius I onwards. These are ideologies which could not have gone unnoticed by the Judaeans. These more overtly political sources, moreover, need not be ignored in the investigation of influence: political and religious ideas can interact in numerous ways, or have mutual influences on the expression of the other.[198] An example of iconography which may carry both religious and political overtones is the so-called winged disk.

Winged Disk
One of the most ubiquitous symbols of the Achaemenids is the winged disk (see Figure 8). It is perhaps the only symbol which is used more often than the bull and/or lion. The symbol is generally considered to be borrowed via Assyria from the Egyptian solar disk. It appears on reliefs, coins, and seals. Sometimes it is merely a winged disk; sometimes the disk contains the upper half of a bust of a crowned male figure, holding a ring of power. Sometimes the lower part of the ring has an eagle tail.

As the winged disk borrowed the ninth-century Assyrian representation for either Aššur or Šamaš,[199] many scholars have assumed that in Persian contexts the symbol stands for Ahura Mazda, the god mentioned in many royal inscriptions.[200] Shahbazi, however, demonstrates that the

196.   Kent, *Old Persian*, 116–57; cf. Skjærvø, "The Achaemenids and the Avesta," 52–53; Bianchi, "Mithra and the Question of Iranian Monotheism," 39–40; Skjærvø, "Avestan Quotations," 1–64.

197.   Skjærvø, "Avestan Quotations," 57. However, Hintze, "Frašō.kərəti," 190–92, considers the word *fraša-* to have no eschatological content in OP; cf. Bailey, *Zoroastrian Problems*, viii.

198.   For example, note the use of eschatological rhetoric for political ends by Xerxes I as argued by Kingsley, "Meetings with Magi," 173–209. See now Strawn, "'A World Under Control'," 85–116.

199.   Root, *King and Kingship*, 210–13, cf. 178; Kuhrt, "The Achaemenid Concept of Kingship," 158.

200.   For examples, see: Root, *King and Kingship*, 213; Skjærvø, "Avestan Quotations," 43; Briant, *From Cyrus to Alexander*, 248–49; cf. Shahbazi, "An Achaemenid Symbol I: A Farewell to Fravahr and Ahuramazda," 135.

identity of the winged disk with Aššur was based upon an assumption of the identity of it in Persia with Ahura Mazda, and the identity with Ahura Mazda later supported by the identity with Aššur.[201] He further argues that beyond the circular logic, the identification in fact is questioned by four considerations: (1) it contradicts the evidence of Greek authors; (2) it is questioned by the variety of forms in which the symbol appears; (3) it ignores that the symbol is sometimes subordinate to other divine symbols; (4) it ignores the dissimilarity to known depictions of Ahura Mazda in post-Achaemenid Iranian art.[202]

Figure 8. *The Winged Disk on the So-Called Seal of Darius*
(British Museum AN23386001).

Shahbazi instead proposes that the winged disk symbol was intended as a representation of *Xᵛarənah*—both the Royal/Kingly and Iranian Glory (OP *Farnah*).[203] Both de Jong and Boyce concur.[204] *Xᵛarənah* in the Zoroastrian writings is a complex concept; closely linked with one of the later systematized *Aməša Spəntas* (*Xšaθra*, "kingdom"), *Xᵛarənah* was a political and religious concept, and its precise translation is debated. The entire *Aštād Yašt* (18) is devoted to the praise of the *Xᵛarənah* of the Aryans, although Hintze considers the *Zamyad Yašt* (19) to be the most important text for understanding the concept.[205] It has been translated as

---

201.   Shahbazi, "An Achaemenid Symbol I," 139–40.
202.   Ibid., 141–44.
203.   Ibid., 119–47.
204.   Jong, *Traditions of the Magi*, 299–301, prefers to understand the symbol as the king's *xvarənah* as does Boyce (Boyce, *HZ II*, 102–5).
205.   Hintze, *Zamyād-Yašt*, 17.

"glory," "fortune," "dignity," "luck," and by Hintze as "Glücksglanz."[206] It was possessed by the Mazdayasnian religion (what the Zoroastrians call their religion), the Aryans and the Aryan lands, heroes, and the king. According to the *Zāmyād Yašt* (19.34–36) and the *Shahnameh*, the *X⁽ᵛ⁾arənah* departed from the mythical primal king Yima when he "found delight in words of falsehood and untruth" in the form of falcon.[207] And, according to the same *Yašt*, §§11–12, 19–20, 23–24, 89–90, it is the *Aməša Spəntas* and their *X⁽ᵛ⁾arənah* which will renew the world by ending decay and death.[208] Indeed, the *Zāmyād Yašt* strongly links *X⁽ᵛ⁾arənah* to the *Saošiiant*, the eschatological savior or "overcomer,"[209] who will inaugurate the final age when evil is no more. While Hintze argues that *frašā* does not have an overtly eschatological connotation in OP as it has in Avestan,[210] it is tempting to speculate that Darius chose this symbol to allude to this victory of Ahura Mazda's *frašā* world at *frašō.kərəti*—as he describes his palaces in his incriptions. The rule of Iran cannot be held without the Iranian *X⁽ᵛ⁾arenah*, and it can only be given, not seized,[211] certainly a convenient idea for a monarch. It also echoes Darius's frequent pronouncements of Ahura Mazda's aid (e.g. the remarkably religious and political Bisitun inscription).[212] If the winged disk was intended to depict the royal *X⁽ᵛ⁾arənah*, it is difficult to know how much of its resonances would have been known to the average Persian subject, whether devotees of Ahura Mazda or not. Yet, that the idea was certainly known in the empire is demonstrated by its appearance as a theophoric element in names.[213] It certainly would have been easily recognizable as a royal symbol, but the array of ideas associated with *X⁽ᵛ⁾arənah* would only be suggested to those who knew the intended referent. Shahbazi suggests

---

206. Scholars translate the term variously: "(God given) Fortune"—Shahbazi, "An Achaemenid Symbol II," 121; "the desired thing, fortune"—Bailey, *Zoroastrian Problems*, 2–75; "Dignity"—Zaehner, *The Teachings of the Magi*, 26; "Glücksglanz" (with a review of scholarly positions)—Hintze, *Zamyād-Yašt*, 28–32. Cf. Greppin, "The Xvarənah as a Transfunctional Figure," 232–42.

207. Hintze, *Zamyād-Yašt*, 191–202; *Zend-Avesta II*, 293. In the later *Shahnameh* IV.1, this is described simply as "Allah's Grace," rather than a falcon (Firdausī, *Shāhnāmeh*, 1:135).

208. Hintze, *Zamyād-Yašt*, 109–28, 148–49, 365–68.

209. See 19.88–97 (Hintze, *Zamyād-Yašt*, 364–400); Hintze suggests the translation of "overcomer" (Überwinder) for *Saošiiant* to avoid the Christian connotations of "savior" (157).

210. Ibid., 107.

211. Ibid., 26–27, 32.

212. Kent, *Old Persian*, 116–34; see also Schmitt, *The Bisitun Inscription*.

213. For a convenient list, see Shahbazi, "An Achaemenid Symbol II," 146. One (פרנדת) is also listed by Porten, "Persian Names," 186.

that veneration of *Xᵛarənah* can be seen in Isa 65:11, but this is unlikely: even if the Achaemenid cult of *Xᵛarənah* was assimilated with the Greek τύχη and the Aramaean גדה in places, it is more likely that Third Isaiah simply intended the old Aramaean cult.[214] Still, if the connection is correct, it is evidence of both the dating of the eschatological ideas and of their importance at least in the royal cult.

The case of the winged disk, then, illustrates both the remaining work to be done on the ideological matrices of the Achaemenid period, as well as the necessity to expand the discussion beyond "Zoroastrian" texts *per se* without excluding them. Political ideology—with its inherently religious coloring—is not to be excluded from the remit of potential Iranian influences. Much more work towards these ends remains to be explored, with the traditions surrounding (and promoted by?) Cyrus perhaps the most outstanding.[215]

Summary

The scholar looking for sources on Iranian religion during the Achaemenid period has plenty to investigate, even if the evidence requires significant reconstruction and complex case-building. Achaemenid texts and artifacts, Greek authors, and the Avesta provide reliable sources of information on the period before Alexander and can be used together to reconstruct some of the ideas which were current at that time. Even though the extant Iranian manuscripts are very late, they can provide invaluable perspectives on ideas which most likely circulated in the Achaemenid Empire when investigated in conjunction with the other sources. Linguistic considerations show that the latest parts of the Avesta can be securely dated to the Achaemenid period; various Classical texts, OP inscriptions, and Elamite texts attest to contemporary practices. The late, Pahlavi sources can be useful when attesting lost Avestan texts, or when explaining otherwise enigmatic classical sources. The investigation is greatly aided if not confined to a search for a monolithic, "orthodox" tradition, but is willing to see the variety which inevitably presents itself. The following chapter deals with the issues of the potential settings for interaction.

214. Shahbazi, "An Achaemenid Symbol II," 129; Blenkinsopp, *Isaiah 56–66*, 274, 278–79.

215. Cf. Anföldi, "Königsweihe und Männerbund," 12, 14; Kuhrt, "Making History," 347–61. See the Excursus in Chapter 2.

Chapter 2

THE ACHAEMENID CONTEXT

There were many opportunities for Judaeans and other Yahwists to
come in contact with Iranian peoples, within Israel and in the diaspora.
The exact location where Jews were influenced by Persian ideas cannot
be proved—indeed, they were probably absorbed over time and in a
variety of locations—but the opportunity for such absorption can be
amply demonstrated. As the entirety of the Yahwistic world lived under
Achaemenid rule for roughly 200 years, there are too many scenarios to
discuss each in detail; the following four broad geographical areas
(Babylonia, Media and Iranian lands, Egypt, and Palestine) highlight
likely locales where Iranian presence and Judaean/Israelite presence can
be surmised.[1] Given the number of potential historical contexts in which
Judaean-Iranian interaction was possible, complete segregation of the
two peoples would require remarkable proof.[2]

Babylonia[3]

Nebuchadnezzar deported Judaean exiles to the region of Nippur, on the
Chebar Canal (Tel Abib; Ezek 1:1, 3; 3:15; 10:15, 20, 22). From the
conquest of Cyrus, or at the latest, Darius I, Nippur also housed estates
of Persian nobles and Iranian colonies. These estates included the lands
of Prince Achaemenes, his son Phradates, and the Egyptian satrap
Aršam.[4] Indeed, Dandamaev suggests that entire districts around Nippur

---

1. Several other regions could also be discussed (Asia Minor, various islands).
2. Decisions on any of the discrete items discussed here are not necessary for the
present purposes; they merely demonstrate that historical interactions between the
two populations had ample opportunities within the Achaemenid Empire, fulfilling
the historical criterion for influence set forth above.
3. Cf. Oded, "The Settlements of the Israelite and Judean Exiles," 91–103.
4. Dandamaev, "The Domain-Lands of Achaemenes in Babylonia," 123–27. For
Aršam, see Zadok, *On West Semites in Babylonia*, 13; Bickerman, "The Babylonian
Captivity," 344–45.

were held by Persian nobles.[5] Beyond official colonies, the Neo-Babylonian and Achaemenid periods saw increasing immigration into Babylonia from the Iranian Plateau.[6] This could partially be explained by
Dandamaev's suggestion that Nippur's importance increased under the
Achaemenids.[7] Further studies on Achaemenid Babylonia are likely to
illuminate more adequately the details of Iranian presence within the
region.

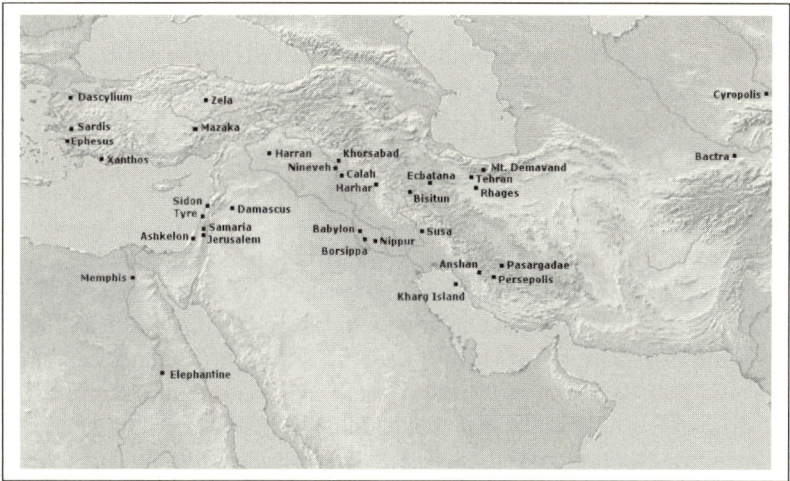

Figure 9. *Map of the Achaemenid Empire*

The Jewish community at Nippur is partially illuminated by the
Murašu Archive. While making ethnic or religious identifications based
solely on names is problematic, onomastics can be used for some general
probabilities. Zadok opines that the scribes of the Murašu Archive were

5. Dandamaev, "Domain-Lands," see esp. 127. Cf. Dandamaev, "Babylonia I,"
331. He also posits a nearby paradise, based on the Murašu archive; Dandamaev,
"Royal Paradeisoi in Babylonia," 113–17. Oppenheim, "The Babylonian Evidence
of Achaemenian Rule in Mesopotamia," 579, includes a settlement of Magi, citing
BEI X.88.4. Cf. Zadok, "Iranians and Individuals Bearing Iranian Names in
Achaemenid Babylonia," 100–106, 126.

6. Zadok, "On the Connections between Iran and Babylonia," 66–67. Dandamaev, "Data of the Babylonian Documents from the 6th to the 5th Centuries B.C. on
the Sakas," 107, even claims a Saka colony was established at Nippur; he also
claims that Median refugees were in Babylon from Nebuchadnezzar's time,
Dandamaev, "History of Babylonia," 327.

7. See Dandamaev, *A Political History of the Achaemenid Empire*, 186. However,
see a refutation in Kuhrt and Sherwin-White, "Xerxes' Destruction of Babylonian
Temples," 69–78.

more familiar with *YHW* [*sic*] as a deity than other Babylonian scribes, obliquely indicating the important presence of Yahwists in the region.[8] According to Daiches, at least 70 Jews can be identified in the records, two of whom had Persian names;[9] Zadok counts 64 with Yahwistic names, but allows for up to 100 persons represented in the archive in total.[10] Some of these Yahwists served as servants to Persians, some as royal officials, including one who was "over the birds of the king."[11] One Judaean was a servant of a Persian and son of an interpreter-scribe.[12] There is also evidence that Jews owned horse- and bow-fiefs.[13] The Jewish community quite naturally represented all social strata, many of which required interaction with the local Persian officials.

Several names in the archive indicate at least the beginnings of Persian borrowing: Judaeans borrowed the Persian or Neo-Elamite word *tiri* for the formation of several names.[14] Since the Persian language was largely spoken only among Persians,[15] this is evidence of some commingling. Indeed, the occupation of interpreter-scribe for the Persian authorities was held by at least three or four Judaeans in the Nippur region.[16] The position of interpreter-scribe is ideally positioned for exposure to Persian ideas and ideologies; they were essential for the functioning of the Persian administration and present at all official communications. OP was primarily a spoken language, Aramaic (and Elamite) the languages of the administration, and local languages still used locally; interpreter-scribes received oral commands in Persian and wrote them in Aramaic, or received written communications and read them out in Persian or the local language.[17] Hence one can expect familiarity with the system of

---

8. Zadok, *The Jews in Babylonia*, 9; Coogan, *West Semitic Personal Names*, 49–53.

9. Daiches, *The Jews in Babylon*, 27–70. Cf. Zadok, *Jews in Babylonia*, 33–34.

10. Zadok, *Jews in Babylonia*, 14, 79.

11. Daiches, *The Jews in Babylon*, 29; Oppenheim, "Babylonian Evidence," 580.

12. Zadok, *Jews in Babylonia*, 65.

13. Ibid., 66–68.

14. Daiches, *The Jews in Babylon*, 16–17; cf. a different name using *tiri* in 1 Chr 4:16 (תיריא); see Coogan, *West Semitic*, 86. Daiches incorrectly cites *tiri* as meaning "power"—rather it is a name of a deity. The word does not appear in either Avestan or OP (cf. Kent, *Old Persian*, and Bartholomae, *Altiraniranisches Wörterbuch*, neither of which list *tiri*), except as an obscure deity who received a day name in the Zoroastrian Calendar. The name *Tiriya* does appear in the Persepolis Tablets, so perhaps it is a Neo-Elamite name. Cf. Hallock, *PFT*, 762–63.

15. Briant, *From Cyrus to Alexander*, 77.

16. Zadok, *Jews in Babylonia*, 69.

17. Olmstead, *History of the Persian Empire*, 177. See also Briant, *From Cyrus to Alexander*, 507–10; Gershevitch, "Old Iranian Literature," 5; Lewis, "The

administration, at least, among the interpreter-scribes, perhaps even knowledge of OP and the traditions shared thereby.

Tablets (so-called TAYN tablets) have recently been discovered which reveal the presence of other Judaean communities in Babylon—at ālu ša Našar and al-Yahudu, both probably near Borsippa.[18] Pearce believes that these new tablets provide evidence of what she refers to as an "administrative fiscal district" composed largely of Jews.[19] If this is true, such a community would likely have had at least periodic contact with Persian officials, even if the tablets so far only evidence two Persian names.[20] At the very least, it would be reasonable to expect a familiarity with the mechanisms and ideologies of the administration which they served.

Smith posits the presence of pro-Cyrus propagandists in Babylonia prior to its fall.[21] It is clear that Cyrus (II) was known before his advance in 539 B.C.E. Much has been written on the (un-)historicity of the *Nabonidus Chronicle* and the *Cyrus Cylinder*,[22] but it is reasonably clear that Cyrus was known in Babylon from his battles with Astyages, king of Media (550 B.C.E.).[23] The prophecy in Jer 51 seems to confirm some expectation.[24]

Perhaps the enigma of "Darius the Mede" in Dan 5:31 also reflects this situation in an oblique manner. While the use of any Daniel passage for Neo-Babylonian or Achaemenid period history is problematic, the use of Iranian terms within it evidences some form of interaction by the time Daniel was written.[25] To the non-Iranian world, Cyrus's defeat of Astyages was viewed more as an internal coup than the rise of a new

Persepolis Tablets: Speech, Seal and Script," 18. Now see an OP administrative docket, Stolper and Tavernier, "An Old Persian Administrative Tablet," 1–28.

18. Pearce, "New Evidence for Judeans in Babylonia," 403. Two volumes with the relevant tablets are apparently forthcoming.

19. Ibid., 405.

20. Ibid., 404.

21. Smith, "II Isaiah and the Persians," 415–21.

22. While Olmstead, *History of the Persian Empire*, 36–55, largely accepts the documents as historical, Kuhrt, "Nabonidus and the Babylonian Priesthood," 117–56, discounts their validity. Cf. the discussion in Vanderhooft, "Cyrus II, Liberator or Conqueror?," 351–72.

23. Briant, *From Cyrus to Alexander*, 31–33. Cf. Glassner, *Mesopotamian Chronicles*, 235.

24. Cf. Vanderhooft, "Cyrus II, Liberator or Conqueror?," 365. Holladay considers the Jeremiah references to be glosses which predate the Cyrus's invasion; see Holladay, *Jeremiah 2*, 397, 398, 405, 407, 427. Cf. Levine, "Prelude to Monarchy," 43; Cameron, *History of Early Iran*, 222.

25. Cf. the discussion in Chapter 4.

empire—Greeks continued long afterwards to confuse the distinction between "Mede" and "Persian."[26] While the final redactional reason for the designation "Mede" in the book of Daniel was likely to fit the four-empire scheme, the historical confusion between Media and Persia certainly did not hinder such use, and it may be part of the reason it was later found unproblematic by commentators.[27] Further, Zadok has argued that the new names given to Daniel's friends Hananiah and Mishael—Shadrach and Meshach—are also Iranian names, placing the Danielic traditions into some form of relationship with Iran.[28] In any case, the possibility for knowledge of Persian ideas among the Babylonian exiles exists from at least the fall of Babylon, if not before.

Ezra 8:15–20 records that Ezra could identify distinct communities of Levites and temple servants still intact at Casiphia, an unknown location presumably different from the communities around Nippur.[29] Even without further information, it, along with the new "TAYN" tablets, indicate that the Yahwistic exiles were not exclusive to Nippur. Therefore, they could have come into contact with Persians throughout Babylonia.

Media and Iranian Lands

There is also evidence of Judaeans and Israelites living in Iranian lands during the Achaemenid period. According to 2 Kgs 17:6, Assyria exiled Israelites to unnamed cities in Media (721 B.C.E.); these cities may have been Harhar and Kišessu, in the former Kingdom of Ellipi.[30] The book of Tobit, if it reflects its setting at all historically,[31] implies an Israelite community around the Median cities of Ecbatana and Rages, both of which feature in the narrative (Ecbatana is about 50 miles from Harhar).

---

26. On Greek confusion, see Graf, "Medism: The Origin and Significance of the Term," 15–30; Dandamaev, *A Political History of the Achaemenid Empire*, 19. Cf. Diakonoff, "Media," 147.

27. See the comments in Collins, *Daniel*, 30–31.

28. Zadok, "Die nichthebräischen Namen," 396. He derives Meshach from *Maiša-ka-*, "little lamb" and Shadrach from *Čiθra-ka-*, "light, glowing." Cited by Demsky, "Double Names in the Babylonian Exile," 2:30.

29. Some suggest that המקום in Ezra 8:17 indicates the presence of a temple or sanctuary, but there is no evidence for it. See Brockington, *Ezra, Nehemiah and Esther*, 100; Blenkinsopp, "Temple and Society in Achaemenid Judah," 52–53.

30. See Diakonoff, "Media," 82; Younger, "The Deportations of the Israelites," 223.

31. Boyce and Grenet, *HZ III*, 414; Moulton, *Early Zoroastrianism*, 246–53. On the dubiousness of historical information in Tobit, see Grabbe, "Israel's Historical Reality After the Exile," 13.

As Bauckham notes,[32] more Northern Israelites were exiled than Judaeans, so their continuance as a community is not impossible. Indeed, he argues that Tobit was written to convert the deportees' descendants to a Jerusalem-centered faith.[33] It is not out of bounds to suggest, therefore, the possibility that these former exiles were in contact with their Judaean counterparts. Zadok even suggests that several of the clans which are recorded in Ezra–Nehemiah are descendants of the deportees to Media.[34] Judaeans from Lachish were settled in the region of Nineveh (701 B.C.E.), which was conquered by the Medes (612 B.C.E.), and these also could have been in contact with other exiles either in Media or Babylonia.[35] The relationship between Judaeans, Israelites, and emerging Judaism is difficult to elucidate, but these hints suggest that the groups related to the biblical traditions were broadly dispersed and in contact with each other, even in the sixth century. The mention of Rages (Raga), later an important Zoroastrian center,[36] may be significant: the appearance of "Asmodeus" in Tobit as a demon (from *Aēšma-Daēuua*, the only demon in the *Gāthās*) is one of the few generally agreed Iranian borrowings.[37]

The book of Nehemiah (1:11) preserves the tradition of Nehemiah serving as a cup-bearer to the king in Susa. The position of cup-bearer was extremely high and important, as it represented the king at his most

32.   Bauckham, "Tobit as Parable for the Exiles of Northern Israel," 156. Lawson Younger, "The Deportations of the Israelites," 201–27, 215, he suggests that the biblical text has conflated multiple deportations.

33.   Bauckham, "Tobit as Parable for the Exiles of Northern Israel," 159.

34.   See Zadok, *Jews in Babylonia*, 41–44. Bickerman, "Babylonian Captivity," 342–58, makes no mention of these.

35.   See Figure 117 and Figure 180 in Collon, *Ancient Near Eastern Art*, 142–44 and 215, respectively.

36.   See Boyce, "Persian Religion," 281. Cf. Boyce, *HZ II*, 7–8; Moulton, *Early Zoroastrianism*, 247. Zaehner, *The Dawn and Twilight*, 33, places Zarathuštra himself in Rhages [*sic*], although this is impossible from a linguistic perspective. Gnoli, "Avestan Geography," 44, claims there is no basis for this identification; Skjærvø, "The Avesta as Source for the Early History of the Iranians," 165, claims it is tenuous.

37.   Schwartz, "Religion of Achaemenian Iran," 682; Boyce and Grenet, *HZ III*, 414; Moulton, *Early Zoroastrianism*, 250; cf. Yarshater, "Iranian Common Beliefs and Worldview," 348. However, Ginzberg, *Legends of the Jews*, 6:299 (nn. 83–85), rejects this for an Aramaic origin. Ahn, "Dualismen in Kontext von Gegenweltvorstellungen," 131–32, accepts the parallel, but only as an example of how selective it is. For Sundermann, "Zoroastrian Motifs," 155–60, it is a Parthian borrowing reflecting *Aēšma*'s hostility to next-of-kin marriage. Thanks to Dr. Hintze for the latter reference.

vulnerable.[38] Even if the accuracy of this title were doubted, Nehemiah's
position must have been sufficiently high to merit two appointments to
govern Yehud. Such a high position of a Judaean in Susa, one of the
imperial capitals, could indicate the presence at least of a small community in the area; indeed, Nehemiah's memoir (1:2) records the presence
of his "brother," Hanani (חנני), and "certain men from Judah." Briant
suggests that Hanani may be the same official as the Hanni [*sic*] (חנניה)
mentioned in correspondence of the Elephantine community,[39] which
would suggest a tradition of at least one family serving in the Persian
civil service. Nevertheless, Hananiah is a very common name. The book
of Esther also implies a Jewish community around Susa (the clan known
as עילם?).[40] Neo-Babylonian inscriptions on alabaster and an oblique
reference in the Talmud imply that Susa long held a Yahwistic community.[41] In any case, if no one else, Nehemiah himself had frequent and
intimate contact with his Persian lords. Boyce argues that this contact
would have not only familiarized Nehemiah with Zoroastrian purity
laws, but would have required his observance of them;[42] she points out in
this connection that one of the major themes in his memoirs is the observation of religious purity. Whether or not it is justifiable to go so far,
Nehemiah's position would have exposed him to Persian court ideas.

Lipiński argues that there is some evidence from the Persepolis tablets
of Judaeans working in the Persian heartland itself, although this is
limited to a few potentially Yahwistic names.[43] As the Persians utilized a
wide variety of ethnicities to work on the extensive building projects of
the kings, it is hardly surprising to find evidence of at least a few Jewish
workers among them.[44] The existence or non-existence of a full community is impossible to ascertain from Lipinski's evidence, however.

38.   Briant, *From Cyrus to Alexander*, 264.

39.   Referring to the "Passover Papyri," ibid., 586; the reconstructed Aramaic text
may be found in Porten, *Archives from Elephantine*, 311, and in English reconstruction, 128–33, as well as in idem, *The Elephantine Papyri in English*, 125–26.
Hanani also appears in Cowley, *Aramaic Papyri*, Papyrus no. 38 (135–36). A similar
name (חננה) appears on bullae found in Yehud. See Avigad, *Bullae and Seals*, 4–5.

40.   Zadok, *Jews in Babylonia*, 43.

41.   For the inscriptions, see Lidzbarski, *Ephemeris für Semitische Epigraphik*,
3:7–48. For the Talmud, see *b. Sanh.* 94a (available in Epstein, ed., *Tractate
Sanhedrin*, Tractate Sanhedrin XI, n.p.).

42.   See Boyce, *HZ II*, 189.

43.   Lipinski, "Western Semites in Persepolis," 101–12.

44.   E.g. DSaa, DSz (Kent, *Old Persian*, 142–44). Cf. Briant, *From Cyrus to
Alexander*, 172.

The sources presented so far evidence at least a minimal presence of Judaeans in three major centers of Achaemenid Iran: Ecbatana, Susa, and Persepolis. This is highly significant for Judaean–Persian interaction, even if these groups were relatively small. It should be remembered that the authors of the received text of the traditions were also probably a relatively small group. But whatever the size of the groups in this period, some Jews did remain in Iranian lands into the Roman period and beyond (cf. Acts 2:9)—perhaps partly descended from the communities hinted at here.[45]

Egypt

The military colony at Elephantine has drawn considerable attention due to the archives found there.[46] The papyri show a remarkable level of governmental interaction in the affairs of the garrison, including religious affairs. It is likely that direct contact between the two was common. As Porten notes, Bagavahya's endorsement of the Elephantine temple's reconstruction only addresses Persian officials;[47] Porten even claims that all the leading positions around Elephantine were held by Persians.[48] The Yahwists of Elephantine wrote to the Governors of Judah and Samaria, assuming they had jurisdiction or influence regarding their affairs.[49] Thus, not only does it seem that the various groups were in contact with the Persian administration, but also that they were in contact with each other. Indeed, an apparent Judaean was sent by the government to regulate a festival.[50] The political complexities of the empire are nicely demonstrated by the correspondence over the destruction of the colonist's temple in 410 B.C.E.; several levels of local, Persian, and kinsmen authorities (Judaean, Samaritan) are involved in the decisions and petitions. It is worth noting as well that the island of Elephantine is across the Nile from Syene, a town which housed the *fratarak* (פרתרך) of Upper

---

45. E.g. Sarshar, ed., *Esther's Children*. See also Levy, *Comprehensive History*. Hirschberg, "The Oriental Jewish Communities," 193–96; Zand, "Bukhara VII: Bukharan Jews," 531–32.

46. See in particular the history of the colony in Porten, *Archives from Elephantine*, 278–98.

47. Cowley, *Aramaic Papyri*, no. 32 (122–24); cf. Porten, *Papyri*, 148–49.

48. Porten, "Persian Names," 175.

49. Cowley, *Aramaic Papyri*, no. 30–32 (107–24); cf. Porten, *Papyri*, 139–49.

50. See the discussion above on Hananiah. The "Passover Papyrus" is sadly lacunose.

Egypt.[51] Persian officials are frequently referred to in many capacities in the papyri, which is consonant with being near an administrative center. One of the papyri confirms that the Persians brought their religion with them by mentioning the presence of a "Mazdayasna" (מזדיזן).[52] The satrapy, particularly around Elephantine, seems also to have hosted a large mix of Iranians of various descriptions besides Persians proper as well.[53] These papyri make clear that this particular community had ample contact with various Iranians as well as other Yahwistic communities.

Besides the Yahwistic colony at Elephantine, the Hebrew Bible indicates the presence of Judaeans in Egypt in a variety of places, from several times and for varying reasons. Isaiah 11:11 expects a recall of Jews from Egypt, Pathros, and Nubia (כוש, פתרוס, מצרים), and Jeremiah prophesies to the Jews in Migdol, Tahpanhes, Noph and Pathros (מגדל, ארץ פתרוס, נף, תחפנחס). Jeremiah curses the Jews of Egypt (24:8; 44), but was himself taken to Egypt with fleeing Judaeans (ch. 43).[54] These passages imply at least nominal Jewish groups throughout Egypt. At least one of these locations definitely had a Persian presence—Memphis, the seat of the Egyptian satrapy.

Even during rebellions, the Persian presence in Egypt was not entirely eliminated. In one of the extant papyri, Aršam commands his servants to protect his holdings from the insurgents.[55] The presence of ethnic Iranians therefore cannot be excluded during the interruptions in Persian rule. It is also possible that Persians remained behind in Egypt after Alexander, just as they did in Asia Minor; the term *Mtj* (either Mede or Persian), at any rate, remained in use in Egypt into the third century B.C.E.[56] Thus Egypt offered another location for Yahwists to interact with Persians on various levels in the Achaemenid Period, and possibly into the Ptolemaic.

---

51. Bresciani, "Egypt, Persian Satrapy," 364–65. Cf. Cowley's papyri nos. 20, 27, 30.

52. Cowley, *Aramaic Papyri*, no. 37 (132–35); cf. Porten, *Papyri*, 127–28. That this is a proper name rather than a title is confirmed by a newly published seal inscription; see Garrison and Dion, "The Seal of Ariyāramna," 4–5, 17. *Mazdayasna* means "worshipper of Mazda," which is consonant with Zoroastrianism—and their self-designation—but does not necessarily require it. Cf. Bartholomae, *Altiranisches Wörterbuch*, 1160–61; Benveniste, "Le terme iranien *mazdayasna*," 5–9. However, a stele from Syene commemorates the construction of a **brazmandāna*, an Iranian shrine. See Hallo, ed., *COS* 2:163 (2.41).

53. Porten, "Persian Names," 176–77.

54. Porten, "The Jews in Egypt," 375.

55. Driver, *Aramaic Documents of the Fifth Century B.C.*, Doc. 7 (23–25).

56. Bresciani, "Egypt, Persian Satrapy," 372.

Palestine

Within the land of Palestine there were several opportunities for contact with Iranians. The coast was heavily fortified and provisioned.[57] Gaza had a garrison large and loyal enough to resist Alexander thoroughly (although Arrian attributes the resistance to Arab mercenaries: *Anabasis* II.25.4–26.7).[58] Even in the technically unadministered areas of Sinai and the Negev, permanent Persian garrisons are attested.[59] Briant notes that remains in Idumea attest a "very thorough mingling" of populations, including Persians and Judaeans,[60] and Amiran posits the "significant role" of Achaemenid elements in the culture of Palestine and the empire as a whole.[61] Nehemiah turned Jerusalem into a fortified garrison town (בירה), implying a direct Persian presence.[62] In this respect, it may be significant that the governor of Judah to whom the Elephantine colonists wrote had the Persian name Bagavahya (בגוהי), perhaps a Persian or Judaean with a Persian name.[63] Even during the periods of Egyptian independence, Persian control reached into the Negev.[64] Indeed, Lipschits considers the Egyptian revolt to be the impetus for increased Persian interest in Yehud in Nehemiah's time.[65] In addition to military installations, the Persian king likely held crown lands in Yehud (as in other provinces), perhaps what was previously held by the Davidic monarchy. Ackroyd thinks the "king's forest" (literally "paradise"—הפרדס אשר למלך) in Neh 2:8 refers to these lands.[66]

Excavations at Ashkelon have revealed an extraordinary number of dog burials, the vast majority from the Persian period; every site at

---

57. Stern, "New Evidence," 222.

58. Briant, *From Cyrus to Alexander*, 716; Arrian, *Anabasis Alexandri, Books I–IV*, 213–19.

59. Stern, "New Evidence," 223; cf. Lipschits, "Achaemenid Imperial Policy," 26.

60. Briant, *From Cyrus to Alexander*, 717.

61. Amiran, "The Persian–Achaemenid Impact on Palestine," 3017–23.

62. For the present purposes, the presence of a garrison is more pertinent than the strategic-administrative details. See Carter, *The Emergence of Yehud*, 44–45; Hoglund, *Achaemenid Imperial Administration*, 200–210; Lipschits, "Achaemenid Imperial Policy," 26; Edelman, *The Origins of the "Second" Temple*, 340–51.

63. Cowley, *Aramaic Papyri*, no. 30 (108–19); Porten, *Papyri*, 139.

64. Graf, "The Persian Royal Road System," 183–84.

65. Lipschits, "Achaemenid Imperial Policy," 38; cf. Hoglund, *Achaemenid Imperial Administration*, 210, 243–44.

66. Ackroyd, "The Written Evidence for Palestine," 215.

Ashkelon attesting Persian presence also attests dog burials.[67] Dog burials have also been found in several other sites in Persian-period Palestine, albeit not in such spectacular numbers.[68] These finds are provocative, especially as regional attitudes towards the dog were generally negative or, at best, ambivalent (Deut 23:19; Prov 26:11, 17; Qoh 9:4; Matt 7:6). The exceptions were Egypt and Persia, where dogs were esteemed.[69] Due to Egypt's long history in the coastal region, one would suspect Egyptian influence, especially as dog burials and mummification are found there. However, no such burials are attested in Ashkelon for any of the periods of Egyptian control.[70] It is significant that all the parallel Palestinian dog burials listed by Wapnish and Hesse are in the Persian period. While they acknowledge a solitary dog burial in Achaemmenid Iran in what may be a fire temple, they dismiss the relevance of Iranian veneration for dogs due to Sassanian period scruples over the burial of bodies.[71] However, according to Boyce, the Zoroastrian veneration of dogs did sometimes include burials.[72] As Ashkelon possibly housed the Persian governor of the Ashdod province,[73] it is possible that the dog burials evidence either significant Persian residency or high acculturation during the Persian period. However, dog burials are also attested in earlier Crete, Greece, and Sardis, which may be significant for the Levantine coast.[74]

The province of Samaria evidences some Iranian presence. According to Stern, the Persian period strata of the city of Samaria was nearly obliterated, so not much evidence has been found in the city itself.[75] However, the finds at Wâdī ed-Dâliyeh have produced some typical Persian seals.[76] The papyri also revealed an interesting name—יהובגה.[77]

---

67. Wapnish and Hesse, "Pampered Pooches," 60.

68. Ibid., 67–69. One of the other sites includes Arad, a location known to have been a site of a station of the Royal Road (on the Royal Road, see below). See Eph'al, "Changes in Palestine," 177.

69. Collins, ed., *A History of the Animal World*, 292, 301–3. She also mentions the Ashkelon burials 419 and 420; Wapnish and Hesse, "Pampered Pooches," 71–73.

70. Wapnish and Hesse, "Pampered Pooches," 71.

71. Ibid., for the Iranian burial, 70; for Zoroastrian custom, 72.

72. Boyce, *HZ I*, 302–3.

73. Stern, "New Evidence," 222.

74. Day, "Dog Burials in the Greek World," 21–32.

75. Stern, *Material Culture*, 29.

76. Available in Winn Leith, *Wadi Daliyeh I*, particularly 191, 193, 199, 204, and 209–31, and associated plates. Cf. Cross, "The Papyri and Their Historical Implications," 17–29, as well as the plates 62 and 63.

This is another example of the use of a Persian word to create a new, Yahwistic name (using OP *baga*, "god'). Although the cultural significance of material culture is difficult to assess, Samaria evidences some finds typical of Achaemenid style. An imported Achaemenid vase and a bronze throne leg in clear Achaemenid style have been found.[78] Stern mentions the presence of "Irano-Scythian" arrowheads which appear in the Persian period.[79] Three clearly Achaemenid objects have also been found north of Samaria; Amiran even claims to see echoes of the winged disk motif on one.[80] Although meager, this confirms that the province of Samaria was not isolated from the rest of the empire. Stern claims that the mountainous region of Palestine shows higher "eastern" affinities than others in the Persian period,[81] even suggesting that tombs near Shechem indicate the possibility of Iranian colonists.[82] Uehlinger also suggests the possible presence of Persian colonists in Samaria, based on "powerful Persianisms" on Samarian coins.[83]

If there were Iranians or Iranian influences in Samaria, it is likely they reached Yehud as well. Knoppers argues convincingly that the break between Samaritans and Jews was not decisive until well after the Persian period, despite the attitude of Nehemiah, and that their mutual contacts may have been significant. He considers the separation between them a matter more of administration/politics than religion or culture.[84] In fact, Ezra–Nehemiah seems to confirm close relations between the two communities, despite attempts to prevent them (particularly Neh 2:19; 3:33–35; 4; 6:17–19; 10:31; 13:1–9 and Ezra 4:1–5; 9:1–10:44). Yehud clearly was not exempt from interactions with its northern *medinah* and that *medinah*'s influences.

---

77. WDSP 7,7 and 7,10 of Gropp et al., *Wadi Daliyeh II*, 80–81; cf. Knoppers, "Revisiting the Samarian Question in the Persian Period," 276.

78. Stern, *Material Culture*, 142 (vase—although he denies the significance); 143–44 (bronze throne leg). Cf. the mention in Lipschits, "Achaemenid Imperial Policy," 31. Orig. pub. Tadmor, "Fragments from an Achaemenid Throne From Samaria," 37–43.

79. Stern, *Material Culture*, 154–56.

80. Amiran, "Achaemenian Bronze Objects from a Tomb at Kh. Ibsan in Lower Galilee," 135–38.

81. Stern, "Between Persia and Greece," 444.

82. Stern, "Achaemenian Tombs from Shechem," 90–111, which differs from *Material Culture*, 154–56; Ahlström, *The History of Ancient Palestine*, 827.

83. Uehlinger, "'Powerful Persianisms'," particularly 178–79.

84. Knoppers, "Revisiting the Samarian Question," 278–79. Cf. Cross, "Aspects of Samaritan and Jewish History," 201–11; Cross put forth similar arguments in his article cited above.

It is often noted that Palestine lies in a strategic location between Mesopotamia and Egypt. Any group traveling between the two of necessity would pass through the land. The history of the Achaemenid Empire contains several large-scale operations which brought armies and baggage trains through Palestine.[85] Cambyses conquered Egypt in 525, and it is likely preparations for the invasion began in the reign of Cyrus.[86] Revolts and reconquests required repeated military incursions into Egypt (486–484, 460–454; revolt in 405, which was followed by unsuccessful attacks in 373, 350, and reconquest in 342). Prior, during, and after these campaigns, the various *medinahs* along the route to Egypt must have often hosted Persian officials and troops. Indeed, the Great King himself sometimes participated in the campaigns (Cambyses, ca. 525; Xerxes I, ca. 484; Artaxerxes III, ca. 345–342).[87] Wherever the king went, including into battle, the entirety of his court—with the associated pomp, courtiers, and Magi—followed.[88] At the very least, such royal caravans would have been ideal situations for the dissemination of royal ideology and for the locals to demonstrate their loyalty. Even if there were no permanent Iranian residents within Palestine (and there clearly were), traveling Iranians were no novelty in the region.

The Royal Road and Royal Mail

One final point remains for discussion of potential locations for Persian contact, one which properly involves all the regions so far discussed. Herodotus describes a complex network known as the Royal Road from Sardis to Susa (V.35, 52–53; VIII.98).[89] He describes this massive distance as stationed with fortresses, hostelries, and riding-posts (ἀγγαρήιον) at a day's journey distance. This system included rapid royal couriers

---

85. In addition to military excursions to Egypt, scholars have often appealed to Yehud's participation in various revolts, although the significance (or reality) of the impact on Palestine is debated. Barag, "The Effects of the Tennes Rebellion on Palestine," 6–12; Schmitt, "Artaxerxes III," 658–59; Betlyon, "Archaeological Evidence of Military Operations," 39; *The So-called "Great Satraps' Revolt,"* 9–14; Eph'al, "Changes in Palestine," 109, sees little in ostraca.

86. Briant, *From Cyrus to Alexander*, 49.

87. Ahlström, *The History of Ancient Palestine*, 852, would add Darius I to this list, before his reconquest of Egypt (519), and removing Zerubbabel.

88. Briant, *From Cyrus to Alexander*, 186–89. Aperghis, "Storehouses and Systems at Persepolis," 158, suggests that the "J" Persepolis texts relate to the kings' movements.

89. Herodotus, *Wars V–VII*, 39, 57–61; idem, *Wars VIII–IX*, 97.

(ἀγγέλοι or *pirradaziš*), escorts for travels on official business,[90] paved sections,[91] and even fire-signals.[92] Yet the royal road and mail were not limited to the route between the central capital and the Greek-inhabited lands of primary interest to Herodotus; the entire empire was connected by it. Indeed, one part of it ran through Palestine to Memphis. Use of this road required a "passport" or *miyatukkaš*, just as in Neh 2:7.[93] A papyrus from 'Aršam, Satrap of Egypt, records an order for the precise provisioning of one on official business, indicating the duty of the local provincial leaders for the upkeep of the stations within their jurisdiction.[94] The local administrators, be they local dynasts or Persian appointees, would thus be required to maintain regular contact with the couriers, escorts, and officials passing through on official business. Such a complex system, able to provision various qualities of grain, wine, beer, and sheep, as well as provisions for the horses (presumably including blacksmiths), implies a substantial local involvement in the provisioning of these hostels and ἀγγαρήιον.[95] It is likely that many of the officials using this system were Iranians and that both Ezra and Nehemiah also used it while traveling. Thus this network provides one more locus where populations and groups could interact, including Judaeans, Israelites, and Iranians.

Summary

The above evidence shows how possible it was for Yahwists and Iranians to come into physical contact with each other throughout the Achaemenid Empire and even well into the Hellenistic period. So far, this

90. Mallowan, "Cyrus the Great (558–529 BC)," 402–3. Cf. Ezra 8:21–23; Neh 1:9.

91. Mustafavi, "The Achaemenid Royal Road," 3008.

92. Graf, "The Persian Royal Road System," 168.

93. Hallock, "New Light from Persepolis," 248; Briant, *From Cyrus to Alexander*, 357–70; on "passport," 364. Cf. Graf, "The Persian Royal Road System," 168–69.

For the *miyatukkaš/halmi* in the Persepolis Fortification Tablets, see Hallock, *PFT*, 40, and his list of relevant tablets, 733–34.

On the relevance of the Persepolis Tablets to Ezra–Nehemiah generally, see Williamson, *Studies in Persian Period History and Historiography*, 212–31. Garrison, "A Persepolis Fortification Seal on the Tablet MDP 11 308 (Louvre Sb 13078)," 15–35, confirms the wide-ranging travelers of the royal road based on ration documents (33).

94. Driver, *Aramaic Documents*, Document 6 (20–23).

95. Cf. Graf, "The Persian Royal Road System," 188. Aperghis, "Storehouses and Systems at Persepolis," argues that there were two overlapping systems, a "regional" one and one for work groups.

chapter focuses on instances and situations where actual, physical interactions were likely or possible. In addition to these practical factors, the
scholar must also consider the less-physical dynamics of *Zeitgeist* and
word-of-mouth transmission of ideas. Since religious and cultural influences are more often a matter of prolonged contact and of unconscious
absorption and/or reaction, it is highly probable that any instances of
influence happened gradually and differently in various Judaean and
Israelite communities. As debate grew and continued on what it meant to
be Jewish, with various communities holding their own interpretations of
their traditions, it behooves the scholar to ask which is more likely—that
this process was in dialogue with the Persian elements in the cultural and
religious context, or that it was completely segregated from them?

In the context of cultural-religious interaction and influences, it is not
necessary to find a single, definitive location. Any interactions would
have necessarily been gradual, widespread, and sporadic. This context
implies multiple locations for a variety of levels of interaction, from
superficial to extensive. This needs to be taken into account when discussing textual questions and the overall import of discrete analyses.

Excursus: Elamites and Iranians in Anšan and Darius's Coup

Although not directly related to the juxtaposition of Yahwists and Iranians, the
ethnic situation of the region today called Fars (Greek Περσίς, Elamite *Anšan*, OP
Parsa) may be relevant when considering the import of Eastern Iran and its tradi-
tions for the Achaemenids generally, and for Second Temple Judaism specifically.
If one analyzes the implications of Darius I's rise, one can posit a context for under-
standing both the ambiguity and plurality of the evidence for religious practice in
Fars. Following several recent studies,[96] it can be argued that Darius represents a
"Persian coup" over the indigenous Elamite elements in the region.

The question of the arrival of the Persians into Southwest Iran is long-debated and
uncertain.[97] Without digressing into all the complications, several pieces of evidence
combine to suggest the dynamics which were operating in the region at the dawn of
the empire. First, Cyrus (II) the Great always referred to himself as "King of Anšan,"
and the Babylonians typically followed suit.[98] "Anšan" is the old Elamite name for

96. In particular, following Waters, "The Earliest Persians in Southwestern Iran,"
99–107; idem, "Cyrus and the Achaemenids," 91–102; Potts, "Cyrus the Great and
the Kingdom of Anshan," 7–28; Vogelsang, *The Rise and Organization*; cf.
Stronach, "Anshan and Parsa," 35–53.

97. Cf. Cameron, *History of Early Iran*, Chapters 9–11; Olmstead, *History of the
Persian Empire*, 22–33; Briant, *From Cyrus to Alexander*, 13–28; Waters, "The
Earliest Persians," 99–107.

98. Gadd and Legrain, *Ur Excavations: Texts*, 1:xix, 58; Kent, "The Oldest of the
Old Persian Inscriptions," 210. The relevant sections of the Nabonidus Chronicle

the region, which once functioned as part of the typical Elamite titulature, "King of Anšan and Susa"; no other Persian king uses this title.[99] Cyrus appears to have descended from a line which had ruled Anšan from at least 646 B.C.E., in the context of a fragmented Elamite polity.[100] Second, Cyrus and his father, Cambyses, seem to have deliberately made ties with leaders of the Iranian elements within and around their kingdom. According to Herodotus, Cyrus was both the son of the Median King Astyages's daughter and also had married the daughter of a noble from the Achaemenids, which Herodotus calls a clan.[101] Third, Cyrus's name (*Kuruš*), is not an Iranian name.[102] Thus, it would seem best to understand Cyrus as the scion of an Elamite dynasty which had nevertheless "persianized."[103]

In contrast to Cyrus, Darius I emphasized his Iranian ethnicity in his inscriptions.[104] It is telling that Darius claims Cambyses—but not Cyrus—as his "family" (*taumā*), as Cambyses was the son of an Achaemenid noble.[105] From these indications one may posit that the Achaemenids were a traditionally noble clan of the Persians, that Cyrus had politically benefited from intermarrying with them, and that when Bardiya (Cyrus's, but presumably not Cassandane's, son) rebelled, the Achaemenid clan took steps to ensure their continued centrality. Once in power, Darius proceeded to write Cyrus into the Achaemenid clan (and to promote his own ancestors to kings). Cyrus and Darius therefore represent the two main groupings within first-millennium Southwest Iran, the Elamites and the Persians.

When one recalls that the names of Darius, his father, his son, and Cyrus's daughter, Atossa,[106] have names which are Iranian and have potentially Avestan resonances, an eastern origin for his "family" is not impossible. If one posits an Elamite derivation for Cyrus's family and an Eastern one for Darius and his clan, this helps

---

and Sippar Cylinder are given in Kuhrt, *The Persian Empire*, 50, 56; cf. Dandamaev, "Cyrus: iii. Cyrus II the Great," n.p.; Shahbazi, "Cyrus: ii. Cyrus I," n.p.

99.   Waters, "Cyrus and the Achaemenids," 94.

100.   Waters, "The Earliest Persians," 104, 102; Briant, *From Cyrus to Alexander*, 17.

101.   On Mandane, Cyrus's mother, I.107–108 (Herodotus, *Wars I–II*, 138–39).

On Cyrus's wife (and Cambyses's mother), Cassandane, as an Achaemenid, III.2 (idem, *Wars III–IV*, 4–5). On the Achaemenids as a noble tribe, I.125 (idem, *Wars I–II*, 165).

102.   Kuhrt, *The Persian Empire*, 48, 55, thinks the name Elamite; however, Schmitt, "Cyrus: i. The Name," n.p., thinks that it is OP.

103.   Stronach, "Anshan and Parsa," 39.

104.   Most notably, on his tomb DNa §2, "a Persian, son of a Persian, an Aryan, of Aryan lineage' (*Pārsa Pārsahyā puça, Ariya Ariya ciça*); available in Kent, *Old Persian*, 138; Kuhrt, *The Persian Empire*, 502. Cf. DPe §3 and DZc §3 (Kent, *Old Persian*, 136, 147, respectively).

105.   DB I §10 (Kent, *Old Persian*, 119); cf. Waters, "Cyrus and the Achaemenids," 97.

106.   For Hystaspes: Kent, "The Name of Hystaspes," 55–58; Darius: Schmitt, "Darius i. The Name," n.p.; Atossa: Waters, "The Earliest Persians," 99 n. 57; Xerxes: Schmitt, "Artaxerxes," 654.

explain the mixture and ambivalence between the two in the Persepolis tablets. Vogelsang has argued that familial ties between the Medians and Scythians enabled Median control over the vast areas of the east;[107] if this is accurate, an eastern origin (with remaining familial ties) for the Achaemenids would help explain the strong support Darius I received from the eastern satrapies during his coup.[108] Understanding the story behind the Behistun inscription as a "Persian coup"[109] contextualizes the complexity in Parsa evidenced on the ground. More significant for this study, however, such an understanding brings the so geographically distant eastern satrapies (and their traditions) much closer to the imperial center, both geographically and for imperial ideology.[110]

The dynamic argued above implies a strong eastern affinity for the dynasty post-Darius, but still leaves the Anšanite dynasty in a murky, "persianizing" status. Two of the points argued in Chapter 1 are, however, strengthened by it: first, the relevance of the eastern traditions (i.e. the Avesta and heroic sagas) and, second, the diversity of traditions which one ought to expect within the empire.

General Theological and Sociological Affinities Between Jews and Persians

Even with centuries of potential contact, there is no guarantee or requirement for the Jews to be receptive to foreign ideas. If there were no similarities or potentials for rapprochement, interaction could have remained solely superficial or only have occurred in negative ways. What is more important, there are several categories of theological and sociological affinities between the Judaeans and the Persians which increase the likelihood that Persian ideas could be seen in a favorable light or viewed as latent within Judaism itself. While such parallels do not *require* influence to occur, they serve as points of orientation, helping to dissolve an overly dichotomistic view of interaction and to identify potential "hooks" for borrowings.

Post-exilic Judaism was partially characterized by a struggle between strict monotheism and varying forms of "syncretism." This is well-illustrated by the colony at Elephantine and the supposed Jewish inscription

---

107. Vogelsang, *Rise and Organization*, 311.

108. Ibid., 306.

109. Potts, "Cyrus the Great and the Kingdom of Anshan," 23.

110. Darius's Behistun account is dubious at best. This has been a much-debated matter. See Olmstead, *History of the Persian Empire*, 108–18; Briant, *From Cyrus to Alexander*, 107–27; Tuplin, "Darius' Accession in (the) Media," 217–44; Balcer, *Herodotus and Bisitun*.

Besides the version in Kent, the inscription itself is available in three critical editions (for the OP, Akkadian, and Aramaic): Schmitt, *The Bisitun Inscription*; Greenfield et al., *The Bisitun Inscription*; von Voigtlander, *The Bisitun Inscription*.

which swears by Bel and Nabu in Asia Minor.[111] It is impossible to know the details of the struggle, but it is beyond doubt that strict monotheistic and other less-monistic forms of Yahwism co-existed and competed, perhaps for many centuries. The religious situation in Iran included the demonization of previously worshipped deities. If Xerxes's *Daēuua* Inscription (XPh) is any indication, the controversy ran well into the Achaemenid period, and certainly could not have gone unnoticed to interested observers. Jeremiah and Second Isaiah's mockeries of the foreign idols[112] share in purpose and tone what the opponents of the *Daēuuas* must have used in their polemics. For those advocating a stricter monotheism and separation from foreign cults, the polemics against the *Daēuuas*—the ideology of denying them the very category of divinity—must have been very useful and appealing. Many Yahwists were surrounded by the Babylonian and Assyrian beliefs in gods and maleficent demons, whose cults threatened to subsume the Judaeans' and to deny the uniqueness of YHWH. An ideology which neutralized the threat of these cults by denying them the status of divinity while admitting their existence, albeit as mere demons, seems perfectly well-suited to their situation.

Partisans on either side of the divide could thus have found within the Persian traditions useful arguments to use in their own polemics. Commentators frequently suggest that Second Isaiah utilized Persian traditions to argue for his Creation-theology;[113] unrecorded debates lost to history quite probably did the same. Forms of rhetoric as much as ideas can be borrowed. For a Judaism still struggling with this question, a tradition with unknown centuries of debating a similar question was available for comparison and perhaps emulation. The potential for analogous rhetoric to be used within internecine debate should therefore be considered.

The purposefulness of history in the Hebrew prophets is oft noted.[114] History is the field in which YHWH exercises his will and power and ensures that not only can he punish his people with exile, but he can effect their return. The essential purposefulness of history is also central

---

111. Lipiński, "Obadiah 20," 368–70.

112. E.g. Isa 40:18–20; 41:6–7; 44:9–20; Jer 10:1–16; 51:15–19.

113. Smith, "II Isaiah and the Persians," 415–21; Olmstead, *History of the Persian Empire*, 55; Moulton, *Early Zoroastrianism*, 221; Mills, *Zarathuštra, Philo, the Achaemenids, and Israel*, 276–77; Boyce, *HZ II*, 43–65.

114. Heschel, *The Prophets*, 214–17, and references there; Muilenburg, "The Biblical View of Time," 225–52, seems to take a more "canonical' view and conflates the ideas of the Hebrew Bible and the New Testament.

to the traditions of Iran, although in a much more radical way than in pre-exilic Judaism. Physical creation itself is described as being for the purpose of defeating Angra Mainyu;[115] history is the field where the cumulative ethics of man will overcome the evil one, and where Ahura Mazda will be proven to be the only god. History is the method whereby the *cosmos* is perfected. The similarities and differences between these two views, different as they are from the other conceptions current in the ancient Near East, are subtle yet profoundly important.[116] Inherent in the Iranian view of history is the *eschaton* of history—history's very *telos* is to destroy evil and thus exhaust its use. History is known as *zruuan-darəyō.xᵛaδāta-*, "limited time,"[117] a term implying its end. Nowhere in the pre-exilic prophets can this end to history be intimated; it certainly is *not* latent or inherent.[118] Yet, the importance of history, the divine purpose in history, is the same in both traditions, and this is so similar in the two traditions that the logic of the end in Iranian traditions could over time have appeared to various Jews as also inherent in their own tradition.[119]

Beyond these more purely theological affinities lay some more purely sociological factors to consider, in particular, the implications of Persian administration (both in Yehud and more broadly). A more complete study of this aspect is reserved for the future; for the present purposes only a few minor comments must suffice.[120] An important yet elusive occurrence in post-exilic Palestine is the rise of the High Priest as ruler. While in some other areas of the Persian Empire peoples were ruled by local dynasts underneath a satrap (at least for a while—i.e. Lycia, the Phoenician city-states, Samaria), Yehud eventually came to be dominated by a "theocracy."[121] The book of Ezra–Nehemiah claims that the re-installation of the priesthood and rebuilt temple was due to royal

115. *Gr. Bund.* 1.24–28 (Anklesaria, *Zand-Ākāsīh*, 9; Boyce, *Textual Sources*, 45–46).

116. Cohn, *Cosmos, Chaos*, 1–115.

117. Bartholomae, *Altiranisches Wörterbuch*, 696.

118. On the question of a/the "Day of YHWH," see Chapter 6.

119. This is, of course, the main thrust of Cohn's argument; see Cohn, *Cosmos, Chaos*.

120. For a variety of views on this contentious topic, see Fried, *The Priest and the Great King*; Edelman, *Origins of the "Second" Temple*; Lipschits and Oeming, eds., *Judah and the Judeans in the Persian Period*; Betlyon, "A People Transformed Palestine in the Persian Period," 4–58; Lipschits et al., eds., *Judah and the Judeans in the Fourth Century B.C.E.*

121. For a discussion of this term as it relates to Yehud, see Cataldo, *A Theocratic Yehud?*

decree and favor. Historical study of the Achaemenid administration shows that Persian "toleration" was dependent on the beneficiaries being loyal. No priesthood within the empire could be or remain established without royal support, and more importantly, loyalty to the person of the king.[122] An example of the relationship between the Great King and religious specialists in the empire can be illustrated by the well-known letter of Darius I to Gadatas, although the authenticity of this is questioned.[123] If this is paralleled to the famous story of the pro-Cyrus Delphic oracle, it may indicate the kinds of relations religious foundations could expect to enjoy *vis-à-vis* the Persians,[124] provided they offered services to the Great King.

Beyond the hierarchic benefit the priestly classes received, one should consider the patronization and authorization of their law. Much has been written on the supposed Persian authorization of the Torah, and no real scholarly consensus on this point exists.[125] Without going into a detailed analysis on this point, it is pertinent to note that the government implemented local law as well as imperial law (cf. Egypt),[126] and that Darius I seems to have had an interest in its codification (if not to the extent advocated by Olmstead).[127] No law could operate in Yehud without (implicit) royal permission. Dozeman even argues that in Ezra–Nehemiah the former role of the Davidic monarch in Yahwism is replaced by Persian law.[128]

As noted by Boyce, purity laws play a significant role in Zoroastrianism.[129] Over time, what probably originally related only to the ritual precinct and priesthood became applied to the believers as a whole. A similar development can be seen in Second Temple Judaism. The gradual

---

122.   Root, "From the Heart," 5–6. However, for alternate views, see Ackroyd, "The Biblical Portrayal of Achaemenid Rulers," 1–16, and Gruen, "Persia through the Jewish Looking-Glass," 90–104; Nykolaishen, "The Sway of the Persian Sceptre."

123.   Briant, *From Cyrus to Alexander*, 491, 583–87, accepts it, though, in the introduction he retracts this view; the text of the inscription can be found in Crawford and Whitehead, *Archaic and Classical Greece*, 197–98 (No. 95b); and in Meiggs and Lewis, *A Selection of Greek Historical Inscriptions*, 20–22.

124.   Although the story in Herodotus I.53, 90–91 is legendary, it is likely Cyrus would have rewarded an oracle which had been favorable to him.

125.   Watts, ed., *Persia and Torah*, contains debates on this theory.

126.   Briant, *From Cyrus to Alexander*, 474, 510–11.

127.   Olmstead, *History of the Persian Empire*, 119–28.

128.   Dozeman, "Geography and History," 449–66.

129.   Boyce, *HZ I*, 294–324; cf. Williams, "Zoroastrian and Judaic Purity Laws," 72–89.

extension of purity laws from the priesthood to the people possibly underlies some of the conflict in Ezra–Nehemiah[130] and between the so-called Hellenizers and Hasids in the Maccabean period.[131] While these are most likely parallel developments, they create situational affinities which could be useful for polemical use on either side. Priests or scribes attempting to impose stricter purity laws on the populace ("people of the land"?) had a source to plunder for inspiration.

Earlier the importance and role of Ahura Mazda as "the Wise Lord" was mentioned. For Judaeans interested in wisdom traditions, the idea of god as primarily a god due to his wisdom could be quite compelling. Perhaps the personification of wisdom would even be less threatening than a more overtly naturalistic or anthropomorphic god. One may wonder about the extent of Persian scribal activities (at least among non-noble Iranians), but surely aspects of a god of wisdom would appeal to scribal schools.

There are two more possible but extremely speculative similarities between Second Temple Judaism and Iranian religion. Both were supposedly aniconic, but experienced tension between the rule and the reality. While various stories and myths are clearly depicted in Jewish structures (such as the later synagogue at Dura Europas),[132] YHWH was not; similarly, while Artaxerxes II instituted a cult statue for Anāhitā, Ahura Mazda was not represented,[133] and the aniconism of Persian religion was a feature noteworthy to Greek observers.

Recent scholarship has posited that the impetus behind some of the visions in prophetic, apocalyptic, and merkabah literature were real visionary experiences.[134] Artificially induced (or encouraged) mystical experiences are common throughout the world, and the possibility of this type of mysticism lying behind at least some of these visions cannot be excluded out of hand. Iranian tradition knows of a stimulant used by poet-priests, *Haoma*. The use of this in the Achaemenid Empire is indicated by the mortar and pestles found at Persepolis and is characteristic of the Iranian religion both before and after Zarathuštra. Could the Jews have learned of its use from the Persians, or perhaps could they have emulated the idea of a mystical journey from it? Even without such a connection, a mutually similar approach in both could have increased a sense of affinity between adepts of each.

130. See Olyan, "Purity Ideology in Ezra–Nehemiah," 1–16.
131. Hellerman, "Purity and Nationalism," 401–21.
132. See Gutmann, ed., *The Dura-Europos Synagogue*.
133. Following Shahbazi, "An Achaemenid Symbol I," 135–44, and Shahbazi, "An Achaemenid Symbol II," 119–47.
134. Stone, "A Reconsideration of Apocalyptic Visions," 167–80.

In all these examples, the nature of religious influence must be kept in mind. Influence is not a matter of wholesale adoption of strange ideas, but of how the continual process of reinterpretation occurred in dialogue with foreign ideas which came to be perceived as latent within the Jewish tradition itself, whether consciously or subconsciously.[135] When evaluating this issue, care must be taken not to force everything into an Iranian mold, but rather to examine carefully the nature and extent of Persian borrowings, and how they were used on their own terms within their new Jewish context. Before moving on to textual evidence, the communicative contexts of the emergence of apocalyptic and of the Achaemenid Empire must be considered.

135.   Cf. the Prolegomena.

Chapter 3

THE MEDIA OF INFLUENCE:
ORALITY, LITERACY, AND CULTURAL INTERACTION

The issue of orality[1] and literacy in the ancient Near East during the periods of prophetic and apocalyptic literature is a vexed one. Scholars have varied widely in their opinions and appropriations of the understanding of orality, to the point that one may wish to eschew the quagmire altogether.[2] Nevertheless, understanding the roles of orality and literacy is essential not only to understanding the context of the emergence of the apocalypse, but to the very nature of cultural interaction, and thus to the methodology needed for investigating Iranian influence. The issues of the interplay and natures of orality and literacy are issues of basic and largely subconscious *Weltanschauung*, and thus must be understood prior to tackling questions of more explicit dynamics such as socio-economics, colonialism, or theology. Orality and literacy affect how one understands the social situation, the formation of texts, the transmission and alteration of traditions, and the nature of religious authority. Ultimately, it is an issue of hermeneutics, of how "religious specialists"[3] interpret received tradition in light of contemporary circumstances.

Past attempts at delimiting the oral layers and traditions from the various sections of the Hebrew Bible have been criticized significantly and are characteristic of an older scholarly paradigm.[4] The work on the so-called oral "Überlieferungsgeschichte" was largely based on extensions

---

1. As Ong has pointed out (Ong, *Orality and Literacy*, 10–15), the term "(oral) literature" is inappropriate for works originating in an oral medium. Cf. Powell, *Writing and the Origins of Greek Literature*, 16.

2. Kelber, "Orality and Biblical Studies: A Review Essay," n.p.

3. To borrow the catch-all phrase used by Grabbe, *Priests, Prophets, Diviners, Sages*.

4. Niditch, *Oral World and Written Word*, 8–9, 110–14; Whybray, *The Making of the Pentateuch*, 133–85, particularly 138–39; Nielsen, *Oral Tradition*, 12–17, 94–103; Aaron, *Etched in Stone*, 28–40. The author is grateful to Professor Philip Davies for the last reference.

of Wellhausen's "Documentary Hypothesis";[5] similar work has been done on "Q" in the New Testament as well. However, the incessant search for "source documents," whether it be J, E, D and P, Q, or רז נהיה,[6] itself betrays a modern, post-print literate misunderstanding of the dynamics of orality. At issue is not the detailed microanalysis of hypothetical documents, but of traditional oral milieu. The present chapter does not call for a return to an outdated paradigm; rather, it argues three main points: (1) the cultural and cognitional difference between the modern, scholarly milieu and the world dominated by orality and emerging literacy; (2) the importance of the increasing "interiorization" of writing on the scribal elite and culture in general and for the rise of the apocalypse in particular; and (3) the importance of these considerations for understanding prophecy, apocalyptic, and Iranian interactions. Given the limited resources extant for ancient Judaism, it is not possible to reconstruct a history of oral traditions; such an endeavor could only be possible through an extended anthropological study of the given oral tradition of a kind which is impossible with an extinct society. Scholars must be content with working with the textual indices extant, while understanding the dynamics which make it different from later, more thoroughly literate (interiorized), contexts. First, an overview of relevant Oral Theory and its relation to influence is discussed. Afterwards, one aspect of Oral Theory (interiorization) is applied to the emergence of the apocalypses. Finally, the last section problematizes the traditional literary methodology utilized in Biblical Studies for questioning influence by raising questions begged by Oral Theory.

The Importance of Orality and Its Role in Influence

Oral Theory
The origins of Oral Theory belong to Classics and Comparative Literature, particularly Parry and Lord in Homeric Studies.[7] However, the

---

5. E.g. Gunkel, *What Remains of the Old Testament*, 13–56; Gunkel, *Genesis*, in particular xlviii–lxix; Noth, *A History of Pentateuchal Traditions*; Wellhausen, *Grundrisse zum alten Testament*; Ahlström, "Oral and Written Transmission," 69–81.

6. Harrington, *Wisdom Texts from Qumran*, 49; ibid., "The Raz Nihyeh in a Qumran Wisdom Text," 549–53; rejected by Goff, "Pedagogical Ethos of 4QInstruction," 61 n. 19.

7. See Parry, *The Making of Homeric Verse*; Lord, *The Singer of Tales*; Havelock, *The Greek Concept of Justice*; Havelock, "The Coming of Literate Communication to Western Civilization," 90–98; Peabody, *The Winged Word*; Anderson, "The Significance of Writing in Early Greece," 73–90; Powell, *Origins of Greek Literature*; cf. the overview in Ong, *Orality and Literacy*, 5–7, 16–30.

following overview takes its departure from the field of Communication and Media Studies.[8] The focus is on the effects of the media themselves, rather than poetry or formulicity *per se*, as has so occupied some scholarship. Before proceeding, the terms which appear in this overview are defined; they will be further discussed subsequently. A *medium* is the format in which communication proceeds (speech, writing, television, etc.). *Orality* is the technology of speech-listening. This has three main forms: *Primary Orality*, the condition of peoples in which verbal communication only occurs oral-aurally, which prevails before the invention of writing and in various isolated communities today; *Residual Orality*, the form of orality that persists subsequent to writing; and *Secondary Orality*, the resurgence of aspects of primary orality post-electronics. *Literacy* is the technology of writing and reading. There are various levels of literacy, and it consists of several independent but related skills: reading, writing, and composition. *Interiorization* is the process whereby a technology becomes integrated into individual and societal psychological processes and becomes part of the cognitional and functional norm. Finally, *Amplification* is the phenomenon whereby aspects of a previous technology are at first increased by the advent of a new technology.

McLuhan demonstrates the life- and consciousness-shaping aspects of communicative technology.[9] His famous dictum "the medium is the message" declares the fundamental shifts created by media technologies in society and psychology. He shows that it is not just the *context* or *content* of a message which gives meaning, but that the very *medium* in which it is given carries an implicit message, regardless of the intentions of the user. This message is one of change in social organization and patterns of thought—after all, communication is in many senses synonymous with society and thought. Because of the structural ramifications of communicative technology, "the message of any medium or technology is the change of scale or pace or pattern that it introduces into human affairs."[10] It is this effect—of the medium independent of its content— which is too often ignored by biblical scholarship, intent on the ideology or historicity of the content as it is. The very fact that *texts* are gaining religious authority in the period in which the investigation of Iranian influence is concerned must be as significant as the texts themselves. McLuhan puts this point forcibly:

---

8. The length of this discussion is due to its general unfamiliarity in Biblical Studies. The present author is only aware of one biblical scholar noting McLuhan's work (Schniedewind, *How the Bible Became a Book*, 2).

9. McLuhan, *Understanding Media*; idem, *The Gutenberg Galaxy*.

10. McLuhan, *Understanding Media*, 8.

> It is the medium that shapes and controls the scale and form of human association and action. The content or uses of such media are as diverse as they are ineffectual in shaping the form of human association. Indeed, it is only too typical that the "content" of any medium blinds us to the character of the medium.[11]

McLuhan uses the light bulb to illustrate his point, as it contains no verbal message to cloud the issue, unlike other media. The light bulb transforms society and the manner of human associations by eliminating the difference between day and night—no longer must practical limitations of daylight or candle wax determine lifestyles. This effect is independent of whether the light bulb is used for Midnight Mass or a sporting event[12]—the patterns of daily life are just as altered. It is important to note that, while the light bulb appears to be a frivolous example, this "technological change alters not only habits of life, but patterns of thought and valuation."[13] To stay with the example of the light bulb, this little device increases the hours available for work and recreation, reduces the need for candles, and increases the demand for ophthalmology. Even peoples who reject the new technology must adjust to the changes around them.[14] Even with media that carry explicit contents, such as television or print, the effect of the media themselves—in the formation of new patterns of association, valuation, and thought—parallels the effect of the light bulb. Effectively, a paradigm shift[15] occurs with each new technology—a shift which alters both those accepting of and those resistant to the new medium. The new technology does not create thought *ex nihilo*, but it changes *how* people think and how they *relate* to one another. These principles also apply to two of the greatest revolutions in human society—the phonetic alphabet and print.

The phonetic alphabet transforms the word from sound to sight, but it does this in a way more revolutionary than the way in which ideograms or hieroglyphs do—it completely separates sound from meaning.[16] The principles of the phonetic alphabet are fragmentation and decontextualization. It does this by reducing speech to visualized sounds which are meaningless on their own, which is unlike cuneiform, hieroglyphs, or ideograms, all of which retain residual pictorial qualities. McLuhan

11. Ibid., 9.
12. Ibid., 9.
13. Ibid., 69.
14. For example, the Amish, who do not themselves use light bulbs, must still use reflectors on their buggies and roadside barns to defend against the light bulb-using cars.
15. Cf. Kuhn, *The Structure of Scientific Revolutions*.
16. Cf. Ong, *Orality and Literacy*, 46, 73.

illustrates the type of transformation implicit in the advent of the written word by comparing the American flag with the words "American flag" written on a piece of cloth:

> To translate the rich visual mosaic of the Stars and Stripes into written form would deprive it of most its qualities of corporate image and of experience, yet the abstract literal bond would remain much of the same. Perhaps this illustration will serve to suggest the change tribal man experiences when he becomes literate. Nearly all the emotional and corporate family feeling is eliminated from his relationship with his social group. He is emotionally free to separate from the tribe and to become a civilized individual, a man of visual organization who has uniform attitudes, habits, and rights with all other civilized individuals.[17]

This illustration helps to demonstrate the effects of differing media on the same abstract content; while the written words "American flag" and the actual item technically contain the same *content*, the media they use and the likely reactions they provoke differ. The violent, emotional debates over flag-burnings are hard to imagine for a piece of cloth with the words printed upon it. The latter invites a decontextualized, non-participatory, analytical response.

It is the creation of a visually uniform conception of rationality that so shockingly changes society. The alphabet creates patterns of linearity, visual uniformity, increased specialization and individuation.[18] This pattern of thought creates new expectations and new types of relationships with previous traditions. The link of writing with bureaucracy is here telling.[19] Writing aids the increased complexity and uniformity on which bureaucracy and empire depend. It is no accident that the spread of the alphabet in the ancient Near East coincided with the largest empire it had yet seen, or that the advent of literacy in Greece preceded Alexander and Rome.[20]

The situation of contemporary technology places the scholar in a position in which it is both easier and more difficult than for earlier generations to relate to the change created by the transition from orality to literacy as mediated by the phonetic alphabet. The radical message of fragmentation and repeatability propagated by print technology has

17. McLuhan, *Understanding Media*, 89. This is exactly the personal experience described by Akinnaso, "Literacy and Individual Consciousness," 73–94, even though he explicitly denies this.

18. McLuhan, *Understanding Media*, 91.

19. Cf. Schaper, "Death of the Prophet," 63–79.

20. Cf. Ong, "Orality, Literacy and Medieval Textualization," 6; Achtemeier, "Omne verbum sonat," 11; Swearingen, "Oral Hermeneutics," 142; and the discussion below.

dominated Western tradition for centuries.[21] Print fosters the identification of logic with the linear, and amplifies the effect of the alphabet. The Western scholarly paradigm is formed with a print mentality. Academic standards of consistency and logical reasoning are entirely based upon a print-centered mentality. McLuhan notes, "We have confused reason with literacy, and rationalism with a single technology."[22] Literacy does not *create* logic; it does, however, promote a link between logic and *linearity* and a focus on closed, contextless systems. It fosters individuality and specialization, enabling detailed analysis to the detriment of situational context; in other words, the close analysis enabled by writing makes it easier to miss the forest for the trees.[23] This study itself, by its very printedness, is testimony to the power print technology has in modern scholarship. Yet, the advent of electronic media has to some degree broken the hegemony of the printed word and reinstated a type of "secondary orality." The phenomenon of "postmodernity" as compared to "modernity" is more linked to the advent of electronic media against print than often realized. Radio, television, film, and the Internet reinstate a kind of immediacy and "tribal interconnectivity" which threatens the linear, visualist orientation of print. But this "secondary orality" is one which is subsequent to, and dependent upon, print literacy; therefore the comparison with "primary orality" is limited.[24]

The importance of the printing press for human history is often acknowledged. The implications of that technology on social structures and patterns of thought is less so. Modern academia takes the typed word for granted; it operates using carefully indexed, labeled, sorted, and classified typographic information.[25] All of this information is neatly

---

21. McLuhan, *Understanding Media*, 173. Cf. idem, *The Gutenberg Galaxy*.

22. McLuhan, *Understanding Media*, 16.

23. Ibid., 135.

24. See Ong, *Orality and Literacy*, 137; cf. Killingsworth, "Product and Process, Literacy and Orality," 30; Tyler, "On Being Out of Words," 133, 136. Modern skeptics of orality theory betray a misunderstanding of the nature of contemporary scholarship; while it is indeed true that "postmodernism" is in vogue in many parts of academia, it is little recognized that this postmodernism occurs within the radically print-literate milieu of scholarship. While modern (print) paradigms are shifting, academia is more inherently print-oriented than society at large, and therefore the influence of print is more fundamental. As Ong (*Orality and Literacy*, 134) notes, "Unlike members of a primary oral culture, who are turned outward because they have had little occasion to turn inward, we are turned outward because we have turned inward."

25. Ong, "Orality, Literacy and Medieval Textualization," 1–2; idem, *The Presence of the Word*, 85–86; idem, *Orality and Literacy*, 128.

ordered, both on the page in neat textual rows and on the bookshelves in neat physical rows; it all invites careful visual comparison and analysis. The drive towards standardization can be seen in the print-fostered birth of dictionaries, standardized spellings, and national languages.[26] The Enlightenment-era (modernist) patterns of thought associated with many of these features are often challenged by post-modernist critiques, but the extent of their support in the medium of print receives much less attention.

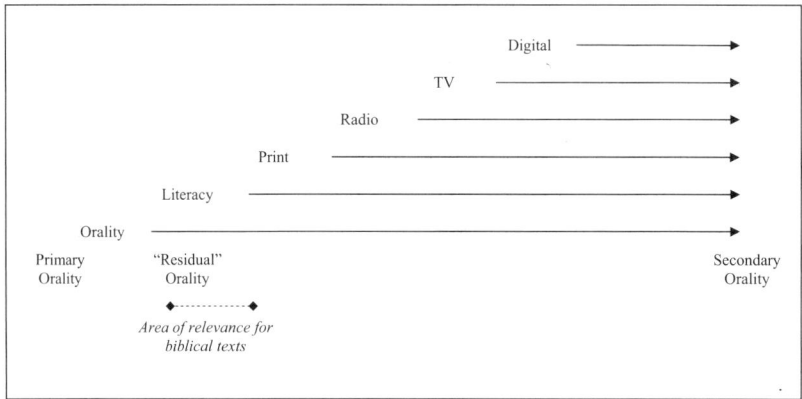

Figure 10. *Media and Their Overlaps*

The print paradigm is currently shifting with the advent of electronic media such as the Internet and email. These media encourage immediate access to and dissemination of bits of information. Information can be hyperlinked to other information, and it can be instantly saved or passed on; it offers an ever-expanding horizon of information. This instanta-neousness, however, has the effect of eliminating both depth and context; it is the medium of the "sound-byte" *par excellence*. New types of social interaction based on hyperlinks rather than proximity (or necessarily even of personal choice) are also created. The changes in society and the possibilities and tensions created thereby should be recognizable to the contemporary scholar.[27] As a model of the societal and mental shifts of technological revolution, it is revealing; as technology which is still dependent upon print, it is misleading.

Ong takes the lead of McLuhan and further explores the implications of the technology of the alphabet on society and modes of thought.

26. McLuhan, *The Gutenberg Galaxy*, 229–231; Ong, *Orality and Literacy*, 128.
27. Cf. Killingsworth, "Product and Process," 31.

Perhaps the primary consequence of writing is "objectivity" and "distance," or to use other terminology, "alienation." Word as speech is of necessity tied to the existential;[28] it indicates the current present-ness of the speaker. Indeed, it more directly indicates the presence of the speaker than any other sense: "Sound is more real or existential than other sense objects, despite the fact that it is also more evanescent."[29] Before the advent of literacy, humankind related to each other and to reality primarily through speech–sound. Speech necessitates the presence and direct interaction of the other; one cannot communicate with another without being in their presence. Writing changes this. "Writing introduces a whole new set of structures within the psyche: communication which lacks the normal social aspect of communication, encounter with one who is not present, participation in the thought of others without commitment or involvement."[30] This contrasts with the original (in historical and personal terms) method of communication. "The paradigm of communication is dialogue, a two-way transaction in a world of sound, which is the world of response, of echo. Vision by contrast is of itself a one-way operation."[31] It was this non-existential aspect of writing which Ong notes was a major cause of the resistance to Sophism in Greece.[32]

Awareness of the changes implicit in the new medium of the alphabet was partially apprehended already in the Achaemenid period. Plato's dialogue between Phaedrus and Socrates is very intriguing for its comment on the effects of literacy.[33] Socrates cites an Egyptian myth to indict writing for causing loss of memorizing-skills, true instruction, and creating the appearance of false wisdom. He claims that written words are inferior to spoken as they can neither be questioned nor can explain nor defend themselves. He further claims that the serious philosopher will not waste his time with writing, bar providing for the "forgetfulness of old age"; writings are, therefore, never to be taken seriously. This passage presumes that written works are still considered somewhat of a novelty and disruptive of traditional methods of education and learning. Socrates cites loss of context and proper instruction, and (implicitly) potential loss

---

28. The term "existential" (lower case) here simply refers to "in relation to the moment" rather than the body of (although related) philosophy known as 'Existentialism.' For a concise explication of this difference set within a history of Western philosophy and theology, see Tillich, *A History of Christian Thought*, 539–41.

29. Ong, *Presence of the Word*, 111.

30. Ibid., 126.

31. Ibid., 167.

32. Ibid., 57.

33. Plato, *Phaedrus* 274B–278C (*Plato I*, 561–75).

of traditions (due to lack of true memory). Of course this appears ironic, as the rejection is itself written. Yet, it is instructive to see how this critique of literacy parallels critiques of the computer upon its introduction.[34] Just as the computer and other electronic media threatened the print paradigm, so literacy threatens the oral paradigm.

A further implication of writing is the process of education. The manner and function of pedagogy is radically altered by the introduction of writing. Without writing all learning by necessity must come from a master or sage, who personally imparts the relevant wisdom, skill, or knowledge to (chosen) pupils. While the skills of writing and reading must be taught, they impart to the pupil the ability to study the thoughts and works of others independently of a pedagogical relationship with them. This was a major reservation of Plato's Socrates noted above.[35] It also adds a dimension of artisanship to the position of sage—writing requires training amanuenses as much as it requires "philosophers." Over time, writing shifts authority and gravity away from the wise *person* to the wise person's *text*, and from wisdom as situated in a tradition to individual interpretation and appropriation of a text. This tension between holy keepers of tradition and holy texts is paralleled with various developments of the Protestant Reformation. Eventually writing gives birth to the "author" as an isolated genius rather than a shaper and transmitter of tradition.[36]

The advent of the letter has further effects. After separating words from immediate context and participation, the linearity and visual nature encourages the dissection and comparison of the content in a manner not encouraged orally. As Ong states, "Abstractly sequential, classificatory, explanatory examination of phenomena or of stated truths is impossible without writing and reading."[37] Two oral stories quite simply cannot be compared in the same manner as two textual variants can be. A visualist orientation transforms ideas of logic, time, and persuasion. It is not that writing creates logic, it changes it to a new form or pattern. This fostering of new types of abstraction leads on from the decontextualization of language from existential concerns. A field study conducted by Luria nicely demonstrates the difference between contextual-existential and

---

34. Ong, *Orality and Literacy*, 79–83; cf. Swearingen, "Oral Hermeneutics," 144.

35. Cf. similar reservations in his letters; see Plato, *Seventh Letter* 341c–d, 344c (*Plato IX*, 531–32, 535, 541); also *the Second Letter* (415–17, in the same volume).

36. Cf. Ong, *Orality and Literacy*, 22; Schniedewind, *How the Bible Became a Book*, 7–8; van der Toorn, *Scribal Culture*, 23, 47–48.

37. Ong, *Orality and Literacy*, 8.

decontextualized-abstract logics. Both literates and oral peoples were given cards with four items (an axe, a saw, a hammer, and a log) and asked to separate them into two groups. Literates separated out the log; oral people refused to remove the log from the list of items the literates classed as "tools."[38] The existential perspective quite naturally links the axe, saw, and hammer with that with which they are used (the log); the "detached" view links the axe with other 'useful' items in general. Neither association is 'illogical,' they simply operate on different assumptions and in different contexts. This principle must be seriously considered when approaching texts which likely come from a residually oral background: the logic may be less abstractly systematic than a modern interpreter may desire.

The movement towards comparison and analysis flows from the nature of writing. By placing words visually before a person in sequential order—but frozen in that order—writing enables the comparison of passages repeatedly and in non-sequential order. Two speeches heard back-to-back can be compared in content, style, and theme; but it is much easier to analyze detailed differences with the transcriptions of those same speeches placed visually side-by-side. The eye is able to separate and reconnect any segment of each speech as it wills; the ear can only hear the words in the flow of context. The element of time creates a paradox—while orality is linear (i.e. sequential and evanescent), by its nature it is relational and fosters relational thought; writing, by removing the sequential element of time, allows the stable information to be dissected (i.e. analyzed and decontextualized) and reassembled into logical rows.[39]

This difference between writing and speaking can still be observed on some level today. One has different expectations for consistency in a spoken, narrated story than from a novel. If the (oral) narrator makes a mistake and corrects it later, the audience is more likely either to miss it or accept it in passing than if it were written on paper. Tannen critiques Oral Theory in reference to scholarly conferences, but her critique fails to understand the concept of "primary orality" or that academic thought has a literacy which is highly interiorized, such that scholars' use of orality is therefore highly influenced by literate modes.[40] Indeed, the concept of an academic paper presupposes a pre-prepared text, itself

---

38. Luria, *Cognitive Development*, 45–79.

39. Ong, *Orality and Literacy*, 9, 103.

40. Tannen, "The Commingling of Orality and Literacy in Giving a Paper at a Scholarly Conference," 34–43.

based on the reading of other texts. It is important to note with her that orality never vanishes; new media change the relation to, rather than replace, predecessors.

Ong discusses orality in three different modes: what he calls "primary orality," "residual orality," and "secondary orality" (defined above).[41] To compare secondary orality, which is based upon the previous 'interiorizing' of literacy, with primary orality is to completely ignore or misunderstand how writing (and in particular, print) reshapes thought. Tannen's critique therefore misses the point.[42] Indeed, much criticism stems from literacy's tendency to analyze and dichotomize dialectics (relationships).[43] The work of communications theorists such as McLuhan, Ong, and Goody emphasizes the necessity to understand the relation between the emerging technology (in this case literacy) and the previous "technology" (in this case speech) and how complex that situation truly is.[44] This relationship varies in contexts, but has certain similar and recognizable features: it amplifies or *intensifies* certain aspects of the previous technology to a degree higher then they were before; and it creates a tension between the new modes of thought/technology and the older one.[45]

In noting the changes literacy effects, there are three basic categories to understand: orality, literacy, and the interaction between the two. It is of course the latter which is pertinent to most investigations (and for Iranian influence) and the most difficult to elucidate. Both McLuhan and Ong point to a paradoxical relationship between a new technology and the previous form: the new technology does not replace the previous one, but *changes the way in which a society relates to it.*[46] Indeed, a new technology tends to increase certain tendencies of the previous technology before its own hegemony sets in.[47] To understand this, one only

41. Farrell confuses the categories of "residual" and "primary" orality, though his overview is otherwise useful; Farrell, "Kelber's Breakthrough," 27–46.

42. Cf. Tyler, "On Being Out of Words," 132; Killingsworth, "Product and Process," 30; Linda Woodbridge, "Add Context and Stir, or, the Sadness of Grendel," 23–24.

43. Tyler, "On Being Out of Words," 32–33. Cf. Kierkegaard's critiques of Hegelian dialectic; Kierkegaard, *Philosophical Fragments; Johannes Climacus,* 108–9; *Either/Or.*

44. Cf. Ong, "A Comment on 'Arguing about Literacy'," 700–701.

45. Cf. McLuhan, *Understanding Media,* 8, 28, 71; Ong, "Orality, Literacy and Medieval Textualization," 1–12.

46. McLuhan, *Understanding Media,* 28; Goody, *The Domestication of the Savage Mind,* 15; Ong, *Orality and Literacy,* 79.

47. Cf. Ong, *Presence of the Word,* 53–87.

need recall how the personal computer was initially expected to eliminate the use of paper, but instead at first grossly increased its usage. Thus, particularly as literacy begins to be interiorized in a society, it *both transforms the nature of orality while extending its patterns.*[48] This principle is very important, but often neglected by scholars. Many of the criticisms of the work of Ong, McLuhan, and Goody ignore this dynamic; when scholars critique Oral Theory by claiming that a mixture of oral and literate is more typical than pure orality, they miss both this phenomenon of intensification as well as the fact that in order for orality and literacy to interact, literacy must already be present.

Some scholars dismiss Oral Theory through anti-colonialist critique, claiming inadequate anthropological proof, or linking the two.[49] Oral Theory, however, does not equate literacy with intelligence or logic—it, rather, points out how the *literate, scholarly world* has equated logic with literacy. Orality is not illogical, it has a *different type* of logic, one which is suited to its medium.[50] Print (and modernity) associated logic with the linear and the analytic; orality has a situational and relational logic. Indeed, in many aspects, Ong and McLuhan's work can be seen as a critique of literacy as much as, if not more than, one of orality. This is explicitly stated by Ong as a reason for his use of *orality* instead of *preliterate* or another term which would presuppose literacy.[51] However, even if Oral Theory has been used in racist or colonialist terms by some scholars, the validity of a theory is independent of its potential uses or misuses. Indeed, the anthropological data support it,[52] and it must be remembered that the description of difference is a separate matter from valuating that difference.

---

48. Cf. Ong, *Orality and Literacy*, 80, 150.

49. See in particular Botha, "Cognition, Orality-Literacy, and Approaches to First-Century Writings," 37–63; Loubser, "Moving Beyond Colonialist Discourse," 65–82; Camp, "Oralities, Literacies, and Colonialism in Antiquity and Contemporary Scholarship," 193–217.

50. Powell, *Origins of Greek Literature*, 22–23, misses this point.

51. Ong, *Orality and Literacy*, 13.

52. Scriber and Cole claim the effect is due to schooling, but they fail to note how literacy demands schooling, and schooling, in their sense, demands literacy. See Scribner and Cole, *The Psychology of Literacy*. Cf. Goody, *The Domestication of the Savage Mind*; idem, *The Interface between the Written and the Oral*; idem, *The Power of the Written Tradition*; Luria, *Cognitive Development*. Akinnaso, "Literacy and Individual Consciousness," 73–94, explicitly challenges Goody (75, 92), but his own personal experiences are classic examples of decontextualization and linear analysis (particularly 90). See also Holbek, "What the Illiterate Think of Writing," 183–96.

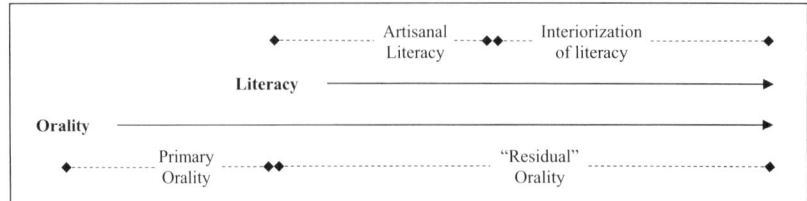

Figure 11. *Orality and Literacy*

In his work Ong notes a variety of characteristics of primary Orality.[53] For the present purposes only a few of these characters are discussed. Particular emphasis will be placed on the "existential" vs. detached dynamics, holistic understanding vs. analysis, and the idea of visual uniformity. These issues are particularly relevant in connection with the questions of sources and traditional redaction criticism—and, therefore, of influence and its impact on text creation. These characteristics are carried into the early stages of literacy and are amplified before their dialectically opposite tendencies begin to take hold among the literate classes.

Niditch applies orality–literacy considerations to the biblical texts in her *Oral World and Written Word*. She proposes an "oral–literate continuum" under which it is possible to analyze orality and literacy in the Hebrew Bible in a more nuanced manner.[54] Instead of treating oral traditions as textual chunks of a distant past or treating Israelites as modern literates, she explores how orality is evidenced well into the biblical period. She notes that writing has various functions, many of which operate within an "oral register" where the written word contains religio-numinous implications. She shows that the archeological evidence towards the use of writing reveals how supposed evidence of literacy is better understood as highlighting typically oral thought-patterns, and that the basic supposition of an original source text is problematic. Her analysis leads her to reject the documentary hypothesis on the grounds that it too heavily represents literate thinking.

Niditch's work is an excellent starting point and heralds a more fruitful use of Oral Theory in Biblical Studies. In exploring the sources of apocalyptic, it is important to note the interaction and natures of communicative media, and to see how the radical changes in society and thought-patterns are influenced, and perhaps even partially determined, by the changes in media. These changes would have affected all of

---

53. In *Interfaces of the Word*, 102, Ong notes seven general characteristics; in *Orality and Literacy*, 36–57, he offers nine.
54. Niditch, *Oral World and Written Word*, 3–7.

society, not just the few who were literate. The structure of authority, the nature of education, and the division of labor are all affected by the advent of literacy, just as the transmission, alteration, and preservation of traditions is altered.

All this theory can be distilled into a few methodological principles. The first is that oral and written modes vary in their relationship to previous traditions; orality is contextual and aggregative, while writing is more critical and distant. All oral performance is in a shared context; writing decontextualizes previous traditions. It is therefore important to analyze the logic inherent in a text before deciding that it is "illogical" or poorly redacted: it could be the record of an oral performance. Second, the concept of verbatim quotation is a very literate idea and largely anachronistic for a largely residually oral culture. This is due to the evanescent nature of orality itself as well as the physical difficulty of consulting passages in rare, unwieldy, and expensive scrolls or tablets. Third, the introduction of writing alters social structures and patterns of thought; this is most easily recognizable in the development of bureaucracy and new types of education. This is a dialectical process, however, and proceeds through interiorization and amplification.

Implications for Methodology
The type of scholarship commonly known as text-critical, as exemplified by Fishbane's *Biblical Interpretation in Ancient Israel*, potentially misunderstands the dynamics of the oral and literate media. Fishbane extensively documents cases of scribal alterations and textual quotations in the received biblical text. However, the type of analysis which he uses presupposes an entirely (modern) literate mindset. While he acknowledges that oral transmission must have occurred,[55] he analyzes as if the written tradition which is extant originated, was transmitted, and was altered solely as a written tradition. The legal materials of the Hebrew Bible serve as an apt example. It is commonly recognized that "frequent lacunae or ambiguities"[56] in the text make it inoperable as a law code; indeed, Fishbane admits it is "but an expression of a much more comprehensive oral law."[57] It is dubious to analyze the text solely in reference to itself, and to read it is as if the scribes who wrote it did the same. It is much more plausible that the legal materials were written in reference to the (common knowledge) oral tradition which, over time, was lost. It is immaterial whether or not the laws were written as innovations,

---

55. Fishbane, *Biblical Interpretation*, 23.
56. Ibid., 92.
57. Ibid., 95

clarifications, or examples of justice; what may be more important to the understanding of the texts is the change in the attitudes of the scribes towards various texts as their surrounding oral traditions and imperial contexts either alter, fade, or disappear—in other words, when the scribes begin to treat the texts as self-sufficient.[58]

There is no doubt that scribes altered texts. Nor is the complexity of textual transmission to be understated. There is a serious question, however, as to whether every "deviance" or "variation" is due to exegetical or scribal written innovation—it could simply reflect (now lost) oral tradition, the typical vagaries of human memory, or, more significantly, that the original author/editor might not have recognized a difficulty or contradiction at all. To cite just one example, Fishbane claims that Jer 17:21–22 is an exegetical innovation based upon Deut 5:12–14.[59] He claims the similarities and differences between the wordings of the two passages on the Sabbath reveal a need by ancient Israel "to camouflage and legitimate its exegetical innovations."[60] The differences between the two, however, are more *visual* than *aural*, specific rather than general. In the prophetic passage Jeremiah takes a general principle (not to do work on the Sabbath) and in good hortatory fashion applies it to a specific ("existential") situation: the carrying of burdens into the city on the Sabbath. In the context of the extant book of Jeremiah, the presentation of this critique to the people at the city gates presages the entry of the city by foreign invaders as punishment for such violations. So, rather than being a scribal innovation disguised as an ancient quotation, the passage might be better understood as the typical work of a religious orator— applying principles to the here-and-now of the audience. This understanding is underscored when the two passages are read aloud, rather than viewed side by side (as Fishbane indeed presents them): as heard, the passages appear to be more parallel than they appear to be contradictory. Even if the passage in Jeremiah is intended to allude to Deut 5:12–14, it is likely the variations are due to the nature of memory rather than calculated variance.[61] The attempt to treat them in so exacting, verbatim a manner is more likely to be misleading than illuminating.[62]

---

58. Cf. Kraus, "Ein centrales Problem," 283–96; Fitzpatrick-McKinley, *The Transformation of Torah*, 146–82; Niditch, *Oral World and Written Word*, Chapter 8.

59. Fishbane, *Biblical Interpretation*, 131–34.

60. Ibid., 134.

61. McIver and Carroll, "Experiments," 667–87.

62. Cf. Ong, "Maranatha," 433: "To think of memory as essentially verbatim is to resort to an unreal model for memory fostered by literacy and its practice of transcribing texts." Aaron, *Etched in Stone*, 36, also sees this as too "narrow," although he still sees Oral Theory as "hopelessly circular" (170–72).

The above example demonstrates that to think that all "quotations" must refer to a previous *text* is to think like a modern literate scholar, not like an inhabitant of a largely residually oral culture.[63] As the Hebrew Bible increasingly became a recognized canon, the likelihood increased that teachers and preachers, be they priest, prophet, or scribe, would directly quote the authoritative text. But even here, it is important to note that before print the notion of quotation itself is much more fluid and closer to modern concepts of paraphrase than verbatim quotation. Even after the "canonization" of texts, quotation on most occasions would be from memory rather than direct visual copying.[64] Scrolls were expensive and rare, and it was likely even the most literate and papyrus-laden of scribes more often drew on memory than on actual visual reference to a text.[65] In addition, phrases taken from a scriptural milieu can simply be used as part of a communal vocabulary without direct, intended reference to the original passage; consider, for example, the career of the phrase "hewers of wood."[66] The usage of stock phrases and epithets is here cautionary.[67]

In discussing biblical material where texts appear to have similar language, content, or form, a literary dependence, in one direction or another, is generally assumed. While direct literary dependence is *possible*, it is not always *necessary* when dealing with "traditional" materials. It is fairly clear that an Exodus tradition existed in pre-exilic Israel. At various times this tradition and its motifs were used and appropriated in the Hebrew Bible, something which must have been a common occurrence. When approaching a text which appears to utilize Exodus motifs, it is appropriate to ask whether the use is a literary quotation, or whether it is simply another use of the general tradition. Was the text in question performed orally or was it originally written? If performed orally, would the audience have viewed it as a quotation of *x*, or merely have understood it within the "Exodus" tradition? In any given society traditional stories, motifs, proverbs, and so on, will be used, reused, and refashioned by various members of that society for various purposes. All of these adaptations of the traditions may occur independently or in tandem, but

---

63. Similar concerns are expressed by Schultz, *Search for Quotation*, in particular 109–12.

64. Cf. Achtemeier, "Omne verbum sonat," 26–27.

65. Van der Toorn, *Scribal Culture*, 23; cf. Niditch, *Oral World and Written Word*, 41; Ong, *Orality and Literacy*, 93; Carr, *Writing on the Tablet of the Heart*, 4, 40.

66. Elliott, *The Catholics of Ulster*, 343; a search on Google Scholar reveals a large number of contexts for the phrase's usage.

67. Cf. Niditch, *Oral World and Written Word*, 10–20.

they all operate within a milieu which is understood on a broader scale than any single given representation of the tradition. In other words, an individual textual occurrence of a story, motif, or phrase is not necessarily the wellspring or touchstone of its constituent tradition. This is equally true when investigating parallels between cultures.

Further, an oral tradition does not cease to exist orally once it is written down, nor does the writing of the tradition need to have an immediate impact on the oral form of a tradition (indeed, it is likely not to). The same tradition can be written more than once, each time recording the same strand of tradition in various oral forms, without any knowledge or dependence on previous or simultaneous written forms. It is therefore problematic to declare or assume *literary* dependence between texts dealing with traditional motifs without clear reasons to do so. Linking the date of a text to the date of a tradition (or form of a tradition) is equally problematic.

The influence of a literate "scribality" should be understood in concert with the above considerations. The scribes were operating within an oral tradition; they were also operating in a new milieu—the increased use and hegemony of writing both for the creation and preservation of tradition. As written traditions become more normative, more of the overall culture will refer to them—developing the phenomena of re-oralized texts, the ideal of verbatim memorization, and textual hermeneutics—which seems to be the situation of the Persian and Hellenistic periods. "It is the mechanism of writing and its virtually immediate effect of decontextualization that over time opens these texts (unlike speech) to reformulation, critical attention, reflection and commentary."[68]

The scribal situation—in the context of the oral world—was a relatively new one. Yet, the collection of texts created a new situation, one which had to alter the ways in which the scribes thought (even while their thought processes were closer to primary orality then post-print mentality). The situation of writing—to which these scribes most likely dedicated their lives—offered these scribes a new window to evaluate, reflect upon, and edit their religious and cultural traditions. Perhaps they even discovered traditions that had been generally forgotten. It has long been noted that the apocalyptic literature is scribal in character, and it has been postulated that one of the differences between prophetic and apocalyptic literatures is their original orality and literacy, respectively. Grabbe has recently challenged this distinction, however, by claiming

---

68. Fitzpatrick-McKinley, *The Transformation of Torah*, 15–16.

that both literatures and phenomena evidence orality and literacy.[69] To what extent does the increasing interiorization in the ancient Near East generally and in the scribal class in particular play a role in the difference between prophetic and apocalyptic literatures, if any?

It is clear from both the Hebrew Bible and ancient Near East parallels that prophets operated primarily orally, even when their oracles were written.[70] These written oracles served more as monuments to the gods or reports in lieu of presence than records in the modern sense.[71] But to what extent do the prophetic books reflect original oral oracles, and how much later scribal redaction? Suffice it to say that the increasing authority of the text evident in Judaean religion had an impact not only on the genres and forms of religious expression, but on the social structures and thought patterns: it is in this context that prophetic literature "died" and the apocalypse was born.[72]

Two examples will illustrate the relevance of Oral Theory to the present study. The first, Jer 36, demonstrates the complex relationship the extant text has with literacy; the second, Second Isaiah, introduces how media analysis should inform questions of sources and foreign influence.

Jeremiah 36. A famous crux for the development of prophetic literature and of orality and literacy is Jer 36 (LXX 43). In this passage Jeremiah dictates all of his oracles to Baruch the scribe, who then reads them to the people in the temple during a fast. Another scribe present for this recitation reports the event to the officials. Upon hearing this, they have Baruch read the scroll again to them. The officials store the scroll, tell Baruch and Jeremiah to hide, and report it to the king. The king has the

---

69. See his various articles in Grabbe and Haak, eds., *Knowing the End from the Beginning*, 11, 30–31, 109, 116, 119–24.

70. See van der Toorn "Mesopotamian Prophecy between Immanence and Transcendence," and Nissinen "The Socioreligious Role of the Neo-Assyrian Prophets" both in Nissinen, ed., *Prophecy in Its Ancient Near Eastern Context*, 71–114. Cf. the primary sources edited in Nissinen, *Prophets and Prophecy*. In this context it is interesting to consider Davis's theory that Ezekiel was the first *writing* prophet. See Davis, *Swallowing the Scroll*. However, Odell, "'You Are What You Eat'," 242, 244, denies that the scroll Ezekiel eats stands for writing *per se*, but rather the symbolic permanence of judgment (and thus squarely in the "oral mode").

71. Niditch, *Oral World and Written Word*, 104–5.

72. Nissinen, "The Dubious Image of Prophecy," 26–41. It is to be wished that these considerations would have been included in Floyd, "The Production of Prophetic Books in the Early Second Temple Period," 276–97.

scroll read in his presence, cutting off and burning four columns as it is read. In response, Jeremiah again dictates the oracle collection to Baruch, adding a further oracle of condemnation and more similar things (ועוד נוסף עליהם דברים רבים כהמה).

Van der Toorn sees in this passage a scribal obfuscation of the growth in prophetic collections.[73] Niditch sees evidence of a still largely oral setting in the late monarchy.[74] Whatever the relationship between the historical formation of the Jeremiah corpus and this passage, it is still revealing in its attitudes towards writing.[75] The narrative assumes that while people can read, the standard paradigm is still the spoken word: even the group of scribe-officials have Baruch *read out* the scroll to them, rather than reading it themselves. After this reading they store the scroll and verbally report the contents to the king. Only upon royal request do they actually read the text themselves. While the passage clearly takes the existence of the written word for granted, it utilizes texts in two very residually oral manners. First, the scroll functions primarily as an aide to oral pronouncement in the absence of Jeremiah, and, secondly, the scroll itself functions as a witness against the king's intransigence.[76] The scroll's physical destruction and recreation doubly guarantee the efficacy of the threat.

It is further worth noting the pericope's lack of concern for verbatim repetition. Indeed, while Jeremiah is able to recreate his oracle collection at will—presumably with no prior writing of his oracles—he is able to expand and add to it without violating the essential continuity of the second version with the first. This mindset is reminiscent of oral singers observed by Lord, who are able to note differences between separate performances while seeing no real significance in the fact.[77] Again, verbatim replication is a literate concern.

Second Isaiah. In a well-known article, Smith proposes influence of an Iranian prophecy upon the first half of Second Isaiah (chs. 44–48).[78] This passage offers a valuable example of the ways in which Oral Theory can inform the weighing up of potential influences.

---

73. Van der Toorn, *Scribal Culture*, 186–88.

74. Niditch, *Oral World and Written Word*, 104–5; cf. Carr, *Writing on the Tablet of the Heart*, 146–47, who makes points similar to the ones below.

75. Or, in Barstad's parlance, "phenomenologically true"; see Barstad, "No Prophets?," 59, cf. 46.

76. Cf. Nielsen, *Oral Tradition*, 71.

77. Lord, *The Singer of Tales*, 27–29.

78. Smith, "II Isaiah and the Persians," 415–21.

In the context of the Servant Texts,[79] the anonymous prophet proclaims Cyrus as the coming agent of Babylon's deserved destruction
(44:24–45:13; 46:11; 48:14–16). Cyrus is depicted as YHWH's anointed
(משיח), servant (עבד), and shepherd (רעה),[80] and the prophet expects
Cyrus to destroy the city of Babylon and to return the Judaeans home.
These expectations are placed within a greater theological construct of
monotheism, creation theology, punishment and restoration.[81] These
passages are unmistakably related to several Neo-Babylonian texts, the
Cyrus Cylinder, *The Verse Prophecy of Nabonidus*, and the *Nabonidus
Chronicle*.[82] The coincidences between these texts have led several
scholars to conclude that Isaiah's prophecies are in fact dependent on
either the *Cyrus Cylinder* itself or on the pro-Cyrus propaganda which
lay behind it.[83] In addition to the Neo-Babylonian political parallels,
Smith finds a parallel to Second Isaiah's creation theology and rhetorical
questions in one of the *Gāthās*, *Yasna* 44.[84] He therefore concludes that
behind *Yasna* 44, the *Cyrus Cylinder*, and Second Isaiah lays an oral,
pro-Cyrus oracle. Rather than discuss the historical probability, for the
present purposes only the media-related aspects of the proposal are
explored.

The first question involves the nature of Second Isaiah itself: is it a
literary text, the record of oral performance(s), or a combination of the
two?[85] For whom was it initially created: a circle of followers, fellow
scribes, inhabitants of a particular settlement, or was it meant for a wider,
oral dissemination? The Servant Texts are a long-standing puzzle, but the
presence of residual orality must be considered; this bears heavily on the
question of the redaction-history of the section, a question by necessity
bypassed here.

79. "Servant Texts" rather than 'Servant Songs' is used following the discussion
of Conroy, "Recent Studies of the Enigmatic Servant Texts in Isaiah."

80. The MT has רעי, which could be understood as "my friend" or "my shepherd,"
depending on pointing. The Mesopotamian parallels to "shepherd" as a royal designation prompt many commentators to prefer "shepherd." Cf. Blenkinsopp, *Isaiah
40–55*, 244; Goldingay, *The Message of Isaiah 40–55*, 259.

81. Cf. Baltzer, *Deutero-Isaiah*, 33–44.

82. All three are translated in *ANET*, 305–7, 312–16. A translation including an
additional fragment of the *Cyrus Cylinder* is available in Hallo, ed., *COS*, 2:314–
316; cf. Kuhrt, *The Persian Empire*, 70–80.

83. Blenkinsopp, *Isaiah 40–55*, 249; Boyce, *HZ II*, 43–65.

84. Smith, "II Isaiah and the Persians," 419. Smith's retention of the oracular
genres is certainly preferable to Parpola's attempt to see them as extispicy queries.
Parpola, "The Originality of the Teachings of Zarathustra," 373–83.

85. Discussed by Gitay, "Deutero-Isaiah: Oral or Written?," 185–97, although he
ultimately discounts the import of the question (197).

As noted by Niditch, the use of standard epithets or phrases does not necessarily indicate textual dependence.[86] That both the *Cyrus Cylinder* and Second Isaiah use the same terms and even phrases to depict Cyrus as a legitimate king does not require a literary explanation on its own.[87] The use of rhetorical questions or a dialogical format, like *Yasna* 44, points towards a more oral setting as well. The common timeframe and referent for the two texts, however, may still justify Smith's search for a shared background in Persian propaganda.

Secondly, the same question must be posited of the sources behind the text. If one wishes to see Persian psychological warfare as a source, one must confront the forms this would have taken. It is *prima facie* unlikely that such propaganda would or could have been disseminated in writing unless carried by messengers: how would they get into Babylonia, in what language, and to whom would such texts be given?[88] One rather thinks of a scenario similar to the one in 2 Kgs 18, where the officials of Shalmaneser yell propaganda to the populace in their own language. If such an occurrence could inspire the Cyrus texts, one would expect the original utterances to be formulaic, diplomatic speeches rather than prophetic oracles. It would also require Judaean presence in a besieged city. Of course, different questions would need to be posed if one wished to follow Albertz in seeing the intended monarch as Darius I.[89]

It is clear from the *Nabonidus Chronicle* and the *Sippar Cylinder of Nabonidus*[90] that Cyrus was known in Babylonia prior to his assault on said kingdom. Nabonidus claimed to have had a dream in which Marduk promised to raise Cyrus to defeat Astyages (550 B.C.E.), enabling the reconstruction of the temple in Harran.[91] Although Nabonidus initially seems to have favored Cyrus as weakening his main rival Astyages, this attitude may not have long survived; as Briant notes, the extant textual indices appear to compress the period of hostilities between the kings.[92] Residents of the Neo-Babylonian Empires had plenty of advance notice of the ascendancy of Cyrus, and it is not inconceivable that Second Isaiah's prophecy draws the Judaean conclusion simply from the political situation of the day. Although evidence for *avant-garde* propagandists

---

86. Niditch, *Oral World and Written Word*, 10–20.

87. Contra Smith's assertion, Smith, "II Isaiah and the Persians," 417.

88. Cf. Greene, *Messenger and Message*, 8–43.

89. Albertz, "Darius in Place of Cyrus," 371–83. Also argued in idem, *Israel in Exile*, 399–404.

90. Translated in Hallo, ed., *COS* 2:310–13.

91. In the *Sippar Cylinder*.

92. Briant, *From Cyrus to Alexander*, 41–43.

is lacking for Cyrus's campaign,[93] it is likely that the King of Anšan engaged in war propaganda of the time-venerable kind: he appears to have brutally sacked the city of Opis in a manner which prompted the subsequent surrender of Sippar (and then Babylon?).[94] If such actions had come before, the prophet's vindictive hopes for Babylon are easily understandable without recourse to more verbal propaganda. In any case, the prophecies must pre-date 539, since Cyrus did not destroy Babylon, and one must consider which media a minority would have used in a besieged empire.

Cultural Interactions in the Light of Orality and Literacy

The question of Iranian influences on Judaism must be considered in the context of the primarily oral milieu discussed above as well as the increasingly important role of literacy. The import of orality affects the analysis by broadening the manner in which texts and ideas are compared and borrowings considered. Judaeans who came into contact with Persian ideas most likely came into contact with them in an oral setting: in *discussion* with other Judaeans, with Persians, with other peoples, rather than by *reading* Persian sacred texts (whether these were available for reading or not). Perhaps they heard the *Gāthās* or Herodotus's θεο-γονίην chanted and explained; perhaps they observed Persian officials practice or discuss their religion; perhaps they heard a minstrel perform songs of Iranian mythology; perhaps it was part of the general *Zeitgeist*. Because even the scribes were more orally oriented than today, the discussion of influence and its manifestations in literature needs to be alert for this subtle media-context.

Importance of Interiorization for the Context of the Apocalypses

Most important for understanding the shift in communication media is the concept mentioned above, the "interiorizing" of a technology. The shifts created by a new technology do not happen immediately, but have a cumulative effect as more and more of a society's thought and social

93. Kuhrt, "The Cyrus Cylinder and Achaemenid Imperial Policy," 83–97, would understand the cylinder as an after-the-fact piece of propaganda. Kelly, "Persian Propaganda," 173–219, argues that the Persians did indeed utilize advance propaganda, but not until Xerxes's campaign in 480.

94. *Nabonidus Chronicle* 7.iii.12–13 (*ANET*, 306, although the translation supplies a misleading parenthesis implying Nabonidus did the massacring; see the relevant snippet in Hallo, ed., *COS* 1:468; cf. Kuhrt, "Nabonidus and the Babylonian Priesthood," 133; Briant, *From Cyrus to Alexander*, 41).

patterns are assimilated to it. New technologies become, over time, accepted as parts of/extensions of the human body itself: writing extends the eye, telephone extends the ear, and so on. Because the media are extensions of the human body they alter the ratios of use between the senses.[95] These extensions to the body create new psychological ratios between mental faculties, just as people with physical impairments cope through the increased reliance on the other senses. The systemic and psychological stress occasioned by the internalization of new media rather recalls the distress often associated with the advent of apocalyptic or millenarian groups.[96]

Perhaps the Hebrew language itself gives a hint of the gradual interiorization of literacy, in the culture in general and among scribes in particular. The word קרא means both "to call" and "to meet." It seems likely that its use to mean "to read" is related to an analogue with the obviously oral-personal meanings of "calling" and "meeting." As late as Augustine written works were read by being pronounced aloud, in private and in public.[97] A person, then, who קרא was calling the words out of the text. Similarly, ספר offers an interesting hint. סָפַר is to count and סֹפֵר is a scribe. This seems to pick up the historical situation that writing originated as accounting and administrative dockets.[98] The use, similarly, of סֵפֶר, "book," evolved from dockets to literary works. These are only speculative considerations, but they are suggestive of the progress of the interiorization of the new medium.

The overlap, or *intensification*, between the appearance of writing and its complete interiorization is perhaps what Niditch intended to convey with her concept of the "oral–literate continuum."[99] Within this overlap Ong points to the curious effect whereby tendencies of a previous technology are initially intensified before being altered or eliminated by the new technology. This can be illustrated through two examples. Mnemonic lists are characteristic of oral societies; early literature is characterized by often excessively long and detailed lists (e.g. *the Táin*,

---

95. McLuhan, *Understanding Media*, 3–6; cf. Ong, *Presence of the Word*, 131–35.

96. E.g. Talmon, "Millenarian Movements," 28–29; Hanson, *The Dawn of Apocalyptic*, 408–9. Compare with McLuhan, *Understanding Media*, 5, 35, 45–52; Ong, *Presence of the Word*, 133–38, 211; idem, *Orality and Literacy*, 68.

97. Achtemeier, "Omne verbum sonat," 15–17; cf. Ong, *Orality and Literacy*, 113.

98. Fischer, *A History of Writing*, 1–11; Goody, *The Domestication of the Savage Mind*, 79–82.

99. Niditch, *Oral World and Written Word*, 4.

Numbers).[100] The word has numinous connotations in oral society; in early writing this numinousness even gets projected onto script, making the individual letter a powerful talisman.[101] To give a modern analogue, the Internet first functioned as an expansion of print media before it took on its present multimedia form.

What Niditch labels the "oral–literate continuum" could perhaps be nuanced in terms of the increasing internalization of literacy. The use of the alphabet transforms thought and social patterns, but it does so gradually and cumulatively; the more the written word is used, the more it becomes the dominant paradigm in its users' thought. Hence, the overlap of oral and literate use and mentality which Niditch so carefully notes as well as the increased tendency towards the literate end of the continuum in the later texts are interrelated.[102] This means that the effects of literacy would have been varied both synchronically and diachronically, as well as hierarchically (i.e. levels of education). Niditch notes several times the sense of the numinous, quasi-magical or efficacious nature which the use of the written word implies in the Hebrew Bible; this point has significant ramifications for the present study, although only two examples are cited here: (1) the possibility of oracles being written down as "sign acts" (mostly oral mindset) and then later collected and viewed as if intended as archives (more literate mindset); (2) the transfer and concomitant interiorization of the texts' numinousness and efficaciousness by scribes as literacy becomes increasingly interiorized by them. The scribes' sense of authority increased as they appropriated the growing authority (rather than numinousness) of the texts.

Perhaps a better word to describe this overlap or interaction than "continuum"—which may imply an ease and smoothness of transition, as well as completeness—is "dialectic." Dialectic—in the Kierkegaardian sense rather than in the Hegelian—implies the co-existence of two related, but distinct, entities which are in perpetual tension. Orality and literacy are related, of course, because literacy comes out of and transforms oral modes. They are in tension because oral modes in some form *always remain* and have certain tendencies which contradict literate tendencies. Since all human beings are born into orality and only subse-

---

100.　Cf. Yates, *The Art of Memory*, 6–8.

101.　E.g. the Aramaic incantation bowls and later Kabbalistic letter-mysticism. Noted in Hezser, *Jewish Literacy in Roman Palestine*, 220–22.

102.　Niditch, *Oral World and Written Word*, mentions that the reference to divine record books increases in later literature (81); increased importance of written sources in general (98); earlier prophetic texts seem to cite visions, later ones letters (91).

quently can enter into literacy, an individual's psychology will have various levels of tension between literate and oral modes, varying on the level of the interiorization of literacy.

When discussing the interiorization of literacy, it is important to note that there are shades and levels of literacy, from rudimentary ability to scratch out one's signature to the ability to compose *The Lord of the Rings*. Although modern literates expect one to be able to read and write, these two skills are strictly speaking separate; the Western ideal of universal ability to read anything is highly idiosyncratic in historical and numerical terms.[103] The gradations of literacy (from "artisanal" to complete) must be kept in mind when considering the variable of residual orality. Thus, the mere cataloguing of archaeological finds with writing on them fails to grapple with the distinction in types between highly interiorized (print) literacy and less complete (minimal) forms.[104] This can easily be seen (though often unappreciated) by Paul's use of his signature.[105]

Consequently, in the periods when prophetic literature was surrendering to the apocalypse, many changes may not be so much in the *content* of the text as in the *authority* of *written* texts themselves. Important in this respect is the formation of a scribal class—working with traditional materials which are at the same time given an independent (textual) existence from oral tradition—which was beginning to codify, assimilate, and question a textual tradition. It was in a situation where "prophetic words are no longer predominantly living speech, but rather inscribed and inscrutable data whose true meanings are an esoteric mystery revealed by God to a special adept and his pious circle"[106] that literate mentalities among a scribal elite began to notice *literate* tensions between the canonized traditions. This increasing tension was a situational dynamic beyond the class and sociological implications of scribal authorship. It implies a different origin and literary quality to texts where created *qua* text from texts which were redacted into texts. It is a context where hermeneutes gain a new speciality—no longer do adepts of traditions have merely to interpret the signs of the times (as did an Amos, Isaiah, or Jeremiah), but they had to interpret the meaning of *texts* in the light of the current situation. While one could adequately function as a

103.   See the useful overview by MacDonald, "Literacy in an Oral Environment," 49–118.

104.   For example, approaches such as the one taken by Millard, *Reading and Writing in the Time of Jesus*.

105.   Keith, "'In My Own Hand'," especially 46–58.

106.   Fishbane, *Biblical Interpretation*, 484.

priest or prophet in a wholly oral context, one cannot exegete texts without advanced scribal training.[107] Whatever the nature of prophetic training, there is no doubt that the training and societal expectations of a scribe were very different.

Enochic Literature

The Enochic literature offers a good example of the change in mind-set encouraged by the scribal enterprise and the resultant change in cultural-religious attitudes and traditions. In the Enochic literature a trend towards the linking of scribality with righteousness can be detected. The angels, the righteous dead, and even YHWH himself are increasingly depicted as scribes; the heavenly system of justice depends heavily on books which record the deeds of humanity.[108] The effectiveness of YHWH's power is evidenced less by his presence and more by his literate bureaucracy; indeed, YHWH becomes increasingly distant.

1 Enoch 12:4 explicitly calls Enoch a "scribe of righteousness"; this identification is repeated in 13:4 and 15:1. Writing is deemed so important for the identity of Enoch that learning to write is listed as one of two momentous life-events, the other being his marriage (83:2).[109] In distinction to Deut 4:9, where the Israelites are admonished to remember and to pass their memory on to their children, *1 En.* 81:6 equates the teaching of the law with the *writing* of it. In 103:2 Enoch is justified because he has "seen the heavenly tablets and the holy writings." Knowledge of tradition is no longer sufficient without command of the textual versions of it.

A shift from the admonitory and "existential" aspects of prophetic material is illustrated in *1 En.* 89:62–64, 69. In these verses the sins of the shepherds are written down and recorded for future judgment, but the text explicitly states that the shepherds are not to be admonished for their sins. Rather than the immediate function of oration and the instantaneous demand which it represents, here writing functions as a score-card of sorts, enabling YHWH to keep record until the final judgment; the Day of the Lord is coming rather than present. Indeed, the sapiential idea of

---

107. Over time, the scribal training itself becomes insufficient, requiring supplementation. Cf. Jaffee, *Torah in the Mouth*, who argues that the Rabbis became self-conscious of their oral interpretations, seeing exegesis alone as nothing. The present author is grateful to Professor Niditch for this reference.

108. Cf. *1 En.* 81:1–82:4; 89:70–71; 90:17; 91:14; 93:2; 97:7; 98:6–8; 104:7; 106:19; 107:1.

109. This was pointed out at an SBL session of "Orality and the Formation of the Hebrew Bible" section in Philadelphia 2005, but the author cannot recall whose comment it was.

recompense appears to be wholly suspended until the *eschaton*. Earlier in the current collation of *1 Enoch* this tendency is implicit; Enoch writes a memorial prayer in 13:4, so that the supplicants will be remembered in the future.

1 Enoch 69:8–10. An apparent aberration in scribal glorification appears in *1 En.* 69:8–10. Here the watcher Pinem'e is condemned for teaching people "about writing with ink and papyrus," claiming that "humans were not born for this purpose, to confirm their trustworthiness through pen and ink." At first glance these comments appear to show an oral culture's reservations over the changes created by writing, similar to Plato's comments in *Phaedrus*. However, in the context of the passage and of the collection as a whole, the comments need to be read differently. The following verses claim it is "through this, their knowledge, they are perishing." Clearly it is not knowledge *per se* which condemns, but false knowledge. In the context of scribal traditions, this polemic makes sense in terms of an "elitist" view towards writing and the written text. It is not writing itself which is wicked (after all, Enoch is a scribe and the condemnation is itself written), but the use of writing and reading by non-scribe-sages, and therefore the misunderstanding and misappropriation of the knowledge. Writing makes heresy and falsity more difficult and problematic by *making it permanent*. An idea which might have passed away unnoticed, once written, gains a new authority, an authority inappropriate for those who are not worthy of it. This interpretation is bolstered with reference to 104:9–14; sinners here are indicted for inventing fictitious stories and writing "books in their own names."[110] This strikes a scholar as bizarrely ironic in a pseudepigraphical book, but it shows how residually oral even highly literate scribes could still be; Lord notes that fidelity to a perceived tradition (in this case, the Enochic tradition) is more important than individual authorship among oral tradents.[111] The passage continues by wishing these false scribes would have written faithfully, neither adding nor taking away, and then they would know the joy of the Scriptures. *1 Enoch* 104:10–13, when read with 69:8–10, clearly links sin with "false scribality," which perhaps may be understood as scribal traditions other than the authors'.

---

110. Various readings; see Nickelsburg and VanderKam, *1 Enoch*, 163; however, Stuckenbruck, *1 Enoch 91–108*, 582, 591, sees a reference to translation here; cf. Isaac, "1 (Ethiopic Apocalypse of) Enoch," n. 85.
111. Lord, *The Singer of Tales*, 28–29.

This link between false scribality and wickedness is made explicit in 98:15,[112] "Woe to those who write lying words and words of error; they write and lead many astray with their lies."

These passages, then, seem to evidence some of the tensions created by the interiorization of writing; while it gives these scribes the access to secret heavenly knowledge, it removes the existential and communal controls on traditions and teaching, opening them up to divergent interpretations. Indeed, the problems associated with the verification of prophecy return,[113] only now writing makes them even more permanent.[114] The Enochic myth of demonic teaching belongs in this tension.

2 Enoch. The scribal tendencies visible in *1 Enoch* are radically extended in the *2 Enoch* materials. Enoch is depicted as the scribe *par excellence*, transcribing 366 books in 30 days and nights, including "everything that is appropriate to learn" (22:11–23:6; cf. 68:2).[115] His work as a scribe ("own handwriting") testifies to YHWH (33:5, 8), will bring glory to those who read it (35:2–3), and cannot be contradicted (53:2–3).

The text projects writing back into creation; Adam was the first scribe (33:10). The text echoes the sentiment of Qoh 12:12 in noting the proliferation of texts (since creation), but instead of cynically eschewing them it points to Enoch as the scribal guide to righteousness (47:2). Indeed, the author envisions an almost exclusively text-based righteousness; in 48:6, 8, Enoch is enjoined to pass on his books to future generations, much like Deut 4:9 enjoins the Israelites to pass on Torah. The "J" text again equates reading with personal instruction (36:1).

Like *1 Enoch*, *2 Enoch* envisions a record-based final judgment.[116] Chapter 65, however, extends this motif in a curious manner. According to this chapter, YHWH created time in order to allow man to "think of his sins and so that he might write his own achievement, both good and evil" (65:4). Here, instead of angels or the deity, each person writes the record of his own life. Accountability is linked to one's knowledge of one's achievement, and how it compares to Enoch's writings (65:5). There is a finality in this which seems to forestall the possibility of forgiveness:

---

112. Nickelsburg and VanderKam, *1 Enoch*, 151; Stuckenbruck, *1 Enoch 91–108*, 372.

113. Cf. Carroll, *When Prophecy Failed*, 198–203.

114. Interestingly, this chasm opened by writing was the impetus for the formulation of the Rabbinic concept of the "Orah Torah." See Jaffee, *Torah in the Mouth*, particularly 10.

115. J redaction.

116. *2 En.* 44:5 (A); 50:1; 52:15; 53:2–3.

actions (including sinful ones) are recorded, making them permanent. Salvation is partially dependent on the ability to analyze one's life in regards to Enoch's, a very literate skill.

Further testimony to the increasing hegemony of literate thought within the Enochic strand can be seen in the later *3 Enoch* as well. Taking up the strands of the earlier Enochic literature, *3 Enoch* transforms *1 En.* 69:15–25's account of creation, where everything is created by an oath (illegitimately taught to humans by the Watchers), into an account where everything is created by letters (*3 En.* 13:1; 41). The power of letters continues to the end of the world, where the letters of the Torah and of the alphabet testify against Israel (44:9–10). Although the dominant paradigm for these authors is increasingly writing, writing retains an oral aura of numinousity and power.

Daniel

The book of Daniel also has an interesting relationship with writing. The book explicitly begins by claiming that Daniel and his colleagues were taught the literature and the language of the Chaldaeans (1:4). It may be important that the text mentions that the language and literature is of the Chaldaeans, the scribal class, rather than the Babylonians in general.[117] The character Daniel is clearly associated with the written tradition of learning, and the Danielic author with a mysterious scribal group called the משכילים (11:33; 12:3, 10). The Lord's favor was not the only way in which Daniel was exceptional: Daniel's world as presented in the book is clearly a rarified and literate one. The law is conceived of as a written collection by the time of Daniel; Daniel reads the book of Jeremiah (9:2) and prays on the basis of what is written in the law of Moses (9:13). Additionally, YHWH runs heaven like a bureaucrat: deeds are inscribed in the book of truth (10:21), and the righteous are found written in the book (12:1). However, the collection also notes that writing was not universally expected, even for kings. Several aspects of the collection still betray oral presuppositions.

In the story of the writing on the wall (ch. 5), the text notes that the king was unable to read the writing inscribed on the wall (v. 8). Daniel's interpretation of the enigmatic writing (vv. 25–27) emphasizes both the oral tendency of the word's numinousness as well as Daniel's skills in mastering it.[118] Further, Dan 6:8, 15 considers written decrees permanent, even though the king himself only signs the law (v. 9). This seems to reflect both the increased importance of writing for bureaucracy, as well

---

117. Collins, *Daniel*, 137–39.
118. Cf. Niditch, *Oral World and Written Word*, 80–81.

as the awe in which it continued to be held. In a stimulating study, Polaski analyzes how writing informs the stories in Dan 5 and 6 and the ways in which it and its virtuosi are inscribed with power.[119] Indeed, he notes that the text even depicts scribal ability as obviating the need for revelatory vision!

> Daniel simply does his (former) job as a royal official; he needs no help in reading a text. God, via scribal mediation, addresses a recalcitrant king and his bureaucracy, again showing the extent to which notions of power are "textualized" in the thought world of the book of Daniel.[120]

Perhaps this is telling for the oft-commented visionary nature of the apocalypses. Not only can a shift from "word" to "vision" be found in Daniel and other apocalypses which is consonant with the shift from oral to written, ear to eye, but a shift in the source of authority over both, that is, the scribal ability to write, read, and comment upon both utterance and vision. It is not just the ability to receive revelations, but the ability to correctly write, read, and comment upon them that matters.

It seems likely that apocalyptic literature is more thoroughly literate and scribal then prophetic, regardless of the potential reality of visions. In a very stimulating discussion, McInver and Carroll suggest that the apocalyptic passages in the Gospels are some of the few text-based sources which appear in the Synoptic Gospels.[121] This seems to have very important implications for apocalyptic literature—it may, in essence, be a wholly literate, scribal phenomenon (the phenomenon of apocalypses, not millenarianism). This link helps situate the relationships between apocalyptic and sapiential literature; wisdom and apocalyptic share a scribal origin rather than a common political or theological tradition *per se*. Perhaps this can be tied to the reduction of directly existential concerns which accompanies writing and is evident to some respects in apocalyptic literature.

Perhaps one "apocalyptic" community in Second Temple Judaism helps confirm this suspicion. The community at Qumran was a remarkable group in Second Temple Judaism. In particular, the level of literacy appears to have been quite high, especially in contrast to the general population.[122] The intensity of scribal and literate activity was significant for their organization, self-understanding, and daily activities.[123] It

---

119. Polaski, "Mene, Mene, Tekel, Parsin," 649–69.
120. Ibid., 659.
121. McIver and Carroll, "Experiments," 682–83.
122. Hezser, *Jewish Literacy in Roman Palestine*, 465–66.
123. Ibid., 47, 465.

certainly had an effect on their theology and relation with the Jewish texts extant in their days. Whatever the situation of libraries or archives prior to this community, its concentration of literates—let alone literate "sages"—devoted to textual study was unprecedented in antiquity.[124] Considering the sparsity of Torah texts even into the Rabbinic period, a community with such a library is phenomenal.

When approaching the issues of the emergence of the apocalypse, the worldview which appears therein, and the potential role of external influences, one needs to consider the dynamics of media carefully. First, one must recognize that the role of the scribe is structurally different from the role of a priest or a prophet, and that the scribal role changes as a society becomes increasingly literate. Concomitant with the increased role of literacy and scribes is the rise and importance of *textual* hermeneutics in addition to the hermeneutics of traditions and times; this is supremely important in the fading of prophetic literature and the emergence of new genres. While it is important to recognize the effects of literacy, care needs to be taken to distinguish between oral-like elements and elements of scribal redaction. Even the most profoundly literate scribes in the ancient world were pre-print literates and a minority in their world. This means, lastly, that oral modes of discourse influence all forms of interaction and textual formation in the period. Because of this, analyses for the levels and types of influence must recognize that the subjects operate within a context which is not primarily textual: verbatim, linear, and analytic criteria are likely to misconstrue the data. Once the nature of interaction and scribal creation is recognized, it remains to be seen what evidence of interaction can be discerned in the surviving texts.

Implications for Investigation of Influence

The Persian period (as well as the Greek and Roman periods) represents a very complex interplay between Persians, prophets, (proto-)apocalyptics, scribes, orality and literacy within Judaism. New and old traditions were being written, adapted, and related to each other in the context of the Persian Empire; new forms of religious structure were evolving, and old forms had to be adapted and re-understood in a new context. In this context, a very important and defining difference between people and groups was *theology*, or general religious worldview, and the medium which they used to express it. Some Judaeans likely accepted various

---

124.   E.g. Pedersen, *Archives and Libraries*; Brosius, ed., *Ancient Archives and Archival Traditions*; Frame and George, "The Royal Libraries of Nineveh," 265–84.

Iranian ideas and integrated them into their understanding of Israel's heritage; if so, they would have done so as part of the increasingly important project of (re-)interpreting previous Judaean traditions.

The question of Iranian influence must be considered within two important communicative contexts. First, the high residual orality of the period and implications thus carried for the creation, reception, and adaptation of ideas and traditions must constantly be weighed. Second, the evident increasing interiorization of literacy among at least certain circles must be considered in the evaluation of the genesis of the apocalypses. The newly important tradition of textual exegesis must be appreciated in this regard. The new importance of textual hermeneutics offered ample scope for finding "hooks" within Judaean traditions for new ideas. It is with both of these perspectives that a few sample texts can be approached to probe for potential Iranian influences.

Chapter 4

TEXTUAL ANALYSES:
BIBLICAL LITERATURE

To begin a preliminary re-investigation of Iranian influence, a sample of texts are here analyzed, each representing important stages in the development of apocalyptic. Three canonical texts (Ezek 37:1–14, the Valley of the Bones; Ezek 38–39, Gog of Magog; and Dan 2, the Vision of the Statue//Dan 7) and the collection of texts known as *1 (Ethiopic) Enoch* are analyzed on their own and in their respective positions towards Second Temple Judaism.

Ezekiel 37:1–14 (The Valley of the Bones)

[7]So I prophesied as I had been commanded; and as I prophesied, suddenly there was a noise (קול), a rattling (רעש), and the bones came together, bone to its bone. [8]I looked, and there were sinews on them, and flesh had come upon them, and skin had covered them; but there was no breath in them. [9]Then he said to me, "Prophesy to the breath (הרוח), prophesy, mortal, and say to the breath: Thus says the Lord GOD: Come from the four winds, O breath, and breathe upon these slain (הרוגים), that they may live." [10]I prophesied as he commanded me, and the breath came into them, and they lived, and stood on their feet, a vast multitude (חיל גדול מאד מאד).

This passage presents a good test for Iranian influence, with its vivid imagery of bones reconstituted and re-given רוח חיים, a picture reminiscent of bodily resurrection. In fact, Lang offers an interpretation of this oracle as inspired by the Zoroastrian practice of the exposure of the dead, explaining the references to burial in vv. 12–13 as later interpolations.[1] His most convincing argument for this is the complete lack of purity concern in the passage—while earlier Ezekiel shows clear concern for ritual purity (cf. Ezek 4:12–15), his presence among a field of bones goes unmentioned. Later in the book the defiling aspect of human bones is

---

1. Lang, "Street Theatre, Raising the Dead," 310–14. Cf. Russell, "Ezekiel and Iran," 1–15.

dwelt upon somewhat at length (39:11–16), but no mention of it is made in this context. Lang rightly notes that according to Zoroastrian law, while dead bodies are defiling, dry bones are not.[2] However, the likelihood of Ezekiel having actually seen exposing grounds of bones, as Lang claims, is low for several reasons: the extent of the use of the rite of exposure among Zoroastrians at that early of a date is questionable; even when left for exposure, the bones were possibly collected into ossuaries, if not kept in structures such as later became known as *daxmas* or "Towers of Silence"; and any Zoroastrian strict enough to practice exposure certainly would not have left the funeral rites or remains easily accessible to non-co-religionists.[3] In his commentary, Greenberg considers Lang's thesis unlikely, preferring to look to Mesopotamian battle reliefs and annals.[4] Considering the supposed early exilic setting of this oracle, this is a very likely immediate source, if one beyond the cited saying ("Our bones are dried up, and our hope is lost; we are cut off completely") is needed.

As Greenberg and Fox note, vv. 1–14 are a well-structured unity, making Lang's appeal for the redactional addition of the graves unnecessary and unlikely.[5] Both the structure of the passage and its (con)textual setting make it clear that the vision promises a national restoration to the Land of Israel and is not preaching the idea of bodily resurrection; indeed, as Fox rightfully points out, the entire rhetorical force of the passage depends on the assumption that "the audience regards corporeal resurrection as basically absurd."[6] In the final context this passage is clearly about national restoration: ch. 36 is about the desolate hills of Israel and the nations mocking YHWH, both of which drive him to return Israel; 37:14–28 describes how both Judah and Israel will be united in the land of Israel.[7] Verses 1–14 clearly, therefore, are a prophecy for the

2. See *Vidēvdāt* 8.33, available in English translation in *Zend-Avesta I*, 103; cf. Lang, "Street Theatre, Raising the Dead," 310.

3. See Figure 12. Cf. Inostrantsev, "On the Ancient Iranian Burial Customs and Buildings," 1–28; Boyce, *HZ II*, 25–26, 54, 168; Briant, *From Cyrus to Alexander*, 94–95; Shahbazi, "The Irano-Lycian Monuments," 174–89; Russell, "Burial III: In Zoroastrianism," 562, mentions two burials as far east as Bactria and Sogdia. The antiquity of exposure is a much debated question. See Grenet, "Burial II," 559–61. Shahbazi, "Astōdān," 851, notes that *daxma* means "to bury."

4. Greenberg, *Ezekiel 21–37*, 748.

5. Fox, "The Rhetoric of Ezekiel's Vision," 1–15; Greenberg, *Ezekiel 21–37*, 747–48; cf. Zimmerli, *Ezekiel 2*, 257.

6. Fox, "The Rhetoric of Ezekiel's Vision," 11.

7. The general consensus; cf. Zimmerli, *Ezekiel 1*, 62–65; Cooke, *Ezekiel*, 396–97; Eichrodt, *Ezekiel*, 509; Spronk, *Beatific Afterlife*, 295; Collins, *The Apocalyptic Imagination*, 25.

proper internal response to the promise of return to the land. Yet, this poses an interesting dilemma: the early history of interpretation of the passage clearly saw a reference to bodily resurrection in this section.[8] Here, Lang's example of the mural at the synagogue at Dura Europos may be revealing: while the passage clearly speaks of bones (עצמות), the mural on the wall depicts "anatomical fragments."[9] He suggests that the Jews of Dura Europos saw a similarity between Ezek 37 and Zoroastrian religion, and thus attempted to create what he calls "artificial dissimilation." The early interpreters of the vision at Dura saw that the passage could be seen as consonant with other local traditions, and thus changed the bones into body-parts. This may not be as far-fetched as it first sounds; as Birkeland remarks, the "foreignness" of the idea of bodily resurrection was still felt well past the Persian period; this is evident in Qoheleth, Ben Sirah, and the Sadducees.[10]

Figure 12. *Human Burial at Persepolis (Chicago Oriental Institute P-61007). Courtesy of the Oriental Institute of the University of Chicago*

8. Greenberg, *Ezekiel 21–37*, 749–51.

9. Lang, "Street Theatre, Raising the Dead," 313–14; a drawing of the image is available in Kraeling, "The Meaning of the Ezekiel Panel in the Synagogue at Dura," 14; see also Gutmann, ed., *Dura-Europos Synagogue*.

10. Birkeland, "The Belief in the Resurrection of the Dead in the Old Testament," 77.

In fact, the imagery of this passage does recall various aspects of the Zoroastrian tradition. The wording of Ezek 37 is very precise in the language it uses to describe the scenario: רוח חיים, עצמות. This wording is strikingly different from the language of Gen 2, a passage with which one would expect similarities from a textual-redactional approach. The creation account in Gen 2 uses נפש, נשמת חיים, עפר, none of which occur in this passage.[11] Greenberg suggests a terminological affinity with the flood account, but this is minimal.[12] The use of *spirit, breath,* and *bones,* however, does have a resemblance to Zoroastrian usage.

One of the *Gāthās, Yasna* 30.7, remarks that, "Piety gave body and breath,"[13] and in *Yasna* 34.14, another *Gāthā,* a request is made for "the prize desirable for body and breath."[14] This language often appears in the context of immortality and health (*Amərətat* and *Haurvātat*).[15] That at least the Zoroastrian tradition expected bodily resurrection is quite clear. In the *Zāmyād Yašt,* a Young Avestan hymn, the refrain "...when the dead will rise, when life and immortality will come..." appears four times.[16] A later Zoroastrian fragment of a prayer has Ahura Mazda command, "Let the dead arise...let bodily life be sustained in these now lifeless bodies."[17]

In the *Greater Bundahišn* 34.4–8/*Shorter Bundahišn* 30.4–6, Zoroaster queries Ahura Mazda how bodily resurrection is possible. After relating a list of the feats he performed during creation, Ahura Mazda responds, "Observe that when that which was not was then produced, why is it not possible to produce again that which was? For at that time one will demand the bone from the spirit of the earth..."[18] This claim is directly followed in the text with a section in which it is the *bones* of the first man and women which are raised first, followed by the remainder of humankind. All people "rouse up from the spot where its life departs... all material living beings assume again their bodies and forms..."[19] It

---

11. Zimmerli, *Ezekiel 1,* 63, and idem, *Ezekiel 2,* 261, admits dissimilarity of language, but still posits a creation parallel; indeed, there is a distant creation parallel, but it is Zoroastrian rather than Jewish.

12. Greenberg, *Ezekiel 21–37,* 743, connects רוח חיים with Gen 6:17 and 7:15.

13. Insler, *The Gathas of Zarathustra,* 35. Cf. *Yasna* 31.11, 39.

14. Ibid., 59.

15. Ibid., 169–70.

16. *Zāmyād Yašt* §11, 19, 23, 89 (Hintze, *Zamyād-Yašt,* 109, 148, 158, 365; *Zend-Avesta II,* 290, 291, 292, 307).

17. *Zend-Avesta III,* 391–92 (Fragment 4).

18. *Sh. Bund.* 30.4–6 (*Pahlavi Texts I,* 121–23); cf. *Gr. Bund.* 34.4–8 (Anklesaria, *Zand-Ākāsīh,* 284–87); Boyce, *Textual Sources,* 52.

19. *Gr. Bund.* 34.7–8 (*Pahlavi Texts I,* 123).

may be significant that in this passage the bones are explicitly raised first and the bodies are recreated in the spot at which the person had died. This description is quite reminiscent of the rhetorical style of Ezekiel's vision, with the bare bones receiving flesh and standing in the spot where they were left. However, the *Bundahišn* itself is late, so any parallels require additional corroboration.

In his discussion of 37:1–14 Russell comments on the role which both the "good" and "evil" *Vayu*s (Spirits of the Wind) play in death and resurrection: the evil Vayu overcomes and kills, while the good Vayu revivifies at the resurrection. Russell finds the description of the dead as "killed" (הרוגים, v. 9) in line with this thinking.[20] Because death is unnatural and unoriginal to Ahura Mazda's creation, in Zoroastrian traditions it is always attributed to the onslaught of the evil powers, often the demon of death, *Astō.vīδātu*.[21] The use of הרוגים does appear strange in the context of the vision, as the simple rhetorical logic of the passage merely requires מתים. However, an understanding of death as unnatural, as is found in Iranian traditions, would render it a logical choice. Note that v. 7 does describe a קול and a רעש as the bones come together. These noises could be related to the coming of the *Vayu* or storm-wind.[22] A play between wind and spirit is evident in v. 9, so the text's repetition of רוח certainly could be seen to echo the Zoroastrian use of the (good) wind imparting life. It can also be seen to fit within a traditional Hebrew understanding of wind/breath/spirit.[23] However, as Greenberg notes, all the truly parallel passages are also post-exilic (Jer 49:36; Zech 6:5; Ezek 42:16–20), perhaps implying the idea entered in the post-exilic period.

Ezekiel 37:10 describes the revivified group as a very vast army (חיל גדול מאד מאד). In the context, neither in 37:1–14 nor in the broader section of chs. 36–37, is there a martial reference to explain the use of "army."[24] It clearly cannot be referring to the army in chs. 38–39, as the army there is the army of Gog and not of reconstituted Israel. The reference to an army, however, may make more sense in the context of Iranian traditions. The final resurrection of humankind occurs in the context of the defeat of Angra Mainyu and the *Daēuuas*, with humankind

20. Russell, "Ezekiel and Iran," 7; cf. Wikander, *Vayu*, 1:2, 7.
21. See *Vidēvdāt* 5.8–9; cf. 4.49 and 15.29 (*Zend-Avesta I*, 50–51, 46, and 212, respectively).
22. Cf. *Vidēvdāt* 5.8–9 (*Zend-Avesta I*, 50–51); Boyce, *HZ I*, 79–80.
23. Greenberg, *Ezekiel 21–37*, 744; Eichrodt, *Ezekiel: A Commentary*, 509.
24. Cooke, *Ezekiel*, 400, sees a battlefield image; Eichrodt, *Ezekiel: A Commentary*, 509, sees it as a reference to the "forces of death"; Greenberg, *Ezekiel 21–37*, 748, derives it from the inspiration of Mesopotamian battle reliefs.

having an especial role to play in the victory of Ahura Mazda. In the *Greater Bundahišn* 3.23–24/*Shorter Bundahišn* 2.10–11, Ahura Mazda gives the guardian spirits of humans the choice of "contending in bodily form"; and then being resurrected perfected and immortal at the end of the world; they consent.[25] The entire purpose of the embodiment of the human *frauuašī* (or pre-existent spirit) is to contend with, and ultimately defeat, the forces of Angra Mainyu; the final success of this enterprise will be evidenced when humanity's bodies are reconstituted out of the earth and made immortal.

While Greenberg may be right in pointing to the initial Mesopotamian inspiration for Ezekiel's vision, it cannot be denied that the overall shape of this discourse proves very similar to various Iranian rites and beliefs to which subsequent Judaean audiences/readers would have been exposed; a very good example of this is the mural at Dura Europos, as Lang notes. It is also possible, given the various parallels noted in the text, that Ezekiel intended to borrow Iranian resurrection motifs as part of his rhetorical strategy. The intended message of the passage clearly refers to a national and unified restoration to Israel, but the vision itself may have helped to give a "canonical" or authoritative springboard which made Iranian ideas of bodily resurrection appear less foreign, even if the initial audience (or indeed the prophet himself) did not see it that way.[26] Perhaps if "Ezekiel" is amended to "Ezekiel's inheritors" Lang's following statement can be useful: "The Iranian connection enabled Ezekiel to transcend the limits of Jewish belief current in his day."[27] While it may be remotely possible to see a negative influence here in Ezek 37, the significance of the Iranian parallels are more in their likely long-term effect among the inheritors of the text. It is worth noting how this pericope was conflated with chs. 38–39 and interpreted eschatologically and concerning resurrection in the *Pseudo-Ezekiel* literature in the Dead Sea Scrolls.[28] Later generations more familiar with the concept of bodily resurrection and hostile, demonic forces could easily see this idea already embedded in Ezekiel's vision and thus more easily assimilate them to their understanding of the text.

25. Anklesaria, *Zand-Ākāsīh*, 45; *Pahlavi Texts I*, 14.

26. One may even be tempted to see a polemic with Zoroastrianism, like Block, *The Book of Ezekiel: Chapters 25–48*, 384–86; if so, Ezekiel purposefully appropriated the language and imagery of the Magi's or other Iranian priests' rhetoric to argue YHWH's strength and ability to restore Israel. Thus the vision could serve two functions—to deny the theology of the Zoroastrians and to affirm the prerogatives of YHWH. This, however, is very speculative.

27. Lang, "Street Theatre, Raising the Dead," 313.

28. Hogeterp, "Resurrection and Biblical Tradition," 59–69.

Ezekiel 38–39 (Gog of Magog)

Many commentators consider this dramatic and difficult passage as either apocalyptic or proto-apocalyptic; it certainly influenced later apocalyptic texts.[29] For the moment, the question of the authorship of the section is irrelevant: whether attributed to Ezekiel or redactors, if Iranian material can be detected, it is evidence of Iranian influence at some point.[30] The prophet here describes a divinely thwarted invasion of reconstituted Israel by a coalition of armies from the North, led by "Gog of the land of Magog, chief prince of Meshech and Tubal" (גוג ארץ המגוג נשיא ראש משך ותבל, v. 2).[31] Gog is often connected with the Assyrian *Gugu* or the *Gagaia* of the Amarna Letters, in either case a reference to Lydia.[32] The meaning or significance of Magog has found little agreement; it has been interpreted as "Land of Gog," an alliteration based on Gog, or a gloss based on Genesis or 1 Chronicles.[33] By the time of the Qumran communities, the two were seen as separate peoples.[34]

It is common to associate Ezekiel's use of "far north" in 38:6 and 39:2 with an "Enemy from the North" tradition, which is also associated with

---

29. Calling it apocalyptic: Blenkinsopp, *History of Prophecy*, 178; Heider, *The Cult of Molek*, 356; Cooke, *Ezekiel*, 406; Arthur, *A Smooth Stone*, 274.

Proto-apocalyptic: Cook, *Prophecy and Apocalypticism*, 85; Ackroyd, *Israel Under Babylon and Persia*, 99, who compares it to apocalyptic; Zimmerli, *Ezekiel 2*, 300, 304.

Rejecting the label: Block, *The Book of Ezekiel: Chapters 25–48*, 427–28. On the use of this in later texts, see Bøe, *Gog and Magog*, particularly 235–382; Manning, *Echoes of a Prophet*, 34–37.

30. Cf. Kohn, "Ezekiel at the Turn of the Century," 9–12; McKeating, *Ezekiel*, 122; Zimmerli, *Ezekiel 1*, 65–66; idem, *Ezekiel 2*, 300, 304; Cooke, *Ezekiel*, 407; Cook, *Prophecy and Apocalypticism*, 103; Albertz, *Israel in Exile*, 352, 354.

31. The Greek rendering Ῥως is a misunderstanding of ראש, which is clearly a title (albeit in an unusual formation) rather than a name. Some scholars do still see ראש as a toponym. E.g. Price, "Rosh: An Ancient Land Known to Ezekiel," 67–89.

32. Referring to *Gagaia*, Curtis and Madsen, *Books of Chronicles*, 60; Hüsing, "Gūgu (678–643)," 299–303. Cooke, *Ezekiel*, 408, views either as possible. However, Astour, "Ezekiel's Prophecy of Gog," 569–70, rejects this identification. See also Delitzsch, *Wo lag das Paradies?*, 246–47; Zimmerli, *Ezekiel 2*, 301.

33. As from Akkadian "Māt Gūgi," see Astour, "Ezekiel's Prophecy of Gog," 569; Klein, *1 Chronicles*, 64. From Assonance with Gog: Curtis and Madsen, *Books of Chronicles*, 60.

As a gloss: Cooke, *Ezekiel*, 409; Zimmerli, *Ezekiel 2*, 301–2; Toy, *The Book of the Prophet Ezekiel*, 99.

34. 4QpIsa[a] 8.20 and 4Q523 1.5 both reference Gog and Magog as separate peoples. *DSSSE*, 317, 1049.

Jeremiah and Isaiah.[35] The passage is therefore read as a reinterpretation and combination of the unfulfilled prophecies of Jeremiah and Isaiah, partially basing this upon 38:17. Block notes that both of the supposed antecedents of the Ezekiel passage were already fulfilled in the minds of the earlier prophets, and probably in the mind of Ezekiel—namely by Assyria and Babylon.[36] In both of these cases, the enemy in question is a real, historical enemy who entered Israel from the geographic north.[37] There seems to be little in common which could be called a "tradition" beyond the similarities of topic (an army entering from the north). While the north may have had mythic or numinous implications for the Babylonians, there is no need to read this into the passages in Jeremiah, Isaiah, or Ezekiel. In fact, Ezek 38–39 need not be seen as claiming to reinterpret previous prophecy at all. If one follows the MT of 38:17 (with Block) YHWH's statement becomes "Are you the one of whom I spoke...?"—a rhetorical question with an implied "no." When read in that manner, this passage ceases to be about reinterpreting a past tradition and posits a wholly new event. There is an inevitable terminological affinity due to the common topos of battle, but there is no real reason to appeal to an "enemy from the north" tradition in this passage.[38] If Ezekiel is not reinterpreting previous oracles, is there a specific context for this passage outside a general or mythological enemy from the north?

Diakonoff interprets this passage as a reference to the Median–Lydian war of 590–585 B.C.E.[39] He reads the nations in vv. 2, 5–6 as Phrygia and Tabal (משך ותבל), Asiatic Thrace (he reads תרס instead of פרס), Nubia (כוש), Pontus (פוט), Cimmerians/Scythians (גמר), and the Melitene dynasty (בית תוגרמה). His textual emendation of the text is unnecessary:

---

35. Zimmerli, *Ezekiel 1*, 65–66; idem, *Ezekiel 2*, 299–303; Cooke, *Ezekiel*, 406; Childs, "The Enemy from the North," 178–98; Cook, *Prophecy and Apocalypticism*, 91–94; Block, "Gog in Prophetic Tradition," 165–67; Fishbane, *Biblical Interpretation*, 477.

36. Block, "Gog in Prophetic Tradition," 168; cf. Hyatt, "The Peril from the North in Jeremiah," 507–11.

37. Cf. Childs, "The Enemy from the North," 192, 195.

38. Block, "Gog in Prophetic Tradition," 170–72.

39. See Diakonoff, "Media," 126; two other works by this author are translated from the Russian in Astour, "Ezekiel's Prophecy of Gog," 570–71. Galambush, "Necessary Enemies," 254–67, also argues for a contextualization in the Medo-Lydian War, but uses this to argue for an identification of Gog with Nebuchadnezzar (260–61). Even if one accepts her reading of "ruler *over* the Prince of Meshech and Tubal," this does not privilege an identification with Nebuchadnezzar, who could not have claimed such status.

most scholars identify פרס with Persia, which was a vassal of Media until 550 B.C.E.[40] The inclusion of Nubia in this list of Anatolian/Iranian powers is strange; however, כוש may refer to the "land of the Kaššu" along the Araxes River, which would fit the Anatolian grouping well.[41] 1 Chronicles 1:8–9 and Hab 3:7 seem to indicate several relatively homonymic "Cushes" in the ancient Near East.[42] Astour finds this contextualization problematic for several reasons:[43] first, he objects that the Median–Lydian War never threatened Palestine, with Judah's imperial lord, Babylon, even mediating the peace deal in 585; second, the Kingdom of Judah was still real in 590; third, that Ezekiel wanted the existing (Judaean) state to be destroyed to make way for the new one. A slightly broader (prophetic?) view of the historical circumstances, however, vitiates these objections. Yamauchi discusses the possibility that Indo-Iranian Scythians (the גמר of Ezekiel is generally identified as the Scythians) may indeed have threatened Palestine, either in independent raids in the seventh century B.C.E. or as mercenaries in the service of the Neo-Babylonian Empire in the sixth.[44] Even if no immediate threat to Palestine is referred to or expected, the Median–Lydian War would likely have threatened Ezekiel's real audience—Israelites and Judaeans living in exile. As was noted earlier,[45] deported Israelites and Judaeans were likely living around the regions of Ecbatana, the Median capital, and Nineveh, the former Assyrian capital; Media conquered Calah and

---

40. *HAL*, 969; Herodotus I.123–30 (*Wars I–II*, 160–71); cf. Glassner, *Mesopotamian Chronicles*, 235; Briant, *From Cyrus to Alexander*, 31.

41. See Delitzsch, *Wo lag das Paradies?*, 31–32, 53–57, 127–29; cf. *HAL*, 467; Speiser, "The Rivers of Paradise," 177.

42. Knoppers, *1 Chronicles 1–9*, 275, suggests two different Cush traditions have been combined here. The "Cushan" in Hab 3:7 is problematic, cf. Andersen, *Habakkuk*, 312, but כושן could be emended to כוש. It is interesting to note in this connection the various Kaššu-peoples tentatively associated by Herzfeld; see Herzfeld, *Archaeological History of Iran*, 2; cf. Frye, *The Heritage of Persia*, 63–64. Also note a possible reference to a group of Elamites in the Zagros; see Curtis and Madsen, *Books of Chronicles*, 63.

43. Astour, "Ezekiel's Prophecy of Gog," 571.

44. Yamauchi, "The Scythians: Invading Hordes from the Russian Steppes," 90–99, particularly 95; cf. Phillips, "The Scythian Domination in Western Asia," 129–38. If correct, this would satisfy Galambush, "Necessary Enemies," 259, who argues that Gog must be *returning* to Palestine.

Note Vogelsang's contention that the Scythians/Saka played a major role in the establishment of the Median Empire. See Vogelsang, *The Rise and Organization*, 305.

45. Cf. Chapter 2.

Arrapha in 614 and participated in conquering Nineveh in 612.[46] Thus it is likely that some of the text's intended audience were living under Median rule, and thus very aware of the war. Additionally, awareness of the Medes as a power and potential threat was not limited to Ezekiel—Jer 51:11, 27–28 expects an invasion of the Medes and Anatolian allies to conquer Babylon. While Holladay considers these references to be glosses, he admits that they have to predate 550;[47] in any case, *someone* considered Media a credible force. It may be significant that 51:11 uses שלטים, "quivers": the Scythians were renowned for their skill as archers.[48] Further, Jer 25:25–26 possibly links the Scythians, Medians, and Elamites together with "all the kings of the North."[49] Ezekiel's more defined description of these northern forces suggests, at the very least, a closer and more detailed understanding of the Anatolian political situation. Astour's final objection ignores the preceding context of rehabilitation and restoration in the final book. The prophet has just prophesied that Edom will be destroyed and Israel returned for YHWH's glory (ch. 36); that the scattered remains of David's kingdom will be restored and unified (ch. 37); now in chs. 38–39 he demonstrates the completeness and inescapability of YHWH's plans to restore Israel. This message has nothing to do with the existing vassal Kingdom of Judah; it has everything to do with the upcoming restoration.[50]

When the geographical terms are read in this manner, Ezekiel's use of "north" applies as much to the real geographical position of the nations mentioned as it does to a quasi-mythical "foe from the north." If the Median–Lydian War can possibly be accepted as a contextual background, what is its significance to reading the passage? Beyond indicating a general context for the author and intended audience, it serves as a hint to look for the use of Iranian-inspired imagery in the pericope.

Irwin argues that Ezek 38–39 paints a picture of Molek sacrifice.[51] While the passage, particularly 39:17–20, clearly invokes the language

46. Cf. Glassner, *Mesopotamian Chronicles*, 221–23; Levine, "Prelude to Monarchy," 43–44; Frye, *The Heritage of Persia*, 73.

47. Holladay, *Jeremiah 2*, 397, 398, 405, 407, 427.

48. Ibid., 422–23; Yamauchi, "The Scythians: Invading Hordes from the Russian Steppes," 94. Cf. Zutterman, "The Bow in the Ancient Near East," 119–65, especially 135, 140–41.

49. Holladay, *Jeremiah 1*, 671, 675, considers this reference a later gloss, and זמרי to be an "athbash" for Elam. This makes little sense with Elam mentioned in the next verse. The suggested emendation to גמרי "Gomer" makes more sense, Peiser, "Miscellen," 350.

50. Cf. Block, "Gog and the pouring out of the Spirit," 266–67.

51. Irwin, "Molek Imagery," 93–112.

of sacrifice, the motives for using Molek imagery in this context are unclear. The passage in Isa 30:27–33, to which Irwin compares Ezek 38–39, prophesies the destruction of Assyria in terms of a sacrifice to Molek (in the context of Isa 30–31). This is in the context of Judah's idolatry and predicated on her return to the worship of YHWH; in fact, it seems to be a promise that *if* Judah will cease offering to Molek, YHWH *himself* will offer sacrifice to Molek, with Assyria as the victim.[52] This focus on idolatry with Molek is not in view in chs. 38–39. Further, Molek's cult seems to have been a largely Jerusalem-centered cult,[53] but no mention of Jerusalem, Zion, or the temple appears in chs. 38–39. If the location of Ezekiel's vision is meant to be the Jezreel Valley rather than the Hinnom Valley, as Irwin claims and seems possible,[54] the logic for the prophet's use of the Molek imagery seems slim. Irwin's point on the use of זבח גדול in 39:11 is, however, compelling. He notes that in the two other places where זבח גדול occurs (Judg 16:23; 2 Kgs 10:19) it is used in the context of (human) sacrifice to foreign gods.[55] He fails to note, however, that in each of these cases the foreign imagery is ironic—both times the worshippers of the foreign god are themselves sacrificed to their own god (the Philistines to Dagan and the priests of Baʿal to Baʿal). Even if the Median–Lydian war is not the context of this passage, *Miθra* is more likely to be a deity of the nations listed than is Molek.[56] In this context, particularly in light of the possibility of the Iranian background to the

52. Heider, *The Cult of Molek*, 322.

53. On Molek's association with Jerusalem and its environs, see Day, *Molech*, 55. Day considers Molek to be a Jubusite cult (29–31), although he may have been equated with Nergal (46–49). Heider, *Cult of Molek*, 356–58, sees Molek imagery in Ezek 39:11, but on the basis of identification with the Hinnom Valley. Also see Torrey, "Armageddon," 237–48, who links all apocalyptic battles with the Jerusalem environs.

54. Irwin, "Molek Imagery," 98–103. His argument is based on a parallel with Jer 7:1–34, which is debatable; however, his arguments against the Hinnom Valley are convincing. There is nothing in chs. 38–39 referencing Jerusalem. However, the Plain of Megiddo has often been the scene of battles, real and mythological. These battles are often over the control of Palestine, suiting the content of chs. 38–39 well. Additionally, the Jezreel Valley is a major trade route, much more suiting a reference to blocking travelers than any valley around Jerusalem.

55. Irwin, "Molek Imagery," 107. Also in Neh 12:43, but in the plural.

56. Even if one wishes to equate Nergal and Molek as Bivar, "Religious Subjects on Achaemenid Seals," 99–103, does, the evidence for human sacrifice in Mesopotamia is ambiguous at best. Cf. Heider, *Cult of Molek*, 204–10, 378. Green, *The Role of Human Sacrifice*, 201, however, considers the practice of human sacrifice widespread in the ancient Near East, albeit in times of crisis.

original oracle, it may be more likely that the intended sacrifice is to *Miθra* rather than Molek.[57]

Before discussing Irwin's suggestion and the language of chs. 38–39, a few relevant details about *Miθra* should be noted. The phenomenon of *Miθra*-worship is a complex one,[58] but there are several things which can be said with relative certainty. First, sidestepping the issue of its relation to "orthodox" Zoroastrian worship, *Miθra* was a decidedly (Indo-)Iranian deity and his cult comes out of old (pre-Zoroastrian) Iranian tradition. Second, *Miθra*'s primary association was with the contract, perhaps with political and international overtones.[59] Third, his cult was sometimes linked with blood sacrifice, at least at Persepolis. This may have included even human sacrifice among certain Anatolian Scythian groups.[60] In his later western incarnation as Mithras (whatever the precise link with *Miθra*) he was even especially associated with bull-sacrifice.[61] Fourth,

57. Although, interestingly, Bivar, "Religious Subjects on Achaemenid Seals," 99–103, and idem, "Mithra and Mesopotamia," 285, claims a relationship between Nergal, Molek and (Roman) Mithras. However, also note that Mit(h)ra was known in the Northern Mesopotamian/Anatolian area for many years: cf. the famous Mitanni treaties, discussed in Thieme, "The 'Aryan' Gods of the Mitanni Treaties," 301–17. Earlier, Scheftelowitz argues that *Miθra*-worship spread throughout the ancient Near East early and quickly syncretized, which seems incredible. Scheftelowitz, "Die Mithra-Religion der Indoskythen," 293–333. For evidence of his wide appeal, at least among those with Iranian names, see Schmitt, "Die theophoren Eigennamen," 395–456.

58. Cf. Hinnells, ed., *Mithraic Studies*; Duchesne-Guillemin, ed., *Études Mithriaques*; Boyce, "On Mithra's Part in Zoroastrianism," 10–34; Gershevitch, *Hymn to Mithra*, 1–74.

59. Thieme, "Mithra in the Avesta," 501–11; Gershevitch, *Hymn to Mithra*, 59–60, 77, 109. Abdi, "Bes in the Achaemenid Empire," 121 (following Griziani), suggests that Bes was assimilated to *Miθra* throughout the empire. Sadly, he does not take up this theory further in his subsequent article, Abdi, "Notes on the Iranization of Bes in the Achaemenid Empire," 133–62.

60. Herodotus IV.62, 71–77, 103, implies ritual human sacrifice, though the recipients are unclear (*Wars III–IV*, 261, 209–73, 305). Dhalla appeals to *Yašt* 10.119; see Dhalla, *History of Zoroastrianism*, 190, 255. Cf. Yamauchi, "The Scythians: Invading Hordes from the Russian Steppes," 98, and Sulimirski and Taylor, "The Scythians," 563, 569. Zaehner, *The Dawn and Twilight*, 123–24, links *Miθra*-worship to Plutarch's night sacrifices; cf. Moulton, *Early Zoroastrianism*, 128–30; on livestock sacrifice and *Miθra* at Persepolis, see Razmjou, "The *Lan* Ceremony," 103–17. However, Pirart, "Le sacrifice humain," 1–36, argues that human sacrifice was only rhetorical or in contexts of capital punishment among the Indo-Iranians.

61. Boyce, *HZ I*, 172–73; cf. idem, "On Mithra's Part in Zoroastrianism," 17, who suggests that the taurocotny came from Haoma and was absorbed by Mithras

Miθra was associated with war; this association seems to be an early one linked with his defense of the contract. Additionally, both of the *yazatas* most closely associated with him in Zoroastrian tradition, *Sraoša* ("obedience") and *Vərəθragna* ("victory"), were often described in decidedly martial aspects. *Vərəθragna* was sometimes incarnated as an eagle or bird of prey, and *Sraoša* was associated with the rooster.[62] Fourth, even in pre-Zoroastrian traditions, *Miθra* was given the role of judge, largely connected to his role as arbiter of contracts.[63] In Zoroastrianism, this role is highly developed and important, extending even into primeval contract to limit the warfare between Ahura Mazda and Angra Mainyu. As Boyce has succinctly put it:

> He keeps a daily record of men's sins, and is their impartial judge at the Činvat Bridge. Those who have taken a false oath, or otherwise done wrong, he punishes strictly, both at the individual judgment and also at the end of the world, when he will smite the Evil Spirit. The Evil Spirit will appeal to him to uphold the ancient contract between Ohrmazd and himself, for even the powers of darkness acknowledge Mihr's [(*sic*), Pahlavi for *Miθra*] unswerving equity; but the divine contract which the great *yazata* guards will by then have run its course.[64]

(but not *Miθra*); idem, "Haoma, Priest of the Sacrifice," 80 (cf. 73). Cf. Cumont, *The Mysteries of Mithra*. A newer interpretation of Mithras can be found in Beck, "The Mysteries of Mithras," 115–28; cf. Lincoln, "Review: Mitra, Mithra, Mithras," 200–208; Rudolph, "Mitra, Mithra, Mithras," 309–20.

    62. See *Vidēvdāt* 17.15–16 (*Zend-Avesta I*, 193); *Yašt* 10.119 (Gershevitch, *Hymn to Mithra*, 133; *Zend-Avesta II*, 150–51); *Gr. Bund.* 13.22 (Anklesaria, *Zand-Ākāsīh*, 122–23).

    Cf. Bartholomae, *Altiraniranisches Wörterbuch*, 458, 259, 1634–36; Goodell, "Bird Lore in Southwestern Iran," 146; Gershevitch, *Hymn to Mithra*, 62; Carnoy, "Iranian Mythology," 292; Boyce, *HZ I*, 89–90; Peters, "The Cock," 363–96; Kreyenbroek, *Sraoša in the Zoroastrian Tradition*, 118, 172; Gnoli, "Bahrām I," 510–13. Kreyenbroek, *Sraoša in the Zoroastrian Tradition*, 176, believes that *Sraoša*'s position in the Zoroastrian calendar near *Miθra* and *Rašnu* indicates that their association dates at least to the Achaemenid period. On his links with war: see Olmstead, *History of the Persian Empire*, 25; Briant, *From Cyrus to Alexander*, 251–53.

    63. See especially the *Mihr Yašt*; Thieme, "The Concept of Mitra in Arian Belief," 22–23, and Frye, "Mithra in Iranian History," 64, both in Hinnells, ed., *Mithraic Studies*, 21–39 and 62–67, respectively; Boyce, *HZ I*, 31.

    64. Boyce, "On Mithra's Part in Zoroastrianism," 23; the references cited there seem to follow a different numbering than those in the SBE series. She seems to be referring to the following: *Wahman Yašt* (also known as *Zand ī Vohuman Yašt*) 3.31–36 (*Pahlavi Texts I*, 227–29); *Vidēvdāt* 19.15 (*Zend-Avesta I*, 208); *Mēnōg-ī Xrad* 2.118 (*Pahlavi Texts III*, 18); *Dēnkard* 9.10.4–5 and 9.39.9–10 (*Pahlavi Texts IV*, 210, 277–78).

One of the earliest Avestan sources for *Miθra* even characterizes the relationship between *Miθra* and Ahura Mazda as *pāyūčā θwōrəštārā*, "the protector and the fashioner" (*Yasna* 42.2).[65] The antiquity of *Miθra*'s role as judge and his related war-like and warrior attributes are visible in the *Mihr Yašt*, which is one of the oldest of the extant Iranian hymns. The *Yašt* refers to *Miθra* "with a thousand ears, well-shapen, with ten thousand eyes, high, with full knowledge, strong, sleepless, and ever awake."[66] He is depicted with implacable wrath towards violators of contracts (§§19–21) and as protecting those who honor them (§§22–24).[67] Thus, while *Miθra*'s role in the eschatological judgment seems to have developed in Zoroastrianism with the triplication of eras,[68] even in non- or pre-Zoroastrian Iranian traditions *Miθra* had deep associations with judging and war. The antiquity of these associations may also be implied by the continued association of *Miθra*, through his festival *Mihragan*, with the ancient Iranian heroes *Θraētaona* and *Kərəsāspa*.[69]

These various aspects of *Miθra* offer more parallels to understanding the imagery of this passage than Irwin's appeal to עברים in v. 11 as a link to Molek. Irwin claims עברים in 39:11 is a technical term, indicating "passing through" the fires of sacrifice and thus to Molek.[70] Verse 11 is highly problematic, with the meaning (and proper pointing) of the word in dispute. *BHS* recommends the emendation of the Masoretic הָעֹבְרִים to הָעֲבָרִים, as does Eichrodt and Cooke.[71] Zimmerli rejects the emendation's implied location in Moab, but otherwise makes no clear choice.[72] The word העברים occurs 25 times in the Hebrew Bible; of those not indicating "Hebrew" or the name of a mountain, it indicates a form of "transgression" as well as a form of "passing through" or "traveling."[73] In light of the context, it seems more likely that the use of העברים in Ezek 38–39

65. *Pahlavi Texts III*, 291; Boyce, "On Mithra's Part in Zoroastrianism," 33; Gershevitch, *Hymn to Mithra*, 54.

66. *Yašt* 10.7 (*Zend-Avesta II*, 121; Gershevitch, *Hymn to Mithra*, 76).

67. *Zend-Avesta II*, 124–25; Gershevitch, *Hymn to Mithra*, 84–86.

68. Boyce, *HZ II*, 242–43; idem, *HZ I*, 232–33. Cf. idem, "Apocalyptic (that which has been revealed) i. In Zoroastrianism," 155–56; idem, "Astvat.ərəta," 872.

69. Boyce, "On Mithra's Part in Zoroastrianism," 26 n. 82. The stories of Θraētaona (Feradun) and Kərəsāspa (Sam/Garshasp) can also be found in the *Shahnameh*, vol. 1. Cf. Morrison, "Persian Literature (Belles-Lettres)," 23, 39–40; Jong, *Traditions of the Magi*, 371–77; Frye, "Mithra in Iranian History," 64–65.

70. Irwin, "Molek Imagery," 104–5, 110.

71. Eichrodt, *Ezekiel*, 517, 528; Cooke, *Ezekiel*, 419.

72. Zimmerli, *Ezekiel 2*, 317.

73. Cf. *HAL*, 779 (§7); BDB, 716–20. It could it also be repointed to "Valley of the Hebrews."

is play on these two meanings, as it is in Jer 34:18–19, rather than a technical use indicating child sacrifice to Molek. A play on "passing through" and "transgression" would fit the context, and need not be a secondary addition.[74] Any argument based on the use of העברים seems dangerous, however, since the LXX drops the first reference to the valley.[75] If one insisted on a reference to "passing through" in העברים, the idea of "passing through" fire is at least as applicable to *Miθra* as it is Molek, perhaps even more so in the context of judgment. Ordeal by molten metal was a method for testing the innocence of the accused in Iranian lands,[76] and was a standard component of the final judgment/purification.[77] As guardian of the contract and a judge, *Miθra* was associated with this event;[78] it was believed that the innocent would be protected and the guilty consumed. An allusion in this section could imply that Gog and his allies were forced to "pass through" the ordeal, and failed the test.

It is worth quoting the explicitly sacrificial section (39:17–20):

> [17]As for you, mortal, thus says the Lord GOD: Speak to the birds of every kind and to all the wild animals (צפור כל כנף ולכל חית השדה): Assemble (הקבצו) and come, gather from all around to the sacrificial feast that I am preparing for you (זבח לכם), a great sacrificial feast (זבח גדול) on the mountains of Israel, and you shall eat flesh and drink blood. [18]You shall eat the flesh of the mighty, and drink the blood of the princes of the earth—of rams, of lambs, and of goats, of bulls, all of them fatlings of Bashan. [19]You shall eat fat (חלב) until you are filled, and drink blood until you are drunk, at the sacrificial feast I am preparing for you (אשר זבחתי לכם). [20]And you shall be filled at my table (על שלחני) with horses and charioteers, with warriors and all kinds of soldiers, says the Lord GOD.

Irwin parallels the use of birds and beasts feasting in Jer 7 and Ezek 39, but the phrases used in each place are quite different. Jeremiah 7:30–33 uses the terms עוף השמים and בהמת הארץ, but Ezekiel (vv. 4, 17) uses צפור כל כנף and חית השדה. Jeremiah's use is much more stereotypical

---

74. Zimmerli, *Ezekiel 2*, 318

75. In v. 11a the Greek reads, τόπον ὀνομαστὸν μνημεῖον ἐν Ἰσραὴλ τὸ πολυάνδρειον τῶν ἐπελθόντων πρὸς τῇ θαλάσσῃ, but later in the verse it does refer to a ravine (θάραγγος) for the MT's גיא המון גוג. However, the *Targum Pseudo-Jonathan* reads the valley as "the Valley of the Pass" (חילת-מגזת), which fits the idea of the Jezreel Valley, even though the verse as a whole is quite glossed.

76. Boyce, *HZ I*, 35–36, 242; Lincoln, "'The Earth Becomes Flat'," 136–53.

77. See *Yasna* 30.7; 32.7; 50.9 (Insler, *The Gathas of Zarathustra*, 35, 47, 105, respectively). See also *Sh. Bund.* 30.17–20 (*Pahlavi Texts I*, 125–26).

78. Boyce, *HZ I*, 35–36.

poetic/parallelistic speech; Ezekiel's usage, however, appears to be singular in this particular combination.[79] The "birds of every wing" (צפור כל כנף) is odd in parallel to "beasts of the field"; is it possible that the variety of flesh-eating birds is intended to be emphasized? Geyer suggests that there may be mythological overtones to the term, but given his large enumeration of obscure creatures, one might expect more to appear in ch. 39 if that were the intention in the passage.[80] As noted above, *Miθra* has associations with a variety of birds, mythical and real, largely through his association with *Sraoša* and *Vərəθragna*. *Miθra* is also associated with cattle, the open field, and cosmological origins. Further, in the *Mihr Yašt* 119 the small and large cattle, together with the birds and fowls that fly on wings are described as worshipping *Miθra*.[81] Is this choice of vocabulary significant? The term "wild animals" is חית השדה. While this is a general meaning of this phrase, Koehler and Baumgartner note that חיה can refer to "beast-like" creatures,[82] and that שדה can refer to pastures, open fields, meadows or hills.[83] Both Job 40:20 and Ezek 31:6, 13 use חית השדה in mythical contexts. Considering the liminal and dangerous quality of the field/wilderness in the ancient Near East,[84] this choice could be significant. The standing epithet of *Miθra* is "of wide pastures,"[85] and in a context of battle-imagery, the *Mihr Yašt* praises

---

79. It is more of a stock phrase to use "beasts of the field and birds of the air"; Hos 2:20 and 4:3 parallel חית השדה and עוף השמים; Gen 1:30, חית הארץ and כל עוף השמים. A parallelism between עוף השמים and חית השדה occurs in Ezek 31:6, 13, in the context of Egypt as the World-Tree, where it also uses המון. Cook considers צפור כל כנף to be an Ezekielian phrase, citing 17:23, but does not mention חית השדה. Cook, *Prophecy and Apocalypticism*, 102 (§33). This particular phrase seems to be unique in the Hebrew Bible.

80. Geyer, "Desolation and Cosmos," 49–64, 61–62 on Ezek 39.

81. Gershevitch, *Hymn to Mithra*, 133.

82. *HAL*, 310; BDB, however, reads "unclean beasts" for Ezek 39, see 312.

83. *HAL*, 1307–8; BDB, 961.

84. E.g. Henze, *The Madness of King Nebuchadnezzar*, 90–99.

85. Gershevitch idiosyncratically translates this as "cattle-magnet." Gershevitch, *Hymn to Mithra*, from 74. See especially the *Mihr Yašt*, dedication, §3, 60, etc., in *Zend-Avesta II*, 119, 120, 134). Benveniste, "Mithra aux vastes pâturages," 421–29, argues that this epithet reveres *Miθra* as one who makes these open spaces safe for humans and their cattle (429: "De là est née l'invocation typique *mithro vouru.gaoyaoitiš* « Mithra à la vaste gavyuti », ce qui fait de Mithra non le dieu « aux vastes pâturages », mais celui qui offre un vaste asile aux hommes et aux troupeaux" ["Thus arose the typical invocation *mithro vouru.gaoyaoitiš* …this makes Mithra not a god of "wide pastures" but one that offers a wide asylum to men and herds"]).

Miθra for turning "plains and vales to pasture grounds."[86] If mythical allusions are indeed intended by these phrases, then it is certainly consonant with Mithraic content.

The translation in vv. 17 and 19 has "preparing for you" for זבח לכם/ זבחתי לכם. Importantly, however, the use of ל with זבח normally indicates the god to whom the sacrifice is made.[87] Thus the wording has YHWH sacrificing *to* the birds and beasts in this section. Indeed, they are described as consuming the fat and blood, which were traditionally YHWH's portion of the sacrifice.[88] As noted above, *Miθra* was associated with a bird-like deity, *Vərəθragna*, as well as with cattle; if there is any validity to the reading of the birds and beasts, then this has YHWH offering Gog to the representatives of *Miθra*. The possibility of this nuancing may also be visible in v. 20; there the rare word translated "my table," שלחני, could also refer to a grass mat spread out for sacrifice and meals.[89] The traditional method of offering sacrifice in Iranian tradition, including to *Miθra*, was to spread a grass or twig mat on the ground to lay the victim upon.[90]

Within the logic of the passage, *Miθra* would be within his rights to claim retribution from Gog as the protector of the covenant. As noted above, Block argues that 38:17 does *not* claim to redefine previously unfulfilled prophecy.[91] He takes the ה to indicate a rhetorical question with an implied "No!" While Gog and his allies may think they are functioning in YHWH's service like others before, they are merely misusing prophecy for financial gain. The exile to Babylonia has already fulfilled the covenant curses; once restored, Israel has again a covenant of peace—the covenant of punishment is over. Gog may attempt to justify his attack by claiming to be a fulfillment of foretold punishment, but this is hubris.[92] Because Gog has violated YHWH's new covenant, rather than fulfilled an already fulfilled one, he comes under *Miθra*'s wrath, the protector of covenants *par excellence*.[93] Ezekiel 38–39, then,

86. *Yašt* 10.112 (*Zend-Avesta II*, 148; Gershevitch, *Hymn to Mithra*, 130).

87. *HAL*, 261; cf. BDB, 257 (§3).

88. Lev 3:11, 17; Zimmerli, *Ezekiel 2*, 309; Cooke, *Ezekiel*, 421.

89. *HAL*, 1520. This word only occurs here and in Ezek 44:16; Mal 1:7, 12. Cf. Zimmerli, *Ezekiel 2*, 309.

90. Boyce, *HZ I*, 167.

91. Block, "Gog in Prophetic Tradition," 154–72; contra: Zimmerli, *Ezekiel 2*, 297; Eichrodt, *Ezekiel: A Commentary*, 516, 524–25.

92. In this respect Gog's pride parallels the pride of the King of Tyre in Ezek 28:1–19.

93. In the Zoroastrian cosmology, *Miθra* even guards the primeval contract between Ahura Mazda and Angra Mainyu (see the cosmic contract in *Sh. Bund.*

paints the image of *Miθra* as the recipient of the זבח גדול protecting YHWH's covenant of peace with restored Israel and which was promised in 37:15–23. Gog and his allies are offending the covenant of peace (contract, *miθra*) and thus fully within the wrath of *Miθra*. The judgment which Gog deserves is indicated by the usage of קבץ, "to assemble," in v. 17, which can have connotations of judgment.[94] This connection with the fulfillment of the previous covenant and the institution of a new one is made explicit in vv. 22–28. Such an understanding better parallels the other ironic uses of זבח גדול than if Molek were the recipient.

Irwin claims that the use of מקום in 39:11 alludes to Jer 7:32, implying the need to shift the location from the Hinnom Valley to the Jezreel Valley for sufficient room.[95] The phrase מקום־שם קבר בישראל has occasioned debate, as it is often considered strange or bad Hebrew syntax.[96] In the context of *Miθra* sacrifice, however, the phrase "a place of graves in Israel" could be an ironic punishment on an Army which considers it a sin to be buried.[97] Although the *Vidēvdāt* clearly makes it a sin to be buried, it is unclear how early this development is; however, many scholars see it as a Median or "Magian" introduction, which would be consonant with the peoples listed by Ezekiel.[98] These connections are all very speculative, however, and hinge on the understanding of זבח גדול situated in a reference to the Median–Lydian War.

Bøe advances an interesting parallel to this interpretation for *1 En.* 56:5–8's use of Ezek 38–39.[99] Against the common assertion that the Enochic author intends to allude to the Parthian invasion (40 B.C.E.), he argues that instead the writer understood the passage as a final, eschatological attack, with the terms "Parthians and Medes" representing a more current terminology than "Gog and Magog" for the same kind of assault.[100] The Enochic author adds many features consonant with the *Similitude*'s interests,[101] but the overall method of interpretation is quite similar. Just like the author of Ezek 38–39, the author of the *Parables*

1.17–18, *Pahlavi Texts I*, 7); once the contract expires, however, he participates in *Angra Mainyu*'s destruction (see Boyce, "On Mithra's Part in Zoroastrianism," 23).

94. *HAL*, 1063.

95. Irwin, "Molek Imagery," 96–98.

96. Zimmerli, *Ezekiel 2*, 291; Cooke, *Ezekiel*, 419; BHS notes that the LXX replaces שֵׁם for שָׁם.

97. See *Vidēvdāt* 1.13; 3.8, 12, 36–39 (*Zend-Avesta I*, 8, 15–16, 25, 31–32).

98. Briant, *From Cyrus to Alexander*, 94–95; Boyce, *HZ II*, 113–14; Shahbazi, "Monuments," 174–89; Moulton, *Early Zoroastrianism*, 182–253.

99. Bøe, *Gog and Magog*, 178–84.

100. Ibid., 180.

101. Ibid., 182.

uses historical, political configurations to depict a future (eschatological?) attack on Jerusalem. Not only does this parallel the methods used in Ezekiel and help make the above interpretation more plausible, it suggests how the text itself was re-used later by hearers and readers.[102]

The Gog pericope was very significant for the later development of apocalyptic imagery and literature.[103] It possibly served as a template or inspiration for Joel and Revelation. But it is also significant, at least in its current placement in the text, for positing a "Day of the Lord" (although that phrase is not actually used) which is in many respects larger than those posited in previous oracles. This day occurs after Israel is restored; it is not imminent but set in the distant future (38:8, 16). It links this action with earthquakes, the tumbling of mountains, pestilence, hail, and sulfur (38:19–23). These phenomena all become stock elements in later apocalyptic literature.[104] Childs has seen in the use of רעש a development of the chaos motif in the post-exilic period,[105] but the usages of this term in the Hebrew Bible is more connected with theophanies and battles than with chaos.[106] It is important to note that they all appear together here in a passage which may show Iranian influence.

The passage does not yet show apocalyptic theology or genre: there is no narrative framework, no *angelus interpres* (indeed, even missing common concerns like general judgment, afterlife). However the expectation of YHWH's action is pushed into the distant future, and his judgment is expanded towards cataclysmic proportions.[107] It *is* certainly significant that chs. 38–39, when read together with ch. 37, leaves a larger impression of both Iranian ideas and ideas to become standard in apocalyptic literature. The lack of a call towards repentance is notable

102.   Erho, "The Ahistorical Nature of *1 Enoch* 56:5–8," 23–54, similarly posits an ahistorical reference to the Parthians.

103.   See Bøe, *Gog and Magog*, 16–18, 178–83, 388; Dimant, "The Apocalyptic Interpretation of Ezekiel at Qumran," 31–52. Wacholder, "Ezekiel and Ezekielianism," 186–96, focuses very little on 37:1–14 or chs. 38–39.

104.   Cf. Cook, *Prophecy and Apocalypticism*, 94. Ezekiel 38:19–23 contains a list of signs which do not appear combined elsewhere in the Hebrew Bible. These are internecine fighting, earthquakes (רעש), blood (דם), pestilence (דבר), inundating rain (גשם שוטף), hail (אלגביש), fire (אש), and brimstone (גפרית). These verses take a term generally used in (later?) contexts of judgment (גפרית) and expand it. This combination of terrors, unique for its time, can be seen in Iranian sources.

105.   Childs, "Enemy from the North," 187–98.

106.   In theophanies: 1 Kgs 19:11; Isa 29:6; Ezek 3:12–13; in battles: Jer 10:22; 47:3; Nah 3:2. Amos and Zechariah each use it for a historical earthquake.

107.   E.g. Bodi, *The Book of Ezekiel and the Poem of Erra*, 223: "It [chs. 38–39] is an apocalyptic vision of the final, miraculous defeat of the forces of evil in the land of Israel."

in chs. 38–39 as well. The hint of a deterministic or unwitting use of a powerful leader by the Lord reminds one both of the hardening of pharaoh before the exodus and of the *Animal Apocalypse* in *1 Enoch*. If conscious, negative Median influence can be seen in this passage, then the beginnings of influence are much earlier than the Hellenistic period. Such an influence also highlights the potential importance of negative influence.

Daniel and the Four Kingdoms

Daniel 2 and 7 contain visions which present an overview of history using a scheme of four progressively inferior empires. This trope has long been identified as deriving from Iran, although the scheme itself is a scholarly flashpoint.[108] The present section seeks to evaluate the likelihood of Iranian influence on the current form of the scheme as it appears in Daniel, as well as to assess the relative import of such influence.

The visions themselves appear in 2:28–45 and 7:2–27, both of which are in the Aramaic section.[109] Although the imagery and narrative setting for the two visions are quite divergent, both recount a series of four kingdoms which are ultimately destroyed, and scholarship has tended to see the same concept as underlying both.

The Vision of the Statue (2:28–45)

> [31]You were looking, O king, and lo! there was a great statue. This statue was huge, its brilliance extraordinary; it was standing before you and its appearance was frightening. [32]The head of that statue was of fine gold (דהב), its chest and arms of silver (כסף), its middle and thighs of bronze (נחש), [33]its legs of iron (פרזל), its feet partly of iron and partly of clay. [34]As you looked on, a stone was cut out, not by human hands (די־לא בידין), and it struck the statue on its feet of iron and clay and broke them in pieces. [35]Then the iron, the clay, the bronze, the silver, and the gold, were all broken in pieces and became like the chaff of the summer threshing floors; and the wind carried them away, so that not a trace of them could be found. But the stone that struck the statue became a great mountain and filled the whole earth.

---

108. See Rowley, *Darius the Mede*, 67–184; Swain, "The Theory of the Four Monarchies," 1–21; Eddy, *The King is Dead*, 16; Collins, *Daniel*, 162–64, 166–70; Koenen, "Greece, the Near East, and Egypt," 1–34; Flusser, "The Four Empires," 148–75; Bryan, *Kosher Mentality*, 59–61; Niskanen, *The Human and the Divine*, Chapter 2; Koch, *Daniel 1. Teilband Dan 1–4*, 126–38, 203–7.

109. See Collins, *Daniel*, 12–24.

Daniel recounts a dream of Nebuchadnezzar in which he saw a statue with a head of gold, breast and arms of silver, loins and thighs of bronze, and legs of mixed clay and iron. A stone strikes the statue and destroys it, itself then growing into a mountain and filling the earth. Daniel subsequently interprets this dream as a succession of kingdoms, beginning with the reign of Nebuchadnezzar. Two basic aspects of this vision are noteworthy: the use of a series of metals ordered in decreasing value and a scheme of history based on the transition of power between four empires. A further aspect which requires attention is the appearance of "the end of days" (אחרית יומיא) in the interpretation (v. 28) and whether or not this implies an eschatological interpretation.

The image utilizes some traditional prophetic tropes. The description of judgment/destruction in terms of chaff, threshing floors, and/or wind appears often in the Hebrew Bible.[110] The use of these images recalls the judgment oracles of the prophets, even though the subsequent interpretation focuses more on succession than judgment. Additionally, the mountain which ultimately replaces all four kingdoms echoes the motif of the "mountain of the Lord" found throughout the Hebrew Bible, be it Sinai or Zion.[111] A Judaean audience would no doubt connect such language with promises of the restoration of Jerusalem. Neither of these aspects are particularly dwelt upon in text's own interpretation, however, and certainly do not exhaust the pericope's imagery.

Prominent is the use of a series of precious metals ordered by descending value: gold, silver, bronze, iron mixed with clay (נחש, כסף, דהב, פרזל). Similar series of metals ordered by decreasing value do appear in earlier biblical texts in a variety of contexts,[112] and one even appears in a context of judgment (Ezek 22:20).[113] Nevertheless, these antecedents do not apply the series to history, let alone to a succession of earthly kingdoms.[114] Using the relative values of metals as a method of arrangement is logical and likely universal, yet this has no necessary connection with historical processes and is—since it places Nebuchadnezzar at the pinnacle—rather surprising in a Judaean story.[115] A tempting interpretation is to understand the original referents to be kings rather than

---

110. For example, using chaff (מץ), Pss 1:4; 35:5; Isa 17:13; 29:5; also using the image of the threshing floor (גרן), Hos 13:3; Isa 41:15; cf. 2 Kgs 13:7.

111. For example, Exod 3:1; 15:17; Pss 48:1; 68:16; Isa 2:2; 25:6.

112. 1 Chr 22:16; 29:2 and 2 Chr 2:6, 13; Num 31:22 adds tin and lead; Josh 6:19, 24; 22:8 list all four, but in different orders; Isa 60:17.

113. Although the list starts with silver and adds tin and lead.

114. Contra Fröhlich, *Time and Times*, 28.

115. Cf. Collins, *Daniel*, 169.

kingdoms, thus belonging to a (Persian?) anti-Nabonidus polemic,[116] which was altered to kingdoms at a later stage of the tradition. However, since five kings reigned from Nebuchadnezzar until Cyrus, this still demands an explanation for the shift to a fourfold scheme.[117]

Further, a scheme of four eras or kingdoms which precede a final, everlasting kingdom appears to have no biblical precedent. This concept is intimately intertwined with the apocalyptic quagmires of determinism and eschatology.[118] The pericope's use of the term באחרית יומיא draws the fourfold scheme linguistically into the "Day of YHWH" tradition and its relation to the development of eschatology in Second Temple Judaism. Collins's reading of the eschatology in this chapter is very judicious: while an eschatology must be considered integral to the chapter, it is not an eschatology of the same type as in the second half of the book.[119] It is therefore necessary to consider whether this eschatology was adopted with the four-kingdom motif or whether it was added by the tale's Danielic creator. This will be further dealt with below.

The identification of the four kingdoms has occasioned much discussion, although most modern scholarship accepts the intended series (both here and in Dan 7) as Babylon, Media, Persia, and Greece.[120] Several considerations make this fairly certain. The text identifies the first kingdom clearly as Babylonia (v. 38), and the reference to marriage in v. 43 is generally understood as a reference to the competing Greek kingdoms of the Ptolemies and Seleucids. The reference to the "world dominion" of the third is consonant with the Persian Empire. Finally, the scheme Babylon–Media–Persia–Greece is an important structural motif for the current book.[121]

Several scholars note the chapter contains a number of Iranian loanwords (as well as Greek words).[122] Two of these are well-known and

---

116.   As argued by Bickerman, *Four Strange Books of the Bible*, 61–65; Fröhlich, *Time and Times*, 28–34.

117.   Cf. Rowley, *Darius the Mede*, 166–73.

118.   See Chapter 6.

119.   Collins, *Daniel*, 174.

120.   Rowley, *Darius the Mede*, 61–84; Montgomery, *Daniel*, 174–77, 185; Collins, *Daniel*, 166–70; Koch, *Daniel 1*, 198–202.

121.   Rowley, *Darius the Mede*, 146, 176–78; Collins, *Daniel*, 32; Grabbe, "Another Look at the *Gestalt* of Darius the Mede," 212–13; Koch, "Dereios, der Meder," 296.

122.   Koch, *Daniel 1*, 124; Brown, *Israel and Hellas III*, 234, 238. On Aramaic loanwords generally, see Greenfield, "Aramaic II: Iranian Loanwords in Early Aramaic," 256–59. Cf. Zadok, "On Five Iranian Names in the Old Testament," 246–47.

uncontested: רז ("mystery") and דת ("law"). Koch also identifies the words אזדא, הדמין, זמן, and the name אריוך as Iranian.[123] Further, the title "King of Kings" (v. 37) belongs to an Achaemenid milieu despite the supposed Neo-Babylonian setting.

The Vision of the "Mischwesen" (7:2–27)

The vision of ch. 7 is considerably different from that in ch. 2, although it is clearly related to it. In this "night vision"[124] the metallic imagery is replaced by four fantastic "beasts from the sea" (v. 3),[125] adding a throne vision and the controversial "Son of Man" (v. 13). A succession of four kingdoms followed by an eternal kingdom remains, although the idea of serial inferiority is lost. A few of the details of the ch. 2's visions are recalled in ch. 7: the dominion given to the leopard recalls the dominion of the third kingdom (2:39),[126] the iron composition of the fourth beast's horns (the only remaining metal),[127] and perhaps even the toes of statue.[128] Additionally, the vision's main concern is evidently with the last empire, the other three barely receiving censure;[129] the mention seems more to conform to a fourfold scheme than with a serious critique of the previous three *per se*.

Four-Period Schemes in the Ancient Near East

The sudden appearance of the four-kingdom and four-metal tradition in Daniel has long caused scholars to seek a parallel elsewhere. A variety of allegedly relevant schemes have been adduced; before discussing their relative merits and potential lines of transmission, the various passages are presented below.

Hesiod. One of the more oft-cited parallels occurs in Hesiod's *Works and Days*, lines 109–201.[130] Here the poet describes a succession of five generations or races of men: a golden race, a silver generation, a brazen race "sprung of ash trees," a fourth race of semi-divine heroes, and a fifth generation of iron, to which the poet claims to belong. Two features immediately strike the casual reader: the strong moral characterizations of each race or generation (in a declining succession) and what appears

---

123. Koch, *Daniel 1*, 124.
124. Collins, *Daniel*, 159–60.
125. See Bryan, *Kosher Mentality*, 218–34; Collins, *Daniel*, 280–94.
126. Also noted by Collins, *Daniel*, 298.
127. Cf. Collins, *Daniel*, 299.
128. Bryan, *Kosher Mentality*, 218.
129. Collins, *Daniel*, 304.
130. Evelyn-White, ed., *Hesiod, Homeric Hymns, Epic Cycle, Homerica*, 11–17.

to be an interruption of a fourfold metallic scheme with a generation of heroes. It seems likely that the poet has adapted an older fourfold scheme to accommodate Greek epic heroes.[131] Besides the interruption of the metallic sequence, the additional detail ascribed to the bronze race that they were "sprung of ash trees" likely dates the concept to Indo-European times; the Norse epic poem the *Vǫluspå* §§17–18 also describes the creation of humankind from driftwood of ash.[132] The passage here is concerned with ritual and ethical decline, and the author is unconcerned with the passing of empires.

Ovid. A passage similar to Hesiod appears in Ovid's *Metamorphoses.*[133] He describes a fourfold series of metallic races of increasing wickedness. To this series he appends a race of blood, whose violence prompts a deluge for their destruction. Finally, Ovid identifies the current human race with a race created from stone by the two lone flood survivors. The large number of mythic motifs and stories which are interwoven here leaves the impression that the second two races (of blood and stone) are creations of the poet and do not reflect an older tradition of six races.[134]

Herodotus. In his account of the rise of Cyrus, Herodotus claims obliquely that the rule of Asia was passed from Assyria to Media and thence to Persia.[135] It is important to note, however, that he did not make a clear distinction between the Assyrians and the Babylonians (e.g. I.178, 193; though he seems aware of a distinctness in I.102).[136] For authority Herodotus explicitly claims as his source Persians who "desire not to make a fine tale of the story of Cyrus but to tell the truth" (I.95).[137] He

131. Cf. Collins, *Daniel*, 162.

132. Dronke, *The Poetic Edda II: Mythological Poems*, 11 (text), 122–23. Cf. Widengren, "Leitende Ideen," 131. Mallory claims there was an original Indo-European threefold scheme of white–red–black; see Mallory, "Cosmology," 130–31. Gamkrelidze and Ivanov, *Indo-European and the Indo-Europeans*, 615–19, has a triad of yellow/gold, white/silver, and red/copper.

133. Ovid, *Metamorphoses* I.89–162, 396–416 (*Ovid III*, 9–13, 31).

134. According to Anderson, the race of blood is unparalleled elsewhere, and the creation of men from stones after the flood is a traditional Greek idea. Anderson, *Ovid's Metamorphoses Books 1–5*, 166–67, 180–81. Virgil's *Fourth Eclogue*, lines 4–10, describes the beginning of a golden age which follows upon an iron race, implying a cyclical overturning of the scheme, although Virgil appeals to a "Cumaean song." See Virgil, *Eclogues* (*Virgil I*, 49).

135. I.95, 130 (*Wars I–II*, 125–27, 169).

136. Herodotus, *Wars I–II*, 221, 243, 133.

137. Μετεξέτεροι λέγουσι, οἱ μὴ βουλόμενοι σεμνοῦν τὰ περὶ Κῦρον ἀλλὰ τὸν ἐόντα λέγειν λόγον.

claims that the Assyrians ruled for 520 years, the Medes for 128 years, and then the Persians up to his time (I.95, 130). While it is true a historical sequence with Media before Persia appears here, Herodotus takes no significance from the number, succession, or order of the empires; rather, he simply includes it as part of his tale of Cyrus's rise. However, the two passages are still significant in that they attest to an Iranian view of history which imparted world rule to the Medians. Further, since Herodotus was well known in the Hellenistic world, it is quite reasonable to infer that the later presence of Assyria–Media–Persia in historical lists is due to his history.

Oracle of Hystaspes and Zand-ī Wahman Yašn. Both the *Oracle of Hystaspes* and the *Wahman Yašt* are highly problematic as both currently exist only in citations and commentaries, largely in Lactantius for the former and the *Zand-ī Wahman Yašn* for the latter. Not enough of *Hystaspes* has survived to ascertain the majority of its contents or whether it also contained a fourfold scheme; although Lactantius mentions a scheme of empires in contexts in which he also quotes *Hystaspes*, it appears to be taken from the *Sibylline Oracles*.[138]

The text *Zand-ī Wahman Yašn* is more readily accessible, though the relevant tradition history is problematic.[139] This text is normally understood to be a précis and commentary (*zand*) on a lost hymn to *Vohu Manah* (*Wahman Yašt*), one of the important divine figures in Zoroastrianism.[140] Since it cites *Zand*[141] it is already at two steps removed from the original. Most scholars, however, accept that the text comments on real texts, even though they are not extant.[142] In the extant text, two

138.   Lactantius, *Divine Institutes* XV.13 (trans. Bowen and Garnsey, 423). Justin Martyr, *First Apology* 44, merely mentions the name of the work approvingly (incidentally, also in conjunction with the Sibyl; ANF, 1:178).

139.   Currently available in English in three translations, Anklesaria, *Zand-î Vohûman Yasn*; *Pahlavi Texts I*, 189–236; and Cereti, *The Zand-ī Wahman Yasn*.

140.   See Widengren, "Leitende Ideen," 105–19; Hultgård, "Bahman Yasht: A Persian Apocalypse," 114–34; Gignoux, "Bahman II: In the Pahlavi Texts," 488; Sundermann, "Bahman Yašt," 492–93; Hultgård, "Zoroastrian Myth in Bahman Yasht," 15–27; Eddy, *The King is Dead*, 26–32; Collins, "The Persian Apocalypses," 207–17.

141.   *ZBYt* 2.1, 3.1 (Anklesaria, *Zand-î Vohûman Yasn*, 102) =1.6, 2.1 (*Pahlavi Texts I*, 193–94). On *Zand*, see Boyce, "Middle Persian Literature," 35–36.

142.   Widengren, "Leitende Ideen," 77–162; Sundermann, "Bahman Yašt," 492–93; Hultgård, "Bahman Yasht: A Persian Apocalypse," 114–34; Hultgård, "Zoroastrian Myth in Bahman Yasht," 19–20. The main opponent is Gignoux; cf. Gignoux, "Bahman II: In the Pahlavi Texts," 488.

metallic sequences are presented. In the first version, Zoroaster is shown a tree with four branches of gold, silver, steel, and one of iron mixed with dust.[143] The interpretation given is of four periods, the first identified with the period of Zoroaster and his royal patron *Vīštāspa*, the next two with legendary reigns of kings (Ardaxšīr, Husraw), and the last with "the evil sovereignty of the demons with disheveled hair of the race of Wrath."[144] In the second version Zoroaster sees a tree with seven branches of gold, silver, bronze, copper, tin, steel, and iron mixed with dust. These are again interpreted as ages of the world, all of which are identified with reigns, from that of *Vištāspa* to that of the badly coiffed, angry demons.[145] The doubling of the metallic progression, its expansion from four to seven, and the changes in the interpretation clearly evince a later updating of a fourfold prophecy to fit subsequent history. The interpretation of the second vision understands the final demons to refer to the Arab invasion of Iran at the end of the Sassanian Empire, and this is clearly a reinterpretation of a previous prophecy. While the dating of this interpretation (and thus the current text) is clearly very late, the question remains as to how ancient the original fourfold metallic vision is. Hultgård adduces five reasons why a supposed *Wahman Yašt* existed behind the current text: (1) the other three cited sources are real; (2) at the time of the compilation, extensive materials were available, so forging would be difficult; (3) there are hints of liturgical formulas, suggesting a *Yašt*-like *Vorlage*; (4) the literary character suggests an underlying *zand* like the *Vidēvdāt*; (5) it also preserves epic fragments of other lost Avestan sources.[146] Eddy suggests that the original prophecy intended the disheveled hair to refer to the Greeks—or more specifically, depictions of Alexander—which would likely date the idea to the Hellenistic period.[147] Since the Achaemenid Empire was the last Iranian empire destroyed by a foreign invasion, this identification is plausible. Besides questions of dating, however, important to note is that the text explicitly applies a fourfold metallic scheme to successive reigns. Interestingly, while the succession appears to agree with the version in Dan 2 in mixing the last element, it also differs in the use of steel for bronze.

---

143.   See Cereti, *Zand-ī Wahman Yasn*, 172; Boyce, "The Poems of the Persian Sibyl," 73; Boyce and Grenet, *HZ III*, 386.

144.   *ZBYt* 1.6–11 (Anklesaria, *Zand-î Vohûman Yasn*, 101–102) = 1.3–5 (*Pahlavi Texts I*, 192–93).

145.   *ZBYt* 2.14–22 in West's translation (*Pahlavi Texts I*, 198–201); 3.19–29 in Anklesaria's (Anklesaria, *Zand-î Vohûman Yasn*, 104–6).

146.   Hultgård, "Zoroastrian Myth in Bahman Yasht," 19–20.

147.   Eddy, *The King is Dead*, 19 and plate 1 (between 21–22).

The Sibylline Oracles. A variety of historical schemes organized by world empires appear in several of the extant *Sibylline Oracles*, a Byzantine collection of miscellaneous texts which contains a variety of older oracles.[148] The closest parallel to the version in Daniel appears in Book IV, lines 49–114, which likely dates to the early Hellenistic period.[149] In this text a series of empires rule the world from the flood until the sibyl's time for decreasing lengths of times: the Assyrians rule for six generations, the Medes for two, the Persians for "one generation of prosperous rule," the Macedonians (for an unspecified period of time), and the Romans. Rather than a subsequent heavenly kingdom, the text predicts a world-destroying conflagration (160–61, 171–78). Several characteristics are here worth noticing. The text posits a five-fold division of decreasing length (at least until the Persians), but there is no explicit condemnation of these empires; each receives judgment through conquest, but they are not directly accused of evil. The text focuses on the horrors of war and other disasters rather than on the relative moral qualities of the empires. Finally, a scheme of Assyria–Media–Persia–Macedonia–Rome is evidenced, which could logically be an update for an older fourfold scheme. Flusser adduces that this is the case since the addition of Rome interrupts the ten generations interwoven into the description of the first four.[150]

Several other Sibyllines also break history into succeeding empires, although they are much more varied and removed from any relation to history. *Sibylline Oracles* III.159–61 gives a list of eight empires in the order Egypt, Persia, Media, Ethiopia, "Assyrian Babylon," Macedonia, Egypt, and Rome.[151] This list is notable for three things: its Egyptocentrism, the flipping of Persia and Media, and the equation of Assyria with Babylon.[152] *Sibylline Oracles* VIII.5–9 gives a very similar list of Egypt,

---

148. Collins, "The Sibylline Oracles," 317–472. Cf. Walde, "Sibylle (Σίβυλλα), lat. *Sibylla*)," 499–501, and Sehlmeyer, "Sibyllini libri, Sibyllina oracula," 501–2, both in Cancik and Schneider, eds., *Der Neue Pauly Enzyklopädie der Antike*, vol. 11; Collins, "The Jewish Transformation of Sibylline Oracles," 181–97.

149. Collins, "The Sibylline Oracles," 385–87; dating, 381. Cf. Bartlett, *Jews in the Hellenistic World*, 38.

150. Flusser, "The Four Empires," 150–51.

151. Collins, "The Sibylline Oracles," 365. Flusser argues this also represents a fourfold scheme, if the text intends the second empire to be the combined empire of Persia–Media–Ethiopia–Assyrian Babylon. See Flusser, "The Four Empires," 160 n. 49.

152. Cf. *Sib. Or.* III.268 where the Assyrians are said to conquer Jerusalem and III.300–304 where it refers to "Babylon and the race of Assyrian men" (Collins, "The Sibylline Oracles," 368; cf. n. e2).

Persia, Media, Ethiopia, "Assyrian Babylon," Macedonia, and Rome.[153] Finally, the eleventh Sibylline offers a list of Egypt, Persia, Media, Ethiopia, Assyria, Macedonia, Egypt, and Rome, although equating Assyria with the Jews.[154]

Qumran Fragments. While several documents discovered at Qumran have clear relationships with the canonical Daniel, none of the extant sections preserve either a scheme of kingdoms or metals.[155] However, the *Animal Apocalypse* in *1 En.* 89–90 contains a fourfold periodization within its era of seventy shepherds,[156] and this text is likely roughly contemporary with Dan 7. Unlike the Danielic texts, however, *1 Enoch* simply uses the fourfold division as a structural device, placing no emphasis on the number four nor giving clear indications to the significance of the eras.

The Origin of the Four-Empire Scheme
Scholars have often considered an Iranian milieu for the origin of the four-empire motif, though positions vary widely.[157] There are three

153.   Collins, "The Sibylline Oracles," 418.

154.   *Sib. Or.* XI.19–314; Collins, "The Sibylline Oracles," 434–42.

155.   See Collins, "Prayer of Nabonidus," 83–94, and Collins and Flint, "Pseudo-Daniel," 95–164.

156.   Denied by Nickelsburg, *1 Enoch 1*, 391–92; in his review of Nickelburg's commentary, Tiller asserts the likely relevance of the four-period trope; see Tiller, "Review: *1 Enoch 1*," 577. Although fragments of the *Animal Apocalypse* were found (4QEn^c 4), they do not correspond to the section of the seventy shepherds. See Milik, *The Books of Enoch*, 204–6.

157.   Anti-Seleucid Iranian diaspora in Anatolia: Swain, "The Theory of the Four Monarchies," in particular 3–11. Agnostic: Lambert, *The Background of Jewish Apocalyptic*, 9; Day, *God's Conflict with the Dragon*, 153 n. 26. Mixed Persian and Babylonian: Kvanvig, *Roots of Apocalyptic*, 490–91. Hesiod with Iranian reaction: Flusser, "The Four Empires," 148–75. Cf. Boyce and Grenet, *HZ III*, 384–86, 402–4, especially n. 190. She posits that while the Persians borrowed the metals from the Greeks, Daniel borrowed the idea from Persia. See Boyce, "On the Antiquity of the Zoroastrian Apocalyptic," 70–72; idem, "Persian Sibyl," 73–74. Of a similar opinion is LaCocque, *The Book of Daniel*, 48–49. Urartian or Babylonian: West, *The East Face of Helicon*, 312–19. Brown also seems to posit a vague "oriental" source; see Brown, *Israel and Hellas*, 301–202; idem, *Israel and Hellas III*, 74–75, where it is given an implied Persian imperial setting.

Iranian: Winston, "The Iranian Component," 189–90; cf. Hartman, "Datierung der junavestischen Apokalyptik," 61–64.

Iranian and Seleucid: Koch, *Daniel 1*, 137–38, 206–7.

Cautiously Persian or ancient Near East: Collins, *Daniel*, 164. Collins, however, was earlier more positive towards a Persian origin; see his "Jewish Apocalyptic

aspects of the motif as it appears in Daniel which need to be kept in mind and considered both independently and in combination: the four-empire scheme alone and as understood in the form Babylon–Media–Persia–Greece, the four metallic eras, and the implied eschatology.

Four Kingdoms or Kings. A motif of four significant periods was known in the ancient Near East well before Daniel. Its appearance in Hesiod presents a *terminus ante quem* in the eighth century; Koch even suggests a similar idea can be found in earlier Hurrian/Hittite mythology.[158] Indeed, it seems likely that a similar idea was held by Proto-Indo-Europeans.[159] A possibility, therefore, that the idea was widely disseminated in the ancient Near East cannot be wholly discounted. Nevertheless, four generations or eras and four world empires are not necessarily parallel ideas, and one could wonder whether the latter is not a separate or at least subsequent tradition to the former.

A historical sequence of empires presented as Assyria, Media, Persia, Greece originally represents an Iranian (or perhaps an Eastern Anatolian) perspective. Two points indicate this: only Iranian lands experienced such a sequence, and Herodotus's presentation of the said sequence explicitly names Persian sources. Although Herodotus is probably to be credited with its dissemination in Greek-speaking lands, the concept must have been borne among either Medes or Persians. However, the sequence attested in Daniel replaces Babylon for Assyria. While from a Mesopotamian point of view this is problematic, it is less so from two of the likely sources for the Danielic author, viz., Iran or Greece. The Greek

Against Its Hellenistic Near Eastern Environment," 29. Yet, even earlier, he seems to posit an original Babylonian oracle; see his *The Apocalyptic Vision of the Book of Daniel*, 37–42; an idea which he again entertains in idem, *Daniel*, 169.

Herodotus: Wiesehöfer, "The Medes and the Idea of the Succession," 391–96, who sees a common source and independent development in Daniel.

Judaean and Babylonian: Fröhlich, *Time and Times*, 26–36. Cf. Bickerman, *Four Strange Books of the Bible*, 61–65; Lucas, "The Origin of Daniel's Four Empire Scheme Re-examined," 185–202.

158.   Koch, *Daniel 1*, 186–87.

159.   The Greeks, Iranians, and Hittites were all Indo-European peoples. To reinforce the idea of a pan-Indo-European idea, the Norse *Vǫluspá* §44 mentions a variant which identifies these four ages: an axe-age, a sword-age, a wind-age, and a wolf-age. These are, however, eschatological. See Dronke, *Mythological Poems*, 18–19. In this regard, it is interesting to note that the *Zand-ī Wahman Yašn* describes the final age as the passing of the wolf-age into the lamb-age (8.3, Anklesaria, *Zand-î Vohûman Yasn*, 125; 3.40, *Pahlavi Texts I*, 230). Cf. Griffiths, "Archaeology and Hesiod's Five Ages," 116; Mallory, "Cosmology," 130–31.

authors appear to have had no clear conception of a differentiation between Assyria and Babylon; for the Persians, Babylon was combined with *Aθurā* in a single satrapy.[160]

Contra commentators who see a problem in the shift from king to kingdoms in Dan 2, the ambiguity is no basis for insisting on an adaptation of an older, dynastic prophecy. Kings can easily represent their domain just as their jurisdiction can symbolize their own power.[161] A rule of a dynasty is not easily separated from the rule of one of its members. This is particularly true in an era before the modern nation-state when the idea of borders was more fluid and a kingdom more directly tied into the person of the monarch.[162] In this context, the "you" of Dan 2:38 could simply be understood as rhetorical flattery before a king, rather than the remnant of a previous Babylonian dynastic prophecy.[163] In theory, therefore, the inspiration for Daniel's vision could have been either a sequence of empires or individual kings representative of them.

Wiesehöfer comments that a sequence of Asian empires of increasing inferiority would be peculiar as Achaemenid ideology, but fits well within Herodotus's concept of spiraling decadence.[164] If the concept of increasing inferiority were sustained in Daniel as in Herodotus or in Hesiod, this argument would be compelling; however, the passage as it stands in ch. 2 is clearly only concerned with the fourth empire and its divided nature. Verse 39 briefly mentions that the second is inferior to the first, but then quickly moves on. If a post-Achaemenid Persian reaction is posited, the paradox implied by the inferiority becomes less acute: the focus is on the last empire, which is itself going to be replaced.

Four Metallic Eras. The two most relevant metallic parallels to Dan 2 are striking both in their similarities and their differences. Daniel shares the four metals with Hesiod, while altering the last metal, iron, by having

160. See Herodotus and the Sibylline Literature above; for Persia, see Briant, *From Cyrus to Alexander*, 544, 719; Dandamaev, "Assyria II: Achaemenid Aθurā," 816; Elayi and Sapin, *Beyond the River*, 15–18.

For the OP nomenclature, cf. DNa §3 and DSe §26 where *Aθurā* (the country) is used and DSf §32 and the minor DN inscriptions, where *Aθuriya* (the people) is used (Kent, *Old Persian*, 137–38, 141–42 and 142–44, 140, respectively).

161. In any case, the difference between the two in Aramaic is only a matter of pointing (both מלכיא), and the same OP word covers both "reign" and "empire" (*xšaça-*); Schmitt, "Artaxerxes, Ardašīr und Verwandte," 62. Cf. Kent, *Old Persian*, 181; Bartholomae, *Altiranisches Wörterbuch*, 542, 551.

162. Cf. Wright, "Remapping Yehud," 67–90.

163. Contra Colless, "Cyrus the Persian as Darius the Mede," 120.

164. Wiesehöfer, "Idea of the Succession," 393.

it mixed with clay. This addition breaks with the metallic imagery and must in itself be significant. One could wish to see this change as an innovation of the Danielic author to suit the *pešer*, but this simple solution is complicated by the evidence of the *Zand-ī Wahman Yašn*. This text also has iron mixed with dust/clay last. While such a parallel might indicate a relationship between these two, the *Zand*'s use of steel instead of bronze as the third metal and the problematic dating complicates whatever relation may exist.

Boyce believes that the metallic sequence was adapted in Iran from Greece during the wars of the *Diadochi* and from thence was adapted by Daniel.[165] She originally argued that the "mixed iron" of the *Yašt* refers to iron ore still containing dross, which better fits the idea of decline as well as parallels the traditional Iranian conception of the current era as a mixture of good and evil.[166] The author of Dan 2 would have then misunderstood the meaning of "mixed iron" and understood it as clay. In this she has been followed by Koenen, who further believes the sequence to have been a Greek innovation (though prior to Hesiod).[167] However, she has since modified her position according to a suggestion by Gignoux and sees the Pahlavi phrase to mean "iron mixed with dust/clay,"[168] making the phrases nearly identical and requiring some kind of explanation for the coincidence. Boyce's solution accounts for the "mixed iron" but fails to explain (a then doubled) switch between bronze and steel.

Both the Greeks and Iranians are Indo-European peoples, so one could wish to argue that a four-period scheme was a mutual inheritance; indeed the use of "ash" by Hesiod would seem to indicate that possibility. However, the four-metal scheme could not have been developed before the separation of the Indo-Europeans, as that likely occurred before the Iron Age.[169] The metallic version most likely predates Hesiod, although perhaps not by much.[170] The evidence available is insufficient to decide, but either a borrowing of the metal sequence from Greece to Persia, parallel developments (each adding a fourth metal to an inherited three-metal scheme), or the borrowing of both from a third, unknown source is possible. A switch between reigns and kingdoms is unproblematic since

	165.	Boyce, "On the Antiquity," 71–72; cf. idem, "Persian Sibyl," 73–74; Boyce and Grenet, *HZ III*, 386, 402.

	166.	Also Van der Merwe, "Investigating Apparent Commonalities," 107.

	167.	Koenen, "Greece, the Near East, and Egypt," 12–13, 24–25.

	168.	Boyce, "Persian Sibyl," 73; Boyce and Grenet, *HZ III*, 386; cf. Cereti, *The Zand-ī Wahman Yasn*, 172.

	169.	Cf. Fortson, *Indo-European Language*, 39, 44; Gamkrelidze and Ivanov, *Indo-European*, 614–15, 761.

	170.	Koenen, "Greece, the Near East, and Egypt," 25 n. 59.

they represent similar concepts. A change from races to kingdoms might be more so, although if the kingdoms are understood as belonging to different nations, then again this idea is analogous. The form of either the Greek or Iranian versions is therefore not a hurdle. This does not solve the question of Daniel's sources, however.

Niskanen strenuously objects to an Iranian explanation,[171] preferring a Herodotean source. Niskanen's arguments are highly suggestive and helpful—not because they are persuasive—but because they prompt a more thorough investigation of the potential Iranian sources.[172] Therefore, his arguments will be used as a foil in an attempt to reconstruct what traditions may underlie the *Zand-ī Wahman Yašn* and thus what may or not be comparable to Daniel.

Daniel 2 combines two separable concepts: a sequence of four empires and a series of four metals, yet only the former receives much interpretation in the text. Niskanen argues that their combination here is misleading, since it is likely that Daniel combined two separate sources.[173] However, the very fact which he notices—that Daniel seems to ignore the implications of the four metals—argues rather that he is adapting a sequence of empires *which already utilized the metallic imagery*. If Dan 2 were drawing directly on a Herodotean tradition, one would expect the vision to eliminate the metallic imagery, or, if the author were combining sources, for the metals to take a more prominent place in the *pešer*. This impression is reinforced if one considers that the second half of the book (chs. 7 and 11) dispenses with the metallic imagery. Niskanen's appeal to these later visions to reinforce a Herodotean derivation for ch. 2 ignores the likelihood that the source and authorship of these two is quite probably divergent from ch. 2; if ch. 11 derives the idea of four Persian kings from the Greeks, that does not have any necessary bearing on the vision in ch. 2.[174] The background of ch. 2 is a different one from the second half of the book and is probably one which already combined the two fourfold motifs. This consideration, then, justifies the examination of the only other extant source which combines the two fourfold ideas, the *Zand-ī Wahman Yašn*.

171. Niskanen, *The Human and the Divine*, 31–34.
172. The present study is much indebted to Niskanen's; until reading it, the author was on the verge of concluding the impossibility of deciding a source, although leaning towards a Greek source. Ironically, it was Niskanen's argument for Greek influence which consolidated thoughts about the supposed Persian source and lead to the argument set forth below.
173. Niskanen, *The Human and the Divine*, 31.
174. Contra ibid., 41–42.

Niskanen is correct to note that the extant text of the *Zand-ī Wahman Yašn* is late; however, he appears to miss the fact that the text is clearly composite, containing two distinct metallic sequences, the second of which is clearly a later updating of the former. He appeals to details consonant with the Turkish invasion in the second version (the sevenfold version) to discredit Eddy's arguments based on the "tousled hair" as selective;[175] however, these details are clearly an updating of the earlier Arab invasion, which is likely an update of one based on the Greek invasion. The impression that the original core of the vision was based on the Macedonian conquests is actually reinforced by deeper considera-tion of two of his objections to this thesis: that the kings listed are all Iranian and that a reference to Greece is unlikely in a Persian text.[176] The first objection forgets a few relevant points. The sequence Assyria–Media–Persia–Greece already contains two Iranian empires (Media and Persia), and Assyria was viewed by the Achaemenids as a legitimate ruler of Iran.[177] Further, the *Zand* first uses *Vīštāspa* as the representative, who was sometimes considered a foreign king.[178] Thus, the Iranian list better fits the Macedonian situation than the post-Macedonian one. The latter objection ignores two points. First, if the Persian scheme was origi-nally a reaction to the Macedonian invasion, then it would be expected to contain a reference to the Macedonians; second, the later portions of the text do contain what appear to be vague memories of Alexander.[179] The two notices of Alexander appear in the text in the second metallic sequence and in the subsequent elaboration of eschatology.[180] Specifi-cally, the last reinterpretation of the sequence places "*Aleksandar-ī Kilīsāyīg*" in the fourth (copper) era. This would imply that this reinter-pretation was based on a text which mentioned Alexander as part of the

175.   Ibid., 32–33.

176.   Objections are in ibid., 32, 34, and 41 n. 59.

177.   Cf. the comments in Stronach, "Anshan and Parsa," 45; cf. the editor in the introduction, 12–14. In addition, Cyrus appeals to Assurbanipal as a precursor in the *Cyrus Cylinder* (Hallo, ed., *COS* 2:314–16). See also Stronach, "Icons of Domin-ion," 380, 382, 384, 386.

178.   Cf. Humbach, et al., *The Gāthās of Zarathushtra*, 1:47–49; Boyce, *HZ I*, 186–88.

179.   This last point is actually noted by Niskanen, *The Human and the Divine*, 34, especially n. 31.

180.   The two most commonly cited publications of the texts are numbered differently; the two relevant verses are in 4.4 and 7.32 in Anklesaria's edition (Anklesaria, *Zand-î Vohûman Yasn*, 105, 124) and 2.24 and 3.34 in West's (*Pahlavi Texts I*, 200, 228). More recently Cereti, *Zand-ī Wahman Yasn*, follows Anklesaria's numbering.

fourth empire. If these objections can be dispensed with, then the task remains of reconstructing as much as possible the vision which finds its *zand*s in the *Zand-ī Wahman Yašn*.

Reconstructing the Ur-form of an Iranian Vohu Manah Yašt. The following attempt is necessarily hypothetical; however, the lateness and layers of reinterpretation which are clearly evident in the extant *Zand-ī Wahman Yašn* require that an effort be made, if an Iranian prophecy is to be compared with Daniel at all. Only once a version which can be reasonably understood to be roughly contemporaneous or prior to Dan 2 is reconstructed can a consideration of its relevance be undertaken. If this task fails, then the investigation must conclude that further evidence is required.

The primary starting point ought to be the fourfold vision, as that is likely to be closer to the original version of the vision. It is pertinent to note that the *Zand* gives a series of three reigns followed by a race.[181] The names given are *Vīštāspa* (the legendary patron of Zoroaster), *Ardaxšīr* "the Kayan King," Husraw son of Kevād, and the Race of *Xēšm* "with disheveled hair" (*dēwān ī wizārd-wars ī xēšm-tōhmag*). These names deserve investigation.

The name of the second king (*Ardaxšīr*) is the Pahlavi form of the most common Achaemenid throne name, Artaxerxes (*Artaxšacā* in OP).[182] Boyce argues that Ardašīr, the founder of the Sassanian dynasty, deliberately chose his name to claim continuity with the previous empire ruled from Fars, in particular with Artaxerxes II;[183] two other sources (Syncellus and several inscriptions from Nisa) support this.[184] Even if this is incorrect and the Sassanians had no knowledge of the Achaemenids except through Greek materials as Yarshater argues,[185] the linguistic coincidence of the names is striking. More recently, Arjomand has argued further that the names which appear as "Ardaxšīr the Kay who

---

181. *ZBYt* 1.8–11 (Anklesaria, *Zand-î Vohûman Yasn*, 101–2; Cereti, *Zand-ī Wahman Yasn*, 133, 149) = 1.3–5 (*Pahlavi Texts I*, 192–93). West translates *tōhmag* as "race"; Anklesaria as "seed."

182. Schmitt, "Artaxerxes, Ardašīr und Verwandte," 61–72; idem, "Artaxerxes," 654–655; idem, "Thronnamen bei den achaimeniden," 422–25. There were five Artaxerxeses, if one includes Bessus.

183. Boyce, *HZ II*, 263.

184. Schmitt, "Artaxerxes II," 658. He cites Syncellus 1.539.16f D, and Pahlavi inscriptions, listed by Gignoux, *Glossaire des inscriptions Pehlevies et Parthes*, 46, as "Artaštāvanak," from eight inscriptions at Nisa.

185. Yarshater, "Were the Sasanians Heirs to the Achaemenids?," 520–31.

will be called Wahman ī Spandyādān" in the *Zand-ī Wahman Yašn* and "Ardaxšīr who is called Vahuman" in the *Bundahišn* are both actually Artaxerxes II Mnemnon.[186] This is based on understanding the Greek surname which was attached to Artaxerxes II, "Mnemon" ("having good memory"), as a translation of a Persian surname "*Vohu Manah*" ("Good Thought"), which is *Wahman* in Pahlavi. Thus, the Ardaxšīr-Wahman of the epic cycles is really Artaxerxes II.[187] Ardašīr's claim of descent would also correspond with other, previous dynasts claiming descent from Artaxerxes II (e.g. Antiochus I and the Arsacids).[188] The appearance, then, of "Artaxšīr the Kayan King" in the current *zand* would appear to be a conflation of a historical name and an epic tradition, facilitated by the identity of the names. Indeed, if Artaxerxes II was completely forgotten and morphed into the Kayanid epic cycle, a Sassanian understanding of the name as Ardašīr is even more understandable.

It has long been noted that the name of Zoroaster's patron is identical to Darius I's father's.[189] It is also the pseudepigraphal author of the elusive *Oracles of Hystaspes*, which purportedly contained apocalyptic material.[190] Additionally, it is a name which was held by a number of Achaemenid nobles.[191] While a historical connection between Darius's father and Zoroaster's patron is unlikely, it is certainly telling that a text which is generally considered to be a reaction against foreign imperialism takes as its pseudepigraphal author a significant king in the religious traditions which also happens to coincide with a name from Achaemenid

186. Arjomand, "Artaxerxes, Ardašīr, and Bahman," 245–48.

187. Cereti, *Zand-ī Wahman Yasn*, 173, prefers to identify him with Artaxerxes I.

188. Arjomand, "Artaxerxes, Ardašīr, and Bahman," 245; Garsoïan, *The Epic Histories*, 356–57.

189. Cf. Herzfeld, *Archaeological History*, 43, and Olmstead, *History of the Persian Empire*, 102–3, who both even identified the two people. For discussion (without identification), see Kent, "The Name of Hystaspes," 55–58; Koch, *Daniel 1*, 135.

190. For an attempt at reconstructing an *Oracle of Hystaspes*, see Flusser, "Hystaspes and John of Patmos," 12–75. See also Collins, "The Persian Apocalypses," 210; Hinnells, "The Zoroastrian Doctrine of Salvation in the Roman World," 125–48.

191. Balcer, *A Prosopographical Study of the Ancient Persians*, 105, 149, cf. 269, 67–69, gives two occurrences of the name *Vīštāspa* besides Darius I's father: one a son of Darius I and the other a son of Xerxes I. He cites Herodotus, VII.64.2 (*Wars V–VII*, 379), Thucydides, *History of the Peloponnesian War* I.115.4 (*Thucydides I*, 191), and Diodorus Siculus, *Library of History* II.69.2 (*Diodorus of Sicily IV*, 305). Xerxes's son also appears in Ctesias (Photius, *The Bibliotheca*, 59). However, it appears that the *Vīštāspa*, father of Sardis's satrap, in Thucydides could be another person. Cf. Boyce, *HZ II*, 41.

history. This point will need further consideration. It is also worth noting that while the *Zand* places Vīštāspa first, the *Dēnkard* places his reign second.[192]

It is often noted that the third name that the *Zand-ī Wahman Yašn* gives, Husraw son of Kevād, is the name of a Sassanian king.[193] However, both "the son of Kevād" (Kai Kaus) and Kai Husraw are mythical characters from the Iranian epic tradition with many attached stories.[194] The antiquity of both of these characters is confirmed by their appearance in the Avesta and in India.[195] It appears that the Sassanian King Husraw deliberately modeled himself on these legendary characters and/ or modeled the epic traditions on himself.[196] This adaptation seems to have effected two things: the transformation of the priestly term *kavi* into a dynastic term, and the inclusion of King Husraw in the list of the *Saošiiant*'s companions.[197]

The last reign given is a race born of the demon *Xēšm* (Avestan *Aēšma*), who are famously described as having wild hair.[198] *Aēšma* is an important demon in Zoroastrian tradition, the personification of Wrath, and related to destructive warfare.[199] Indeed, he is the only demon to appear in the *Gāthās*.[200] In later Iranian, Alexander is also associated with

192. *Dēnkard* 9.8.1–6 (*Pahlavi Texts IV*, 180–81).

193. Reigned 531–579 C.E. Cf. *Pahlavi Texts I*, 193, 199; Niskanen, *The Human and the Divine*, 32; Cereti, *Zand-ī Wahman Yasn*, 173–74; Frye, "The Political History of Iran Under the Sasanians," 151, 153–62.

194. The first has many stories associated with him under the name "Kai Kaus" in the *Shahnameh*. See Firdausī, *Shāhnāma*, 2:29–43, 82–106, 336–412. It is in his version, however, combined with the Rustam cycle.

For Husraw: Firdausī, *Shāhnāma*, 2:336–end. He also appears in a variety of Pahlavi texts. See *Dēnkard* 7.1.39 (*Pahlavi Texts V*, 14); 9.23.1–7; 9.58.10 (*Pahlavi Texts IV*, 223–26, 355); *Mēnōg-ī Xrad* 2.95; 27.59–63 (*Pahlavi Texts III*, 15, 64).

Cf. Yarshater, "Iranian National History," 359–416 and 436–40, 444–53 (on Husraw and the Kayanids); Boyce, *HZ I*, 105.

195. *Yašt* 5.45, 49; 9.18, 21; 13.121, 132; 14.39; 19.71; 23.2 (*Zend-Avesta II*, 65, 114–15, 216, 222, 241, 303, 328); Yarshater, "Iranian National History," 436–40.

196. Wikander in Timus, "Les 'Haskell Lectures'," 297–98, 311. Jamzadeh opines the stories are reflexes of Xerxes I, Jamzadeh, "A Shahnama Passage in an Achaemenid Context," 383–88.

197. Timus, "Les 'Haskell Lectures'," 316.

198. See Eddy, *The King is Dead*, 19, plates between 21 and 22.

199. Asmussen, "Aešma," 479–80; cf. Pines, "Wrath and Creature of Wrath," 76–82; Lincoln, *Priests, Warriors, and Cattle*, 127; Boyce, "Priests, Cattle and Men," 524.

200. *Yasna* 29.2; 30.6; 48.12 (Insler, *The Gathas of Zarathustra*, 29, 33, 93); cf. Boyce, *HZ I*, 87, 201.

him.[201] It is certain that this detail, both in the first version and its subsequent reinterpretations, refers to a foreign military invasion. While the text of the *Zand* as it now stands regards these invaders as the Turks and/or the Arabs, it is likely that earlier interpreters understood the demonic race as the foreign invaders of their respective days, the Arabs and the Greeks. Indeed, most commentators accept the Macedonians as the original referent, since they were the first army to remove Iranian sovereignty.[202] The text as it stands seems to confirm that this was an ancient interpretation: the fourth reign of the second vision includes that of "*Aleksandar-ī Kilīsāyīg*," generally understood to be Alexander the Great.[203]

With the exception of the third, each one of the above referents appears to combine several levels: a political level suitable to a post-Achaemenid period, legendary religious references, and Sassanian references. Given likely Sassanian re-interpretation, the text as it now stands would appear to combine two fourfold schemes: a political and a religious, a combination which was updated in the Sassanian period. That religious fourfold schemes existed is demonstrated by the *Dēnkard*'s précis of four religious eras.[204] Further, the religious connotations of the Achaemenid names and their re-use by the Sassanian dynasts would appear to facilitate their conflation. If the conflated schemes of the *Zand-ī Wahman Yašn* are separated, the two schemes as understood by the Sassanian commentators were:

"Religious":
Zoroaster—Vīštāspa—Aturpad son of Maraspend—Period of Apostasy

"Political":
Zoroaster and Vīštāspa—King Ardašīr—King Husraw—The Arabs

The first one is attested independently in the *Dēnkard*, and it is clearly influenced by the developments of the Sassanian and post-Sassanian era. If the Sassanian identifications are removed from the two series, the following two schemes immediately present themselves:

---

201.   The *Dēnkard* passage (679.14) is transliterated and translated in Bailey, *Zoroastrian Problems*, 154; Pines, "Wrath and Creature of Wrath," 76; *Pahlavi Texts V*, 83 (labeled 7.7).

202.   Cf. Hultgård, "Zoroastrian Myth in Bahman Yasht," 16, and the references cited there.

203.   Boyce and Grenet, *HZ III*, 384; *Pahlavi Texts I*, 200 n. 1.

204.   *Dēnkard* 9.8.1–7 (*Pahlavi Texts IV*, 180–81, 451–52); Cereti, *Zand-ī Wahman Yasn*, 171.

"Religious":

Zoroaster—Vīštāspa—Saošiiant—Final Battle

"Political":

Darius (Son of Hystaspes)—Artaxerxes II Memnon—Unattested—Alexander

The first of these is a simple sequence which can easily be derived from the *Gāthās* before the triplication of millennia under Babylonian influence.[205] The second presents itself once the OP forms are used instead of the extant Pahlavi forms.[206] Important to note in this respect is the Sassanian tradition of the occultation of Husraw, an idea which appears in the epic tradition, but for which widespread Indo-European parallels are attested.[207] It would appear likely that the tradition of Husraw's occultation in the *Zand-ī Wahman Yašn* is a replacement for the previous (Achaemenid) dynast, who perhaps was also understood to have been "occulted." The immediate candidate would, of course, be Darius III, but could in theory be any of the later kings.[208] If this theory is accepted, the root political concept behind the first chapter of the *Zand* is a threefold Achaemenid dynasty supplanted by Alexander. Since the concept of reign and empire are easily compatible, this series would have been easy to combine with the concept of world empires once the Achaemenid Empire had fallen. Further, the negative attitude taken to the Macedonians facilitated a religious interpretation of the significance of their victory over the Iranians, seeing it as a sign of the end of Zoroaster's millennium.

It was already noted that the succession of empires attested from Assyria to Greece is an Iranian perspective and would suit a reaction to the fall of the Persian Empire. It can be objected, however, that this could not have been combined with the metal scheme by the Persians, since it would reflect negatively on the Achaemenid dynasty.[209] However, the idea of inferiority appears not to be the primary intention of the imagery,

205.   Cf. Boyce, *HZ I*, 284–87, 291–92; Hintze, *Zamyād-Yašt*, 371.

206.   Boyce argues that Cyrus was assimilated to Hystaspes, as he ruled prior to Darius and Darius's father was known to be Hystaspes, explaining Cyrus's eclipse in later Iranian tradition. See Boyce, *HZ II*, 68–69.

207.   Timus, "Les 'Haskell Lectures'," 316–18.

208.   An older theory understood Cyrus as the original background behind the Kaus-Husraw legends (Yarshater, "Iranian National History," 447–48). If this Cyrus is understood as Cyrus the Younger, then perhaps one would wish to see the disappointed supporters of Cyrus occulting him, and their Anatolian descendants using it as part of their anti-Seleucid propaganda. This is, of course, nothing but pure speculation.

209.   Cf. Wiesehöfer, "Idea of the Succession," 393.

either in the Iranian context or in Daniel. First, in the *Zand-ī Wahman Yašn* the first three kings receive no censure; indeed, they are all positive. Only the last is negative—which is characterized as evil and demonic. Within the context of traditional Zoroastrian imagery, the metals utilized bear this out: metals were part of the good creation, belonging to the *Amǝša Spǝnta Xšaθra* ("Dominion"), particularly appropriate for a symbol of successive reigns.[210] Only the last, the "mixed" iron, carries a negative connotation. As Boyce has commented, the idea of mixed iron is an appropriate image for a period of the mixing of good and evil.[211] In this context, the choice to use metals to represent the eras fits perfectly a religious-political reflection on the fall of Darius's dynasty.[212]

In light of the above considerations, it is probable that the extant *Zand-ī Wahman Yašn* combines Sassanian reflections on combined religious and political fourfold schemes. The political version could have contained either dynasts, empires, or dynasts as representative of empires. It would have used the four metals, with only the last one carrying a negative connotation. The tree may or may not be original, but this does not affect the overall form of the concept. It is this version which must be compared to Dan 2.

Although hypothetical, the above reconstruction makes sense in the overall context of Iranian developments. It also very closely parallels the vision in Daniel. It shares a fourfold political scheme, four metals in declining order while only stressing the inferiority of the last, and an eschatological and theological overall interpretation of the significance. It even shares a fictive chronological setting *vis-à-vis* the vision, that is, occurring in the first era of the vision. It shares the detail of iron mixed with dust/clay and finds significance in this. Finally, both likely share a revelatory context. A difference between bronze and steel, remains, however. This may be less of a problem than it appears now. The sevenfold version of the *Zand*'s vision lists the metals as gold–silver–bronze–copper–lead–steel–mixed iron, with bronze in the third position. All that differs from the more well-known fourfold scheme is the insertion of copper–lead–steel. It seems probable that the underlying Persian scheme was, therefore, gold–silver–bronze–iron mixed with dust, and that, after

---

210. Cf. Boyce, *HZ I*, 204.

211. Boyce, "On the Antiquity," 71–72; idem, "Persian Sibyl," 73.

212. Perhaps understood as Hystaspes/Assyria, Artaxerxes/Media, Darius?/Persia, Alexander/Macedon. Note that several fake inscriptions purporting to be by Arsames and Ariaramnes but assigned to an Artaxerxes have been found in the region of Ecbatana. Listed as AmH and AsH in Kent, *Old Persian*, 116; cf. Schmitt, "Old Persian," 77, where he assigns it to Artaxerxes III.

it was expanded into a sevenfold system, the last metal of the longer version (steel) was retroactively placed into the first one by a scribe more familiar with the longer version. In other words, the second version simply inserted copper–lead–steel to reach seven rather than bronze–copper–lead.[213]

If the above reconstruction is valid, then it must be admitted that the Iranian vision is extremely similar to the dream in Dan 2, a connection between these two visions is probable, and, since the "mixed" detail finds support in an Iranian context, that the direction must be from Iran to Yehud.[214] This borrowing would have to fall into a relatively short time span, long enough after Alexander's conquest for the Iranian scheme to be developed but before either the marriage of Berenice and Antochus II or of Cleopatra and Antiochus III (from post-330 and before either 252 or 193).

Eschatology. A further element which must be considered is the appearance of eschatology in Dan 2. Several phrases within the passage can imply or carry an eschatology: v. 28, "what will happen at the end of days" (מה די להוא באחרית יומיא); vv. 29, 44, 45, "what would be hereafter" (מה די להוא אחרי דנה); v. 44, "it shall stand forever" (והיא תקום לעלמיא). However, the presence of eschatology in the passage is not solely dependent on these phrases as it is implied in the form of the vision itself. In this respect, there are several pertinent aspects to consider. First, the passage reuses the prophetic term "in the latter days" (באחרית הימים). Second, the eschatology would seem to be imported with the vision itself, as it appears to be of little interest to the Danielic author.[215] Third, the eschatology is a "deferred eschatology," quite distinct from the "imminent eschatology" of chs. 7–12.[216] Fourth, this passage plays an important role in the book of Daniel as a whole.

---

213. Hartman, "Datierung der junavestischen Apokalyptik," 62–63, seems to imply a similar understanding (albeit without discussion) in his listing of the *Zand*'s scheme as gold, silver, copper, iron.

214. Moses of Khoren (*History of Armenia* 1.26) relates a fourfold vision very similar to the ones in Dan 2 and 7, supposedly received by the Median king Astyages, whom he assimilates to *Aži Dahāka*. While the vision clearly alludes to both Daniel and Revelation, it seems to contain an older, pre-Christian core which the author was biblicizing. See Khorenats'i, *History of the Armenians*, 114–21. Cf. Gamkrelidze and Ivanov, *Indo-European*, 420–23; Russell, "Early Armenian Civilization," 34–36, cf. 28.

215. Collins, *Daniel*, 174–75; idem, "The Court-Tales in Daniel," 220–21.

216. See pp. 217–19, 224–25, below. Cf. Collins, *Encounters with Biblical Theology*, 134–36.

The use of the term באחרית יומיא and cognate terms deliberately recalls its use in the writing prophets. This term and the related יום יהוה are exegetical flash points, and can only be briefly discussed here. However, the distinction argued earlier—between future expectation and eschatology—is important for understanding the relation of the passage with previous Judaean traditions and with the subsequent Danielic (and other Judaean) tradition. The passage's imagery does appear to imply an event outside normal historical processes. The four metallic empires all hold in common the fact that they are metals, part of the same statue, and presumably made by man. This contrasts with the fifth empire, which is stone rather than metal, and "not by (human) hands" (די־לא בידין, v. 34). Using language of judgment, the stone destroys and then supplants the four. The historical sequence is not to be repeated.

The eschatology is implicit in the form of the vision itself; yet, since the overall context of the chapter entirely ignores the eschatology to focus on the deity's revelatory powers, it is most probable that the eschatology was inherited from the borrowed vision. The language of the Hebrew prophets was used by the author, but he (perhaps unwittingly) placed a new interpretation onto them.

According to the logic of the chapter, Nebuchadnezzar's dream depicts an *eschaton* which can be no less than three hundred years distant (since the length of the last kingdom is left unspecified). The fall of Babylon and three more kingdoms must first pass by. From the perspective of the author of the chapter, however, the *eschaton* is much closer, although it is still not urgent. He is living in the last kingdom, but sees no sign of the end. The end is to be expected, but more as the result of wisdom than urgency. For the later tradents, however, the scheme takes on utmost importance since they believe that the end is nigh. The shift between Dan 2 and Dan 7 is less the content of the eschatology, but the author's perceived proximity to the *eschaton*. The later authors fully accept the accuracy and import of the eschatology in Dan 2 which, for that author, was incidental to his interests.

From the above considerations, it becomes clear that borrowed ideas can have an impact beyond their borrower's intention and even their own time. If it can be accepted that the author of Dan 2 borrowed an Iranian vision to make a point about the revelatory power of YHWH, it also becomes apparent that an eschatological reinterpretation of traditions also "piggy-backed" its way in. This had major ramifications for the development of subsequent Judaean traditions and played a role in the appearance of the apocalypse.

Four Metallic Kingdoms with an Eschatology. The presence of relatively ignored features in Dan 2—the metals and the eschatology—make it probable that Daniel's source had already combined the ideas of the succession of empires, four metallic ages, and eschatology. Otherwise, one would have expected the author to have utilized them more in his interpretation. The only parallel adduced which combines all three of these ideas is the likely Hellenistic-period source of the *Zand-ī Wahman Yašn* (the presumed *Wahman Yašt*). There is no firm evidence for this source. That "apocalyptic" traditions and even documents existed seems to be confirmed by the references to the *Oracles of Hystaspes* (which must have had an Iranian element).

Conclusion

Although the unfortunate state of the Iranian evidence makes a definitive conclusion impossible, an Iranian source for the four-empire scheme in Daniel best accounts for the available evidence. Not only does it supply the details of the vision, it helps to explain the development of the Danielic worldview itself, one which evidently began well before the historical appearance of the genre apocalypse. Perhaps it can be suggested that the four-empire scheme, understood as Babylon–Media–Persia–Greece, could have appealed to the author of Dan 2 through offering a way of reconciling previous prophecy with historical outcomes. Colless argues that the reference to "Darius the Mede" is intended to show fulfillment of Jer 51:11.[217] However, in the context of a borrowed oracle in ch. 2, it can instead be suggested that the sequence offered the redactor a convenient method for reconciling these traditions—thus explaining its use as a structural device for the present book[218]—as well as encouraging the adoption (of the validated) eschatology.

Excursus: On the Watchers

In his paper in the Warfare in Ancient Israel session of SBL, Smith-Christopher proposed to speak of "an Imperial Gaze" which affects communities (and texts) in an exilic context.[219] By this phrase he wishes to denote the effects of imperial observation upon displaced and subject peoples in a parallel manner to the concept of the "male gaze." He further notes the language of "eyes" and "watching" in several of

217. Colless, "Cyrus the Persian as Darius the Mede," 118, 121.
218. Collins, "Court-Tales in Daniel," 229; idem, *Daniel*, 31–32.
219. Smith-Christopher, "Can We Speak of the Socio-Psychology of Exile in the Bible?" (paper presented at annual meeting of the Society of Biblical Literature, Boston, 24 November 2008), 6–10. The author is deeply grateful to Professor Smith-Christopher for sending him a copy of his presentation for consultation.

the exilic books, considering such language in the context of modern studies of refugees and of prisons. By extension, this insight offers a plausible context for the appearance of the term "Watcher" (עִיר, ἐγρήγορος) in Second Temple Judaism.

The term "Watcher" first appears in the *Book of Watchers* and Daniel, the origin and associations of which are obscure.[220] The early contexts of the term make clear that the עִירִין were understood as a class of angels which functioned in heaven, even if the *Book of Watchers*'s interest is largely on a group of them which fell. This can be seen, for example, in *1 En.* 20:1 and 22:6, where the term "Watcher" or the similar phrase "who watch" is used of the seven archangels in general and Raphael in particular,[221] as well as in the Danielic usage where it is consistently used in conjunction with קַדִּישׁ (4:10, 14, 20). The unfallen Watchers in both traditions appear in contexts of the pronouncement of judgment due to hubris: in Dan 4 the Watcher proclaims the decreed humbling of Nebuchadnezzar and in *1 En.* 9:1–10:15 (cf. 20:1–8), the archangels are in charge of executing punishment upon the Watchers, although the judgment's proclamation itself is given to Enoch. The duties of a Watcher, then, appear to be to survey the heavenly domain and to prosecute delinquents. Such a remit explains the Enochic tradition's choice of the Watcher-class for its fallen supernatural beings: it provides punch to the ironic twist (cf. *1 En.* 15:2),[222] perhaps even playing on the theme of theodicy so important to the tradition.[223] Such a motif can again be seen in both the Enochic and Danielic traditions in the series of seventy shepherds in the *Animal Apocalypse* (*1 En.* 89:59–90:25)[224] and in the four hubristic empires (Dan 2; 7), respectively. To this function the *Book of Watchers* adds an intercessory role on behalf of the righteous. The four "archangels" in *1 En.* 9 appeal, at least partially, for the sake of suffering humankind, and the intercessory role is explicitly charged to the Watchers in Enoch's judgment oracle against them (15:2).[225] The overall impression given of the Watchers, then, is of beings charged with monitoring both praiseworthy and damnable actions and relaying such information above.

A similar concept of "watchful" and prosecutorial heavenly beings appears in Zech 4, albeit without using the word "Watcher." In a somewhat obscure passage, Zechariah sees a seven-lamp lampstand, which the text identifies as "the eyes of the Lord, which range through the whole earth" (אֵלֶּה עֵינֵי יְהוָה הֵמָּה מְשׁוֹטְטִים בְּכָל־הָאָרֶץ, v. 10b). In the previous chapter, the Davidic scion is described as "a single stone

---

220. Cf. Fitzmyer, *The Genesis Apocryphon*, 80; Black, *The Book of Enoch*, 106–7; Montgomery, *Book of Daniel*, 232; Collins, *Daniel*, 224–26; Davidson, *Angels at Qumran*, 38–39, who notes their appearance, but does not give an origin; Wright, *Origin of Evil Spirits*, 20–21; Nickelsburg, *1 Enoch 1*, 140–41. Barr, "Aramaic–Greek Notes on the Book of Enoch (I)," 190, suggests that the term was already obscure to the translators of the LXX.

221. Nickelsburg, *1 Enoch 1*, 40, 42.

222. Nickelsburg and VanderKam, *1 Enoch*, 36.

223. That is, YHWH himself is not unjust, just his corrupted, delegated enforcers make it appear so.

224. Nickelsburg and VanderKam, *1 Enoch*, 129–34; cf. Tiller, *Animal Apocalypse*, 57–58.

225. Nickelsburg and VanderKam, *1 Enoch*, 36.

with seven eyes" (עַל־אֶבֶן אַחַת שִׁבְעָה עֵינָיִם, v. 9), possibly giving the concept a royal context.[226] The setting of these chapters is in the Persian period, and it is plausible to understand such a vision of surveillance as based upon contemporary structures.[227] From there, the apocalyptic literature lifts the idea into an angelic category. It is here suggested, then, that this term is an Aramaic reflex of the Achaemenid "eye of the king" and is a part of *1 Enoch*'s assimilation of YHWH's administration to that of the Great King.[228]

Both Herodotus and Aeschylus briefly mention the existence of a royal Persian appointment to which they refer as "(the king's) eye."[229] Although both of these mentions are in literary rather than historical contexts *per se*, the manner in which they are mentioned imply an office with which the expected audience was already familiar. Without providing historical information on the office, they arguably demonstrate its existence. Plutarch also mentions an office holder by name.[230] In his depiction of Cyrus *cum* philosopher-king, however, Xenophon denies the existence of such a singular informant.[231] The importance of this denial is questionable as its basis is not direct knowledge of the lack of such a system but is rather based on four postulates: (1) the benevolence of Cyrus; (2) subjects acting as if they are continually being watched; (3) people would avoid the company of a spy; and (4) a proverb "the king has many eyes and ears" (δὴ πολλὰ μὲν βασιλέως ὦτα, πολλοὶ δ' ὀφθαλμοὶ). Instead, Xenophon claims that a wide, voluntary system of informing was supported by the Great King's bestowal of gifts and honors. While Xenophon must be right in stressing the importance of gift-exchange,[232] this does not exclude the possibility of a formal position. Indeed, later in the same book Xenophon claims that the kings operated a regular system of satrapal oversight using commissioners, among whom he includes the king's brother, son, and eye.[233] The overseers, however, are charged not only with rooting out malfeasance but also with the reporting of excellence. Tuplin opines that there was an official "eye" who worked alongside an informal network of informants, combining the above Greek information.[234] If one recalls that such modern spying organizations as the CIA operate covertly while utilizing a

226. Tigchelaar, *The Prophets of Old*, 16–46; on p. 31 he finds a reference to royal surveillance probable in v. 10b.

227. Cf. 2 Chr 16:9, "the Eyes of the Lord range over the whole earth" (כִּי יהוה עֵינָיו מְשֹׁטְטוֹת בְּכָל־הָאָרֶץ), ensuring reward or punishment.

228. This connection was already put forward, albeit without discussion, by Teixidor, Review of *The Genesis Apocryphon of Qumran*, 634; Oppenheim, "The Eyes of the Lord," 173–80.

229. Aeschylus, *The Persians*, line 980 (*Aeschylus I: Plays*, 193); Herodotus I.114.2 (*Wars I–II*, 148–49).

230. Plutarch, *Artaxerxes* XII.1 (*Lives*, 153).

231. Xenophon, *Cyropaedia* VIII.ii.10–12 (*Cyr. V–VIII*, 337).

232. Briant, *From Cyrus to Alexander*, 302–4; Hintze, "'Do ut des'," 27–45. Nevertheless, it must be remembered that it is difficult to distinguish between gifts, tributes, and taxes. Cf. Sancisi-Weerdenburg, "Bāji," 23–34.

233. Xenophon, *Cyropaedia* VIII.vi.16 (*Cyr. V–VIII*, 417–19).

234. Tuplin, "The Administration of the Achaemenid Empire," 120; Oppenheim, "The Eyes of the Lord," 173.

variety of intelligence sources with appointed, known directors, then this scenario seems plausible. Although there are no certain Iranian sources for this system,[235] the testimony of the Greek sources and logic argue for its existence, importance, and (in)famy.

Most commentators derive the term "Watcher" itself from the Aramaic root עוּר, "to awake, to be watchful, to rouse," even if they express some dissatisfaction with it.[236] It seems, however, that the potential range of associations in the Hebrew and Aramaic cognate terms is slightly more broad, including protection, guarding, and going "hither and thither." If one is willing to accept the root as Hebrew rather than Aramaic, it may be interesting to note that Ps 35:23 uses the verb form of עיר to ask for vindication for wrongs done.[237] This is the same role imputed to the Watchers in their first literary appearances. Even if the etymology of עיר cannot be directly related to a Persian or Greek word,[238] the implied nuances as well as the context of its appearance in the early apocalyptic literature certainly recall the Greek authors' discussion of the "King's Eye."

If Smith-Christopher's musings on refugees and prisoners are brought into conjunction with this thought, the choice of the word עיר appears to be a logical development. Just as the temporal imperial power has those who watch out for its interests and vindicate wrongs, so the divine imperium has its own mechanism for vindication. This mechanism would, of course, be understood as largely to the benefit of Israel and one which ought to strike fear into YHWH's enemies. The importance of the oversight function also perhaps illuminates the paranoia and purity concerns of certain Judaean circles in the Second Temple period. If this interpretation is acceptable, it represents an instance of influence without linguistic borrowing. A Hebrew term was chosen to represent a heavenly form of Persian, earthly administration, once again melding the "political" and the "religious."

235.   Cf. Briant, *From Cyrus to Alexander*, 343–44; cf. Balcer, "The Athenian Episkopos and the Achaemenid 'King's Eye'," 252–63.

236.   Cf. Nickelsburg, *1 Enoch 1*, 140; *HAL*, 2:1946; Sokoloff, *A Dictionary of Jewish Babylonian Aramaic*, 860; BDB, 1105; Gesenius, *Hebrew and Chaldee Lexicon*, 615, 625; Black, *Book of Enoch*, 106.

237.   Gesenius, *Hebrew and Chaldee Lexicon*, 615.

238.   However, note the various attempts listed by Frye, *The History of Ancient Iran*, 108–9 n. 79. Shaked suggests that the Greek term "King's Eye" could be a corruption of an OP form for *wēnān-pad-tan šābistān*/רואי פני המלך, "(the one) who sees the king." See Shaked, "Two Judaeo-Iranian Contributions," 301–3.

Chapter 5

TEXTUAL ANALYSES:
ENOCHIC LITERATURE

The Book of Watchers *(1 Enoch 1–36)*

The *Book of Watchers* incorporates a diverse variety of material. While it clearly has links with the Torah, Gen 6 in particular, it also contains motifs and ideas for which Gen 6 cannot account. One of the more significant strands is the material collected around the character of the watcher Asael. A myth of forbidden knowledge which explains the existence of culture (*Kulturentstehungsmythos*) and a motif of binding until the eschaton are largely linked with Asael in the book. Both of these strands have parallels in Iranian materials. The character of Asael—even if not "original" to the Enochic tradition—gradually assumed greater notoriety until he became the paradigm of the rebellious angel (54:5; 55:4). The eschatology connected with the idea of a temporary binding is also foundational for much in the work as a whole; indeed, Nickelsburg has argued it is one of the unifying themes of the Ethiopic corpus.[1] Finding sources behind the character of Asael, therefore, will help illuminate the formation of the watcher tradition in both the *Book of Watchers* and in the later Enochic tradition. As Reed notes, the instruction motif is quite central to the form of the *Book of Watchers* as it is now known.[2]

The Motif of Forbidden Knowledge as a Kulturentstehungsmythos
In both the *Book of Watchers* (*1 En.* 8:1–3; 10:7–8; cf. 7:1; 9:6; 13:1–3) and the *Parables* (*1 En.* 69:6–8; cf. 52:8) appears a myth of the human acquisition of forbidden, arcane knowledge, more or less linked with a watcher called Asael or Azazel (עשאל),[3] which explains in some manner

1. Nickelsburg, *1 Enoch 1*, 37.
2. Reed, *Fallen Angels*, 30–34.
3. According to 4Q202, Col. II and 4Q204, Col. II (*DSSSE*, 405, 413). 4Q201 (Col. III), though, gives the homophonic variant עסאל (403).

the state or existence of culture/civilization as it is known (*Kultur-entstehungsmythos*).[4] Hanson argues that the Asael narrative arose from the comparison of the Šemiḥazah narrative in the *Book of Watchers* with the scapegoat given over to the demon Azazel in Lev 16,[5] but this explanation has not been accepted by all scholars.[6] Hanson's point of departure is the appearance of the name "Azazel" in some versions and later parts of *1 Enoch*. Since Lev 16 does not involve any form of rumination on the origins of culture, it is more plausible that the name "Asael" in *Enoch* was later assimilated to the Levitical form, rather than Lev 16 having served as the initial inspiration for the motif as a whole.[7] Indeed, while the Greek versions read "Azazel" here, the extant Aramaic clearly reads "Asael."[8] While Davies cites Milik in defense of seeing Azazel as simply a variant of Asael, the comment he cites is in the context of the later *3 Enoch*, not *1 Enoch* itself.[9] This does not defend an origin of the character from the Levitical ritual. Neither does an appeal to עזזאל in 4QEnGiants[a]; according to Milik, 4QEnGiants was part of a scroll which contained *1 En.* 1–36, 83–90, and 91–107,[10] a manuscript which he dates to 50–51 B.C.E.,[11] considerably later than the original writing of the *Book of Watchers*. Since the name עשאל is more or less homophonic with עזזאל, it is easy to see how the latter variant could be assimilated to עזאזל.[12] If Pinker is correct in claiming that the "scape-goat" in Lev 16 was simply a memory of YHWH's desert origins (as in the Song of Deborah),[13] then it seems most likely the Asael *cum* Azazel tradition evident in *1 Enoch* is the source of the later demonic interpretation of Lev 16 than the other way around. Without the name "Azazel"

---

4. Bhayro, *The Shemihazah and Asael Narrative*, 11, tries to argue that the "Asael Narrative" and the "Angelic Instruction Motif" were from two separate sources. It is unclear, however, what remains "Asaelic" after the removal of the instruction motif.

5. Hanson, "Rebellion in Heaven," 222.

6. Nickelsburg, *1 Enoch 1*, 191–93; Molenberg, "Shemihaza and Asael," 136–46; Newsom, "The Development of *1 Enoch* 6–19," 310–29. Cf. Collins, *The Apocalyptic Imagination*, 38–39; Wright, *The Origin of Evil Spirits*, 109–14.

7. Cf. Black, "The Twenty Angel Dekadarchs," 231–32; idem, *The Book of Enoch*, 121; Molenberg, "Shemihaza and Asael," 143 n. 34; Pinker, "A Goat to Go to Azazel," 1–23.

8. 4Q202, 4Q204.

9. Davies, "And Enoch Was Not," 99 n. 9. He cites Milik, *Books of Enoch*, 131.

10. Milik, *Books of Enoch*, 310.

11. Ibid., 300.

12. This is also the opinion of Dimant, "The 'Pesher on the Periods' (4Q180) and 4Q181," 94 n. 19. Cf. 4Q203 and the comment on the form "Azazel" in Stuckenbruck, *The Book of Giants from Qumran*, 77–79.

13. Pinker, "A Goat to Go to Azazel," 22, 24–25.

Lev 16 becomes unlinkable to the pericope, and the question of the primary source of inspiration for the Asael myth remains.

Scholars generally agree on separate provenances for the Šemiḥazah and Asael stories in the *Book of Watchers*[14] and that the Šemiḥazah motif is the older and the Asael material was interpolated later, even if the details of how this happened vary significantly.[15] This sequence is usually interpreted to indicate the relatively younger age of the Asael tradition, but there is no solid reason for this to be the case. Even if the Asael material was worked into a pre-existing version of the *Book of Watchers* (which itself is not wholly certain) there is no need to assume that the negative *Kulturentstehungsmythos* (of which Asael is the primary Enochic representative) had not been previously circulating in Second Temple Judaism or among scholarly circles; it merely shows that the author/redactor found it useful for his purposes at a later point in his writing.[16] The original inspiration for the motif could well be much older than the text of the *Book of Watchers* itself.[17] The priority of Šemiḥazah or Asael in the writing of the extant book, then, tells little about its original dating or provenance. Since the story in Gen 6:1–4 contains neither motif here considered related to Asael (neither *Kulturentstehungsmythos* nor binding), it is understood here to have been at least partially inspired by a secondary source.

The idea of a divine source for the arts of civilization (*Kulturentstehungsmythos*) is widespread in folklore.[18] Sometimes this impartation of knowledge to humanity has a positive connotation, sometimes a more negative one. Often, these accounts are inherently ambivalent; the information can be beneficial to humanity but against the will of the

14. Collins, "The Apocalyptic Technique," 97; Nickelsburg, *1 Enoch 1*, 165–72; Argall, *1 Enoch and Sirach*, 24–25; Tiller, *Animal Apocalypse*, 90.

15. Cf. Newsom, "Development of *1 Enoch* 6–19," 320–21; Hanson, "Rebellion in Heaven," 220–25; VanderKam, *Enoch and the Growth of an Apocalyptic Tradition*, 124; Nickelsburg, *1 Enoch 1*, 190–91. However, Molenberg, "Shemihaza and Asael," 146, argues that there are no separate traditions behind the strands. Barker, *The Older Testament*, 21–22, argues that the Asael material is older, royal cultic mythology that was replaced by Adam and Eve.

16. Cf. Reed, "Heavenly Ascent," 47–66; Collins, "Methodological Issues in the Study of 1 Enoch," 316.

17. Cf. Dimant, "Biography of Enoch," 25, who suggests the myth is an "ancient midrash." This hesitation, however, is not intended to agree with Barker and Davies, who argue that it is older than Genesis. On this issue, see Hendel, "Nephilim Were on the Earth," and Stuckenbruck, "Origin of Evil," in Auffarth and Stuckenbruck, eds., *The Fall of the Angels*, 11–34 and 87–118, respectively, especially 11, 88.

18. Cf. Thompson, *Motif-Index*, 1:123 (A541); Reed, "Heavenly Ascent," 49.

gods, or the information could itself be detrimental.[19] Indeed, the watcher myth itself appears to have been ambivalent in Judeo-Christian tradition as well.[20] Various aspects of the story extant in *1 Enoch* parallel several sources, so determining primary influence is difficult. Several versions of the myth known in the ancient Near East are analyzed below for resemblances to the *Book of Watcher*'s scenario.

Perhaps most familiar in the Occident is the Prometheus myth.[21] This myth is available in two primary versions, by Hesiod and by Aeschylus. Beyond a basic motif of forbidden, divinely sourced knowledge, Aeschylus's version offers more details than Hesiod's.[22] According to Aeschylus, Prometheus taught men not only the use of fire, but also astronomy, writing, pastoralism, horse-riding, sea-faring, medicine, astrology, dream interpretation, augury, extispicy, and metallurgy.[23] This patronage was an affront to Zeus, who had Prometheus bound to a rock as punishment. Rather than being a curse, the knowledge which Prometheus imparts humanity is described as raising them up from a beast-like condition to civilization.[24] This version of the myth parallels the accounts given in *1 Enoch* in certain arts (astronomy, astrology, various magic arts, writing, and metallurgy), but the context and significance are quite different. For *1 Enoch* the watchers' knowledge is the cause of humanity's miserable and sinful state, or at least contributes to it; in the Greek versions of the story, humanity's difficulty comes not from Prometheus's teachings, but Zeus's attempts to neutralize their benefit. Indeed, Aeschylus's Prometheus suffers wrongly due to the arbitrary authority of Zeus. This indictment of arbitrary authority is totally foreign to the theology of the *Book of Watchers*; *1 Enoch* focuses on the watchers' failure to fulfill their necessary and proper roles *vis-à-vis* humanity. The problem in view

19. See Figure 13.

20. Nickelsburg, *1 Enoch 1*, 196.

21. Parallel most favored. Tiller, *Animal Apocalypse*, 89; Nickelsburg, *1 Enoch 1*, 191–93; VanderKam, *Enoch and the Growth of an Apocalyptic Tradition*, 127; Hengel, *Judaism and Hellenism*, 190, who parallels both the Titans and Prometheus; Bremmer, "Remember the Titans!," 58–60; Wright, *Origin of Evil Spirits*, 115–18, who finds the parallel "attractive" (117); Hanson, "Rebellion in Heaven," 226–27, who is sympathetic to such a parallel, but ultimately prefers a "Semitic" prototype; Reed, *Fallen Angels*, 39–40, who favors a "pan-Greco-Roman" inspiration. Graf, "Mythical Production," 322, sees too many Greco-Roman parallels to choose a single source.

22. Hesiod only mentions Prometheus's stealing of fire and the (better) sacrificial portion and Zeus's reaction. See *Works and Days* §§42–59 and *Theogony* §§507–616 (Evelyn-White, ed., *Hesiod*, 5–7 and 117–25, respectively).

23. *Prometheus Bound*, lines 436–506 (Aeschylus, *Plays*, 255–59).

24. Cf. West, *The East Face*, 581–82.

is the fallen angels, not YHWH's rule; YHWH's judgment is consistently presented as a sign of his justice. Thus, in both intention and focus, the Prometheus myth shows little resemblance to the Asael myth.[25] In light of West's suggestion that the Greek versions of the myth are themselves dependent on an "oriental" prototype,[26] perhaps it is better to look farther east for parallels.

There are several Babylonian variations on the *Kulturentstehungs-mythos*. According to Berossus, a fish-man named Oannes (or Adapa) imparted all the knowledge of civilization to humans.[27] In this version, the knowledge is wholly beneficial—indeed necessary—for humankind and contains no overtones of being illicit. The version of the Adapa story Dalley offers could perhaps be read as slightly more ambiguous. While there is no condemnation of the knowledge *per se*, Adapa offends the gods with its improper use, and Ea must give further knowledge to protect Adapa before them. The story is quite fragmentary, and the final extant episode is ambiguous. It is unclear whether Ea means to protect or punish Adapa with the information which causes him to lose out on eternal life. As Dalley comments, the ambiguity may be intentional "and a crucial *double entendre* may attribute man's folly to a simple mis-understanding."[28] On the whole, however, there appears to be no con-demnation of Ea or Adapa in this version. The fragments presented by Pritchard, however, offer hints of a myth of forbidden knowledge. Fragment B, line 58, may imply that Ea imparted esoteric knowledge to Adapa along the lines of the Asael myth; Fragment D states that Adapa's actions had brought disease and death upon humankind.[29] Fragment D certainly preserves a serious story with more transgressive implications than the other versions of Adapa so far mentioned; however, the council of the gods is quick to rectify any harm caused by Adapa. Ultimately, Adapa's loss of immortality (something to which he had never held claim anyway) is the only misfortune to result.

West also briefly cites the myth of *Lahar and Ašnan* in connection with the Prometheus myth, but it does not offer a useful parallel to Asael.[30] According to Kramer's version, the story depicts the arts of agriculture and pastoralism as divine gifts, or, more correctly, considers

25. See a similar appraisal of the Prometheus parallel in Molenberg, "Shemihaza and Asael," 144.

26. West, *The East Face*, 295, 310–12, 579–85.

27. Burstein, *The Babyloniaca of Berossus*, 13–14.

28. See Dalley, *Myths from Mesopotamia*, 182–88. Comment from 183.

29. *ANET*, 102 and 102–3. Fragment B, line 58 reads, "of the earth the plan disclosed."

30. West, *The East Face*, 582.

their existence to be dependent on the creation of patron deities for each. The myth contains no reference to nor discussion of humanity, forbidden knowledge, nor even the receipt of knowledge.[31] Even if many aspects of Enoch's character parallel Babylonian prototypes,[32] the negative *Kulturentstehungsmythos* motif does not seem to have an adequate Babylonian parallel extant.

The *Kulturentstehungsmythos* appears twice in Iranian traditions, one linked directly to sin, the other with the loss of a golden age. The first version is the story of the first human couple, Mašye and Mašyane (also called Mašya and Mašyānag). The second story deals with the reign and fall of the primaeval king, Yima.

The *Greater Bundahišn* 14.11–34//*Shorter Bundahišn* 15.19–21 describes how, prompted by demons, Mašye and Mašyane discover fire, kill animals, invent metallurgy, make weapons, make clothes, and worship demons.[33] Two things are notable in this story: that the actions are committed by humans on the prompting of evil spirits, and that the couple is described as creating both good things (fire, ritual) and negative things. The story thus also has an ambiguous element; while the author of the *Bundahišn* clearly viewed the couple as inveterate sinners,[34] they also put into place many of the things needed for the functioning of civilization.[35] That the author of the passage deemed them sinners is seen by the use of the term "to lie" (Pahlavi *druxtan, drōz-*, OP *duruj-*). This version of the motif represents a more moralizing reflex than the Prometheus or Adapa versions. At least some of the knowledge is itself wicked, and the protagonists are considered to be held guilty.

The *Kulturentstehungsmythos* also appears in Iran in the stories around the primeval king Yima. The character of Yima (Yama) is Indo-Iranian,

31. Kramer, *The Sumerians*, 220–22.

32. See the explorations in Borger, "Die Beschwörungsserie Bīt mēseri und die Himmelfahrt Henochs," 183–96; Kvanvig, *Roots of Apocalyptic*, particularly 538–613; Orlov, *The Enoch-Metatron Tradition*, 343–54; Collins, "The Sage in the Apocalyptic and Pseudepigraphic Literature," 343–54; VanderKam, *Enoch and the Growth of an Apocalyptic Tradition*, but note the (convincing) critique of the *baru* parallel in Bedenbender, "Jewish Apocalypticism: A Child of Mantic Wisdom?," 189–96. It must be noted in this context that the parallel between Enmenduranki and Enoch is much more plausible than the old appeal to *Gayomarətan* (e.g. Lincoln, "The Indo-European Myth of Creation," 125).

33. *Pahlavi Texts I*, 54–57. Anklesaria, *Zand-Ākāsīh*, 128–33. Cf. Zaehner, *The Teachings of the Magi*, 71.

34. See *Gr. Bund.* 14.16 (Anklesaria, *Zand-Ākāsīh*, 130–31); *Sh. Bund.* 15.9 (*Pahlavi Texts I*, 55).

35. Cf. Boyce, *HZ I*, 96–97, 140.

although his roles in Iran and in India were quite different.[36] In the *Gāthās*, Yima only appears as having sinned, with no explanation of what the sin entailed.[37] In the *Zāmyād Yašt*, however, he appears as a king of a golden age who lost his *Xᵛarənah* ("royal or heroic glory or fortune") through lying.[38] In the *Zāmyād Yašt* version, Yima forces the demons to impart to humankind the positive arts of civilization, listed largely in vague terms (19.32). Yima is able to do this because of his *Xᵛarənah*. His subsequent fall is due to pride at his achievements, which caused him to lie (19.33). Thus, in this version, the acquisition of knowledge was itself a beneficial thing; the sin was the subsequent hubris (lying and pride) rather than an effect of the knowledge.

The *Shahnameh* of Firdausī explicitly links the *Kulturentstehungsmythos* with Yima. Firdausī credits Yima with the discovery of metallurgy, weapons and warcraft; of clothing, castes, and jewelry; of perfume and medicine, and with forcing the demons to serve rather than harm humans. All of his achievements cause him to become prideful and claim to be god, whereupon he loses his glory and fortune.[39] Again, the knowledge is of supernatural origin but is of itself a good thing and reflective of the power of Yima's *Xᵛarənah*; it does not cause Yima's later misfortune. Firdausī's version appears to be largely an expansion of the myth as it is visible in the *Zāmyād Yašt*. It is worth noting in this context, however, the statement in the *Aogəmadaēcā* §§91–93 that Tahmōrup, son of Vīvanghān, acquired "seven kinds of writing and penmanship from Angra Mainyu."[40] The deed is left unevaluated; interestingly, *1 En.* 69:8–11 also attributes diabolic teaching to the creation of writing. The *Aogəmadaēcā* is a Parthian-period liturgy which assembled, translated, and commented on now lost Avestan verses,[41] so a diabolic culture myth certainly did circulate in Iran prior to *1 Enoch*. Yima is also described as the "son of Vīvanghān," so it is possible that the diabolic inspiration comes from another *Kulturentstehungsmythos* tradition associated with Yima. In any case, several versions of the motif of forbidden knowledge circulated in Iran, although attached to a variety of figures;

---

36. For a useful collection of the related Indo-European myths, see Lincoln, "The Lord of the Dead," 224–41. Pages 233–35 note where the Iranian myths depart from the remainder.

37. *Yasna* 32.8 (Insler, *The Gathas of Zarathustra*, 47; *Zend-Avesta III*, 61).

38. *Yašt* 19.30–34 (Hintze, *Zamyād-Yašt*, 173–95; *Zend-Avesta II*, 293).

39. Firdausī, *Shāhnāmeh*, 1:131–35. Note the remarkable similarity of this story to the Rabbinic traditions of Solomon (see Ginzberg, *Legends of the Jews*, 4:123–76).

40. See Jamasp Asa, *Aogəmadaēcā*, 82.

41. Ibid., 9–10.

Boyce sees an alternate protagonist with a similar role in the character of Haošiiaŋha/Hōšang, and she suggests different heroes for different tribes.[42] Haošiiaŋha appears in *Yašts* 5.21–2; 9.3–4; 15.7–8; 17.24–25, the *Dēnkard* 9.13.5, the *Aogəmadaēcā* §§88–89, and in the *Shahnameh* 1.17–20.[43] In all of these texts he is depicted as a primaeval king who defeated demons. In this role he parallels Yima, and the *Zāmyād Yašt* and the *Dēnkard* even have him usurp Yima's role as the first king. However, there seems to be no evidence for a negative *Kulturentstehungsmythos* being connected with Haošiiaŋha. If his myths were associated with royal ideology as Shahbazi suggests, then it seems highly unlikely they were negative in any case.[44] Carnoy, citing *Yašt* 17.25, suggests it was Yima who was the original giver of forbidden knowledge rather than Mašya and Mašyānag.[45] If this were true, then the dating for the sinful *Kulturentstehungsmythos* would be pushed back comfortably into the Achaemenid period; however, the present writer cannot see how such an interpretation can be culled from that text.

Of the two Persian versions, the myth of Mašya and Mašyānag parallels the Asael story in *1 Enoch* more closely than the myths associated with Yima. The focus of the story in *1 Enoch*, however, has shifted from the human protagonists to their demonic inspirations, which is consonant with the Enochic traditions' preoccupation with angelic figures in general. Unfortunately, this parallel cannot as comfortably be considered to be an older survival as the Yima myths can; indeed, Boyce describes Mašya and Mašyānag as a later elaboration.[46] However, one could wish to see an Indo-European reflex in the story of the first human couple, since a story also appears in the Norse text, the *Vǫluspå*.[47] The first human pair, Askr and Embla, are there said to be fashioned from two pieces of driftwood. While it is interesting that this first couple is fashioned from plant material (the *Bundahišn* describes Mašya and Mašyānag's birth from a rhubarb stalk), the association between humanity and driftwood in particular appears to be well situated in Norse tradition itself.[48] One may even wish to see the allusion to the ash tree (*askr*) as Indo-European as it also appears in Hesiod, but it does not

42. See Boyce, *HZ I*, 104; cf. Wikander, *Vayu*, 51–52, 61; Minorsky, *Iranica: Twenty Articles*, 270.

43. See *Zend-Avesta II*, 58–59, 111, 251, 276–77; *Pahlavi Texts IV*, 26–27; Jamasp Asa, *Aogəmadaēcā*, 81; Firdausī, *Shāhnāma*, 1:122–24.

44. Shahbazi, "Hōšang," 491–92.

45. Carnoy, "Iranian Mythology," 296–310.

46. Boyce, *HZ I*, 96–97.

47. Dronke, *Mythological Poems*, 11.

48. Ibid., 122–23.

appear in Iran.[49] Additionally, the manuscript which preserves the *Vǫluspǎ* (the Codex Regius) dates to 1270 C.E.,[50] even later than the manuscripts of the *Bundahišn*. The possibility that the Scandinavian story was influenced by the biblical story of Adam and Eve cannot be eliminated, and while Ström and Hasenfratz may be convinced of the Indo-European origins of both the *Bundahišn* and the *Vǫluspǎ* due to parallels,[51] the parallel of interest here—a negative *Kulturentstehungs-mythos*—is not found in Scandinavia. Thus, despite the excellent parallels with the story in *1 Enoch*, it seems that the negative *Kulturentstehungsmythos* would need to have been associated with characters other than Mašya and Mašyānag to be viable as a source for the *Book of Watchers*.[52]

It is possible that the authors of this story in its Enochic version adapted it from an Iranian source for their own ends. It is also possible they adapted a version of the Prometheus myth, either from Greek sources, or from a Hellenized Persian source (e.g. Commagene). The scant hints make a definitive identification impossible, but an Iranian source for the diabolical *Kulturentstehungsmythos* is at least as likely as a Greek or Babylonian one. Sadly, only vague hints of the Iranian myth survive for comparison. It may be worth noting that Aeschylus's version of Prometheus appears during the Persian period. It has been suggested that the Greeks were quite open to Persian ideas until Darius's or Xerxes's invasions.[53] If this is true, perhaps the choice between a Persian source and a Greek source is, in the final analysis, no real choice at all.

49. See Evelyn-White, ed., *Hesiod*, 13; Dronke, *Mythological Poems*, 122–23.

50. Dronke, *Mythological Poems*, xi.

51. Ström, "Indogermanisches in der Völuspá," 167–208; he even claims influence of the trope on Daniel via Persia, see 197–98; Hasenfratz, "Iran und der Dualismus," 44–45, argues that the parallel proves antiquity; cf. Hultgård, "Persian Apocalypticism," 69. Nielsen, "'*Hver tíðendi eru at segja frá um ragnarøkr?*'," 61–77, argues that the story itself is indeed of ancient Scandinavian origin, even if the current form has a Christian frame.

52. Chenciner, *Daghestan: Tradition and Survival*, 40, 187, cites a "cylindrical bronze" from Daghestan which he claims depicts Mašya and Mašyānag, but unfortunately does not give reference information for the artifact.

53. Cf. Boyce, *HZ II*, 153–54; Dandamaev and Lukonin, *Culture and Social Institutions*, 297, 326; Duchesne-Guillemin, *The Western Response to Zoroaster*, 70; idem, "Fire in Iran and in Greece," 198–266; idem, "Heraclitus and Iran," 34–49; West, *Early Greek Philosophy and the Orient*, 203, suggests an "active period" of interest in things Persian until Xerxes's invasion, though his later work does not mention a definite end; see idem, *The East Face*. However, Kingsley, "Meetings with Magi," 188, rejects an "ending" of Persian influence caused by the Greco-Persian wars.

	Asael Myth	Prometheus (Aeschylus)	Mašye and Mašyane	Adapa (ANET)	Yima (Yašt 19)
Types of knowledge acquired	Weapons, metallurgy, cosmetics, sorcery, astrology, "iniquity"	Fire, astronomy, writing, pastoralism, horse-riding, sea-faring, medicine, astrology, dream interpretation, augury, extispicy, metallurgy	Fire, (bad) sacrifice, clothing, well-making, metallurgy, weapons, cannibalism	Not extant: wisdom not including immortality	prosperity, reputation, flock and cattle, satisfaction and honor
Morality of knowledge	Morally evil	Morally neutral	Some neutral, some evil	Morally neutral	Morally neutral, morally good
Divine sanction	Against will of YHWH	Against will of Zeus	According to the will of the *Daēuuas* (and by implication, against will of Ahura Mazda)	By Ea, unknown to divine council	Against will of *Daēuuas*; by implication, according to will of Ahura Mazda
Giver of knowledge	Asael (Watcher)	Prometheus (Titan/god)	The *Daēuuas* (demons)/Mašye and Mašyane	Ea (god)/Adapa	The *Daēuuas* (demons)/Yima
Results of knowledge for humanity	War, death, sin, birth of the Giants	Civilization	Civilization; both good and bad ritual; increase in demons	Civilization; temporary illnesses	No frost, heat, no death or age, envy
Results of knowledge for the Giver	Bound in abyss until final judgment	Bound to rock and liver eaten (Prometheus)	Souls in hell (Mašya and Mašyānag)	Loss of immortality (Adapa)	Became prideful and lied (Yima)

Figure 13. Kulturentstehungsmythos *Table*

None of the parallels discussed here offer an exact match to the Asael version of the myth. However, each is probably but single reflexes of a variety of oral variations on the *Kulturentstehungsmythos*. Ancient Near Eastern scribes would have come into contact with a variety of oral traditions and most likely would have also known some of the written, scribal traditions. A scribe who wished to use the *Kulturentstehungsmythos* most likely had an eclectic mix of ideas available for use, stemming from around the ancient Near East. One should perhaps posit a scholarly *koine* or stock of tropes from which the scribe could adapt or borrow. In this *koine* it is just as likely that the authors of *1 Enoch* knew the current Persian variations on the myth as the Greek or Babylonian ones.[54]

Excursus: The Šemiḥazah Myth

Most scholars consider the Šemiḥazah myth to be an interpretation of Gen 5–6,[55] which saw in the neutral account in Genesis a myth of the origins of evil. It is impossible to know the extent of the tradition which was referenced/excerpted by Gen 6:1–4 or how much of said tradition survived orally, nor, therefore, how much of the interpretation in *Book of Watchers* is original to the Enochic tradition or was merely an elaboration of lost oral material. It is highly likely the Torah's version was known to them, even if other versions were known as well. Since the story in *1 Enoch* adds narrative causality where there is none stated in Genesis, it is most probable that whomever created the Šemiḥazah myth in the *Book of Watchers* interpreted Gen 6:1–4 negatively as an explanation for the existence of demons as part of their dualistic theodicy. Such an interpretative narrative could have been inspired by a parallel story. It is worth, then, noting a parallel story which may have inspired such a reading of the Pentateuchal account.

An Avestan text, the *Zāmyād Yašt* §§80–81, records a myth of the demonic subjugation of women (and the demons' subsequent defeat by Zarathuštra). The passage is quoted below in a recent translation.

[80]Before that the *daēuuas* would run about in full view.
(Their) pleasures would *take place in full view.

---

54. Cf. Hendel, "The Nephilim were on the Earth," 32, refers to "rich circulation of oral traditions." If the suggestion that YHWH was originally a god of metallurgy is true, this would raise interesting questions for the negative view of that art in *1 Enoch*: Amzallag, "Yahweh, the Canaanite God of Metallurgy?," 387–404.

55. Cf. Nickelsburg, *1 Enoch 1*, 166–67; the majority of scholars in Boccaccini, ed., *Henoch: The Origins of Enochic Judaism*, especially Stuckenbruck ("Genesis 6.1–4," 99–106) would agree; see also Collins, *The Apocalyptic Imagination*, 38–39; VanderKam, "Biblical Interpretation in *1 Enoch* and *Jubilees*," 103–7; Alexander, "Enochic Literature and the Bible," 64–65; Stuckenbruck, "The Origin of Evil in Jewish Apocalyptic Tradition," 87–118. A few scholars reverse the direction of influence. See Milik, *The Books of Enoch*, 31; Barker, *The Older Testament*, 19–20; Davies, "And Enoch was Not," 103, 106.

In full view they would drag off
The women from the humans.
Then the *daēuuas* would by force debase
Them, as they plaintively wept.
[81]Then a single *Ahuna vairiia* of yours (=Ahura Mazda's),
Which orderly Zarathustra chanted...
Drove all the *daēuuas* underground
Depriving them of sacrifices and hymns.[56]

This brief passage describes how Zoroaster ejected the *Daēuuas* from earth with a single recitation of the most sacred Zoroastrian formula, the *Ahuna Vairiia* prayer (= *Yasna* 27.13).[57] The detail of primary interest here is the habitual activity attributed to the *Daēuuas* while on the earth: the violation of human women. This aspect also appears in the version told by Moses of Khoren.[58] Hintze notes that the language of §81 inverts the traditional Indo-European epithets of the *Daēuuas* to underscore their demonic/non-Ahuranic attributes.[59] This suggests a context in which some still viewed the daevic gods as valid deities. It is interesting that illicit relations with human women are discussed in the context of the demonization of heavenly figures; this is largely the same context as the Šemiḥazah narrative in *1 Enoch* (not all Watchers are fallen—*1 En.* 20:1–8 mention the "holy angels who watch").[60] But, contrary to the *Book of Watchers*, the purpose of the *Zāmyād Yašt* passage is not to explain the current situation as under demonic influence, but to explain why the current situation is *not* under demonic influence.

Perhaps, however, in the first Enochic version this is not so much of a difference. Chapters 12–16 describe how the flood will destroy the giants, but their spirits will proceed from them and still inflict humanity. Yet in the first version (chs. 6–11) the watchers themselves were bound while their progeny destroyed.[61] It is afterwards that there is an admission of their continued presence on earth. The Zoroastrian material also does not deny the current presence of evil activity on the earth, though it implies that Zoroaster curtailed the brazenness of their activity. Thus the basic outline is still similar in form—divine beings ravishing human woman are defeated, but still cause havoc in the human world. The *Zāmyād* text, however, makes no mention of giants as progeny. Ultimately, while this passage cannot be used to argue direct influence, it is still suggestive: such a story could plausibly interact with the re-interpretation of Gen 6:1–4.

---

56. Skjærvø, "The Antiquity of Old Avestan," 24. See also Humbach and Ichapora, *Zamyād Yasht*, 54–55; Hintze, *Zamyād-Yašt*, 341, 344.

57. This prayer is notoriously difficult to translate. A translation is available in *Zend-Avesta III*, 281; Humbach et al., *Gāthās of Zarathushtra*, 115. Insler does not include *Yasna* 27 in his edition. Cf. Brunner, "Ahunwar," 683.

58. Moses of Khoren, *History of Armenia* 1.24, 27 (Khorenats'i, *History of the Armenians*, 114, 117).

59. Hintze, *Zamyād-Yašt*, 345.

60. Nickelsburg and VanderKam, *1 Enoch*, 40. Cf. Excursus: On the Watchers (pp. 171–74, above).

61. Cf. Reed, "Heavenly Ascent," 25; Nickelsburg, *1 Enoch 1*, 7.

The Binding of Azazel (Asael) (10:4–8, 11–14; cf. 54:1–6)
In 10:4–8 Raphael is commissioned to bind and imprison Asael until
the final judgment in "the wilderness that is in Doudael (Δουδαήλ/
duda'el)."[62] The Enochic author has Asael (and vv. 11–12 Šemiḥazah and
the other watchers) confined until the eschatological judgment rather
than receiving immediate judgment or destruction like the giants and
wicked humanity (10:9–10, 15). The force of this rhetoric indicates an
emphasis by the author on the coming judgment rather than the one
ostensibly in focus in the passage (the flood). The text describes Asael's
"binding" (δέω; Aramaic not extant) and imprisonment in a pit. Nickelsburg suggests that "bind" (אסר) is a semi-technical term for exorcism.[63]
This is possibly an intended connotation, but the eschatological context
suggests that there could be more to the idea; Asael is not merely exor-
cised, but is held for future punishment. With the possible exceptions of
the "Isaian Apocalypse" and Job 7:12, this motif of *binding* until delayed
punishment does not appear in the Hebrew Bible; typological enemies
are *slain*. This is also true of the primeval enemy *par excellence*, the
dragon.

Nickelsburg parallels the binding motif with the Prometheus myth.[64]
This parallel is not compelling; in addition to the general unsuitability
argued above, Prometheus's fate lacks both the permanence and the
eschatological aspects of Asael's binding. Prometheus is promised hope
of salvation from his punishment; indeed, Hesiod indicates that Heracles

---

62. There is no extant Aramaic. See the discussion in Nickelsburg, *1 Enoch 1*,
215, 220–23; for the reading Δουδαήλ, see 217. Doudael could be read as the Greek
rendering of דוראל ("dwelling of 'El") which misread the resh as a dalet, or perhaps
it could be understood as a rendering of a Hebrew דודיאל ("cooking pot of 'El,"
supported by Black, *Book of Enoch*, 134; Knibb, *The Ethiopic Book of Enoch*, 2:87).

Doudael could also be derived from דודאי, "mandrakes." The mandrake had magi-
cal associations, including exorcism (Josephus, *War* VII.6.3 [*Josephus III*, 556–59]).

Positing an etymology or popular etymology related to mandrakes behind Doudael
offers a sarcastic pun on Asael's teachings: while Asael taught humankind forbidden
knowledge, the forbidden sorcery and divination associated with him would be used
against him, "exorcising" him from the face of the earth. While 8:3 technically
credits Šemiḥazah and Hermoni with teaching sorcery to people, 10:8 and 13:2
blames all of the illicit knowledge on Asael's agency, not just the metallurgic skills
listed in 8:1. Considering the link between the name of the angel Raphael to his
duties of healing in this section (Nickelsburg, *1 Enoch 1*, 221), it is reasonable to
expect the name given to the site of the internment to carry similar thematic import.

63. Nickelsburg, *1 Enoch 1*, 221. Cf. de Moor, *An Anthology of Religious Texts
from Ugarit*, 177 n. 14.

64. Nickelsburg, *1 Enoch 1*, 221–22.

ended Prometheus's binding.[65] Further, if there is an eschatological link to the Prometheus myth at all, it is to the fall of Zeus himself (line 940), not to a future judgment of Prometheus![66] Certainly a threat to YHWH's role is not intended by the Enochic author. The direct link with eschatology which is so present in the myth's context in *1 Enoch* makes a parallel which also shares this concern desirable. The Iranian myth of the binding of Aži Dahāka parallels the binding, a future release to judgment, the theme of violence, and the motif of illicit marriage in the Asael narrative. The myth of the bound arch-demon present here (and recurring in Revelation) is best explained by a post-exilic combination of the Ugaritic/Canaanite *Chaoskampf* motif and the Iranian legends of Aži Dahāka.

In Iran an eschatological myth of a demon-dragon bound until the last days developed around the character Aži Dahāka. Persian sources locate Dahāka's prison inside Mount Damavand (*Qolleh-ye Damavand*), an inactive volcano 42 miles northeast of modern Teheran. This mountain is well-known not only for being the highest mountain in the Near East, but for its volcanic fissures which leave sulfuric deposits and generate warm springs at the foot. Aži Dahāka is consistently portrayed as a monstrous dragon (*ažay*),[67] although the details varied over time. *Yašt* 19 describes him as having three-mouths, three heads, six eyes, one thousand *druj*-like senses, and having been created by Angra Mainyu to destroy the good creation. Significantly, he shares the epithet "of bad religion/conscience" (*duždaēna*) with Angra Mainyu in the Avesta.[68] He was later anthropomorphized into a human king (albeit it with serpents growing from each shoulder), yet Firdausī still periodically describes Dahāka as a dragon.[69] An appeal to this myth can answer several problems in Second Temple Judaism: it not only locates a source for the binding myth, but it also helps explain the rise of eschatology and the re-emergence of Canaanite myth in the post-exilic period.

65. Aeschylus, *Prometheus Bound*, line 1025 (*Plays*, 309); Evelyn-White, ed., *Hesiod*, 117 (lines 520ff.).

66. Aeschylus, *Plays*, 301.

67. Bartholomae, *Altiraninisches Wörterbuch*, 266, gives "Schlange, Schlang enähnliches Untier, Drache."

68. Gray, "A List of the Divine and Demonic Epithets," 110.

69. Firdausī, *Shāhnāma*, 1:139, 146, 155. The anthropomorphizing of Aži Dahāka predates Firdausī, however. It is evident in the demythologizing versions given by Moses of Khoren, *History of Armenia* I.24–30 and the interlude between books I and II (Khorenats'i, *History of the Armenians*, 114–21, 126–28). Moses dates to the eighth century C.E. (cf. 59–60).

The motif of dragon combat is wide-spread in world mythology generally and in Semitic and Indo-European mythologies in particular.[70] In Biblical Studies, much has been made of the fight against the "chaos-monster"/dragon in Ugaritic and biblical materials. Yet in these myths the context is creation, and the emphasis is on the destruction of the monster—the dragon (לויתן, תנין) is often described as *slain* (הרג), a description which precludes a future judgment (see Isa 51:9; Pss 44:18–19; 74:12–17; 89:9–13; Ezek 29:3; 32:2; Job 7:12; 26:5–14). The Ugaritic material is very fragmented, but it appears that there were *two* combat stories: a "recurrent" battle between Ba'al, Mot, and Yam, and a primeval slaying of Leviathan and his dragonic compatriots by either Ba'al or Anat.[71] Both Anat and Ba'al claim to have killed Leviathan, but the Ugaritic tablets describe how Yam is held captive and how Ba'al was unable to overcome Mot.[72] With the possible exceptions of Isa 27:1 and Job 7:12, the biblical material either characterizes the dragon as killed at creation, uses it as a metaphor for historic enemies, or affirms the creature's status as part of YHWH's creation.[73] The primeval defeat is used by biblical authors as evidence of YHWH's kingship and as a guarantee that he is able to defeat the audience's current enemies as well.[74] A needed future defeat would undercut the rhetorical force of such a claim. Indeed, this usage is in contrast with Ba'al at Ugarit, who requires aid in his battles.[75]

In Indo-European tradition, the most prominent aspect of the dragon-battle is either one of primeval defeat or of the initiation of a hero.[76] This reflex is well attested in Iranian literature through all time periods, with the motif using several heroes and dragons as antagonists.[77] The most common in Iran appears to have been of Θraētaona's defeat of the monster Aži Dahāka, to which allusions are found in many Avestan passages (*Yašts* 5.29–35; 19.14, 37, 92; 14.40; 15.23–25; 17.34; *Yasna* 9.7–11).[78]

---

70. Watkins, *How to Kill a Dragon*. Cf. Thompson, *Motif-Index*, 1:191 (A1070).

71. Day, *God's Conflict*, 12–15, 24–25; Watson, *Chaos Uncreated*, 387.

72. For Leviathan's death, see de Moor, *Religious Texts from Ugarit*, 11, 69–71; for Yam and Mot, 38–42, 93–99, 131–34.

73. E.g. Job 3:8; 41:1–34; Pss 77:17–21; 93:3; Dan 7; Nah 1:4; Hab 3:8–9. See Day, *God's Conflict*, 22, 39–40, 72–75; Watson, *Chaos Uncreated*, 389, 392.

74. Day, *God's Conflict*, 22.

75. Cf. de Moor, *Religious Texts from Ugarit*, 95–99, 131–34.

76. Watkins, *How to Kill a Dragon*, 303.

77. Cf. Bagheri, "Prince Mohammad, Fereydun, Thraētaona, and Trita Āptya," 199–201.

78. See *Zend-Avesta II*, 60–62, 113, 242, 254–55, 277, 294, 307; *Zend-Avesta, III*, 233–34. Wikander, *Vayu*, 163–71, however, saw competing eastern and western dragon-slaying heroes.

The typical allusion refers to his "smiting" (*jan*)[79] of Aži Dahāka. Particu-larly interesting is the brief notice of a myth of Aži Dahāka's illicit marriage, which does not occur in the other Indo-European versions of the motif.[80] In *Yašts* 9.14, 5.34, 15.24, and 17.34 Θraētaona prays to a deity to help him free the two women from the dragon's control;[81] the motif of the women, however, is not further elaborated in the Avesta.

This (past) reflex of the Θraētaona/Dahāka myth stands solidly in Indo-European tradition and parallels the Babylonian and Ugaritic primeval conflicts, but it is not the only interpretation available in the sources. The Pahlavi works mention the myth that while Θraētaona *defeated* Dahāka, he was unable to *kill* him due to the defilement of the earth caused thereby. Instead, Θraētaona imprisoned the monster. This is recounted in the *Dēnkard, Book IX*, a late Pahlavi text which sum-marizes the contents of (now) lost Avestan books.[82] Further, the *Dēnkard* recounts that at the eschaton Aži Dahāka will be released upon the earth and the slumbering hero Kərəsāspa will be awakened to finally kill him.[83] The *Bundahišn*, the *Mēnōg-ī Xrad*, and the *Zand-ī Wahman Yašn* also attest the story of Θraētaona's temporary binding of Aži Dahāka to a mountain and Kərəsāspa's final victory over him at the end of history (at *Frašōkərəti*, i.e., the *eschaton*).[84] These Pahlavi texts are late, but there are hints that this interpretation is significantly older than the Pahlavi documents.

Yašt 13.61 (ca. 800–400 B.C.E.)[85] records that Kərəsāspa is asleep and watched over by the *frauuašīs*, implying his later reawakening.[86] Kərəsāspa's association with dragon-slaying is well-attested in the Avesta, although in connection with dragons other than Aži Dahāka.[87]

---

79. Bartholomae, *Altiraniranisches Wörterbuch*, 605, for the forms *jatay, jaidyai, jantay*.

80. Watkins, *How to Kill a Dragon*, 464–68, where the illicit marriage replaces stolen cattle.

81. The *Aban, Goš, Ram*, and *Aši Yašt*s, respectively. See *Zend-Avesta II*, 61–62, 113, 254–55, 277.

82. *Dēnkard* 9.21.8–11 (*Pahlavi Texts IV*, 214).

83. *Dēnkard* 9.15.2 (*Pahlavi Texts IV*, 198–99).

84. In Pahlavi, Θraētaona is known as Fredun, Kərəsāspa as Sam or Garshasp, and Aži Dahāka as Bewaras. See *Sh. Bund.* 12.31 and 29.9 (*Pahlavi Texts I*, 40, 119); *Gr. Bund.* 29.7–9 (Anklesaria, *Zand-Ākāsīh*, 255); *Mēnōg-ī Xrad* 27.38–39 (*Pahlavi Texts III*, 61); *ZBYt* 3.54–62; 9.14–22 (*Pahlavi Texts I*, 233–35; Anklesaria, *Zand-i Vohûman Yasn*, 115, 127–28). Cf. Firdausī, *Shāhnāma*, 135–40, 145–73. Cf. Boyce, *HZ I*, 103; Boyce and Grenet, *HZ III*, 420–21.

85. Malandra, *The Fravaši Yašt*, 1–7; Skjærvø, "Avestan Quotations," 7.

86. *Zend-Avesta II*, 194–95; Skjærvø, "Aždahā I," 196.

87. See *Yasna* 9.7–11 (*Zend-Avesta III*, 233–34).

This indicates an antiquity for the sleeping hero motif, but not for the victim itself. Skjærvø suggests that the bound-until-the-*eschaton*-monster may be of Indo-European antiquity due to the similarity with the Fenris-wolf myth in Scandinavia, although other scholars see independent parallel developments.[88] The important question is the dating of the alteration from slaying to temporary binding: does it date prior to *1 Enoch*? Hintze suggests that the use of the epithet *vərəθra-ja-* (used of the weapon with which Θraētaona killed Aži Dahāka) for the *Saošiiant* (the eschatological savior) in *Yašt* 19 already implies a conscious eschatologization of the hero myth, here associated with the *saošiiant* rather than Kərəsāspa.[89] If this is true, it would date the motif to the seventh or sixth centuries B.C.E. The novel aspect of the Pahlavi descriptions, then, would not be the interim binding of the dragon, but rather Kərəsāspa's identity as the slayer. As Hintze notes, *Yašt* 19 fuses the Indo-European heroic tradition with Zoroastrian religious traditions of the eschatological savior.[90] The eschatological extension of the dragon slain by the hero was a natural development from there.

There are further indications that this dating is correct. One uncertain hint is the festival of **Miθrakana*. In Islamic times, the festival of **Miθrakana* celebrated the binding of Aži Dahāka.[91] The same festival was celebrated in the Achaemenid period, although the sources do not indicate clearly what kind of festival it was nor whether it was already associated with the defeat of Dahāka. If Krasnowolska is correct in linking the festival with an ideal type of kingship, then a link with Θraētaona is certainly possible.[92] Further, the use of the motif of Kərəsāspa and Dahāka in the *Zand-ī Wahman Yašn*—almost certainly originally a reaction to the fall of the Achaemenid Empire—suggests the altered myth predated Alexander. The myth is also hinted at in the *Aogəmadaēca* §§100–101, again implying an Achaemenid dating.[93] Thus, it seems likely that the bound and to-be-killed monster motif dates to the latter

---

88. Skjærvø, "Aždahā I," 191; O'Brien, "Indo-European Eschatology," 297; Ström, "Indogermanisches in der Völuspá," 189–91, 195–96; Dronke, *Mythological Poems*, 16, 18, 19–20 (§§34, 43, 45–46).

89. Hintze, "The Saviour and the Dragon," 77–78; idem, "The Rise of the Saviour," 93–94.

90. Hintze, "Rise of the Saviour," 93–94; idem, "The Saviour and the Dragon," 78.

91. Al-Biruni, *Chronology of Ancient Nations*, 209; Boyce, "On Mithra's Part in Zoroastrianism," 26 n. 82; see also Khaleghi-Motlagh, "Aždahā II," 201.

92. Krasnowolska, "Some Heroes of Iranian Calendar Mythology," 371–82.

93. Jamasp Asa, *Aogəmadaēcā* §§100–101 (85).

Achaemenid period at the latest, though the identification of his slayer with Kərəsāspa came later.

The motif's extensive representation and linkage with eschatology make it an important aspect of Iranian religious tradition, and it fits organically into the overall belief structure. The arch-villain of created creatures is left to await his judgment at the one which will befall all of Angra Mainyu's creations—the same time when Ahura Mazda is finally able to overcome his enemies once and for all. This "suspended" defeat does not sit well with pre-exilic Israelite ideas. Day argues that the conflict myth is—in both the Hebrew Bible and Ugarit—intimately intertwined with the enthronement of the chiefly worshipped deity (YHWH or Ba'al, respectively).[94] If Day is correct about the enthronement context in the Hebrew Bible, then the image must be understood as slaying; the dragon's temporary binding would imply that YHWH's kingship was also only temporary, or at least could be imperiled (indeed, Ba'al's reign was). That is certainly unacceptable in a monotheistic context. It is also foreign to the so-called Deuteronomistic historical-theology which sees YHWH's workings happening within history, rather than deferred into a post-historical time.[95] Indeed, the idea of a binding-until-future-judgment practically requires an eschatology merely to make sense. It would be reasonable, however, for the motif to be borrowed with or formed following the development of the accompanying eschatology.

Nevertheless, the parallel between Asael and Dahāka faces a difficulty: the *Book of Watchers* does not describe Asael as a dragon—rather, he is called a "watcher" (עיר, ἐγρήγορος).[96] Although another heavenly creature, the "seraph," has serpentine associations, it is unlikely that "watcher" carried the same.[97] However, the characters of Asael and Aži

94. Day, *God's Conflict*, 18–38.

95. This characterization still holds true even if the Noll's rejection of the Deuteronomistic history is accepted; see Noll, "Deuteronomistic History or Deuteronomic Debate?," 311–45, particularly Thesis 1 (despite its pan-Persianism).

96. See the Excursus: On the Watchers (pp. 171–74, above).

97. The word "dragon" in Greek (δράκων) was possibly derived from the word δέρκομαι, "to see clearly" (LSJ, 448, 379), even though the Greek translators of the *Book of Watchers* used ἐγρήγορος to translate "Watchers." Perhaps the author's monstrous allusions are the referent of the mysterious usage of Behemoth in 60:8, who is also thrown into Doudael. The text of the *Parables* is corrupt, however, and may originally be from a lost Noachic work. Cf. the discussion by Black, *Book of Enoch*, 227 (translation on p. 56); see a slightly different translation in Nickelsburg and VanderKam, *1 Enoch*, 76. This is not say the fabled *Book of Noah, per se* (for a critique of the *Book of Noah* thesis, see Dimant, "Two "Scientific" Fictions," 231–42).

do have two common traits: supernatural origin and association with blood-thirst. Aži Dahāka is noted for his desire to eliminate all human-kind. In *Yašt* 5.29–31 and *Yašt* 15.19–21, he is depicted praying to gods for the ability to clear the entire earth of inhabitants.[98] After Dahāka's transformation into an (Arab) usurper king, the *Shahnameh* still describes the blood-thirstiness of the serpents which grew from Aži's shoulders, linking the blood-thirst of the serpents with Ahriman's scheme to destroy humanity.[99] Asael is also associated with a critique of violence. Asael is blamed for teaching "swords of iron" and "every instrument of war" (8:1), both obviously linked with violence.[100] The result of all of the watchers' teachings combined caused men to perish (8:4; 9:1); further, their progeny also caused war and bloodshed (7:3–6; 8:4; 9:9c). The critique of violence was certainly associated with Asael, even if it was not the most important aspect of his narrative.[101] Violence is certainly prominent enough to see it as a significant parallel with the character of Dahāka.

Dahāka's monstrous/demonic qualities and his blood-thirstiness combined with his abduction of beautiful human women is certainly suggestive in the Asael context—the *Book of Watchers* is also concerned with illicit marriage and monstrous, numinous creatures.[102] Even though the motif of the illicit marriage is connected with the Šemihazah layer and drawn from Gen 6, it helps to explain why an Iranian myth would be useful for combining the Asael story with the Šemihazah material. A blood-thirsty, woman-defiling demon bound until the final judgment certainly resonates with the *Book of Watchers*'s interests. In this light, it is better to discuss sources of influence rather than source documents. If one speaks of "inspiration" rather than source documents, the possibility arises that the Asael material could well have been more instrumental in the initial compiling of the story than is sometimes considered. Perhaps it was an Asael-like story which inspired the scribe to write the *Book of Watchers* in the first place.

Hintze discusses the motif of the bound dragon in Zoroastrian and Jewish texts, including the passage in *1 En.* 54:1–6.[103] In her opinion, this

---

98.   *Zend-Avesta II*, 60–61, 253–54.

99.   Firdausī, *Shāhnāma*, 138–39; cf. 163.

100.   Further, metallurgy is linked to violence by Josephus, *Ant.* I.64 (*Jewish Antiquities I–III*, 31).

101.   Nickelsburg, *1 Enoch 1*, 190–94; cf. 51; Newsom, "The Development of *1 Enoch* 6–19," 313; Alexander, "Enochic Literature and the Bible," 63.

102.   Cf. the similar opinions in Widengren, "Iran and Israel in Parthian Times," 172, and Boyce and Grenet, *HZ III*, 421.

103.   Hintze, "The Saviour and the Dragon," 72–90.

motif in Judaism was adopted from the old chaos myth motif under the influence of the Iranian model. Thus, the eschatologization of the Ugaritic conflict–kingship motif (and indeed its rise) can be explained through an Iranian backdrop. The Ugaritic myth resurfaces in the post-exilic (Persian) period because the themes associated with the parallel myth in the Persian setting—eschatology, dualism, coming judgment and resurrection—gave them new meaning and relevance. While the polytheistic motif of a warrior god's ascent to kingship loses its vitality in monotheism, the eschatology of dualism returns the motif to prominence *on the behalf of* the deity, that is, the *messiah* or *saošiiant* brings victory on behalf of the increasingly transcendent deity. The Persian parallel, then, does not deny the relevance or importance of the Ugaritic/Canaanite parallels, but it provides a logical catalyst for their resurgence and re-adoption in post-exilic Judaism.[104] Motifs associated with gods like Ba'al were able to be reused in a new monotheistic and future-oriented perspective without threatening YHWH's kingship.[105]

The role of the Messiah in Jewish apocalyptic literature takes over much from the divine warrior traditions of the Hebrew Bible and ancient Near East.[106] In so doing, motifs from the older religious traditions—associated with other deities[107]—were reinterpreted. It is suggested here that the adoption of aspects of the structurally intertwined matrix of the Iranian system helped make such reinterpretation attractive and useful for the Second Temple scribe. The Asael narrative is one example of detailed parallels between Judaean works and Iranian myths. The parallels are at least as striking as the ones with the Prometheus myth, but they have a greater structural affinity to the Enochic work as a whole.

Whether one accepts the Asael material as original or as secondary, it cannot be denied that it was extremely important for the formation of the *1 Enoch* corpus as it is currently known. Even if Šemiḥazah was the "original villain" in the tradition, Asael eventually usurps that role, becoming a kind of embodiment of evil.[108] While part of the origin of the *Book of Watchers* comes from traditions associated with Gen 6, the analyses above suggest that certain aspects of the Asael material for which the biblical verses cannot account—the motif of forbidden, cultural instruction (negative *Kulturentstehungsmythos*) and the temporary,

---

104. Watson, *Chaos Uncreated*, 394.

105. For a revised Ba'al imagery, see Day, *Yahweh and the Gods and Goddesses of Canaan*, 116–27.

106. Cross, *Canaanite Myth and Hebrew Epic*, 91–111.

107. Cf. the suggestion in Watson, *Chaos Uncreated*, 395.

108. Black, "Twenty Angel Dekadarchs," 232.

eschatological binding—are at least partially due to Iranian inspiration. If one credits the responsible scribe(s) with a "persophilic" hermeneutic, the *Book of Watchers*'s differences with Genesis become much more understandable.

Book of Parables/Book of Similitudes *(1 Enoch 37–71)*

Weighing of Souls

The image of human souls being weighed for judgment appears twice in the *Book of Parables* (41:1; 61:8), in neither case elaborated.[109] It appears once in the sapiential tradition of the Hebrew Bible. In Job 31:6 Job asks for his righteousness to be weighed (שׁקל) by YHWH. It also occurs in Daniel (Dan 5:27): Belshazzar's vision weighs him (תקל) and finds him delinquent. The misuse of weights is condemned and occurs often in the prophets as an indicator of justice (Deut 25:13–16; Prov 11:1; 20:23; Hos 12:7; Amos 8:5; Mic 6:11), but it is not applied directly to the judgment of people. Only in Daniel is this image used as a prerequisite or synonym for YHWH's judgment of the wicked, and the influence of Daniel on the *Similitudes* is hard to determine.[110] Some translations read a reference to weighing in the closely parallel verses of Prov 16:2; 21:2, and 24:12, but the word used in each of these verses is תכן, which BDB gives as "regulate, measure, estimate" and Koehler–Baumgartner as "examine, check."[111] The latter further note that the root is cognate with תקן, "to make straight."[112] That the latter may be a better way to read the word is supported by the reading of the LXX for 21:2, Κατευθύνει δὲ καρδίας κύριος, "but the Lord directs/straightens the hearts."[113] The Targum to Proverbs translates 16:2 as "sets ways in order" and 21:2 as "sets hearts aright," suggesting that this is the better way to translate the verses, and that no mention of "weighing" is intended.[114] Thus the verses in Job and Dan are the only clear references in the Hebrew Bible.[115]

---

109. Nickelsburg and VanderKam, *1 Enoch*, 55, 78.

110. Cf. Collins, *Daniel*, 59; VanderKam, "Biblical Interpretation in 1 Enoch and Jubilees," 296.

111. BDB, 1067; *HAL*, 1733.

112. *HAL*, 1784.

113. Arndt and Gingrich, *A Greek–English Lexicon*, 423, gives "make straight, lead, direct" for κατευθυνω. The LXX for ch. 16 is highly defective as a whole, and v. 2 barely resembles the MT.

114. Healey, *The Targums of Proverbs*, 38, 46. Kaminka, "Septuaginta und Targum zu Proverbia," 169–91, does not list either 16:2 or 21:2 as diverging from the MT.

115. Contra Charles, *The Book of Enoch*, 79.

Considering the sapiential influences on *1 Enoch* in general and the *Book of Parables* in particular,[116] one could argue that the idea was taken from the brief mention in Job.[117] The question remains how such a brief mention, however, would be brought into prominence (particularly in the later *Testament of Abraham*).[118] It will be suggested here that this motif was selected out of sapiential tradition under the inspiration of the Iranian preoccupation with the balancing of deeds.[119]

The eschatological weighing of the deeds of mankind holds a fundamental centrality in the Zoroastrian system that is traced to the *Gāthās*. This poetic-ethical idea was later expanded and taken to its logical conclusions by scholar-priests, but it retained its original relevance to Zoroastrian thought.[120] Already in the *Gāthās* a three-fold division of people can be found, between the "truthful," the "deceitful," and the "indifferent."[121] The most prominent image of judgment in the *Gāthās* is the one of the Bridge of Judgment or Separation, over which souls must travel to heaven or fall to hell; this individual judgment precedes the final, eschatological one.[122] The individual judgment is often overseen by either the *yazata* of truth, *Rašnu* ("judge"), or the trio *Miθra, Sraoša,* and *Rašnu*.[123] *Rašnu* balances the actions, words, and thoughts of the deceased within a hair's breadth, sending the person to the appropriate destination.[124] That *Rašnu* was especially associated with judgment can be seen in the fact that the *Yašt* dedicated to *Rašnu* invokes him to come witness an ordeal.[125] The cult of *Rašnu* was known in Achaemenid Persia, demonstrated by the occurrence of his name in the onomastica

---

116.   Nickelsburg, *1 Enoch 1*, 60; von Rad, *Old Testament Theology*, 2:301–15; cf. Nickelsburg, "Enochic Wisdom," and Wright, "1 Enoch in Ben Sira," in Boccaccini and Collins, eds., *The Early Enoch Literature*, 81–94, 159–76, respectively.

117.   While the dating of Job is notorious, it certainly predates the *Parables*; see Habel, *The Book of Job*, 40–42.

118.   See 889–91 of E. Sander's translation in *OTP* (Recension A). The parallel passages in Recension B do not make use of the image (§§8–11, 899–900).

119.   Already suggested by Hinnells, *Zoroastrian and Parsi Studies*, 78.

120.   Boyce, *HZ I*, 236–41; Hintze, "Treasures in Heaven," 15.

121.   *Yasna* 33.1 (Insler, *The Gathas of Zarathustra*, 51).

122.   On the Bridge, see *Yasna* 46.10–11; 51.13. For various allusions, see 31.3, 13, 20; 45.7; 49.10–11 (Insler, *The Gathas of Zarathustra*, 37, 41, 43, 51, 77, 97; Humbach et al., *The Gāthās of Zarathushtra*, 1:126–27, 129, 131, 165, 182).

123.   Cf. *Mihr Yašt* 42–43, 100, 126 (Gershevitch, *Hymn to Mithra*, 95, 123, 135). On the close connections between *Sraoša, Rašnu* and *Miθra*, see Zaehner, *Dawn and Twilight*, 111–13.

124.   See *Mēnōg-ī Xrad* 119–121 (*Pahlavi Texts III*, 18).

125.   *Zend-Avesta II*, 168.

found at Persepolis and Egypt.[126] Later, the *Ardā Wirāz Nāmag* refers to *Rašnu* as the one with "the yellow golden balance" who sends people to limbo/purgatory.[127] Although *Ardā Wirāz* is a late text, the idea of the threefold division of souls (righteous, wicked, and "indifferent") is a Gathic idea (*Yasna* 33.1),[128] even though the Gathic support for a "purgatory" *per se* appears to be about as elusive as it is in the Judeo-Christian tradition.[129] Boyce suggests that the Gathic verse *Yasna* 48.4 refers to a "separate place" for the "indifferent,"[130] but in Insler's translation the text does not clearly refer to three places at all.[131] However, the term *Misuuan Gātu*—denoting a place for the "indifferent"—does appear in the Young Avesta (*Vidēvdāt* 19.36),[132] making its currency by the end of the Achaemenid period most likely. The idea was developed further by the time of the redaction of the *Bundahišn*.[133]

It is not only Zoroastrian religious tradition which displays this preoccupation with balance; indeed, it has even been claimed that Achaemenid jurisprudence closely parallels the conception of justice as the totality of life.[134] Herodotus relates a story of Darius I's justice which appears to support this. After crucifying a judge for accepting a bribe, Darius discovered that the man's "good services to the royal house were more than his offenses," and Darius had the man removed from the cross.[135] While this story may be dubious historically, it is adequately illustrative of jurisprudence as the balancing of good and bad deeds *in toto*, rather than individual deeds or conversion experiences. Diodorus

---

126. Porten, "Persian Names," 184; Hallock, *PFT*, in theophoric names: PF335, PF1509, PF1956, PF2003 (150, 423, 500–501, 605); *Rašnu* also occurs in a place name (Rašnumattiš), PF 1956 (562); cf. Boyce, *HZ I*, 59, 241; Boyce, *HZ II*, 142.

127. Vahman, *'Arda Wiraz Namag'*, 195–96.

128. Insler, *The Gathas of Zarathustra*, 51.

129. That is, 2 Macc 12:38–45, which in no way mentions a "purgatory" but was later taken to imply one.

130. Boyce, *HZ I*, 237.

131. Insler, *The Gathas of Zarathustra*, 91. However, Duchesne-Guillemin, *The Hymns of Zarathustra*, 34–35, sees a mention of a separate place both in his notes and in his translation. Humbach et al., *Gāthās of Zarathushtra*, 1:136, does mention a threefold division, but sees no separate place on 177.

132. Boyce, *HZ I*, 237, citing Bartholomae, *Altiraniranisches Wörterbuch*, 1186–87. Bartholomae cites three references, but the present author could only trace *Vidēvdāt* 19.36 as actually mentioning *misuuan gātu*, which Darmesteter glossed as "all of heaven" (*Zend-Avesta I*, 215); however, Shaked, "Eschatology I," 565–69, accepts the reference.

133. *Gr. Bund.* 30.32–33 (Anklesaria, *Zand-Ākāsīh*, 262–63).

134. Moulton, *Early Zoroastrianism*, 170.

135. Herodotus, VII.194 (*Wars V–VII*, 511).

also offers a story which supports this conception. When Artaxerxes examines three judges' reasoning for the acquittal of Tiribazus, the second judge replies that Tiribazus's benefactions outweighed the accusations against him. This reply seems to have pleased the king.[136] Claims to justice do appear in the OP inscriptions, at least those of Darius (DB I.20–24, IV.61–67, DNb 5–11),[137] but these inscriptions vary little from the stereotypical language of royal ideology in this regard. The idea of balance may have been merely a juridical ideal among the Iranians, however, as it is certainly true that all justice ultimately depended on the king's grace.[138]

The strict application of justice fits well into an Iranian context, but it does not fit so snugly into the Jewish system (e.g. Ezek 3:16–21). While YHWH was a god of justice, Judaism did not tend to picture him as a strict, balancing judge like *Rašnu*. Indeed, there is a strong tradition stretching through the Rabbinic writings which emphasizes the necessity of mercy for the existence of justice itself,[139] and mercy is by definition not strict. It is quite possible, however, under the influence of a Persian preoccupation with balance that the verse in Job was selected out and utilized in the *Book of Parables* as the symbol of the individual judgment.

The image of a divine scale-holder is not limited to Iran; it also occurs in Egypt. The *Book of the Dead* depicts the hearts of the dead being weighed against *Ma'at*, to determine whether or not they are worthy of eternal life,[140] and an Egyptian background is typically conceded for parts of Proverbs.[141] The basic idea is the same in the Persian and Egyptian systems, but the emphasis is slightly different. In the Iranian version, the person's good actions, words, and thoughts are weighed against his or her own bad actions, words and thoughts; in the Egyptian version, the person's heart is weighed against *Ma'at*. Although either could have in

---

136.   Diodorus, XV.11 (*Diodorus of Sicily VI*, 352–54); cf. Briant, *From Cyrus to Alexander*, 317.

137.   For the texts, see Kent, *Old Persian*, 119, 132, 140. Kent's translation of "Ordinance of Good Regulations" in DNb 3–5 appears to be a poor translation for *ubānām hadugām āxšnavaiy*, "until I have heard both of them." Cf. Baghbidi, "Darius and the Bisotun Inscription," 58; Brosius, *The Persian Empire from Cyrus II to Artaxerxes I*, 64.

138.   Cf. Briant, *From Cyrus to Alexander*, 129–30, 302–4.

139.   Neusner, *The Theology of the Oral Torah*, 61–63, 324–26; Segal, "Justice, Mercy and a Bird's Nest," 176–95; Levine, "Looking Beyond the Mercy/Justice Dichotomy," 455–72.

140.   See Quirke, "Judgment of the Dead," 173–77; Silverman, "Divinity and Deities in Ancient Egypt," 48–49, with Fig. 32 on 51; cf. David, *The Ancient Egyptians*, 111, where he describes the heart as weighed against a feather of Thoth.

141.   Whybray, *The Book of Proverbs*, 3.

theory served as a catalyst towards the choice of the scales-image, the Persian version is technically closer in terminology—in both *1 En.* 41:1 and 61:8 it is the *deeds*[142] rather than the hearts of humanity which are weighed. While the possibility that the image derives from Egypt cannot be excluded, at least the version used in *Parables* is closer to the Iranian version. One could imagine that even if the mention in Job ultimately came from Egypt, the Enochic author was reflecting the heritage of an Achaemenid milieu. For this particular detail, then, it is still reasonable to understand it as an example of Iranian influence by the selection of pre-existing ideas (borrowing), even if those ideas had originally been known in Judaean circles from Egypt.

It is unfortunate that the provenance and dating of the *Parables* is so uncertain, but the detail of the weighing of souls offers another example where the re-interpretation and selection of Judaean material could have been in dialogue with Iranian ideas. This particular detail did not have a particularly distinguished afterlife in Judeo-Christian traditions,[143] but it may serve as an indication that further research into the *Similitudes* could prove fruitful.

The Birth of Noah Fragment (1 Enoch 106–107)

1 Enoch 106–107 is an independent unit which perhaps derives from a longer narrative.[144] The fragment's position is old, since it follows the *Epistle* in 4Q204.[145] A similar (longer) narrative also appears in the *Genesis Apocryphon*,[146] although the birth narrative itself is not extant. Nickelsburg considers this section to be a concluding summary of the "whole gamut of Enochic eschatological thought," which served to encourage the reader, who was in the same historical position *vis-à-vis* God's wrath as Lamech.[147] This view is more probable than Milik's contention that chs. 106–107 represent a transition between the Enochic Corpus and the lost Noachic Corpus,[148] since this section summarizes the

142. See Nickelsburg, *1 Enoch 1*, 15.
143. Although Hintze, "Treasures in Heaven," sees it feed into individual eschatology.
144. Stuckenbruck, *1 Enoch 91–108*, 1, 4; Nickelsburg, *1 Enoch 1*, 539.
145. *DSSSE*, 1:418–21. For a convenient overview of the manuscript evidence, see Stuckenbruck, *1 Enoch 91–108*, 17, 20–25, 614–616.
146. Column II, *DSSSE*, 1:28–31.
147. Nickelsburg, *1 Enoch 1*, 540.
148. Milik, *Books of Enoch*, 55–57; cf. the comments in Nickelsburg, *1 Enoch 1*, 541–42.

Enochic tradition so well, and since the phrase "words of the Book of Noah" appear in the *Genesis Apocryphon* after the birth narrative.[149] Whatever the details of the sources used by the author of this section, it most likely dates between the second and first centuries B.C.E. due to the evidence of the Aramaic fragments.[150]

The birth of Noah in *1 En.* 106–107 is described as a profoundly strange incident, requiring the explanation of the departed Enoch. When born, Noah's

> body was whiter than snow and redder than a rose, his hair was all white and like white wool and curly. Glorious was his face. When he opened his eyes, the house shone like the sun. (106:2; cf. vv. 10–11)[151]

He also immediately praised the Lord (vv. 3, 11). This abnormality causes Lamech and Methuselah to suspect that Noah is the illegitimate child of a watcher and to seek an answer from Enoch "at the ends of the earth" (v. 8). This situation enables Enoch to recount the scenario of the watchers (vv. 13–14), the flood and Noah's role in it (vv. 15–18), and the future (final) destruction of evil (106:19–107:1). The basic outline of this scenario is paralleled in the *Genesis Apocryphon* (1QapGen, 1Q19, 1Q20, 4Q537, 4Q538), although the manuscripts are very fragmentary.[152]

While the section contains much material which occurs previously in *1 Enoch*, the details of Noah's birth are new. The child is described as numinous and precocious, with white and red body, white hair, glowing face and eyes, and the ability to speak from birth. The motif of an abnormal pregnancy and precocious child is widespread in folklore, although the motif does not occur in the Hebrew Bible.[153] Rabbinic legends portray Moses as having an extraordinary gestation.[154] Legends

149.   Stuckenbruck, *1 Enoch 91–108*, 611. It should be remembered that the existence of an independent *Book of Noah* is itself dubious. Cf. Dimant, "Two 'Scientific' Fictions," 231–42.

150.   Nickelsburg, *1 Enoch 1*, 542; Alexander, "Enochic Literature and the Bible," 69, appears to date the section to ca. 130 B.C.E.; Stuckenbruck, *1 Enoch 91–108*, 616.

151.   Following the text in Nickelsburg and VanderKam, *1 Enoch*, 164.

152.   *DSSSE*, 1:26–49.

153.   Feldman, "Josephus' Portrait of Moses," 285–328; Brewster, "Some Parallels between the 'Fêng-Shên-Yên I' and the 'Shahnameh'," 118; Lessa, "'Discover-of-the-Sun'," 37. Cf. Holden, *Forms of Deformity*, and Thompson, *Motif-Index*, 5:408 (T585). In his commentary, Nickelsburg discusses a number of parallels, but not to the birth itself, Nickelsburg, *1 Enoch 1*, 542–44; idem, "Patriarchs Who Worry About Their Wives," 144–45.

154.   See Feldman, "Josephus' Portrait of Moses," 301–2. Cf. Ginzberg, *Legends of the Jews*, 2:262–265. White hair is not one of the signs he mentions.

of Zoroaster portray an unusual pregnancy and precocious signs.[155] A parallel passage in *2 En.* 71:1–23 combines both an unusual pregnancy with an unusual child, although the child is not described like Noah is in this passage.[156] While the *child* Noah is remarkable, there is no indication in either the *1 Enoch* text or its expansion in the *Genesis Apocryphon* that the *pregnancy* was in any way abnormal. It is noteworthy, therefore, that only the physical appearance of the child himself is unusual. The particularly notable aspects of the child—white hair and glowing face— are otherwise only used in Jewish literature to describe YHWH himself or his representative.[157] Thus, Nickelsburg suggests a divine characterization of Noah in the passage, but one which is merely in service of the revelation of the section.[158] Similarly Huggins considers it to emphasize Noah's divine role.[159] In a brief note, Bailey suggests that the name of Noah may be related to either an Akkadian or Hurrian god; Koehler– Baumgartner seems to agree and consider it assimilated to the Hebrew נוח, so the image could be an old vestige of the Noah story which appears only here.[160] Stuckenbruck understands the divine imagery to be denying traditions that giants survived the flood by claiming that Noah was not in fact a giant.[161] While this passage does deny Noah's evil pedigree, this does not explain the unique combination of the red and the white skin, white hair, and shining eyes. However, this particular combination of physical features and normal pregnancy is paralleled by the story of the birth of the Persian hero Dastān, better known as Zāl-i-Zar or just Zāl, as recounted by Firdausī in his *Shāhnāmeh*.

When Zāl is born, he has "beauty like the world-illuminating sun," "loveliness of face," "hair as white as snow," and "ruddy cheeks."[162] There appears to have been some ambivalence in the Persian traditions

---

155. See the legends in *Dēnkard* 7.2.47–55 and 3.1–19 (*Pahlavi Texts V*, 28–30, 35–40); cf. *Selections of Zad-Sparam* 13.1–16 (*Pahlavi Texts V*, 138–43). Hultgård, "Das Judentum in der hellenistisch-römischen Zeit," 551, finds this to be an acceptable parallel. Of his discussion of numinous children, only one (Zāl) has white hair. See Yarshater, "The Feared Child in Iranian Mythology," 65–68.

156. Andersen, "2 (Slavonic Apocalypse of) Enoch," 204–6.

157. Cf. Holden, *Forms of Deformity*, 97; Stuckenbruck, *1 Enoch 91–108*, 626–27. The only other instance of which the author is aware is *Jub.* 23:25, which uses the motif of grey-haired children as the symbol for the nadir of decreasing human longevity, which occurs just before the *eschaton*.

158. Nickelsburg, *1 Enoch 1*, 543–44.

159. Huggins, "Noah and the Giants," 109–10.

160. See Bailey's brief note in Lewis, "Noah and the Flood," 225; cf. *HAL*, 684–85.

161. Stuckenbruck, *1 Enoch 91–108*, 633–35.

162. Firdausī, *Shāhnāma*, 1:240–8.

towards the appearance of Zāl's skin, as some sources depict him with dark body and white face, white skin and red face, or red and white skin.[163] When the father, Sām, learns of the child's appearance, he assumes the child has a demonic paternity and abandons him in the wilderness. For the present purposes, the physical features of the child are most relevant. In both stories, the child is described having a radiant face, a strange ambivalence between a red and white body, and white hair, and in both the father suspects demonic illegitimacy. While albinos are often considered suspicious in many pre-modern societies,[164] neither the description of Noah nor of Zāl can properly be described as albino.[165] In both cases, the character involved in the story is situated in a context connected with wisdom. Noah, in the milieu of the Enochic and Noachic traditions, is associated with ancient revealed wisdom; Zāl became in Persian literature a "personification of wisdom."[166] Perhaps most interestingly, Zāl became a "last bastion of hope" for the Iranian monarchy, a fitting parallel for the hero of the deluge.[167]

While this parallel is interesting, it is problematic for two reasons: the date of the *Shāhnāmeh*, and the folkloric nature of the motifs. It is certain that Firdausī's version of the story dates between 936–1026 C.E.,[168] and other known written antecedents to it still appear to date only to the tenth century.[169] While Firdausī's poetic form is very late, much of the legendary material contained within the poem is very ancient; parallels and allusions to the stories fleshed out by Firdausī are found in the Avesta and in the *Bundahišn*, as well as some Indian sources.[170] Indeed, the Rustam cycle, of which the Zāl stories are a part, is generally agreed to have been adopted in Parthia from the Saka/Scythians;[171] nevertheless, there are hints of a poorly remembered Achaemenid history.[172] Colarusso

---

163. Omidsalar, "Rostam's Seven Trials," 267; Firdausī describes Zāl as having a "sunlike face" and "blood-red cheeks"; see Firdausī, *Shāhnāma*, 247.

164. Cf. Krappe, "Albinos and Albinism in Iranian Tradition," 170–74.

165. Omidsalar, "Rostam's Seven Trials," 267; Froggatt, "The Albinism of Timur, Zāl, and Edward the Confessor," 334–35; contra Krappe, "Albinos and Albinism in Iranian Tradition," 172.

166. Omidsalar, "Rostam's Seven Trials," 265.

167. Shahbazi, "Zāl," n.p.

168. Morrison, "Persian Literature," 22; cf. Curtis, *Persian Myths*, 29.

169. Morrison, "Persian Literature," 16, 21.

170. Ibid., 39–40; Curtis, *Persian Myths*, 10, 24.

171. Morrison, "Persian Literature," 23; Hintze, *Zamyād-Yašt*, 34–35; Brewster, "Some Parallels," 115; Shahbazi, "Zāl," n.p.

172. Morrison, "Persian Literature," 29; Curtis, *Persian Myths*, 56; cf. Jamzadeh, "An Assyrian Motif in the Shāhnāma," 167–72; idem, "A Shahnama Passage in an Achaemenid Context," 383–88.

suggests that the whiteness motif is of Indo-European origin due to Irish and Germanic parallels.[173] However, Davis sees the whiteness of Zāl as the mythic reflex of racial tensions from the Indo-Iranian invasions.[174] Thus, while it is difficult to reconstruct early forms of the myths with any certainty from the *Shāhnāmeh*, it is likely that this discrete story refracts older ones. Widengren's suggestion that this detail is evidence of a "Zurvanite" influence on Judaism is even more tenuous, as Zurvanism most probably did not exist as a separate tradition.[175] If the hero's description is indeed an old Indo-European motif, Colarusso's suggestion that this characteristic was related to the possession of "prophetic powers" is certainly provocative in the context of this Enochic passage.[176]

The other difficulty is the possibility of a common folkloric impulse rather than a direct borrowing. Yet, while the story of Dastān/Zāl clearly contains the reworking of folkloric motifs, such a context appears to be lacking in *1 Enoch*. Firdausī's story includes the common motif of the abandoned and rescued child, which is completely absent in *1 En.* 106–107: consultation of Enoch precludes the child's abandonment. The details of Zāl's appearance appear to be designed to highlight his role as wise (rather than purely martial) hero, whereas the details of Noah's appearance take back seat to the need for consultation with Enoch. While it certainly is possible that folk stories circulated about the birth of Noah, some of which may have found their way into the *Genesis Apocryphon* and 1Q19, it is also possible these texts are based on *1 Enoch*. Moreover, the details of Noah's birth do not seem to reappear in any other early Jewish or Christian exegesis of the flood.[177] When *1 En.* 106–107 was composed as a conclusion to the Enochic Corpus as it stood at the time, the author could have picked up the details of Noah's birth from popular folk traditions, invented them himself, or have borrowed them from a Persian source. It is impossible to tell for certain, but considering the Persian motifs which are evidenced throughout the previous Enochic Corpus and in other more or less contemporary Qumranic documents, the possibility of Persian borrowing is quite plausible. However, until an older parallel than Firdausī is found, it must remain only an intriguing possibility. One could argue for the reverse influence of the Enochic

---

173. Colarusso, "The Hunters," 448–49.
174. Davis, "Rustam-i Dastan," 233–34.
175. See his comments, Widengren, "Iran and Israel," 157.
176. Colarusso, "The Hunters," 449.
177. See Lewis, *A Study of the Interpretation of Noah*, particularly Chapters 2, 3, and 6.

passage on Firdausī, perhaps via the Manichaean dissemination of the
Book of Giants,[178] but there is little evidence of the eastern dissemination
of the five main sections of the *Ethiopic Book of Enoch*.

Enochic Conclusions

The *1 Enochic* Corpus represents an extended period of time and a variety
of authors, albeit within what was most likely a continuous tradition. It
is significant that in each of the major sections of the Ethiopic text of
1 Enoch discussed above parallels or points of contact were found with
the Iranian traditions, most of which implied the reinterpretation of native
Judaean ideas. The *Book of Watchers* paralleled the negative *Kulturentstehungsmythos* and the eschatological binding of a (dragon-)demon. The
Parables evidenced influence in the concepts of the weighing of souls,
yet much more remains to be done. Finally, the *Noachic Fragment*
offered an intriguing possibility with Noah's white hair and glorious
visage. None of the parallels are in themselves certain, but the number of
parallels and structural considerations within a single tradition suggest
that they may be more than mere coincidences.

Conclusion

The small number of analyses attempted here evince several potentially
important trends. First, most of the texts could be best analyzed in the
context of multiple traditions; it was not always a matter of *either/or*, but
often of *both/and*. Ezekiel 37 may have been partially inspired by Mesopotamian reliefs, but subsequent audiences were more likely to have
Iranian themes in mind. Daniel 2 likely evidenced dependency upon an
Iranian oracle which itself utilized a variety of motifs, potentially some
from Greece. The *Book of Watchers* used Iranian concepts to rehabilitate
older Canaanite mythology. These examples, then, suggest that in any
investigation of influence few cases will be discrete, "pure" transfers
from one context into another.

Second, every analysis above highlighted how traditions were re-inter-
preted. This was evident in the use of foreign material, native materials,
and in the reception of the materials. Ezekiel 38–39 transformed prophetic threats against Israel into a future promise of protection while
potentially inverting Median rhetoric. Daniel 2 borrowed the language of
the Day of the Lord to color an Iranian oracle, in the process reinventing

---

178.   Milik, *Books of Enoch*, 299; cf. Henning, "The Book of Giants," 66, frag.
D; Reeves, *Jewish Lore in Manichaean Cosmology*, 22, 29, 195, 208–9.

the term's meaning. The *Book of Watchers* transformed its understanding of Genesis in dialogue with a number of traditions, including Iranian ones.

Third, many of the contexts proposed for the parallels were related to Iranian royal ideology. The source behind Dan 2 was a reaction to the loss of Iranian sovereignty. The concept of the Watchers was modeled after Achaemenid functionaries. A supplementary bonus to this result is the potential of alleviating the difficulty inherent in using "religious" sources from Iran; as a rule, material pertaining to the Great Kings is more securely dated and more widely attested. Subsequent research into the effects of Imperial administration on Yehud and the Torah could prove to be highly illuminated by such a trajectory.

For each individual text discussed, the criteria for influence were continually considered; dating (criterion 1); context (criterion 2); relative structural logic (criterion 3); a space or "hook" for the foreign element (criterion 4); discrete, distinctive elements (criterion 5). Wherever possible, an attempt at assessing the relative interpretive or structural change effected by the proposed instance of influence was made. However, a broader canvass in the context of Second Temple Judaism as a whole is needed to consider better the sixth criterion of structural and interpretive change. The next chapter will attempt to situate the individual case studies considered above within an intellectual and sociological context in which influence as defined in the Prolegomena can be profitably explored.

Chapter 6

AN APOCALYPTIC HERMENEUTIC

Introit: The Proposal

After showing that the time is ripe for a reassessment of Iranian influence, discussing the nature of the Iranian evidence, setting the stage in
the Achaemenid Empire, applying principles of Oral Theory, and tentatively analyzing several passages, it remains to assess the framework in
which these considerations may be applied to the continuing study of
Judaean apocalyptic and of Iranian influences. As argued in the Prolegomena, an understanding of influence requires consideration of the
systemic import of any details analyzed and proposed, rather than leav-
ing them as a list of isolated instances of borrowing. Having amassed a
number of potential discrete parallels, a method for understanding their
significance is needed. The best way, it is here argued, to understand and
pursue both the micro- and macroscopic questions is through appeal to
an *Apocalyptic Hermeneutic*. This Apocalyptic Hermeneutic has two
substantial contributions: (1) the relationships between apocalypticism,
millenarianism, and the apocalypses and (2) the "ground zero" for Iranian influences in Second Temple Judaism.

Six criteria for determining influence are proposed in the Prolegomena. Chapter 1 demonstrates the existence of Iranian material pre-dating
apocalyptic (criterion 1). Chapters 2 and 3 present a historical context for
interaction (criterion 2). In the analyses of Chapters 4 and 5, discrete
elements are analyzed in terms of structural contexts in foreign and
Judaean sources, as well as for plausible ways they were utilized (criteria
3–5). The final criterion—interpretive change—remains outstanding. The
Apocalyptic Hermeneutic helps to fulfill that criterion.

A number of the analyses in Chapters 4 and 5 pointed to the importance of the reinterpretation of previous Judaean traditions for their
interaction with Iranian ideas. It is therefore proposed here that the best
place to envision Iranian influence on Jewish apocalyptic is within the
Apocalyptic Hermeneutic.

The "hermeneutic" of the term "the Apocalyptic Hermeneutic" can be defined as

> the point of departure and reflexive personal alignment from which, through which, and by which an individual and/or community receives, understands, interprets, and re-creates traditions, circumstances and ultimately worldview, involving some specific content which supports favored methodologies and media, while occurring with specific reference to a real social context. This may but need not be held exclusively of other hermeneutics by the same individual or group.[1]

This type of hermeneutic is thus differentiated from a worldview by being a mechanism which both creates and comes out of a worldview (via the well-known "hermeneutic circle"); a worldview is more comprehensive and may utilize multiple hermeneutics in its self-creation, sustenance, and evolution. Two important aspects are included in the definition above: methodologies and media, each deserving some comment.

The importance of "methodology" for intellectual thought is axiomatic for the academy, and the results of the application of differing methods upon the same questions can be startling. Very different results are created by application of Rabbinic methods of *midrash* to a text than application of Philonic ideas. It is useful in the context of the human life-world, however, to broaden the concept of methodology from merely the self-conscious application of methods within a particular field to the strategies which people adopt for reception, understanding, and re-interpretation in their lives. In the life of an individual or a community, the application or non-application of ideas or traditions to daily life is as significant as purely "intellectual" methodologies. A community which interprets texts as socially binding laws will differ significantly from one which interprets them as ennobling myths even in the nitty-gritty of life. This sort of application deserves to be included in considerations of methodology. The use of the term "methodology" is meant, therefore, to include intellectual and pragmatic "methods" and values.

Questions of media were discussed at length in Chapter 3, and they hold import here again. The medium or media in which one chooses to respond to a tradition or situation reverberates in the life of the individual and community—does the catalyst prompt a speech, a text, a mosaic floor? Perhaps it involves the carving of a new community, which again could be accomplished via several media; perhaps it prompts the creation of a previously non-existent genre or medium. The question of the media

---

1. Author's own definition.

preferred or ignored for the purposes of hermeneutics ought to be integrated into the way the interpretive process is understood. An individual or group which considers textual study and creation the dominant paradigm will surely differ significantly from one which prefers oral modes— or, indeed, even from one which prefers an architectural response.

Obviously, hermeneutics as defined above will vary drastically between peoples in their sophistication, their self-reflection, and their comprehensiveness. They need not be based purely on rational-logical arguments or principles, and even those which utilize such elements are likely to include some elements (at least) which Fisher would characterize as "narrative" or "the logic of good reasons."[2] In other words, a hermeneutic includes reason, values, and actions. While the formulation above is an intellectual abstraction based on modern understandings of human knowledge, it is meant to describe the real workings of humans, whether "intellectuals" or not. All people by needs must respond to and recreate traditions. This concept of hermeneutics is thus meant to be much more comprehensive than simply the exegesis and expansion of biblical texts, which is so often discussed with regards to Second Temple Judaism.[3]

Before discussing the implications and contours of this proposal, it is necessary to clarify what this Apocalyptic Hermeneutic is and what it is not. The Apocalyptic Hermeneutic is primarily to be regarded as a *shared interpretive framework* which interrelates apocalypticism, the apocalypses, and millenarianism. It is not a shared theology, nor is it a coherent, systematic philosophy. It is a method of receiving and reshaping traditions which shares identifiable aspects while producing noticeably divergent results.[4] It is an intellectual and social paradigm through which many Judaeans of the Second Temple period channeled their concerns, queries, and teachings. By positing a shared framework one is able to account for both the similarities and the differences which are manifested in the extant texts and between various apocalyptic groups; developments in the cultural, sociological, political, and economic, situations will produce corresponding variations in the formulation of specific doctrines and ideas. By primarily placing the locus of Iranian influence in this hermeneutic one is able to understand recurrent motifs which have

---

2. Fisher, *Human Communication as Narration*. Bankston, "Rationality, Choice and the Religious Economy," 311–25, also wants to include considerations above and beyond "rational logic," in his case, communities, noting the complexities involved in their interactions.

3. E.g. Charlesworth, "The Pseudepigrapha as Biblical Exegesis," 139–52.

4. This is perhaps consonant with the "intellectual transformation of prophecy" which Brooke sees in Qumran; see Brooke, "Prophecy and the Prophets in the Dead Sea Scrolls," 158.

Iranian parallels better, as well as discern reasons for the divergences between acceptance and rejection of individual motifs. Ultimately, it offers the potential for a more nuanced appreciation of the levels of influence on individual texts while relating each to Second Temple Judaism as a whole.

It must be stressed that the proposal here called the Apocalyptic Hermeneutic is entirely historiographical rather than prescriptive; it attempts to solve the problems of Iranian influence and its relation to apocalyptic in the Second Temple period. It is based on reflections on the foregoing analyses and methodological considerations.

Towards these ends proceed the following arguments. The first argument examines how the Apocalyptic Hermeneutic relates to the creation of the apocalypses and the potential impact of Iran thereupon. Second, the analyses of Chapter 4 and 5 are drawn upon to flesh out the nature of the hermeneutic and how Iranian considerations impact upon it. Lastly, an attempt to construct a preliminary model of the Apocalyptic Hermeneutic provides a framework for assessment of the significance of the analyses in Chapter 4 and 5. Further considerations of Iranica are reserved for the Metalegomena.

Hermeneutics:
The Re-interpretation and Application of Tradition

The majority of analyses of Chapters 4 and 5 highlighted the importance of (re-)interpretation for the understanding for each passage; this chapter expands that observation.

Relation of Hermeneutics to Apocalyptic

The relation of hermeneutics to apocalyptic and its three manifestations was hinted at in the Prolegomena. A brief overview of how this fits into the phenomena of apocalyptic can here be sketched (cf. Figure 1).

A fairly widespread scholarly consensus distinguishes between apocalypticism (worldview), apocalypses (written genre), and millenarianism (social movement) and cautions against a one-to-one correspondence between any of them. The proper understanding of how these three relate to each other or more broadly to Second Temple Judaism is much more contested. An infuriating ambiguity causes this impasse: each of the three is similar while retaining significant differences; further, none of the three is in itself monolithic. How can the chaos of the details be reconciled without undermining the significance of the multiplicity? Appeal to a shared hermeneutic offers a way beyond this impasse: shared methods, media predilections, and values—rather than particular instances of exegesis—relate the three and their constituents. Such a tie explains the "instinctive" scholarly feeling of a similarity between the apocalypses while simultaneously explaining how individual apocalypses could interpret a tradition and/or circumstances divergently. If this idea is accurate, then one of the great impasses in modern apocalyptic studies can be surmounted. Further, a likely vista for Persian interaction in the Second Temple period is opened. Before attempting to sketch the preliminary outline of this Apocalyptic Hermeneutic in the next section, the function of this hermeneutic needs further explication.

An Apocalyptic Hermeneutic both comes out of and creates apocalypticism. As tradents interpret their traditions and circumstances, they refine patterns of interpretation which in turn form their worldview. Part of this process is the generation and refinement of ideas—doctrines, myths, philosophies, and so on. These discrete ideas form part of the constellation of apocalypticism and are communicable beyond the confines of apocalypticism *per se*; the general culture and broader religious traditions can pick up and adopt ideas from the apocalyptic worldview without adopting it wholesale. If a group adopted the Apocalyptic Hermeneutic—and not just aspects of the worldview—it would likely (but not *necessarily*) begin to generate its own apocalyptic tradition and participate quite fully in apocalypticism. In this respect it is important to remember that apocalypticism can contain multiple apocalyptic traditions, that is, more specific constellations of understandings;[5] Danielic and Enochic traditions can be distinguished within the greater umbrella of apocalypticism.

If a number of individuals who share the Apocalyptic Hermeneutic consciously form a group, they may be considered an apocalyptic movement. If such a movement expects an imminent appearance of the *eschaton*, perhaps taking actions to hasten it, it may be considered millenarian. Even if a group adopts substantial aspects of apocalypticism but does not also adopt the Apocalyptic Hermeneutic, it is unlikely to appear to be an apocalyptic movement: it will function as part of the general tradition more broadly.

As part of the construction and dissemination of their worldview, some apocalyptic tradents write apocalypses. The writing of an apocalypse will be a single instance of the utilization of the Apocalyptic Hermeneutic; different instances will therefore produce differing results. Inasmuch as two historical-critical scholars may reconstruct the history of a text differently while using similar methods, so two apocalyptic

---

5. See the Prolegomena.

writers—even from the same tradition—may write diverging apocalypses. Each, however, share methods of interpretation as well as a common medium.

The construct just described indicates how the Apocalyptic Hermeneutic interrelates the various apocalyptic categories while hinting at how individual catalysts could produce startlingly unique specific results. Since it is clear that apocalypticists were reshaping and receiving traditions, it is in this context that foreign influences—including Persian— should be considered. So doing broadens the concept of interaction and influence from just text-reception and text-creation to oral intercourse and community formation. It now remains to begin to reconstruct the architecture of the Apocalyptic Hermeneutic and how this involves the Iranian question. A few examples from the preceding analyses will help to sketch out such a structure.

The Apocalyptic Hermeneutic's Blueprint

Afterlife and the Resurrection: Ezekiel 37:1–14

Collins proposes to view the apocalypses as a means for the individual's transcendence of death.[6] He does this in the context of debate over the relevance of "apocalyptic eschatology" for the study of the apocalypses. The question of eschatology will be dealt with separately; the first test case is individual post-mortem expectations ("personal eschatology"): afterlife and resurrection.

That a decisive shift in expectations for the individual afterlife occurred between most of the Hebrew Bible and the apocalypses is nearly a scholarly cliché.[7] This has been analyzed in terms of a shift from collective (or nationalist) to individual focus, a response to persecution of the faithful, or the absorption of Greek ideas of a separable soul.[8] Yet

6. See the following works by Collins: "Apocalyptic Eschatology as the Transcendence of Death," 21–43; *The Apocalyptic Imagination*, 11–12; "Eschatological Dynamics and Utopian Ideals in Early Judaism," 74; "Prophecy, Apocalypse and Eschatology: Reflections on the Proposals of Lester Grabbe," 47.

7. E.g. Birkeland, "The Belief in the Resurrection of the Dead," 75; Russell, *The Method and Message*, 353–79; Spronk, *Beatific Afterlife*; Grabbe, *Judaic Religion*, 258, 267–68; see also the first three articles in Avemarie and Lichtenberger, eds., *Auferstehung — Resurrection*; Vidal, "Resurrection in the Israelite Tradition," 47–55.

8. E.g. Charles, *Religious Development*, persecution and nationalism (96, 113); Russell, *Method and Message*, "corporate personality" and Greek pre-existent souls; Mowinckel, *He That Cometh*, 270–1, an increased individualism; Nickelsburg, *Resurrection, Immortality, and Eternal Life*, persecution, although the preface to the

it must be stressed that there is no single or uniform expectation in Second Temple Judaism: the unifying aspect is more the *types* of expectations than the details of those expectations. Part of the Apocalyptic Hermeneutic, then, must pertain to the kinds of afterlife which can be expected by the individual, with room left for the results of such expectations to be refined based on specific apocalyptic worldview of the individual or group in question.

The basic hope for afterlife in the Hebrew Bible had two aspects: a long, prosperous life followed by a good name remembered by one's descendants.[9] These hopes should not be seen as disappearing in later eras and literatures, but they cease to be sufficient for many: additional expectations are added. These additional hopes are a meaningful (beatific) immortality and a final rectification of ideals not fulfilled in earthly life. The latter receives its fullest expression in terms of a Day of Judgment. The exact depiction (content) of these hopes varies.

A simple appeal to deprivation or persecution is insufficient to explain these additional hopes (although they make the ideas more widely palatable)—such considerations appear well before the Antiochean crisis once considered so important for the appearance of apocalyptic.[10] While the roots of such expectations are likely pluriform, there are several aspects which can be profitably analyzed in regards to the Apocalyptic Hermeneutic. First, the new hopes distance perceived cause and consequence. No longer do actions directly proceed via present consequences but via displacement (both temporal and spatial). Second, the hopes are by needs based on a perception of YHWH as just and not capricious. Third, the new hopes carry implicit cosmic implications. These new hopes involve the relation of the individual to the totality of YHWH's creation rather than to just the individual's family, tribe, or nation: the continued existence of the individual with recompense implies a transmundane community which in principle is broader than the existential horizons of any one earthly life. If one takes these three implicit principles, the re-interpretation of Ezek 37 in terms of bodily resurrection can be set in a useful framework.

The imagery of Ezek 37:1–14 is very vivid and strongly implies bodily resurrection *when one accepts such an idea as reasonable*. As discussed

revised edition (5–6) notes that this is now problematic; Setzer, *Resurrection of the Body*, 20, disputes progression in ideas at all. Cf. Nickelsburg, "Where is the Place of Eschatological Blessing?," 53–72.

9. E.g. Job 7:9; Pss 6:6; 21:5; 25:13; 30:4; 39:14; 49:12, 15; 88:11–13, etc.

10. E.g. Russell, *Method and Message*, 16; cf. the recantation in Nickelsburg, *Resurrection*, 5–6.

above, it seems that the similarities of this passage to Zoroastrian conceptions of bodily resurrection were already noted by some Jews in the Parthian Empire.[11] The passage itself, however, declares national restoration for both Israel and Judah. A return to Yehud did indeed later occur, albeit along differing lines.[12] Subsequent interpretations of the text would likely alter the political understanding of the oracle in light of the community in Yehud and in light of the known conceptions of bodily resurrection. What if a subsequent receiver of this text applied the above three principles to this text? A distancing of cause and consequence mean the two stages of revival in the vision (vv. 7, 10) could be interpreted as belonging to different times, places, and protagonists; even if the revival is attributed to a return to the land, the breath of YHWH could come subsequently. The rhetorical addition of graves in vv. 12–13 could also tend towards a secondary, individualized interpretation. The description of the bodies as slain (הרוגים) also invites a re-interpretation along lines which view death as unnatural. Further, since YHWH is just, the idea of a resurrection brings to bear questions of who is resurrected (can only *some* be resurrected, and if so, on what criteria?). Lastly, if YHWH has a *cosmos* broader than Israel, then how do individual Judaeans relate to this greater *cosmos* and the populations there implied? When these questions are added to a non-metaphorical interpretation of the oracle, very clear trajectories for afterlife speculations and ideas of bodily resurrection are thereby created. The potential influence of Iranian ideas of resurrection finds a logical place within the re-interpretation of the passage in the post-exilic period.[13]

For those for whom the older Hebraic hopes for the afterlife were insufficient, Ezek 37 provided a vivid hook whereby ideas of resurrection and immortality could be profitably explored within the Judaean tradition. When these questions are placed within a context of broader cosmological speculation, the development of the ideas of eternal heavenly life and resurrection are quite natural. It must be noted in this regard that Iranian conceptions of resurrection and human immortality are tightly bound up with the eschatological drama which is the *raison*

---

11. See Chapter 4.

12. Proper understanding of the trope of exile and return is highly contentious; see Grabbe, ed., *Leading Captivity Captive*; Scott, ed., *Exile*. The classic study is Ackroyd, *Exile and Restoration*.

13. After writing this analysis, the author was pleased to discover a similar analysis of the passage by Ricoeur in LaCocque and Ricoeur, *Thinking Biblically*, 165–83. Of course, the relation between Judaean transmundane expectations and Egyptian ideas are subject to the same considerations.

d'être of the material creation.[14] The pre-existent, spiritual forms of humans decided to enter physical form, die, and be bodily resurrected to enable the defeat of Angra Mainyu[15]—the bodily resurrection is one of the very mechanisms whereby evil is to be definitively defeated. This is inherently bound up, then, in an understanding of the *cosmos* itself, the relation of the individual to it, and the manner of divine justice and administration. Death itself plays a role in assuring its own defeat, and humanity's happiness is guaranteed by its tardiness. The potential impact of the Achaemenid Empire upon Judaean visions of the divine *cosmos* is periodically noted in Chapters 4 and 5.[16] Rather than attempting to see a one-to-one correspondence between individual Iranian views of the afterlife and Jewish ones, it is pertinent to note the similarities between the structure of the Iranian drama with the *types* of expectation within the Apocalyptic Hermeneutic. If one looks to the hermeneutic, Iranian influence on the questions for which Judaeans were seeking answers appears more likely than upon each individual Judaean's answers to these questions.[17]

Ezekiel 37:1–14 and its likely reception nicely illustrates how the Apocalyptic Hermeneutic helps to find a locus for situating potential Iranian influence within Second Temple Judaism, specifically within apocalyptic traditions. A closely related issue to understandings of the afterlife is the concept of a Day of Judgment, or cosmic Day of YHWH. This will be explored in light of Ezek 38–39.

The Day of Judgment: Ezekiel 38–39

The previous analysis of the Gog pericope proposes a more direct use of Iranian traditions within the passage itself, as well as a subsequent impact upon its interpretation.[18] The direct use of this passage in apocalypses is important (e.g. *1 Enoch*, the *War Scroll*, *Sibylline Oracles* 3, and Revelation);[19] the present analysis, however, intends to discuss how the passage

14. Cf. Chapter 1 and the note below.
15. *Yasna* 26.6 (*Zend-Avesta III*, 279); *Yašt* 13.76 (*Zend-Avesta II*, 198); *Sh. Bund.* 2.10–11; cf. 3.1–7 (*Pahlavi Texts I*, 14–16) = *Gr. Bund.* 3.23–24 (Anklesaria, *Zand-Ākāsīh*, 45).
16. E.g. Excursus: On the Watchers (pp. 171–74, above).
17. While attention to the function resurrection ideas played in communities is important, *a la* Setzer, *Resurrection*, this does not explain the emergence of the ideas in the first place or how anyone first came to espouse them.
18. Chapter 4.
19. Cf. Bøe, *Gog and Magog*, particularly 159–382; on the *War Scroll*, see Manning, *Echoes of a Prophet*, 34–37; to a lesser extent, see Wacholder, "Ezekiel and Ezekielianism," 194–95.

can be understood within the context of a developing Apocalyptic Hermeneutic. Of particular importance is the concept of negative or rhetorical influence, and the re-interpretation of previously present tradition, in this case the "Day of YHWH" traditions.

The Iranian influence proposed upon Ezek 38–39 above was one of appropriation for the sake of rhetorical combat, and as such, could be termed a conscious, negative influence.[20] The author made use of the religious imagery of the north-western Iranian peoples, in an ironic mode, to refute potential religious justifications for an invasion of (yet to be reconstituted) Israel, and thereby to strengthen the preceding prophecies. The rhetoric appropriated, however, became part of the tradition, coloring subsequent discourses within this receiving tradition. Several aspects of the rhetoric of Ezek 38–39 are notable in this regard. First, the oracle is neither predicated on a particular response on the part of Israel, nor is it viewed as imminent; it is a depiction of the revocation of the exile. This is in contrast to the divine threats which appear in other prophetic literature. Further, this distant future is depicted as already determined: there is no *if*. Gog is to marshal his allies for a call which will come, human responses notwithstanding. Lastly, the overthrow of the invading army is described as a purely divine effort in colorful, hyperbolic language, using a number of terms and motifs which would become stock apocalyptic language. The use of divine warrior imagery is drawn upon to its final extent to emphasize the purely divine nature of the war in view.[21] Like the story in Dan 2,[22] this oracle appears to have inadvertently imported an (implied) deferred eschatology in its utilization of imagery to declare the power of YHWH: he is not merely working through history, but has predetermined (at least some) aspects of human history for his intended ends. What would appear to have been intended as a historical guarantee—by its sequential placement in the book and its language—was susceptible to being re-read eschatologically (on eschatology, see below). Further, the apparent use of less-common referents for nations by the author gave rise to a situation where the historically specific grouping could be easily re-read as a universal attack (as, indeed, most modern scholars do).[23] Such a grouping further encourages a re-interpretation on a supra-historical level, particularly if one wishes to posit an eschatological battle.

20. See the Prolegomena and Chapter 4.
21. Miller, *The Divine Warrior in Early Israel*; Shellenberg, "Development of the Divine Warrior Motif in Apocalyptic"; Collins, "The Mythology of Holy War"; Cross, *Canaanite Myth*, 91–111; idem, *From Epic to Canon*, 22, 39.
22. See Chapter 4.
23. E.g. Bøe, *Gog and Magog*, 107; Block, *Ezekiel 25–48*, 439–40.

The use of Ezek 38–39 by the *Parables of Enoch* is extremely suggestive in this regard.[24] Using similar imagery, the Enochic author replaces Gog from Magog with the Parthians and Medes, who controlled a number of the regions identified in Ezekiel.[25] A similar phenomenon can be found in each passage: real, contemporary powers are depicted as playing a predetermined role in an unspecified future.[26] This has several implications for the Apocalyptic Hermeneutic. First, the oft repeated (and criticized[27]) dichotomy between history and myth is inadequate: both of the passages in Ezekiel and *1 Enoch* utilize historical events to describe an ahistorical event which is itself still envisioned as taking place on the earth. This historical typology, however, also utilizes mythological imagery and ideas as part of its self-understanding. In short, "history" and "myth" are fused. Second, both passages tap into the Day of YHWH tradition, yet both passages describe a battle which implies judgment which is both ultimate and final: it is *the* Day of YHWH not just *a* Day of YHWH. This would imply an interpretive process which is in some ways the inverse of the previous one—not only can events or myths be types of events to come, they may also be the shadow of the "real" ones to come. Such an interpretive principle would lead very readily into the abstract speculations which are so significant in many apocalypses.[28]

The Day of YHWH tradition has long been a focus of scholarly rancor as well as a point of appeal for the origins of apocalyptic.[29] It is most probable to understand the pre-apocalyptic tradition as a depiction of a theophany of YHWH, one which was expected both in sacred war on behalf of Israel and in cultic settings.[30] The first thing that can be noticed in this regard is that the very conception of the Day of YHWH embodies the fusion of history and myth which was claimed as characteristic of the

---

24. Bøe, *Gog and Magog*, 178–84.
25. Chapter 4.
26. Cf. Bøe, *Gog and Magog*, 107, 184.
27. Cf. Roberts, "Myth versus History," 1–13.
28. Cf. Rowland, *The Open Heaven*.
29. E.g. Smith, "The Day of Yahweh," 505–33; von Rad, "The Origin of the Concept of the Day of Yahweh," 97–108; Müller, *Ursprünge und Struckturen alttestamentlicher Eschatologie*, 72–85; Sæbø, "יום IV: Theological Usage," 28–31; Barton, "The Day of Yahweh in the Minor Prophets," 68–79.
30. Cf. Weiss, "The Origin of the 'Day of the Lord'—Reconsidered," 29–60; Mowinckel, *He That Cometh*, 145; Jeremias, *Theophanie*, 97–100, would separate the two via the Day of the Lord absorbing theophanic motives; see also Cross, *Canaanite Myth*, 91–111, who centers the motif on the Divine Warrior.

Apocalyptic Hermeneutic: this aspect can be seen in full continuity with earlier Judaean traditions. Yet, two disconnects with the earlier form of the Day can also be seen: a transfer of focus from *a* Day to *the* Day and a concomitant eschatologizing of the idea. Once the Day of YHWH becomes a consummate event, the cosmological and juridical aspects of the idea necessarily increase in importance: the Day of Judgment. The importation of eschatology into the Day of YHWH transforms it from a historical rhetoric (whether promise or threat) into a teleological point to which all other aspects of the Day must refer.

This passage, then, serves as an important crux for subsequent Judaean re-interpretation: it offers the seeds where the particularization of typology could easily occur in its wake. This was done on the basis of previous traditions marshaled against a (presumably) Median rhetoric/ideology. Wide scope was thus open for a variety of speculations on the nature and timing of YHWH's judgment, without any need for the tradent to feel like an innovator. Ample scope is left for individuals and groups to accept or reject more specific Iranian concepts within this sphere.

As repeatedly noted, the concept of a Day of Judgment, whether individual or universal, is intimately intertwined with the problem of the emergence of eschatological thought.

Eschatology: Daniel 2, the Book of Watchers

While the apocalypses are more than just eschatological treatises, eschatology is an essential part of what differentiates them from other genres of revelatory literature.[31] Two important aspects of eschatology are not always sufficiently noticed: the interpretive role of eschatology and the distinction between imminent and deferred eschatology. Eschatology shapes an important part of the Apocalyptic Hermeneutic, as by its very nature eschatology is an interpretive concept. This has been stated very well by Franke:

> It cannot be overemphasized that the very soul and inspiration of apocalyptic is the application to contemporary history of a theologically revealed vision of the end. This intrinsically hermeneutic dimension is the element in which apocalyptic springs to life, and it must be heeded if we are to understand apocalypse at a deeper level than that of its surface imagery, which is indeed meant to horrify and appall, but as a means of pointing out what is actually horrifying and appalling in the realities being lived historically.[32]

31. See the Prolegomena.
32. Franke, "Apocalypse and the Breaking-Open of Dialogue," 74.

The previous analyses of Dan 2 and of the *Book of Watchers* indicate some of the ways this ought to be understood. The analysis of Dan 2 contends that a deferred eschatology was imported along with an Iranian political oracle,[33] in a context which deliberately re-used prophetic language. It becomes apparent, then, that subsequent receivers accepted this eschatology in a context which implied that all previous prophetic uses of the terms related to the Day of YHWH also referred to eschatology. This point highlights a neglected aspect of debate over "prophetic" and "apocalyptic" eschatology: one's presuppositions greatly influence the way the relevant prophetic passages are read; the future expectations of many oracles *can* be read to describe the *eschaton*, but only *when one accepts the concept that there is a coming* eschaton. Once a group of Judaeans accepted the eschatology implicit in Dan 2, it was only a matter of simple extrapolation to read other texts eschatologically. As such, eschatology functions as a hermeneutical principle. That this occurred can easily be seen in extreme form in several of the *pešarim* found at Qumran.[34]

The other important aspect is the distinction between deferred and imminent eschatology, one which cannot be over-stressed. As noted above, the *content* of the eschatology in the two parts of Daniel is quite similar; they differ most prominently on the authors' perceived *proximity* to the *eschaton* itself. In fact, many of the differences between subgroups of various traditions can be understood as reflexes of the perceived imminence of shared eschatological ideas: even if person x and person y agree exactly in the content of eschatology, the importance of the eschatology and the likely modes of expression between the two will drastically vary if x thinks the *eschaton* is tomorrow and y in three thousand years. Urgency of the end would be more likely to produce millenarian groups and new apocalypses than its long-term deferral and more likely to make eschatology more prominent in the authors' works.[35]

The importance of these two points can be seen in some of the more "encyclopaedic" sections of the apocalypses.[36] Enoch's journeys in the

33. See Chapter 4.

34. A convenient collection and translation of the *pešarim* is available in Charlesworth et al., eds., *The Dead Sea Scrolls 6B*.

35. Cf. the history of Darbyism, which continues to see a series of imminent eschatologies; see the essays by Eaton, "Beware the Trumpet of Judgement," and O'Connor, "'Take one, it's FREE!'," in Bowie and Deacy, eds., *The Coming Deliverer*, 119–62 and 163–201, respectively; Newport and Gribben, eds., *Expecting the End*.

36. Also noted by Owen, "The Relationship of Eschatology to Esoteric Wisdom," 122–33.

Book of Watchers are a good example.[37] Enoch travels throughout the *cosmos* and learns arcane knowledge about many aspects of the world, yet much of the vast array of information is united by an orientation towards a deferred eschatology; he sees the prison for the Watchers and erring stars (chs. 19, 21), the place where the dead await judgment (ch. 22), the tree of life (ch. 25), a valley of punishment (ch. 27), and the future paradise (chs. 28–32). The author of this journey certainly had eschatological beliefs, but there is no indication of their imminence; later Enochic authors, however, seem to have interpreted their times as falling much closer to the end (e.g. the *Animal Apocalypse*).[38]

An important aspect, therefore, of the Apocalyptic Hermeneutic is eschatology, as well as the hermeneutes' perception of their own temporal relation to it. Following the rule that the most violent disputes are between those whose positions are most similar, it is to be expected that the interpretation of the temporal relations to the end are a major factor in schism and controversy without negating overall shared features.

Although the Apocalyptic Hermeneutic (as well as apocalyptic) consists of much more than just eschatology, eschatology is an underlying factor for much of it: cosmic, personal, national; afterlife, justice, the interpretation of the Day of the Lord, and so on, are all affected by it, and can be teased out once it is accepted as a principle of interpretation. This will need to be further discussed, making careful distinctions which are sometimes conflated.

(Re-)Constructing the Apocalyptic Hermeneutic (With an Eye Towards Iran)

The thesis advanced here is that the connecting thread between the various apocalypses, apocalypticism, and millenarian groups is an Apocalyptic Hermeneutic which consists of shared interpretive principles and some shared content, and that the most likely locus for Iranian influence is to be found therein. This is not to discount the importance of the likely variety of influences and borrowings in different apocalypses and other, non-apocalyptic Judaean texts; rather, placing the central focus here helps to contextualize and explain the more individual and scattered borrowings or influences which may be found.

Having preliminarily sketched out the concept of the Apocalyptic Hermeneutic above, it remains to describe more adequately its potential

---

37. Cf. Nickelsburg, *1 Enoch 1*, 55–56; Collins, *Seers, Sybils [sic] and Sages*, 50.
38. Tiller, *Animal*, 126.

relations to Iran. This will be attempted in three brief movements: first, a number of potential shared principles and contents will be listed—these are largely understood as dialectics and in relation to earlier extant Judaean traditions; second, the importance of textual and oral hermeneutics will be discussed; and lastly, a few suggested examples of how Iranian concepts can be seen to impact on the principles set forth will be presented.

Shared Principles of the Apocalyptic Hermeneutic
The Jerusalem Temple. Of fundamental importance to Judaean apocalyptic was the Jerusalem temple, a feature shared with most Judaeans. This can be seen in Daniel's indignation over its desecration and in *4 Ezra*'s distress over the temple's destruction. Few scholars would deny this point, but it is worth making explicit as a twofold reminder: first, that references to the sacrificial cult need not necessarily imply a priestly origin,[39] and second, that for all its abstract speculations, the Apocalyptic Hermeneutic relates to people within a concrete historical situation.

Nevertheless, in addition to the concrete elements, the theology/ ideology of the temple was susceptible to reformulation and divergent interpretation by different Judaean circles.[40] It must be queried, then, how these supra-cultic ideas may have interacted with other ideologies within the Achaemenid Empire (and its heirs)—whether along the lines of Imperial policy, official cults, or general Iranian attitudes.

Immanence and Transcendence. An important dialectic for apocalyptic is the immanence and transcendence of the divine. This dialectic is a consequence of the increased importance of monotheism; the one and only deity becomes increasingly transcendent, creating a religious need for more immanent divine manifestations. This gap is susceptible to a variety of solutions, depending on the inclinations of the hermeneute in question. As is commonly noted, angels, a "second power in heaven," and other mediatory figures are methods for reconciling the tension between the immanence and transcendence of the divine.[41] This has several implications which bear on the Apocalyptic Hermeneutic.

---

39. Nor does the absence of priests or temple need imply their rejection. See, e.g., Linville, "The Day of Yahweh and the Mourning of the Priests in Joel," 98–114.

40. E.g. Knibb, "Temple and Cult in Apocryphal and Pseudepigraphal Writings," 401–16; Brooke, "The Ten Temples in the Dead Sea Scrolls," 417–34.

41. Conrad, "The End of Prophecy and the Appearance of Angels/Messengers," 65–79, contends that an angelic solution can be seen in the Persian-period redaction of the Twelve.

First, the radical transcendence of YHWH tends towards determinism: the farther above he is, the less involved in minutiae he must be, and thus control must be predetermined. The second derives from the first; the minutiae of life must relate to subordinate characters, such as angels and demons. This construct not only helps to explain the common fascination with angelology in the apocalypses, it helps to explain their divergences. Depending on the issue in focus, the necessary intermediation will vary. It also offers a space for foreign interactions: the roles and functions of angels and gods of other systems can be re-appropriated to serve YHWH's minutiae.

The increased transcendence of YHWH is also likely to increase the dramatic nature of any posited divine intervention in history: the less immanent his workings, the more external and disruptive his interventions will appear. If the apocalypticist no longer sees YHWH's work directly in each historical moment, when YHWH does intervene in the moment, the consequences are likely to be viewed as catastrophic. Thus, the corollary to the increased transcendence of heaven is the increased uniqueness of the Day of YHWH. If the prophets saw YHWH directly at work behind the historical moment, the apocalyptic hermeneute saw YHWH directing all towards its ultimate culmination.

As mediators and managers for YHWH's celestial Imperium became more desirable, the hierarchical systems of Iran were surely influential (as was argued above for the concept of the Watchers)—both the "secular" system inherited by Alexander as well as the complex of Iranian deities.

Theodicy and Pessimism. Sacchi highlights the importance of theodicy to the *Book of Watchers* and apocalyptic in general—even as he overstates the case[42]—and there can be no doubt that theodicy is an important theme for the apocalypses (as, indeed, for religions in general). While it is true that crises are likely to increase the urgency of theodical concerns, they are problems which occupy thinking peoples of all circumstances. As with the dialectic of transcendence, the principle of monotheism pushes this issue to the fore. This is a problem which the apocalypticists shared with all their Judaean compatriots. However, for them the problem of evil and suffering was more urgent than for others: "apocalyptically important" to use the colloquial phrase. It is this pre-occupation with evil

42. Sacchi, *Jewish Apocalyptic*, particularly 72–87; Collins, "From Prophecy to Apocalypticism," 137.

which exposes the apocalypses—like their prophetic forebears—to the charge of pessimism.[43]

As Russell points out, the charge of pessimism is unfair:[44] a long-term hopefulness can just as rightly be seen in them. YHWH's justice *will* prevail, evil *will* be destroyed. This hope, however, is forged in the face of seemingly intractable evil.[45] A principle of the Apocalyptic Hermeneutic, then, must be the utmost seriousness of the problem of evil. This principle then leaves open a space for consideration of one of the major solutions to theodicy: ontological dualism. Whether it is ultimately accepted or rejected, it is difficult to envision anyone who took theodicy seriously—as do the apocalyptic hermeneutes—to completely ignore a system built upon the seriousness of evil (such as that ascribed to Zoroaster).

In this regard, a dialectic of evaluations of the *cosmos* should perhaps be posited within Second Temple Judaism, one in which Ben Sirah and the *Book of Watchers* would represent opposite poles: whether the world is good though prone to the invasions of chaos or whether creation itself is broken and in need of a fundamental replacement. One's response to this would determine whether the purpose of humankind was to maintain order or to fight evil.

Within this dialectic, a Yahwist who saw evil as a radical problem—for whatever reasons—would be more prone to accepting and utilizing a persophilic theodicy than one who did not. In either case, however, a variety of competing philosophies must have been available and in dialogue.

Teleology. One of the more neglected aspects in the study of apocalyptic is the issue of teleology.[46] The teleology of relevance here is twofold: of history and of the person. The Apocalyptic Hermeneutic moves beyond the teleology found in the prophetic literature: the prophets declare the purpose behind a historical moment or series of moments, while the apocalypses find a purpose behind *history as such*. This represents a major intellectual shift, which has implications for both eschatology and free will/determinism. For Jeremiah the fall of Jerusalem is a work of

43. E.g. Hanson, *The Dawn of Apocalyptic*, 11–12; Koch, *The Rediscovery of Apocalyptic*, 28–33.

44. Russell, *Method and Message*, 18; Rowland, "Apocalyptic Literature," 185; cf. Meeks, "Apocalyptic Discourse and Strategies of Goodness," 402, sees apocalyptic as "obsessed" with the possibility of goodness.

45. Cf. Fuery and Fuery, "The Pharmakon of the Apocalypse," 7–16.

46. Bull, "On Making Ends Meet," 1–6.

YHWH;[47] for Daniel it is merely a step in the progression of YHWH's plan for the earth. For the sages of Proverbs, righteousness will ensure long life;[48] for the *Parables of Enoch* it will ensure eternity with YHWH. The teleological concerns of the Apocalyptic Hermeneutic have expanded. There is a massive leap between claiming that YHWH is at work behind the present moment (and that one knows what this is) and claiming that he is behind the sweep of history.

As teleology expands, the perspective of ethical demands (the so-called Paraenesis) will change: rather than warning that order is being subverted, the addressee must orient to an order which will replace the current one, towards an order which requires a *striving towards*. Covenantal terms thus alter from a return to a prerequisite. This shift in teleology is largely a matter of hermeneutics, and the historical moment loses its importance *qua* moment, and remains merely in relation to time as a whole. Again, this is not merely a question of future expectation nor of history versus eschatology or myth, but of how history is understood and interpreted (i.e. the philosophy of history).

The broadened concept of teleology is much more at home in Iran than in Israel; therefore, ways in which the Iranian conceptions may have intersected with Judaean concepts of history must be considered.

Determinism and Freedom. The dialectic of determinism and free will is no stranger to Western theological or philosophical thought, nor to debates on apocalyptic literature and its antecedents. Nevertheless, it is worth stating that most apocalypses can be understood as preserving the tension between the two: insofar as they hold to the *eschaton*, history is pre-determined; insofar as they make ethical demands on their audience, they affirm free will. Nevertheless, the extant apocalypses place much less stress on the freedom of YHWH than previous Judaean literature and place more on his sovereignty. This is to be expected as a corollary to the increased transcendence of YHWH and the implicit determinism behind a teleological and eschatological theory of history. Such a perspective is conducive towards rampant cosmological speculations about the methods, manners, and details of YHWH's control over his empire. This speculation, of course, must have interacted with the knowledge of the relevant temporal empires: not only Ptolemaic, Seleucid, and Roman, but Achaemenid and Parthian as well.

47. E.g. Jer 1:15.
48. E.g. Prov 9:11.

Eschatology, Imminent and Deferred. The issue of eschatology has been broached several times in this study. The interpretive functions are discussed above, and a discussion of the imminent-deferred dialectic and its implications is overdue. That the world should terminate is not self-evident, nor is the idea that this terminus is the fulfillment of history.[49] Indeed, Cohn would argue that this concept is highly distinctive in the ancient Near East.[50] Be that as it may, the acceptance of the idea of an *eschaton* combined with a *telos* is highly significant for a worldview and its methods of interpretation.[51] However, the centrality of eschatology for a given interpretative system will vary in accordance with the manner in which the interpreter views the *eschaton*'s imminence or remoteness; the closer an interpreter believes the *eschaton* is, the more important it will be in their overall worldview. If it is far from nigh, a calm appraisal of speculations concerning it may be sufficient; if it is tomorrow, then not much else is likely to matter. Much in terms of perceived crisis relates directly to this aspect. An extremely deferred eschatology can even lead to the rhetorical downplaying of its importance.[52]

Not only the relative urgency of the eschatology is altered by its imminence or deferral; the popular acceptability of the concept is also highly affected thereby. The concept of a teleological *eschaton* is much easier to accept as a distant concept than as a present reality. Two things follow from this. First, a general tradition is more likely to adopt a deferred eschatology than an imminent one. Second, the role of crises should be viewed not as *creating* eschatological hopes, but in making their difficult aspects more popularly palatable. A period of intense suffering can be more easily depicted as the end than a blissful one. Thus, the relation of deprivation to the Apocalyptic Hermeneutic is less in the creation of eschatology and more in the ratcheting up of the popularly sensed imminence of an idea already existent.

From the hints adduced by Kingsley,[53] it may be profitable to explore whether the Achaemenid Great Kings propagated a deferred or an imminent eschatology as part of their own ideology (ones which may have been subsequently re-used in reaction to their fall). In any case, a closer look into the interpretive function of eschatology—as a historical

49. Bull, "On Making Ends Meet," 1.

50. Cohn, *Cosmos, Chaos and the World to Come*; idem., "How Time Acquired a Consummation," 21–37; Foster, "Mesopotamia and the End of Time," 23–32.

51. Evidence of this can easily be seen in the history of millenarianism; see, e.g., Cohn, *The Pursuit of the Millennium*; Newport and Gribben, eds., *Expecting the End*; Rowland and Barton, eds., *Apocalyptic in History and Tradition*.

52. Cf. Collins, *Encounters with Biblical Theology*, 134–36.

53. Kingsley, "Meetings with Magi," 174–209.

and philosophical-theological concept—should help to frame the question of whether/how much/where Iranian eschatology influenced its development in Second Temple Judaism better.

Typology, Mythology, and Prediction. The definition of myth is perhaps more fraught than that of apocalyptic;[54] rather than attempting to solve this dilemma, the implications of the apocalypses' use of myth is here explored for their methods of interpretation.

For the present purposes, myth is defined as "an attempt to understand and impart meaning to reality in narrative and symbolic form without regard to empiricist concerns."[55] In this sense, myth is characteristic of almost all Judaean literature. Yet, myths are particularly important in most apocalypses, and their authors' use of them is significant for their hermeneutic.

There are at least two methods of utilizing myth which must be distinguished: typological and predictive. Myths can be used as a way of interpreting an event or person: *this* is like or foreshadowed by *that*. A good example of this is the common use of Exodus motifs to describe a return from exile,[56] or in depicting a prophet like Moses.[57] Here myth is used to explain or characterize something else, much like an elaborate metaphor. As described by Burkert, "Myth usually takes what has happened once as a model for what is now."[58] However, myth can also be used predictively: examples would include expectations of a second Elijah.[59] These two uses are quite distinct, but often conflated in discussion of myth in the apocalypses. There is no reason why typological (or aetiological) use of myth need lead to predictive use of myth. A case in point is the "*Endzeit wird Urzeit*" trope and its often associated *Chaoskampf* motif. When one investigates these, it is appropriate to ask

54. For a variety of views, see the introduction (1–12) of Larson et al., eds., *Myth in Indo-European Antiquity*, with its parade of problematic definitions; see also Bowie, *The Anthropology of Religion*, 267–304; Caspo, *Theories of Mythology*; in the context of apocalyptic, see Grabbe, "Introduction and Overview," 20; Breslauer, "Mythology, Judaism and," 1812–33.

55. Author's own definition; see the explanation in Appendix III. Without digressing into the debate, the definition above was crafted since other current definitions are defective, either placing too much emphasis on one type of myth or excluding more modern forms of myth. This definition corrects the deficiencies of debates over myth, particularly in works such as Hanson, *The Dawn of Apocalyptic*; Arthur, *A Smooth Stone*, 278; or even Scholes et al., *The Nature of Narrative*, 55.

56. E.g. Goldingay, *Message of Isaiah 40–55*, 264.

57. E.g. O'Kane, "Isaiah: A Prophet in the Footsteps of Moses," 29–50.

58. Burkert, "The Logic of Cosmogony," 91.

59. E.g. Mal 4:5; Matt 11:14; 17:10; Mark 9:11.

whether they are being used typologically or predictively. Is the imagery of *Urzeit* hyperbolic or prognostic? Is the situation *like* a return to chaos or predicting an actual return of chaos? The two are cognitively very different even if literarily they can be quite difficult to distinguish.

It is here suggested, then, that an element of the Apocalyptic Hermeneutic is the addition of a predictive element to myth to its inherited typological use. The interpretative principle is an eschatologizing, predictive use of myth rather than merely its use instead of history.

Just like the other ancient Near East societies, Iran had a rich mythological tradition. If investigations into apocalyptic are open to the subtleties possible in the use of myth—to interpret as well as to predict—a wide vista for and broad array of possibilities towards the use of Iranian myths is opened. This need not in any way exclude the use of other mythologies (whether Egyptian, Babylonian, or Greek).

Epistemology. One's hermeneutic is highly impacted by one's epistemology. The apocalypses, by definition, evince a revelatory epistemology. This epistemology, however, has three bases: first, the acceptance of the revelatory nature of the nascent Hebrew Bible; second, the revelatory nature of their interpretations of that scripture; and third, the legitimacy of their own revelatory experiences. The first of these was likely shared with most Judaeans. The second and third, however, were as liable to the problematics of verification as that which attends prophecy.[60]

The importance of this threefold epistemology can be seen in Ben Sirah's reaction to it (34:1, 8).[61] Both the apocalypticists and Ben Sirah agree on the revelatory nature of texts and of their own interpretations; however, they disagree on the nature of their interpretations and on the value of personal revelations (visions, dreams).

If one accepts the possibility of real visionary experiences behind at least some of the apocalypses,[62] then a wide vista for interaction is opened up within the Apocalyptic Hermeneutic. Since the material of visions and dreams is constituted from the life-world of the visionary/dreamer, real visions offer a potential locus for (unconscious?) interactions to surface. Since the apocalypses accept these as revelatory, the content thus received would then become more consciously integrated into the tradents' apocalypticism. In other words, latent ideas have the

---

60. E.g. the discussion of Carroll, *When Prophecy Failed*, 14; Crenshaw, *Prophetic Conflict*; Overholt, *Channels of Prophecy*; Sanders, "Hermeneutics in True and False Prophecy," 23, 27.

61. Cf. Argall, *1 Enoch and Sirach*, 91–98; Wright, "Putting the Puzzle Together," 89–112.

62. E.g. Stone, "A Reconsideration of Apocalyptic Visions," 167–80.

potential of becoming explicit in visions. Vision-accepting groups hold the potential for exhibiting more blatant borrowings than vision-rejecting ones, although one must allow for negative and rhetorical influences on rejecters as well.

Perhaps an investigation into the scholarly paradigms of the Achaemenid Empire would discover parallel divergences in epistemologies elsewhere. "Ecstatic" traditions (such as *Haoma* use) could be explored for their impact either on the deuteronomistic rejections of divination or upon the source of the apocalypses' visions.

Conclusions

A focus on the Apocalyptic Hermeneutic as a locus for Iranian influence correlates disparate, discrete proposed parallels, while pointing towards a way of assessing their overall significance for the evolution of Second Temple Judaism. This is not to revert to abstract parallel-seeking, or to claim a back-door method for non-textual-based theorizing. Rather, focusing on the hermeneutic draws attention to the real-life processes in which these texts were created, the process in addition to the product.[63] Further, it helps bring clarity to a number of terms often used imprecisely, namely, imminent and deferred eschatology, teleology, and mythology. Of course, a similar focus would be equally beneficial for the investigation of influences from other quarters.

The phenomenon of the reinterpretation of traditions, both textual and contextual, offers the best way to understand both the situational context and the unity behind the diversity of the texts and their likely approach to ideas Persian. Paradoxically, the foci of scholarship on either individual apocalypses or on conceptual parallels have obscured how Iranian ideas could inform the process of their creation. It remains for scholarship to investigate more apocalypses individually and to relate them to the Apocalyptic Hermeneutic for a better picture to emerge of just how significant Israel's first encounters with Iran were.

Scholarship still needs, then, more textual analyses to be done and these to be related towards the overall Apocalyptic Hermeneutic. This ought to be done with reference to Achaemenid (and later Parthian) contexts and with careful consideration of the oral-literate dialectic. As such a study advances, it will be possible to answer the question posed here better : What was the significance of Iranian influence upon Jewish apocalyptic?

---

63. Cf. Davies, "Artistic Intentions and the Ontology of Art," 148–62.

METALEGOMENA

The preceding discussion adequately demonstrates the viability of and need for a reappraisal of Iranian influence upon Jewish apocalyptic. A focus on Achaemenid period history and ideology, close attention to Oral Theory, and a recognition of the Apocalyptic Hermeneutic provide a solid grounding for the sub-discipline.

Adopting the Apocalyptic Hermeneutic as a framework for investigating Iranian influence carries a wide-ranging array of fruitful implications. A focus on hermeneutics could very productively interact with Boccaccini's attempts to define "traditions" within Second Temple Judaism;[1] different traditions and/or sects likely operated with different hermeneutics. Each one of these hermeneutics—apocalyptic or not—would have likely interacted with Iranian ideas in divergent ways. Understanding how a group—or its text(s)—interpreted earlier traditions should help clarify the group's openness and potential to adapt from Iran, as well as its differences from other contemporary groups.

Based on the foregoing preliminary analyses, the Enochic tradition appears as a potential candidate for the most thoroughly "Iranicized" of traditions within Second Temple Judaism, evidencing complex interactions throughout its literary history. In contrast, groups like the Sadducees or scribes like Ben Sirah may have had much less (positive) influence, due primarily to the way in which they interpreted Judaean traditions. This does not mean, however, that such Yahwists could not have been unconsciously and negatively influenced.[2]

Further, understanding eschatology as a method of interpretation which was adopted by some in the Persian period has implications for the study of the final form of the Hebrew Bible. For example, perhaps the eschatologizing of the Day of YHWH influenced the final presentation of the Twelve Minor Prophets in the MT.[3]

1. E.g. Boccaccini, *Rabbinic Judaism*; idem., "Finding a Place for the Parables with Second Temple Jewish Literature," 263–89.

2. See the Prolegomena.

3. Cf. the recent trend to see the Twelve as a redacted unity; discussed in Redditt, "Recent Research on the Book of the Twelve as One Book," 47–80. Barton even thinks they evidence a unified eschatology; see Barton, "The Day of Yahweh in the Minor Prophets," 68–79.

This study focused in and advocated a closer engagement with the Achaemenid Empire. Since all Yahwists lived subject to the Great Kings for 200 years, this is historically justified and serves as a healthy balance to foci on the Neo-Babylonian and Hellenistic (Ptolemaic and Seleucid) empires. Nevertheless, Iran's significance is not limited to the direct heirs of Cyrus. The results of the analyses of Ezekiel above suggest that closer, sustained research into the Median Empire could prove rewarding,[4] perhaps in conjunction with the Assyrian exiles of north or south, or later Jewish enclaves.[5] Perhaps Tobit could belong within such a remit. For the study of early Christianity in particular, the role of Parthia and the Parthian period should not be ignored, either. As the major rival to Imperial Rome, Parthia had an important presence in the ancient Near East, an importance which potentially included its religious and imperial ideas.

A complex desideratum highlighted by this study is the need to investigate the effects and dynamics of the gradual interiorization of literacy in the Persian (and Hellenistic) periods, how this related to the emergence of the apocalypse, and how this interacted with the Persian bureaucracy and its heirs. Since Judaeans indeed served within the various administrative systems, these must have had important interactions. Perhaps one of the intersections of Persian interaction and literacy's interiorization will prove to be the Aramaization of the Judaeans' language.[6] If indeed the initial genesis of the apocalypse is a highly literate phenomenon, a final result of this slow progression of interiorization may prove to have been Qumran.

---

4. For Media, see Diakonoff, "Media," 35–148; Stronach, "Tepe Nūsh-i Jān: The Median Settlement," 832–36; Calmeyer, "Art in Iran II: Median Art and Architecture," 565–69; Vogelsang, *Rise and Organization*, who makes much of the role of Media for the rise of the Achaemenids; Summers, "The Median Empire Reconsidered," 55–73; Genito, "The Archaeology of the Median Period," 315–40.

For Parthia, see Boyce, "The Parthian *gōsān* and Iranian Minstrel Tradition," 10–45; Widengren, *Iranisch-semitische Kulturbegegnung*; idem., "Iran and Israel in Parthian Times," 139–77; Yarshater, ed., *CHI*, vol. 3 (in 2 vols.); Curtis et al., eds., *The Art and Archaeology of Ancient Persia*.

5. Cf. an overview of Median sources in Bivar, "Mithraism: A Religion for the Ancient Medes," 341–58; for the archaeology, see Genito, "The Archaeology of the Median Period," 315–40.

6. Of course, the relative roles of Hebrew and Aramaic are still much contested, although the importance of Imperial Aramaic for the administration cannot be gainsaid. It is odd that Aramaic is barely mentioned in Gruber, "Language(s) in Judaism," 1535–50. For a study in this vein (although without reference to Persia), see Block, "The Role of Language in Ancient Israelite Perceptions of National Identity," 321–40.

A commonly postulated locus for Iranian influence—the so-called sectarian documents from the Dead Sea Scrolls—deserves a reconsideration in light of the methodology proposed in this study. Understanding influence as effecting the kinds of questions asked even before individual details should help to nuance the peculiar situation where the most obvious Iranian affinities—at least, on the surface—appear in texts dated well after the Persian period. Whether this would prove to be relatable to the Achaemenids or the Parthians remains to be seen.

A simplistic yes or no to the question posited by this study is no longer tenable; previous studies need to be replaced by a new paradigm founded on the apocalyptic hermeneutic and complex oral-literate interactions situated within the Achaemenid and later Parthian contexts. A wide array of ideas—from sociological affinities to royal ideologies to religion—need to be considered separately and in concert. It is highly likely, however, that the questions which Yahwists asked—of their traditions and their texts—were impacted by the Achaemenid context. With this perspective in mind, once such a broad spectrum of studies has been completed, biblical scholarship should finally be able to synthesize a sound answer to the question "What has Persepolis to do with Jerusalem?"

APPENDIX I:
SOURCES

Iranian Sources

Cf. KELLENS (1989), MALANDRA (1983), SKJÆRVØ (1995); KUHRT (2009).

1. THE AVESTA. The Avesta is a collection of sacred texts. Rather than viewing the Avesta as the "Zoroastrian Bible," it is better to compare it to the Anglican Book of Common Prayer. The only comprehensive translation of these texts in English is still the dated collection in the Sacred Books of the East Series (SBE). In addition, a variety of selected passages are presented in Boyce (1984).

Translations and critical editions:

a. **The Gāthās.** INSLER (1975); HUMBACH, ELFENBEIN, AND SKJÆRVØ (1991). For easily accessible translations, see: DUCHESNE-GUILLEMIN (1992); *Zend-Avesta III*.

b. **The Yasna Haptaŋhāiti.** NARTEN (1986); HINTZE (2008). Humbach's translation of the Gāthās also includes the Haptaŋhāiti. See also *Zend-Avesta III*.

c. **The Vidēvdāt.** (also known as the Vendidad) ANKLESARIA (1949); *Zend-Avesta I*.

d. **The Yašts.** The only comprehensive English translation of all the Yašts remains the SBE edition: *Zend-Avesta II*. A German translation of the complete Avesta (including the Yašts) is WOLFF (1960). See now KOTWAL AND HINTZE (2008). Five of the Yašts are available in critical editions:

   Tištrya Yašt (Yt. 7): PANAINO (1990).

   Mihr Yašt (Yt. 10): GERSHEVITCH (1959).

   Fravaši Yašt (Yt. 13): MALANDRA (1977).

   Vayu Yašt (Yt. 15): A translation is available in the first part (pp. 1–12) of WIKANDER (1941) vol 1.

   Zamyad Yašt (Yt. 19): HINTZE (1994); HUMBACH AND ICHAPORA (1998).

2. VARIOUS PRAYERS AND FRAGMENTS. Various other texts in the Avestan language have survived. A funeral liturgy, the Aogəmadaēcā, quotes both extant and lost Avestan passages.

Translations:

    a. **The Sirozahs and Niyayeš.** *Zend-Avesta II.*

    b. **The Aogəmadaēcā.** JAMASP ASA (1982).

3. THE OLD PERSIAN INSCRIPTIONS. A number of inscriptions in OP cuneiform have been found throughout Iran from the reigns of Darius I to Artaxerxes II.

Translations and Critical Editions:

    a. **General Corpus.** The standard edition, with grammatical discussion, is KENT (1961). More recently, selected translations (without transcriptions) are offered by BROSIUS (2000). For a correction to two of Kent's versions, see SCHMITT (1999).

    b. **Critical Editions and Facsimiles.** For Darius's Bisitun/ Behistun inscription, see the editions of: SCHMITT (1991); GREENFIELD, PORTEN, AND YARDENI (1982); VON VOIGT-LANDER (1978). For Persepolis itself, see SHAHBAZI (1985). For Post-Achaemenid Iranian inscriptions, see GIGNOUX (1972).

4. VARIOUS TABLET ARCHIVES. Most relevant are the Elamite cuneiform archives found at Persepolis (The Treasury Tablets and the Fortification Tablets.) Not all of the tablets have been published to date.

Translations and Critical Editions:

    a. **Persepolis Tablets.** CAMERON (1948); CAMERON AND GERSHEVITCH (1965); HALLOCK (1969; 1977; 1978); BOWMAN (1970); STOLPER (1984); RAZMJOU (2004 [2d ed.]); JONES AND STOLPER (2006); STOLPER AND TAVERNIER (2007); ARFA'I. (2008). Some unpublished texts are discussed in HENKELMAN (2008).

    b. **Babylonian Tablets.** Several Akkadian archives provide information for the Achaemenid Empire. Commonly cited is the **Murašu Archive.** This Archive is published in CARDASCIA (1951). For the Ergibi texts, see ABRAHAM (2004). More recently discovered is the **TAYN** archive, which is discussed in PEARCE (2006).

5. VARIOUS PAPYRI.

Translations and Critical Editions:

    a. **Egyptian Papyri.** A number of collections of papyri from Egypt have been published, see: PORTEN (1996); DRIVER (1954); COWLEY (1967); KRAELING (1953).

    b. **Samarian Papyri.** In the DJD series: WINN LEITH (1997); GROPP ET AL. (2001).

6. THE PAHLAVI WRITINGS. For a list of a variety of other texts and editions, see NYBERG (1964). The only comprehensive English translation is again in SBE.

Translations and Critical Editions:

    a. **The Bundahišn.** "Greater" Bundahišn: ANKLESARIA (1956); The "Shorter" Bundahišn: SBE 5, *Pahlavi Texts I.*

    b. **Zand-ī Vahman Yašn.** CERETI (1995); ANKLESARIA (1957); SBE 5, *Pahlavi Texts I.*

    c. **Ardā Virāz Nāmag.** Facsimiles and translation are available in VAHMAN (1986).

    d. **Dēnkard.** The Dēnkard is not available in its entirety in translation. A facsimile is available in DRESDEN (1966). A variety of scholars offer translations of portions of the Dēnkard, including, BOYCE (1984); BAILEY (1971); ZAEHNER (1956). Two volumes of the SBE offer translations of parts of Books VII and IX. See: SBE 37, *Pahlavi Texts IV*; SBE 47, *Pahlavi Texts V.*

    e. **Mēnōg-ī Xrad.** The only complete English translation of this text is SBE 24, *Pahlavi Texts III.* Selections are also available in ZAEHNER (1956).

7. ARCHAEOLOGICAL SOURCES. Cf. ROOT (1979).

Monumental Remains. Excavations have been conducted at the imperial capitals of Pasargadae, Persepolis, and Susa, but not yet at Ecbatana.

    Reports:

STRONACH (1978); SCHMIDT (1953, 1957, 1970); BOUCHARLAT (2002). For recent salvage excavations in Fars, see the following Achemenet reports: ADACHI AND ZEIDI (2009); CHAVERDI AND CALLIERI (2009); ATAI AND BOUCHARLAT (2009); ASADI AND KAIM (2009); HELWING AND SEYEDIN (2009); HENKELMAN, JONES, AND STOLPER (2004, 2006).

APPENDIX II:
GLOSSARY OF IRANIAN TERMS

When possible, words appear initially in their Avestan form, followed by the Pahlavi in parentheses, e.g., Miθra (Mihr).

Aēšma (Xēšm): Personification of "wrath" and a demon in Zoroastrianism. First appears in the *Gāthās*.

Ahura: Avestan equivalent of Sanskrit "Asura," meaning "lord," designates some Indo-Iranian deities.

Amǝša Spǝnta (Amahraspand): Personified abstractions which emanate from *Ahura Mazda*. Originally a fluid group, by the Young Avesta they were standardized into a group of seven.

Aŋra Mainiiu/Angra Mainyu (Ahriman): "The Devil" of Zoroastrianism, technical name derived from "evil/malignant spirit." He is the inverse of *Ahura Mazda* in all respects.

Aogǝmadaēca: A late Avestan funeral liturgy.

Apadāna: OP word for a columned hall.

Ardā Virāz Nāmag: A ninth- to tenth-century Pahlavi apocalypse, with a tour of heaven and hell. Often described as "the Persian *Divine Comedy*."

Arǝdvī Sūrā Anāhitā (Ardvīsūr): Goddess, probably originally the deification of a spring or river, later assimilated to/identified with Anaïtis and Ištar. One of four deities which appear in OP inscriptions.

Ārmaiti (Spendārmad): Personification of obedience or religious devotion, patron of the earth, and one of the *Amǝša Spǝnta*s.

Arštāt (Aštād): Personification of justice.

Aša: "Truth" or "Order," the good principle of the universe and the quality of all Ahura Mazda's creation. Appears as *Rta* in Sanskrit and *Arta* in OP.

Aša Vahišta (Ardvahišt): The personification of *Aša* as one of the *Amǝša Spǝnta*s.

Aši (Ard): Personification of "Reward, recompense."

Astuuat.ǝrǝta: The given name of the only Saošiiant in the original eschatological framework and of the final Saošiiant in the tripled version.

Astōdān: OP for an ossuary.

Aži Dahāka: Mythical, three-headed dragon who became an arch-accomplice of Angra Mainyu. He was defeated by *Θraētaona*; in some versions he lays bound inside Mount Damavand, awaiting his release and death at the hands of *Kǝrǝsāspa*.

Barǝsman (Barsom): Originally a pile of grass or twigs providing a seat for divinities visiting sacrifices. Later became a bundle of twigs held by the priests during the ceremony, as is visible on a number of Achaemenid remains.

Bundahišn: A ninth- to tenth-century Pahlavi epitome and commentary on the Avestan creation and eschatological myths. Contains the most systematic presentation of Zoroastrian eschatology extant.

Činvatō Pəretu (Činvat Puhl): Bridge over which the newly deceased soul must pass to reach paradise. If the soul is wicked the bridge reduces to a hair's breadth and the soul plunges to hell; if it is righteous the bridge becomes wide.

Daēna (Dēn): Common noun means "religion." As a personification, it represents a deceased soul's conscience, appearing after death to reward or rebuke. Also sometimes personified as a separate *yazata* representing Zoroastrianism itself.

Daēuua (Dēw): Avestan for "demon." Originally denoting Indo-Iranian deities.

Daxma: Originally a grave; after the widespread adoption of exposure became a technical term for the places of exposure later termed "towers of silence."

Dēnkard: A ninth-century Pahlavi work which includes a summary of the contents of the Avestan Nasks and summarizes some of them.

Druj (Drōz): "Lie," "deceit"; the evil principle of the universe; the opposite of *Aša*.

Frašo.kərəti (Frašegird): "Making wonderful," the eschatological restoration of the world to the perfection originally created by Ahura Mazda.

Frauuasi (Fravard/Frawahr): A band of warrior deities, spirits of the ancestors, and the eternal "essence" of a righteous entity; which meaning is intended at a given time is not always clear.

Gāthās: Esoteric religious poems in Old Avestan traditionally ascribed to Zarathuštra which form the central portion of the *Yasna*.

Haoma (Hōm): The juice pounded from an unknown plant and used during the *Yasna*. The mortars and pestles found at Persepolis are usually connected to *Haoma*. "Soma" in Sanskrit.

Haurvātat and Amərətat (Hordād and Amurdād): Personifications of "Health" and "Immortality." respectively and two of the *Aməša Spəntas*. Usually appear together.

Kavi Vīštāspa: The legendary first convert and patron of Zaraθuštra; also the namesake of Darius I's father and the *Oracle of Hystaspes*.

Kərəsāspa (Garšāsp): One of the great heroes of Iranian tradition, known for fighting dragons. In some myths he is asleep to be awoken at the end of time to defeat the bound *Aži Dahāka*.

*Mainiiavaka/*Gaēθiiaka (Mēnōg/Gētīg): Spiritual/Material or intangible/tangible. Ahura Mazda first created the world in a *mēnōg* state and then in a *gētīg* state. This "dualism" does not coincide with the ethical dualism (as in Gnosticism).

Mēnōg-ī Xrad: A ninth-century Pahlavi writing on miscellaneous issues.

Miθra (Mihr): Indo-Iranian deity, personification of "contract," and related to the sun. Appears in Sankrit as *Mitra* and Old Persian as *Miça*. His relationship to the Roman *Mithras* is unclear.

*Miθrakāna (Mihragān): Annual autumnal festival. Al-Biruni reports that it honored the binding of *Aži Dahāka*, and Herodotus reports of a festival in honor of Miθra on which the Great King became drunk.

Nask: A "book" or major division of the *Avesta*. Originally there were 21.

Niyāyeš: Daily prayers for times of the day, largely extracted from the *Avesta*.

Old Avestan: The language of the *Gāthās* and the *Yasna Haptaŋhāiti*. The oldest extant Iranian language.

Pahlavi: The form of the Persian language after OP and before Modern Persian/Farsi.

Rašnu (Rašn): "The Judge"; *yazata* who, with *Miθra* and *Sraoša*, will judge the souls of the dead.

Saošiiant (Sōšyant): "The Over-comer, Savior"; Originally used of worshippers and ultimately for the eschatological savior who will usher in the *Frašo.kərəti*.

Sirozahs: Dedicatory prayers to the patron deities of the Zoroastrian calendar.

Spənta Mainiiu (Spennāg Mēnōg): "The Beneficial/Bountiful/Holy Spirit"; sometimes considered simply an aspect/emanation of Ahura Mazda, sometimes identified with him; usually counted as one of the *Aməša Spəntas*.

Sraoša (Srōš): Personification of "(Religious) Obedience"; one of the *yazatas* who judge the individual soul.

Tīri (Tīr): An obscure Western Iranian deity in the Zoroastrian Calendar and in Western Iranian names. Later identified with the Avestan deity *Tištrya*.

Tištrya (Teštar): Rain deity usually identified with the star Sirius.

Θraētaona (Frēdon): Indo-Iranian hero, associated with the defeat of dragons, especially *Aži Dahāka*.

Vāta (Wād): Indo-Iranian *Yazata* of the winds.

Vayu (Wāy): Indo-Iranian personification simultaneously of the wind, the breath of life, and of death. Was divided in Zoroastrianism into two, a "good *Vayu*" associated with resurrection and an "evil *Vayu*" associated with death.

Vidēvdāt (Vendidād): "Laws against the demons"; a Young Avestan text which compiles a variety of ritual purity laws and some fragments of myths.

Vərəθraghna (Wahrām, Bahrām): Personification of "victory." Often associated with *Miθra*, but with own *Yašt* (14).

Vohu Manah (Wahman): "Best Thought," the *Aməša Spənta* who imparted revelation to Zaraθuštra. Contrasted with the demon *Aka Manah*, "Bad Thought."

Xšaθra Vairiia (Shahrevar): Personification of "rule, dominion." One of the *Aməša Spəntas*.

Xᵛarənah (Khwarr(ah), Farnah): "Glory," "fortune," or "Glückglanz." Usually reserved for kings, heroes, and divinities.

Yasna (Yašn): "Worship." Technical term for the liturgy and sacrifice as well as the Avestan sections recited during the sacrifice.

Yasna Haptaŋhāiti: Seven Old Avestan poems which are surround by the *Gāthās* in the liturgical arrangement of the *Yasna*. Either slightly younger than or contemporaneous with the *Gāthās*.

Yašt: Young Avestan hymns dedicated to various deities, of varying antiquity.

Yazata: Zoroastrian term for anything "worthy of worship" (i.e. from Ahura Mazda).

Young Avestan: The language of the *Yašts*, *Aogəmadaēca*, *Vidēvdāt*, and parts of the *Yasna.* Likely contemporaneous with OP.

Zand: "Interpretation or Commentary." Used of the Pahlavi commentaries to the Avesta.

Zand-ī Wahman Yašn: A ninth-century Pahlavi work, supposedly an epitome and commentary upon a lost Avestan *Yašt*.

Zaoθra (zōhr): Libation or blood sacrifice.

APPENDIX III:
ANNOTATED DEFINITIONS OF TERMS

Dialectic

Definition
Dialectic is the interplay and relationship between two opposites which remain in perpetual tension.

Comments
This understanding of dialectics is based on Kierkegaard and explicitly contradicts the Hegelian and Marxist notion of Thesis–Antithesis–Synthesis (there is no synthesis). It is necessary to distinguish carefully between "dialectic" and "dichotomy." Dichotomies are merely opposites which fail to interact, and thus fail to explain complex relationships.

Eschatology

Definition
Eschatology is a category of beliefs regarding the decisive termination or transformation of the cosmos or the individual, beyond which present historical processes can never recur.

Comments
Conflating future predictions and hopes with eschatology confuses the very different kinds of understanding involved with each. Restricting eschatology to a decisive end does not impinge recognition of the vast array of ends which can be imagined or advocated. The differences between these are involved with teleology (ultimate goal) of either the world or the individual. The idea of purpose, however, is independent from termination.

Hermeneutic

Definition

A hermeneutic is the point of departure and reflexive personal alignment from which, through which, and by which an individual and/or community receives, understands, interprets, and re-creates traditions, circumstances and ultimately worldview, involving some specific content which supports favored methodologies and media, while occurring with specific reference to a real social context. This may but need not be held exclusively of other hermeneutics by the same individual or group.

Comments

The definition describes the way humans practically interpret their traditions and surroundings rather than texts *per se*, as in much of the post-Schleiermacher tradition. Human beings cannot avoid interpretation, and the manner and principles by which this is done—however intuitively or explicitly—is open to analysis and investigation. These hermeneutics are vitally important for understanding any tradition's relationships with previous traditions.

Influence

Definition

Influence designates the reshaping, selection, and/or interpretation of native ideas, stories, characters, or doctrines due to interaction with another culture or tradition which occurs within living traditions.

Comments

This definition highlights the complexity involved in influence and its dialectical rather than dichotomous nature. Influence relates "native" and "foreign," intentionality and unconscious processes, and calls for an analysis of hermeneutics, ideas, and myths.

Interiorization

Definition

Interiorization is the process whereby a technology becomes integrated into individual and societal psychological processes and becomes part of the cognitional and functional norm. The first stage of this is called amplification, the phenomenon whereby aspects of a previous technology are at first increased by the advent of a new technology.

Comments

This concept is derived from McLuhan and Ong and is an important tool for understanding how a technology transforms and is transformed by a society and an individual. Interiorization allows for a nuancing of effects synchronistically and diachronistically due to variations in the extent of its process. A falsely dichotomous "Great Divide" is thus avoided without neglecting the implications—psychologically and communicatively—of technological-communicative change.

Myth

Definition

A myth is an attempt to understand and impart meaning to reality in narrative and symbolic form without regard to empiricist concerns.

Comments

This definition focuses on function not limited to cosmogonic/theogonic myths, an approach reflecting how other stories function symbolically and meaningfully in the same manner. The qualifier "without regard to empiricist concerns" is essential to this definition because it highlights two aspects: (1) myth and history are not dichotomous—they simply relate differently to empirical evidence; (2) a story's mythic and historical natures are independent.

Modern societies have stories which function as myth like ancient ones; the myth of George Washington in America or of the 800 years of English oppression in Ireland have the same culturally defining and orienting function as the myths of Athena or Abraham. When these modern stories are told not as historiography but as explanations for the way things are or ought to be, they are myths. It is this function which is important—the teller is not concerned with the evidence *per se* but with how it explains and imparts meaning to reality, and thus function is mythic regardless of what the teller thinks of the story's historicity.[1]

This definition therefore transcends specific genre categories; the only generic necessity is narrative.

---

1. In some cases, a story's perceived historicity can be used to justify its normativity.

BIBLIOGRAPHY

Aaron, David H. *Etched in Stone: The Emergence of the Decalogue*. London: T&T Clark, 2006.

Abdi, Kamyar. "Bes in the Achaemenid Empire." *Ars Orientalis* 29 (1999): 111, 113–40.

———. "The 'Daiva' Inscription Revisited." *Nāme-ye Irān Bāstān* 6, no. 1–2 (2006): 45–74.

———. "Notes on the Iranization of Bes in the Achaemenid Empire." *Ars Orientalis* 32 (2002): 133–62.

Aberle, David F. "A Note on Relative Deprivation Theory as Applied to Millenarian and Other Cult Movements." Pages 5:7–12 in Hamilton, ed., *The Sociology of Religion*.

Achtemeier, Paul J. "Omne verbum sonat: The New Testament and the Oral Environment of Late Western Antiquity." *JBL* 109, no. 1 (1990): 3–27.

Ackroyd, Peter R. "The Biblical Portrayal of Achaemenid Rulers." Pages 1–16 in *Achaemenid History V*. Edited by Heleen Sancisi-Weerdenburg and J. W. Drijvers. Leiden: NINO, 1990.

———. *Exile and Restoration*. London: SCM, 1968.

———. *Israel Under Babylon and Persia*. Oxford: Oxford University Press, 1970.

———. "The Written Evidence for Palestine." Pages 207–20 in Sancisi-Weerdenburg and Kuhrt, eds., *Achaemenid History IV*.

Adams, Charles J., ed. *Iranian Civilization and Culture*. Montreal: McGill, 1972.

Aelian. *On the Characteristics of Animals*. Translated by A. F. Scholfield. *On the Characteristics of Animals III (Books XII–XVII)*. LCL. Cambridge, Mass.: Harvard University Press, 1959.

Aeschylus. *Suppliant Maidens, The Persians, Prometheus Bound, and Seven Against Thebes*. Translated by Herbert W. Smyth. *Aeschylus I: Plays*. LCL. London: Heinemann, 1922.

Afnan, Ruhi Muhsen. *Zoroaster's Influence on Greek Thought*. New York: Philosophical Library, 1965.

Ahlström, Gösta W. *The History of Ancient Palestine*. Minneapolis: Fortress, 1994.

———. "Oral and Written Transmission. Some Considerations." *HTR* 59 (1966): 69–81.

Ahn, Gregor. "Dualismen in Kontext von Gegenweltvorstellungen. Die rituelle Abwehr der Dämonen im altiranischen Zoroastrismus." Pages 122–36 in Lange and Lichtenberger, eds., *Die Dämonen/Demons*.

Aiken, C. F. "The Avesta and the Bible." *Catholic University Bulletin* 3 (1897): 243–91.

Akinnaso, F. Niyi. "Literacy and Individual Consciousness." Pages 73–94 in *Literate Systems and Individual Lives*. Edited by Edward M. Jennings and Alan C. Purves. New York: SUNY Press, 1991.

Al-Biruni, Muhammad ibn Ahmad. *Athar-ul-bakiya*. Translated by C. Edward Sachau. *The Chronology of Ancient Nations: An English Version of the Arabic Text of the Athâr-ul-Bâkiya of Albîrûnî or 'Vestiges of the Past'*. London: Allen, 1879.

Albertz, Rainer. "Darius in Place of Cyrus: The First Edition of Deutero-Isaiah (Isaiah 40.1–52.12) in 521 BCE." *JSOT* 27 (2003): 371–83.

———. *A History of Israelite Religion in the Old Testament Period.* 2 vols. London: SCM, 1994.

———. *Israel in Exile: The History and Literature of the Sixth Century BCE.* Translated by David Green. Atlanta: SBL, 2003.

Alexander, Philip S. "The Enochic Literature and the Bible: Intertextuality and Its Implications." Pages 57–69 in *The Bible as Book.* Edited by Edward D. Herbert and Emmanuel Tov. London: British Library, 2002.

Allsen, Thomas T. *The Royal Hunt in Eurasian History.* Philadelphia: University of Pennsylvania Press, 2006.

Alvarex-Mon, Javier. "Imago Mundi: Cosmological and Ideological Aspects of the Arjan Bowl." *Iranica Antiqua* 39 (2004): 203–37.

Amanat, Abbas, and Magnus Bernhardsson, eds. *Imagining the End: Visions of Apocalypse from the Ancient Middle East to Modern America.* London: I. B. Tauris, 2002.

Amiran, Ruth. "Achaemenian Bronze Objects from a Tomb at Kh. Ibsan in Lower Galilee." *Levant* 4 (1972): 135–38.

———. "The Persian-Achaemenid Impact on Palestine." Pages 14:3017–23 in Pope and Ackerman, eds., *A Survey of Persian Art.*

Amodio, Mark C., and Katherine O. O'Keeffe, eds. *Unlocking the Wordhord.* Toronto: University of Toronto Press, 2003.

Amzallag, Nissim. "Yahweh, the Canaanite God of Metallurgy?" *JSOT* 33, no. 4 (2009): 387–404.

Andersen, Francis I. "2 (Slavonic Apocalypse of) Enoch." *OTP* 1:91–222.

———. *Habakkuk: A New Translation with Introduction and Commentary.* New York: Doubleday, 2001.

Anderson, Øivind. "The Significance of Writing in Early Greece—A Critical Appraisal." Pages 73–90 in Schousboe and Larsen, eds., *Literacy and Society.*

Anderson, William S. *Ovid's Metamorphoses Books 1–5 Edited, with Introduction and Commentary.* Norman, Ok.: University of Oklahoma Press, 1997.

Anföldi, Andreas. "Königsweihe und Männerbund bei dem Achämeniden." *Archives Suisses des Traditions Populaires/Schweizerisches Archiv für Volkskunde* 47 (1951): 11–17.

Anklesaria, Behramgore T. *Pahlavi Vendidâd (Zand-î Jvît-dêv-dât): Transliteration and Translation in English.* Edited by Dinshah Kapadia. Bombay: K. R. Cama Oriental Institute, 1949.

———. *Zand-Ākāsīh: Iranian or Greater Bundahisn: Text and Translation.* Bombay: Rahnumae Mazdayasnan Sabha, 1956.

———. *Zand-î Vohûman Yasn and Two Pahlavi Fragments: Text, Transliteration, and Translation.* Bombay: Mrs. B. T. Anklesaria, 1957.

Aperghis, G. G. "Storehouses and Systems at Persepolis: Evidence from the Persepolis Fortification Tablets." *Journal of the Economic and Social History of the Orient* 42, no. 2 (1999): 152–93.

Argall, Randal A. *1 Enoch and Sirach.* Atlanta: Scholars, 1995.

Ariel, Yaakov, and Ruth Kark. "Messianism, Holiness, Charisma, and Community: The American-Swedish Colony in Jerusalem, 1881–1933." *CH* 65, no. 4 (1996): 641–57.

Arjomand, Saïd Amir. "Artaxerxes, Ardašīr, and Bahman." *JAOS* 118, no. 2 (1998): 245–48.

Arndt, William F., and F. Wilbur Gingrich. *A Greek–English Lexicon of the New Testament and Other Early Christian Literature. A translation and adaptation of Walter Bauer's Griechisch-Deutsches Wörterbuch zu den Schriften des Neuen Testaments und der übrigen urchristlichen Literatur,* 4th ed. Cambridge: Cambridge University Press, 1957.

Arrian. *Anabasis Alexandri, Books I–IV.* Translated by P. A. Brunt. *Arrian I.* LCL. Cambridge, Mass.: Harvard University Press, 1976.

———. *Anabasis Alexandri Books V–VII; Indica.* Translated by P. A. Brunt. *Arrian II.* LCL. Cambridge, Mass.: Harvard University Press, 1983.

Arthur, David. *A Smooth Stone: Biblical Prophecy in Historical Perspective.* Lanham, Md.: University Press of America, 2001.

Asa, K. M. Jamasp. "Relationship Between Zoroastrianism and Judaism." Pages 340–44 in *Second International Congress Proceedings of the K. R. Cama Oriental Institute (5th–8th Jan, 1995).* Bombay: K. R. Cama Oriental Institute, 1996.

Asmussen, Jes P. "Aešma." *EncIr* 1 (1985): 479–80.

———. "Die Verkündigung Zarathustras im Lichte der Religionsgeschichte." *Temenos* 6 (1970): 20–35.

Astour, Michael C. "Ezekiel's Prophecy of Gog and the Cuthean Legend of Naram-Sin." *JBL* 95, no. 4 (1976): 567–79.

Athenaeus. *The Deipnosophists.* Translated by Charles B Gulick. *Athenaeus VI.* LCL. London: Heinemann, 1937.

Auffarth, Christoph, and Loren T. Stuckenbruck, eds. *The Fall of the Angels.* Leiden: Brill, 2004.

Aune, David E. *Apocalypticism, Prophecy and Magic in Early Christianity.* Tübingen: Mohr Siebeck, 2006.

———. "Transformations of Apocalypticism in Early Christianity." Pages 54–64 in Grabbe and Haak, eds., *Knowing the End from the Beginning.*

Avemarie, Friedrich, and Hermann Lichtenberger, eds. *Auferstehung—Resurrection.* Tübingen: Mohr Siebeck, 2004.

Avigad, Nahman. *Bullae and Seals from a Post-Exilic Judean Archive.* Jerusalem: Institute of Archaeology, Hebrew University, 1976.

Axworthy, Michael. *Empire of the Mind: A History of Iran.* London: Hurst, 2007.

Baghbidi, Hassan R. "Darius and the Bisotun Inscription: A New Interpretation of the Last Paragraph of Column IV." *Journal of Persianate Studies* 2, no. 1 (2009): 44–61.

Bagheri, Mehri. "Prince Mohammad, Fereydun, Thraētaona, and Trita Āptya: Themes and Connections in Persian Narratives." *Folklore* 112, no. 2 (2001): 199–201.

Bailey, H. W. *Zoroastrian Problems in the Ninth-Century Books.* Rev. ed. Oxford: Clarendon, 1971.

Bailey, H. W. et al., eds. *Papers in Honour of Professor Mary Boyce.* 2 vols. Leiden: Brill, 1985.

Bakker, Janine. "The Lady and the Lotus: Representations of Women in the Achaemenid Empire." *Iranica Antiqua* 42 (2007): 207–20.

Balcer, Jack M. "The Athenian Episkopos and the Achaemenid 'King's Eye.'" *AJP* 98, no. 3 (1977): 252–63.

———. "The Greeks and the Persians: The Processes of Acculturation." *Historia* 32, no. 3 (1983): 257–67.

———. *Herodotus and Bisitun.* Stuttgart: Steiner, 1987.

————. *A Prosopographical Study of the Ancient Persians Royal and Noble c. 550–450 B.C.* Lewiston, N.Y.: Mellon, 1993.

Baltzer, Klaus. *Deutero-Isaiah: A Commentary on Isaiah 40–55.* Minneapolis: Fortress, 2001.

Bankston, Carl L., III. "Rationality, Choice and the Religious Economy: The Problem of Belief." *RRelRes* 43, no. 4 (2002): 311–25.

Barag, Dan P. "The Effects of the Tennes Rebellion on Palestine." *BASOR* 183 (1966): 6–12.

————. "Some Notes on a Silver Coin of Johanan the High Priest." *BA* 48, no. 3 (1985): 166–68.

Barclay, John M. G. *Jews in the Mediterranean Diaspora: From Alexander to Trajan (323 BCE–117 CE).* Edinburgh: T. & T. Clark, 1998.

Barker, Margaret. *The Older Testament: The Survival of Themes from the Ancient Royal Cult in Sectarian Judaism and Early Christianity.* London: SPCK, 1987.

Barr, James. "Aramaic-Greek Notes on the Book of Enoch (I)." *JSS* 23, no. 2 (1978): 184–98.

————. "The Question of Religious Influence: The case of Zoroastrianism, Judaism, and Christianity." *JAAR* 53 (1985): 201–35.

Barstad, Hans M. "No Prophets? Recent Developments in Biblical Prophetic Research and Ancient Near Eastern Prophecy." *JSOT* 57 (1993): 39–60.

Bartholomae, Christian. *Altiranisches Wörterbuch.* Strasburg: Trübner, 1904.

Bartlett, John R. *Jews in the Hellenistic World: Josephus, Aristeas, the Sibylline Oracles, Eupolemus.* Cambridge: Cambridge University Press, 1985.

Barton, George A. "The Origin of the Names of Angels and Demons in the Extra-Canonical Apocalyptic Literature to 100 AD." *JBL* 31, no. 4 (1912): 156–67.

Barton, John. "The Day of Yahweh in the Minor Prophets." Pages 68–79 in *Biblical and Near Eastern Essays: Studies in Honour of Kevin J. Cathcart.* Edited by Carmel McCarthy and John F. Healey. London: T&T Clark, 2004.

Basil, Saint. *The Letters.* Translated by Roy J. Deferrari. *The Letters IV.* LCL. Cambridge, Mass.: Harvard University Press, 1934.

Bauckham, Richard. "Tobit as a Parable of the Exiles of Northern Israel." Pages 140–64 in Bredin, ed., *Studies in the Book of Tobit.*

Baumgarten, Joseph M. "The Calendars of the Book of Jubilees and the Temple Scroll." *VT* 37, no. 1 (1987): 71–78.

Bäuml, Franz. "Medieval Texts and the Two Theories of Oral-Formulaic Composition: A Proposal for a Third Theory." *New Literary History* 16, no. 1 (1984): 31–49.

Beck, Roger. "The Mysteries of Mithras: A New Account of Their Genesis." *JRS* 88 (1998): 115–28.

Becking, Bob, and Marjo C. A. Korpel, eds. *The Crisis of Israelite Religion.* Leiden: Brill, 1999.

Bedenbender, Andreas. "Jewish Apocalypticism: A Child of Mantic Wisdom?" Pages 189–96 in Boccaccini, ed., *Henoch.*

Ben Zvi, Ehud, and Michael H. Floyd, eds. *Writings and Speech in Israelite and Ancient Near Eastern Prophecy.* Atlanta: SBL, 2000.

Benveniste, Emile. "Mithra aux vastes pâturages." *JA* 248, no. 4 (1960): 421–29.

————. *The Persian Religion According to the Chief Greek Texts.* Paris: Paul Geuthner, 1929.

————. "Le terme iranien *mazdayasna*." *BSOAS* 33, no. 1 (1970): 5–9.

Berquist, Jon L., ed. *Approaching Yehud: New Approaches to the Study of the Persian Period*. Atlanta: SBL, 2007.

———. *Judaism in Persia's Shadow*. Minneapolis: Fortress, 1995.

Betlyon, John W. "Archaeological Evidence of Military Operations in Southern Judah During the Early Hellenistic Period." *BA* 54, no. 1 (1991): 36–43.

———. "A People Transformed Palestine in the Persian Period." *Near Eastern Archaeology* 68, no. 1/2 (2005): 4–58.

Bhayro, Siam. *The Shemihazah and Asael Narrative of 1 Enoch 6–11: Introduction, text, Translation and Commentary with Reference to Ancient Near Eastern and Biblical Antecedents*. Münster: Ugarit-Verlag, 2005.

Bianchi, Ugo. "Mithra and the Question of Iranian Monotheism." Pages 19–46 in Duchesne-Guillemin, ed., *Étude Mithriaques*.

Bickerman, Elias J. "The Babylonian Captivity." Pages 342–57 in *CHJ* 1.

———. *Four Strange Books of the Bible*. New York: Schocken, 1967.

———. "The 'Zoroastrian' Calendar." *Archiv Orientalni* 35 (1967): 197–207.

Bickerman, Elias J., and Hayim Tadmor. "Darius I, Pseudo-Smerdis, and the Magi." *Athenaeum* 56, no. 3 (1978): 239–61.

Bienkowski, Piotr, Christopher Mee, and Elizabeth Slater, eds. *Writing and Ancient Near Eastern Society: Papers in Honour of Alan R. Millard*. London: T&T Clark, 2005.

Birkeland, Harris. "The Belief in the Resurrection of the Dead in the Old Testament." *ST* 3 (1949): 60–78.

Bivar, A. D. H. "Document and Symbol in the Art of the Achaemenids." Pages 1:49–67 in Duchesne-Guillemin, ed., *Monumentum H. S. Nyberg*.

———. "Mithra and Mesopotamia." Pages 2:275–89 in Hinnells, ed., *Mithraic Studies*.

———. "Mithraism: A Religion for the Ancient Medes." *Iranica Antiqua* 40 (2005): 341–58.

———. "Religious Subjects on Achaemenid Seals." Pages 1:90–105 in Hinnells, ed., *Mithraic Studies*.

Black, Matthew. *The Book of Enoch or 1 Enoch*. Leiden: Brill, 1985.

———. "The Messianism of the Parables of Enoch: Their Date and Contribution to Christological Origins." Pages 145–68 in *The Messiah*. Edited by James H. Charlesworth. Minneapolis: Fortress, 1992.

———. "The Twenty Angel Dekadarchs at 1 Enoch 6.7 and 69.2." *JJS* 1–2 (1982): 227–35.

Blenkinsopp, Joseph. *A History of Prophecy in Israel*. Rev. and enl. ed. London: Westminster John Knox, 1996.

———. *Isaiah 40–55: A New Translation with Introduction and Commentary*. New York: Doubleday, 2000.

———. *Isaiah 56–66: A New Translation with Introduction and Commentary*. New York: Doubleday, 2003.

———. *Prophecy and Canon*. Notre Dame, Ind.: University of Notre Dame Press, 1977.

———. "The Sage, the Scribe, and Scribalism in the Chronicler's Work." Pages 307–18 in Gammie and Perdue, eds., *The Sage in Israel*.

———. "The Social Roles of Prophets in Early Archaemenid Judah." *JSOT* 93 (2001): 39–58.

———. "Temple and Society in Achaemenid Judah." Pages 22–53 in Davies, ed., *Second Temple Studies I*.

Block, Daniel I. *The Book of Ezekiel: Chapters 25–48*. Grand Rapids: Eerdmans, 1998.

————. "Gog and the Pouring out of the Spirit: Reflections on Ezekiel 39:21–29." *VT* 37, no. 3 (1987): 257–70.

————. "Gog in Prophetic Tradition: A New Look at Ezekiel XXXVIII:17." *VT* 42, no. 2 (1992): 154–72.

————. "The Role of Language in Ancient Israelite Perceptions of National Identity." *JBL* 103, no. 3 (1984): 321–40.

Boardman, John. *Persia and the West: An Archaeological Investigation of the Genesis of Achaemenid Art*. London: Thames & Hudson, 2000.

Boccaccini, Gabriele, ed. *Enoch and the Messiah Son of Man: Revisiting the Book of Parables*. Grand Rapids: Eerdmans, 2007.

————. "Finding a Place for the Parables with Second Temple Jewish Literature." Pages 263–89 in Boccaccini, ed., *Enoch and the Messiah Son of Man*.

————., ed. *Henoch: The Origins of Enochic Judaism*. Proceedings of the First Enoch Seminar, Univeristy of Michigan, Sesto Fiorentino, Italy, June 19–23, 2001. Torino: Silvio Zamorani, 2002.

————. *Middle Judaism: Jewish Thought 300 BCE to 200 CE*. Minneapolis: Fortress, 1991.

————. *Roots of Rabbinic Judaism: An Intellectual History from Ezekiel to Daniel*. Grand Rapids: Eerdmans, 2001.

Boccaccini, Gabriele, and John J. Collins, eds. *The Early Enoch Literature*. Leiden: Brill, 2007.

Bodi, Daniel. *The Book of Ezekiel and the Poem of Erra*. Göttingen: Vandenhoeck & Ruprecht, 1991.

Bøe, Sverre. *Gog and Magog: Ezekiel 38–39 as Pre-text for Revelation 19,17-21 and 20,7-10*. Tübingen: Mohr Siebeck, 2001.

Böklen, Ernst. *Die Verwandtschaft der jüdisch-christlichen mit der parsischen Eschatologie*. Göttingen: Vandenhoeck & Ruprecht, 1902.

Borger, Rykle. "Die Beschwörungsserie Bīt mēseri und die Himmelfahrt Henochs." *JNES* 33, no. 2 (1974): 183–96.

Botha, Pieter J. J. "Cognition, Orality-Literacy, and Approaches to First-Century Writings." Pages 37–63 in *Orality, Literacy and Colonialism in Antiquity*. Edited by Jonathan A. Draper. Atlanta: SBL, 2004.

Boucharlat, Rémy. "Pasargadae." *Iran* 40 (2002): 279–82.

Bowie, Fiona. *The Anthropology of Religion*. 2d ed. Oxford: Blackwell, 2006.

Bowie, Fiona, and Christopher Deacy, eds. *The Coming Deliverer: Millennial Themes in World Religions*. Cardiff: University of Wales Press, 1997.

Bowman, A.K., and Greg Woolf, eds. *Literacy and Power in the Ancient World*. Cambridge: Cambridge University Press, 1994.

Bowman, Raymond A. *Aramaic Ritual Texts From Persepolis*. Chicago: University of Chicago Press, 1970.

Boyce, Mary. "Apąm Napāt." *EncIr* 2, no. 2 (1986): 148–50.

————. "Apocalyptic (that which has been revealed) i. In Zoroastrianism." *EncIr* 2, no. 2 (1986): 154–57.

————. "Astvat.ərəta." *EncIr* 2, no. 8 (1987): 871–73.

————. "Ātašdān." *EncIr* 3 (1989): 7–9.

————. "Haoma, Priest of the Sacrifice." Pages 62–80 in Boyce and Gershevitch, eds., *W. B. Henning Memorial Volume*.

————. "Middle Persian Literature." Pages 32–66 in Gershevitch et al., eds., *Iranistik: Literatur.*

————. "On Mithra's Part in Zoroastrianism." *BSOAS* 32, no. 1 (1969): 10–34.

————. "On the Antiquity of the Zoroastrian Apocalyptic." *BSOAS* 47, no. 1 (1984): 57–75.

————. "The Parthian *gōsān* and Iranian Minstrel Tradition." *JRAS* (1957): 10–45.

————. "Persian Religion in the Achaemenid Age." *CHJ* 1:279–307.

————. "The Poems of the Persian Sibyl and the Zand i Vahman Yasht." Pages 59–77 in *Etudes irano-aryennes offertes a Gilbert Lazard.* Edited by Philippe Gignoux and Charles-Henri de Fouchécour. Paris: Association pour l'avancement des études irannienes, 1989.

————. "Priests, Cattle and Men." *BSOAS* 50, no. 3 (1987): 508–26.

————. "The Religion of Cyrus the Great." Pages 15–31 in Kuhrt and Sancisi-Weerdenburg, eds., *Achaemenid History III.*

————. Review of Johanna Narten, *Die Aməša Spəntas im Avesta. BASOR* 47, no. 1 (1984): 158–61.

————. "Some Reflections on Zurvanism." *BSOAS* 19, no. 2 (1957): 304–16.

————. "Some Remarks on the Transmission of the Kayanian Heroic Cycle." Pages 45–52 in *Serta Cantabrigienisa Viris doctissimis clarissimisque qui a die XXI usque ad diem XXVIII mensis Augusti anni MCMLIV congressum internationalem rebus litterisque orientalibus dedicatum Cantabrigiam convenerunt.* Wiesbaden: Steiner, 1954.

————. *Textual Sources for the Study of Zoroastrianism.* Manchester: Manchester University Press, 1984.

————. "Zariadres and Zarēr." *BSOAS* 17, no. 3 (1955): 463–77.

————. *Zoroastrianism: A Shadowy but Powerful Presence in the Judaeo-Christian World.* London: Dr. William's Trust, 1987.

————. *Zoroastrians: Their Religious Beliefs and Practices.* London: Routledge, 2001.

Boyce, Mary, and Ilya Gershevitch, eds. *W. B. Henning Memorial Volume.* Asia Major Library. London: Lund Humphries, 1970.

Boyd, James W., and Donald A. Crosby. "Is Zoroastrianism Dualistic or Monotheistic?" *JAAR* 47, no. 4 (1979): 557–88.

Boyd, Robert, and Peter J. Richerson. *The Origin and Evolution of Cultures.* Oxford: Oxford University Press, 2005.

Bredin, Mark, ed. *Studies in the Book of Tobit: A Multidisciplinary Approach.* London: T&T Clark International, 2006.

Bremmer, Jan N. "Remember the Titans!" Pages 35–61 in Auffarth and Stuckenbruck, eds., *The Fall of the Angels.*

Bresciani, Edda. "Egypt, Persian Satrapy." *CHJ* 1:358–71.

Breslauer, S. Daniel. "Mythology, Judaism and." Pages 3:1812–33 in Neusner, Avery-Peck and Green, eds., *The Encyclopaedia of Judaism.*

Brewster, Paul G. "Some Parallels Between the 'Fêng-Shên-Yên I' and the 'Shahnameh' and the Possible Influence of the Former upon the Persian Epic." *AFS* 31, no. 1 (1972): 115–22.

Briant, Pierre. *From Cyrus to Alexander: A History of the Persian Empire.* Translated by Peter T. Daniels. Winona Lake, Ind.: Eisenbrauns, 2002.

Brockington, L. H. *Ezra, Nehemiah and Esther.* London: Nelson, 1969.

Brooke, George J. "Prophecy and the Prophets in the Dead Sea Scrolls: Looking Backwards and Forwards." Pages 151–65 in Floyd and Haak, eds., *Prophets, Prophecy, and Prophetic Texts*.

———. "The Ten Temples in the Dead Sea Scrolls." Pages 417–34 in Day, ed., *Temple and Worship in Biblical Israel*.

Brosius, Maria, ed. *Ancient Archives and Archival Traditions: Concepts of Record-Keeping in the Ancient World*. Oxford: Oxford University Press, 2003.

———. *The Persian Empire from Cyrus II to Artaxerxes I*. London: Classical Teachers Association, 2000.

———. *Women in Ancient Persia (559–331 BC)*. Oxford: Clarendon, 1998.

Brown, John P. *Israel and Hellas*. Berlin: de Gruyter, 1995.

———. *Israel and Hellas III: The Legacy of Iranian Imperialism and the Individual*. Berlin: de Gruyter, 2001.

Brownlee, William H. "'Son of Man set your face': Ezekiel the Refugee Prophet." *HUCA* 54 (1983): 83–110.

Bruce, Steve. "Religion and Rational Choice: A Critique of Economic Explanations of Religious Behaviour." *Sociology of Religion* 54, no. 2 (1993): 193–205.

Brunner, Christopher J. "Ahunwar." *EncIr* 1, no. 7 (1985): 683.

———. "Geographical and Administrative Divisions: Settlements and Economy." *CHI* 3.2:747–77.

Bryan, David. *Cosmos, Chaos and the Kosher Mentality*. Sheffield: Sheffield Academic, 1995.

Bull, Malcolm. "On Making Ends Meet." Pages 1–17 in Bull, ed., *Apocalypse Theory*.

Bull, Malcolm, ed. *Apocalypse Theory and the Ends of the* World. Oxford: Blackwell, 1995.

Burkert, Walter. "The Logic of Cosmogony." Pages 87–106 in Buxton, ed., *From Myth to Reason?*

Burn, A. R. "Persia and the Greeks." *CHI* 2:292–391.

Burstein, Stanley M. *The Babyloniaca of Berossus*. Malibu: Undena, 1978.

Buxton, Richard, ed. *From Myth to Reason?* Oxford: Oxford University Press, 2001.

Bynum, David E. *The Daemon in the Wood: A Study of Oral Narrative Patterns*. Cambridge, Mass.: Harvard University Press, 1978.

Calmeyer, Peter. "Art in Iran II: Median Art and Architecture." *EncIr* 2, no. 6 (1986): 565–69.

———. "Art in Iran III: Achaemenian Art and Architecture." *EncIr* 2, no. 6 (1986): 569–80.

Cameron, George G. *History of Early Iran*. Chicago: Chicago University Press, 1936.

———. *Persepolis Treasury Tablets*. Chicago: Chicago University Press, 1948.

———. "Persepolis Treasury Tablets Old and New." *JNES* 17, no. 3 (1958): 161–76.

———. "The Persian Satrapies and Related Matters." *JNES* 32, no. 1/2 (1973): 47–56.

Cameron, George G., and Ilya Gershevitch. "New Tablets from the Persepolis Treasury." *JNES* 24, no. 3 (1965): 167–92.

Camp, Claudia V. "Oralities, Literacies, and Colonialism in Antiquity and Contemporary Scholarship." Pages 193–217 in Draper, ed., *Orality, Literacy, and Colonialism*.

Cancik, Hubert, and Helmuth Schneider, eds. *Der Neue Pauly Enzyklopädie der Antike*. Vol. 11, *Sam-Tal*. Stuttgart: Metzler, 2001.

Cardascia, G. *Les Archives des Murašu*. Paris, 1951.

Carnoy, Albert J. "The Iranian Gods of Healing." *JAOS* 38 (1918): 294–307.

Carnoy, M. "Iranian Mythology." Pages 6:253–354, 360–70, 395–404 in *Mythology of All Races*. Edited by Louis H. Gray. Boston: Jones, 1917.

Carr, David. *Writing on the Tablet of the Heart: Origins of Scripture and Literature.* Oxford: Oxford University Press, 2005.

Carroll, Robert P. "Ancient Israelite Prophecy and Dissonance Theory." Pages 377–91 in *The Place is Too Small for Us*. Edited by Robert P. Gordon. Winona Lake, Ind.: Eisenbrauns, 1995.

———. *When Prophecy Failed: Cognitive Dissonance in the Prophetic Traditions of the Old Testament*. New York: Seabury, 1979.

Carter, Charles E. *The Emergence of Yehud in the Persian Period: A Social and Demographic Study*. Sheffield: Sheffield Academic, 1999.

Carter, George William. *Zoroastrianism and Judaism*. Repr., New York: AMS, 1970.

Caspo, Eric. *Theories of Mythology*. Oxford: Blackwell, 2005.

Cataldo, Jeremiah W. *A Theocratic Yehud? Issues of Government in a Persian Period*. London: T&T Clark, 2009.

Cereti, Carlo G. *The Zand-ī Wahman Yasn: A Zoroastrian Apocalypse*. Rome, 1995.

Charles, R. H. *The Book of Enoch, or, 1 Enoch*. Oxford: Clarendon, 1912.

———. *A Critical History of the Doctrine of a Future Life in Israel, in Judaism, and in Christianity*. 2d ed. London: Adam & Charles Black, 1913.

———. *Religious Development Between the Old and New Testaments*. London: Williams & Northgate, 1914.

Charlesworth, James H. "The Pseudepigrapha as Biblical Exegesis." Pages 139–52 in *Early Jewish and Christian Exegesis*. Edited by Craig A. Evans and William F. Stinespring. Atlanta: Scholars Press, 1987.

———. "A Rare Consensus Among Enoch Specialists: The Date of the Earliest Enoch Books." Pages 225–34 in Boccaccini, ed., *Henoch*.

Charlesworth, James H. et al., eds. *The Dead Sea Scrolls 6B: Pesharim, Other Commentaries, and Related Documents*. Tübingen: Mohr Siebeck, 2002.

Chazon, Esther G., David Satran, and Ruth A. Clements, eds. *Things Revealed: Studies in Early Jewish and Christian Literature in Honor of Michael E. Stone*. Leiden: Brill, 2004.

Chenciner, Robert. *Daghestan: Tradition and Survival*. Surrey: Curzon, 1997.

Childs, Brevard S. "The Enemy from the North and the Chaos Tradition," *JBL* 78 (1959): 187–98.

Choksy, Jamsheed K. "Hagiography and Monotheism in History: Doctrinal Encounters Between Zoroastrianism, Judaism and Christianity 1." *Islam and Christian–Muslim Relations* 14, no. 4 (2003): 407–21.

———. "Reassessing the Material Contexts of Ritual Fires in Ancient Iran." *Iranica Antiqua* 42 (2007): 229–69.

———. Review of Norman Cohn, *Cosmos, Chaos, and the World to Come: The Ancient Roots of Apocalyptic Faith*. *Iranian Studies* 29, no. 1/2 (1996): 183.

Clarke, Joanne, ed. *Archaeological Perspectives on the Transmission and Transformation of Culture in the Eastern Mediterranean*. Oxford: Oxbow, 2005.

Clemen, Carolus. *Fontes Historiae Religionis Persicae*. Bonn: Marcus & Weber, 1920.

Clines, David J. A., ed. *The Dictionary of Classical Hebrew*. 4 vols. Sheffield: Sheffield Academic, 1993–1998.

Coggins, R. J., and J. L. Houlden, eds. *A Dictionary of Biblical Interpretation*. Edited by. London: SCM, 1990.

Cohn, Norman. *Cosmos, Chaos and the World to Come: The Ancient Roots of Apocalyptic Faith*. 2d ed. New Haven: Yale University Press, 1995.

———. "How Time Acquired a Consummation." Pages 21–37 in Bull, ed., *Apocalypse Theory*.

———. *The Pursuit of the Millennium: Revolutionary Millenarians and Mystical Anarchists of the Middle Ages*. London: Pimlico, 2004.

Colarusso, John. "The Hunters (Indo-European Proto-myths: The Storm God, The Good King, The Mighty Hunter)." *JIES* 36, no. 3–4 (2008): 442–63.

Colless, Brian E. "Cyrus the Persian as Darius the Mede in the Book of Daniel." *JSOT* 56 (1992): 113–26.

Collins, Billie Jean, ed. *A History of the Animal World in the Ancient Near East*. HO I.64. Leiden: Brill, 2002.

Collins, John J., ed. *Apocalypse: The Morphology of a Genre*. *Semeia* 14 (1979).

———. "Apocalyptic Eschatology as the Transcendence of Death." *CBQ* 36 (1974): 21–43.

———. *The Apocalyptic Imagination*. 2d ed. Grand Rapids: Eerdmans, 1998.

———. "The Apocalyptic Technique: Setting and Function in the Book of Watchers." *CBQ* 44, no. 1 (1982): 91–111.

———. *The Apocalyptic Vision of the Book of Daniel*. Missoula, Mont.: Scholars, 1977.

———. "Cosmos and Salvation: Jewish Wisdom and Apocalyptic in the Hellenistic Age." *HR* 17, no. 2 (1977): 121–42.

———. "The Court-Tales in Daniel and the Development of Apocalyptic." *JBL* 94, no. 2 (1975): 218–34.

———. *Daniel*. Hermeneia. Minneapolis: Fortress, 1993.

———. *Encounters with Biblical Theology*. Minneapolis: Fortress, 2005.

———, ed. *The Encyclopedia of Apocalypticism*, vol. 1. New York: Continuum, 2000.

———. "Eschatological Dynamics and Utopian Ideals in Early Judaism." Pages 69–89 in Amanat and Bernhardsson, eds., *Imagining the End*.

———. "From Prophecy to Apocalypticism: The Expectation of the End." Pages 1:129–61 in Collins, ed., *The Encyclopedia of Apocalypticism*.

———. "Genre, Ideology, and Social Movements in Jewish Apocalypticism." Pages 11–32 in Collins and Charlesworth, eds., *Mysteries and Revelations*.

———. "Introduction: Towards the Morphology of a Genre." *Semeia* 14 (1979): 1–20.

———. "The Jewish Apocalypses." *Semeia* 14 (1979): 21–60.

———. "Jewish Apocalyptic Against Its Hellenistic Near Eastern Environment." *BSOAS* 220 (1975): 27–36.

———. "The Jewish Transformation of Sibylline Oracles." Pages 181–97 in *Seers, Sybils [sic] and Sages*.

———. "Methodological Issues in the Study of 1 Enoch: Reflections on the Articles of P. D. Hanson and G. W. Nickelsburg." Pages 315–22 in *Society of Biblical Literature 1978 Seminar Papers*, vol. 1. Edited by Paul J. Achtemeier. Missoula, Mont.: Scholars Press, 1978.

———. "The Mythology of Holy War in Daniel and the Qumran War Scroll: A Point of Transition in Jewish Apocalyptic." *VT* 25, no. 3 (1975): 596–612.

———. "The Persian Apocalypses." *Semeia* 14 (1979): 207–17.

———. "Prayer of Nabonidus." Pages 83–94 in VanderKam, ed., *Qumran Cave 4 XVII Parabiblical Texts 3*.

————. "Prophecy, Apocalypse and Eschatology: Reflections on the Proposals of Lester Grabbe." Pages 44–52 in Grabbe and Haak, eds., *Knowing the End from the Beginning*.

————. Review of Helge S. Kvanvig, *Roots of Apocalyptic: The Mesopotamian Background of the Enoch Figure and of the Son of Man*. *JBL* 109, no. 4 (1990): 715–18.

————. Review of Norman Cohn, *Cosmos, Chaos, and the World to Come: The Ancient Roots of Apocalyptic Faith*. *TS* 55, no. 2 (1994): 347–48.

————. "The Sage in the Apocalyptic and Pseudepigraphic Literature." Pages 343–54 in Gammie and Perdue, eds., *The Sage in Israel*.

————. *Seers, Sybils* [*sic*] *and Sages in Hellenistic-Roman Judaism*. Leiden: Brill, 1997.

————. "The Sibylline Oracles." *OTP* 1:317–472.

————. "Theology and Identity in the Early Enochic Literature." Pages 57–62 in Boccaccini, ed., *Henoch*.

Collins, John J., and James H. Charlesworth, eds. *Mysteries and Revelations: Apocalyptic Studies Since the Uppsala Colloquium*. Sheffield: JSOT, 1991.

Collins, John J., and Peter W. Flint. "Pseudo-Daniel." Pages 95–64 in VanderKam, ed., *Qumran Cave 4 XVII Parabiblical Texts 3*.

Collon, Dominique. *Ancient Near Eastern Art*. London: British Museum, 1995.

Colpe, Carsten. "Development of Religious Thought." *CHI* 3.2:819–65.

Conrad, E. "The End of Prophecy and the Appearance of Angels/Messengers in the Book of the Twelve." *JSOT* 73 (1997): 65–79.

Conroy, Charles, "Recent Studies of the Enigmatic Servant Texts in Isaiah." Paper presented at Irish Biblical Association Annual Meeting, 24–24 April 2009, Dublin.

Coogan, Michael David. *West Semitic Personal Names in the Murašu Documents*. Missoula, Mont.: Scholars, 1976.

Cook, J. M. "The Rise of the Achaemenids and Establishment of Their Empire." *CHI* 2:200–91.

Cook, Stephen L. *The Apocalyptic Literature*. Nashville, Tenn.: Abingdon, 2003.

————. "Mythological Discourse in Ezekiel and Daniel and the Rise of Apocalypticism in Israel." Pages 85–106 in Grabbe and Haak, eds., *Knowing the End from the Beginning*.

————. *Prophecy and Apocalypticism: The Postexilic Social Setting*. Minneapolis: Fortress, 1995.

Cooke, G. A. *A Critical and Exegetical Commentary on the Book of Ezekiel*. Edinburgh: T. & T. Clark, 1936.

Cowley, A. *Aramaic Papyri of the Fifth Century B.C.* Osnabrück: Zeller, 1967.

Crawford, Michael H., and David Whitehead. *Archaic and Classical Greece: A Selection of Ancient Sources in Translation*. Cambridge: Cambridge University Press, 1983.

Crenshaw, James L. *Education in Ancient Israel*. New York: Doubleday, 1998.

————. *Prophetic Conflict: Its Effect Upon Israelite Religion*. Berlin: de Gruyter, 1971.

Crim, Keith, ed. *Interpreter's Dictionary of the Bible, Supplementary Volume*. Nashville, Tenn.: Abingdon, 1976.

Cross, Frank Moore. "Aspects of Samaritan and Jewish History in Late Persian and Hellenistic Times." *HTR* 59, no. 3 (1966): 201–11.

————. *Canaanite Myth and Hebrew Epic: Essays in the History of the Religion of Israel*. Cambridge, Mass.: Harvard University Press, 1973.

————. *From Epic to Canon: History and Literature in Ancient Israel*. Baltimore, Md.: Johns Hopkins University Press, 2000.

Cross, Frank Moore, Werner E. Lemke and Patrick D. Miller, eds. *Magnalia Dei*. Garden City, New York: Doubleday, 1976.

Culley, Robert C., ed. *Oral Tradition and Old Testament Studies: Semeia* 5 (1976).

Cumont, Franz. *The Mysteries of Mithra*. Translated by Thomas J. McCormick. 2d ed. London: Kegan Paul, 1903.

———. "St. George and Mithra the Cattle Thief." *JRS* 27, no. 1 (1937): 63–71.

Curtis, Edward Lewis, and Albert Alonzo Madsen. *A Critical and Exegetical Commentary on the Books of Chronicles*. Edinburgh: T. & T. Clark, 1910.

Curtis, John E., ed. *Mesopotamia and Iran in the Persian Period: Conquest and Imperialism 539–331 BC*. Proceedings of a Seminar in memory of Vladimir G. Lukonin. London: British Museum, 1997.

Curtis, Vesta Sarkhosh. *Persian Myths*. London: British Museum, 1993.

Curtis, Vesta Sarkhosh, Robert Hillenbrand, and J. M. Rogers, eds. *The Art and Archaeology of Ancient Persia: New Light on the Parthian and Sasanian Empires*. London: I. B. Tauris, 1998.

Curtis, Vesta Sarkhosh, and Sarah Stewart, eds. *Birth of the Persian Empire: The Idea of Iran I*. London: I. B. Tauris, 2005.

Daiches, Samuel. *The Jews in Babylon in the Time of Ezra and Nehemiah According to Babylonian Inscriptions*. London: Jew's College, 1910.

Dalley, Stephanie. *Myths from Mesopotamia: Creation, the Flood, Gilgamesh and others*. Oxford: Oxford University Press, 1991.

Dallmayr, Fred R. *Beyond Orientalism: Essays in Cross-Cultural Encounters*. New York: SUNY Press, 1996.

Dandamaev, Muhammad A. "Assyria II: Achaemenid Aθurā." *EncIr* 2, no. 8 (1987): 816.

———. "Babylonia I: History of Babylonia in the Median and Achaemenid Periods." *EncIr* 3 (1989): 327–34.

———. "Data of the Babylonian Documents from the 6th to the 5th Centuries B.C. on the Sakas." Pages 95–109 in *Prolegomena to the Sources on the History of Pre-Islamic Central Asia*. Edited by J. Harmatta. Budapest, 1979.

———. "The Domain-Lands of Achaemenes in Babylonia." *Schriften zur Geschichte und Kultur des Alten Orients* 11 (1974): 123–27.

———. *A Political History of the Achaemenid Empire*. Translated by W. J. Vogelsang. Leiden: Brill, 1989.

———. "Royal Paradeisoi in Babylonia." Pages 113–17 in *Orientalia J. Duchesne-Guillemin Emerito Oblata*. Leiden: Brill, 1984.

Dandamaev, Muhammad A., and Vladimir Lukonin. *The Culture and Social Institutions of Ancient Iran*. Translated by Philip L. Kohl. Cambridge: Cambridge University Press, 1989.

Daniels, Ted. "Charters of Righteousness: Politics, Prophets, and the Drama of Conversion." Pages 3–18 in O'Leary and McGhee, eds., *War in Heaven/Heaven on Earth*.

David, A. Rosalie. *The Ancient Egyptians: Religious Beliefs and Practices*. London: Kegan Paul, 1982.

Davidson, Maxwell J. *Angels at Qumran: A Comparative Study of 1 Enoch 1–36, 72–108 and Sectarian Writings from Qumran*. Sheffield: JSOT, 1992.

Davies, David. "Artistic Intentions and the Ontology of Art." *British Journal of Aesthetics* 39, no. 2 (1999): 148–62.

Davies, Philip R., ed. "And Enoch was Not, For Genesis Took Him." Pages 97–108 in *Biblical Traditions in Transmission*. Edited by Charlotte Hempel and Judith M. Lieu. Leiden: Brill, 2006.

———. "Divination, 'Apocalyptic' and Sectariansim in Early Judaism." Pages 409–24 in *Berührungspunkte: Studien zur Religions- und Sozialgeschichte des Alten Israel und Seiner Umwelt. Festschrift für Rainer Albertz zu seinem 65. Geburtstag*. Edited by Ingo Kottsieper, Rüdiger Schmitt and Jakob Wöhrle. Munster: Ugarit-Verlag, 2008.

———. "God of Cyrus, God of Israel: Some Religio-Historical Reflections on Isaiah 40–55." Pages 207–25 in *Words Remembered, Texts Renewed*. Edited by Jon Davies, Graham Harvey and Wilfred G. E. Watson. Sheffield: Sheffield Academic, 1995.

———. *Scribes and Schools: The Canonization of the Hebrew Scriptures*. Louisville, Ky.: Westminster John Knox, 1998.

———. *Second Temple Studies I*. Sheffield: JSOT, 1991.

Davis, Dick. "Rustam-i Dastan." *Iranian Studies* 32, no. 2 (1999): 231–41.

Davis, Ellen F. *Swallowing the Scroll: Textuality and the Dynamics of Discourse in Ezekiel's Prophecy*. Sheffield: Almond, 1989.

Day, John. *God's Conflict with the Dragon and the Sea: Echoes of a Canaanite Myth in the Old Testament*. Cambridge: Cambridge University Press, 1985.

———. *Molech: A God of Human Sacrifice in the Old Testament*. Cambridge: Cambridge University Press, 1989.

———, ed. *Temple and Worship in Biblical Israel*. London: T&T Clark, 2005.

———. *Yahweh and the Gods and Goddesses of Canaan*. Sheffield: Sheffield Academic, 2000.

Day, Leslie Preston. "Dog Burials in the Greek World." *AJA* 88, no. 1 (1984): 21–32.

de Boer, P. A. H., ed. *Congress Volume, Uppsala 1971*. Leiden: Brill, 1972.

de Moor, Johannes C. *An Anthology of Religious Texts from Ugarit*. Leiden: Brill, 1987.

Delitzsch, Friedrich. *Wo lag das Paradies? Eine biblisch-assyriologische Studie, mit zahlreichen assyriologischen Beiträgen zur biblischen Länder- und Völkerkunde*. Leipzig: Hinrichs'sche, 1881.

Demsky, Aaron. "Double Names in the Babylonian Exile and the Identitiy of Shesh-bazzar." Pages 23–40 in *These are the Names*, vol. 2. Edited by Aaron Demsky. Ramat-Gan, Israel: Bar Ilan University Press, 1999.

Dequeker, Luc. "Darius the Persian and the Reconstruction of the Jewish Temple in Jerusalem (Ezra 4,24)." Pages 67–92 in *Ritual and Sacrifice in the Ancient Near East*. Edited by J. Quaegebeur. Louvain: Peeters, 1993.

Dhalla, Maneckji N. *History of Zoroastrianism*. London: Oxford University Press, 1938.

Diakonoff, I. "Media." *CHI* 2:36–148.

Dimant, Devorah. "The Apocalyptic Interpretation of Ezekiel at Qumran." Pages 31–52 in Gruenwald, Shaked and Stroumsa, eds., *Messiah and Christos*.

———. "The Biography of Enoch and the Books of Enoch." *VT* 33, no. 1 (1983): 14–29.

———. "The 'Pesher on the Periods' (4Q180) and 4Q181." *IOS* 9 (1979): 77–102.

———. Review of Norman Cohn, *Cosmos, Chaos, and the World to Come: The Ancient Roots of Apocalyptic Faith*. *HR* 36, no. 1 (1996): 79–81.

———. "Two 'Scientific' Fictions: The So-Called Book of Noah and the Alleged Quotation of Jubilees in CD 16:3–4." Pages 230–49 in *Studies in the Hebrew Bible, Qumran, and the Septuagint Presented to Eugene Ulrich*. Edited by Peter W. Flint, Emmanuel Tov and James C. VanderKam. Leiden: Brill, 2006.

DiTommaso, Lorenzo. "Apocalypses and Apocalypticism in Antiquity, Part I." *CBR* 5, no. 2 (2007): 235–86.

———. "Apocalypses and Apocalypticism in Antiquity, Part II." *CBR* 5, no. 3 (2007): 367–432.

Dix, G. H. "The Enochic Pentateuch." *JTS* 27 (1926): 29–42.

Doan, William, and Terry Giles. *Prophets, Performance, and* Power: Performance Criticism of the Hebrew Bible. New York: T&T Clark, 2005.

Dozeman, Thomas B. "Geography and History in Herodotus and in Ezra-Nehemiah." *JBL* 122, no. 3 (2003): 449–66.

Draper, Jonathan A., ed. *Orality, Literacy, and Colonialism in Antiquity*. Atlanta: SBL, 2004.

Dresden, Mark J. *Denkart: A Pahlavi Text*. Wiesbaden: Otto Harrassowitz, 1966.

———. "Survey of the History of Iranian Studies." Pages 168–90 in Gershevitch et al., eds., *Iranistik: Literatur*.

Driver, G. R. *Aramaic Documents of the Fifth Century B.C.* Oxford: Clarendon, 1954.

Drønen, Tomas S. "Scientific Revolution and Religious Conversion: A Closer Look at Thomas Kuhns's Theory of Paradigm-shift." *Method and Theory in the Study of Religion* 18, no. 3 (2006): 232–53.

Dronke, Ursula. *The Poetic Edda II: Mythological Poems*. Oxford: Clarendon, 1997.

Duchesne-Guillemin, Jacques, ed. *Étude Mithriaques*. Leiden: Brill, 1978.

———. "Fire in Iran and in Greece." *East and West* 13 (1963): 198–206.

———. "Heraclitus and Iran." *HR* 3 (1963): 34–49.

———. *The Hymns of Zarathustra: Being a translation of the Gâthâs Together with Introduction and Commentary*. Translated by M. Henning. London: Murray, 1992.

———, ed. *Monumentum H. S. Nyberg*, vol. 1. Leiden: Brill, 1975.

———. "The Religion of Ancient Iran." Pages 323–76 in *Historia Religionum*, vol. 1. Edited by C. J. Bleeker and Geo Widengren. Leiden: Brill, 1969.

———. *The Western Response to Zoroaster*. Oxford: Clarendon, 1958.

Durham, William H. "Applications of Evolutionary Culture Theory." *Annual Review of Anthropology* 21 (1992): 331–55.

Dusinberre, Elspeth R. M. "Satrapal Sardis: Achaemenid Bowls in an Achaemenid Capital." *AJA* 103, no. 1 (1999): 73–102.

Eaton, Kent. "Beware the Trumpet of Judgement: John Nelson Darby and the Nineteenth-century Brethren." Pages 119–62 in Bowie and Deacy, eds., *The Coming Deliverer*.

Eddy, Samuel K. *The King is Dead: Studies in the Near Eastern Resistance to Hellenism, 334–31 B.C.* London: University Microfilms, 1980.

Edelman, Diana V. *The Origins of the 'Second' Temple: Persian Imperial Policy and the Rebuilding of Jerusalem*. London: Equinox, 2005.

Edwards, M. J. "Herodotus and Mithras: Histories I.131." *AJP* 111, no. 1 (1990): 1–4.

Eichrodt, Walther. *Ezekiel: A Commentary*. Translated by Cosslett Quin. London: SCM, 1970.

Elayi, Josette, and Jean Sapin. *Beyond the River: New Perspectives on Transeuphratene*. Translated by J. Edward Crowley. Sheffield: Sheffield Academic, 1998.

Eliade, Mircea. *A History of Religious Ideas*, vol. 1. Translated by Willard R. Trask. Chicago: University of Chicago Press, 1978.

Eliade, Mircea, and Joseph M. Kitagawa, eds. *The History of Religions: Essays in Methodology*. Chicago: University of Chicago Press, 1959.

Elliot, Mark. "Covenant and Cosmology in the Book of Watchers and the Astronomical Book." Pages 23–38 in Boccaccini, ed., *Henoch*.

Elliott, Marianne. *The Catholics of Ulster*. London: Penguin, 2000.

Eph'al, Israel. "Changes in Palestine During the Persian Period in Light of Epigraphic Sources." *IEJ* 48, no. 1–2 (1998): 106–19.

Epstein, I., ed. *Tractate Sanhedrin*. New ed. London: Soncino, 1969.

Erho, Ted M. "The Ahistorical Nature of 1 Enoch 56:5–8 and Its Ramifications upon the Opinio Communis on the Dating of the Similitudes of Enoch." *JSJ* 40, no. 1 (2009): 23–54.

Eslinger, Lyle. "Ezekiel 20 and the Metaphor of Historical Teleology: Concepts of Biblical History." *JSOT* 23, no. 71 (1998): 93–120.

Evans, Craig A., ed. *Of Scribes and Sages: Early Jewish Interpretation and Transmission of Scripture*. 2 vols. London: T&T Clark, 2004.

Evelyn-White, Hugh G., ed. *Hesiod, Homeric Hymns, Epic Cycle, Homerica*. LCL. Cambridge, Mass.: Harvard University Press, 1998.

Falk, H. "Soma I and II." *BSOAS* 52, no. 1 (1989): 77–90.

Farrell, Thomas J. "Kelber's Breakthrough." *Semeia* 39 (1987): 27–46.

Feldman, Louis H. *Jew and Gentile in the Ancient World: Attitudes and Interactions from Alexander to Justinian*. Princeton, N.J.: Princeton University Press, 1993.

———. "Josephus' Portrait of Moses." *JQR* 82, no. 3/4 (1992): 285–328.

Finnegan, Ruth. "What is Orality—If Anything?" *Byzantine and Modern Greek Studies* 14 (1990): 130–49.

Firdausī. *Shāhnāmeh*. Edited by Arthur George Warner and Edmond Warner. *The Shāhnāma of Firdausī*. 9 vols. London: Routledge, 2000.

Fischer, Stephen Roger. *A History of Writing*. London: Reaktion, 2001.

Fishbane, Michael. *Biblical Interpretation in Ancient Israel*. Oxford: Clarendon, 1985.

———. *The Exegetical Imagination: On Jewish Thought and Theology*. Cambridge, Mass.: Harvard University Press, 1998.

———. "From Scribalism to Rabbinism: Perspectives on the Emergence of Classical Judaism." Pages 439–56 in Gammie and Perdue, eds., *The Sage in Israel*.

Fisher, Walter R. *Human Communication as Narration: Toward a Philosophy of Reason, Value, and Action*. Columbia: University of South Carolina Press, 1987.

Fitzmyer, Joseph A. *The Genesis Apocryphon of Qumran Cave 1: A Commentary*. 2d ed. Rome: Biblical Institute, 1971.

Fitzpatrick-McKinley, Anne. "Ezra, Nehemiah and Some Early Greek Lawgivers." Pages 17–48 in *Rabbinic Law in Its Roman and Near Eastern Context*. Edited by Catherine Hezser. Tübingen: Mohr Siebeck, 2003.

———. *The Transformation of Torah from Scribal Advice to Law*. Sheffield: Sheffield Academic, 1999.

Fleming, Daniel E. "Prophets and Temple Personnel in the Mari Archives." Pages 44–64 in Grabbe and Ogden, eds., *The Priests in the Prophets*.

Floyd, Michael H. "The Production of Prophetic Books in the Early Second Temple Period." Pages 276–97 in Floyd and Haak, eds., *Prophets, Prophecy, and Prophetic Texts*.

Floyd, Michael H., and Robert D. Haak, eds. *Prophets, Prophecy, and Prophetic Texts in Second Temple Judaism*. London: T&T Clark, 2006.

Flusser, David. "The Four Empires in the Fourth Sibyl and in the Book of Daniel." *IOS* 2 (1972): 148–75.

———. "Hystaspes and John of Patmos." Pages 1:12–75 in Shaked and Netzer, eds., *Irano-Judaica*.

Foley, John Miles. "Beowulf and the Traditional Narrative Song: The Potential and Limits of Comparison." Pages 117–36; 173–78 in *Old English Literature in Context*. Edited by John D. Niles. London: Boydell, 1980.

———. "Tradition and the Collective Talent: Oral Epic, Textual Meaning, and Receptionalist Theory." *Cultural Anthropology* 1, no. 2 (1986): 203–22.

Fontaine, P. F. M. *The Light and the Dark: The Cultural History of Dualism*, vol. 5. Amsterdam: Gieben, 1990.

Fortson, Benjamin W., IV. *Indo-European Language and Culture: An Introduction*. Oxford: Blackwell, 2004.

Foster, Benjamin R. "Mesopotamia and the End of Time." Pages 23–32 in Amanat and Bernhardsson, eds., *Imagining the End*.

Fox, Douglas A. "Darkness and Light: The Zoroastrian View." *JAAR* 35, no. 2 (1967): 129–37.

Fox, Michael V. "The Rhetoric of Ezekiel's Vision of the Valley of the Bones." *HUCA* 51 (1980): 1–15.

Fragner, Bert G. et al., eds. *Proceedings of the Second European Conference of Iranian Studies (Bamburg, 30 September–4 October, 1991)*. Rome: Istituto Italiano Per il Medio ed Estremo Oriente, 1995.

Frame, Grant, and Andrew R. George. "The Royal Libraries of Nineveh: New Evidence for King Ashurbanipal's Tablet Collecting." Pages 265–84 in *Nineveh: Papers of the XLIXe Recontre Assyriologique Internationale, London, 7–11 July 2003*, vol. 2. Edited by Dominique Collon and Andrew George. London: British School of Archaeology in Iraq, 2005.

Franke, William. "Apocalypse and the Breaking-Open of Dialogue: A Negatively Theological Perspective." *International Journal for Philosophy of Religion* 47, no. 2 (2000): 65–86.

Freyne, Sean. *Jesus, A Jewish Galilean*. London: T&T Clark, 2004.

Fried, Lisbeth S. "Cyrus the Messiah? The Historical Background to Isaiah 45:1." *HTR* 95, no. 4 (2002): 373–93.

———. *The Priest and the Great King: Temple–Palace Relations in the Persian Empire*. Winona Lake, Ind.: Eisenbrauns, 2004.

———. "'You Shall Appoint Judges': Ezra's Mission and the Rescript of Artaxerxes." Pages 63–90 in Watts, ed., *Persia and Torah*.

Froggatt, P. "The Albinism of Timur, Zāl, and Edward the Confessor." *Medical History* 6 (1962): 328–42.

Fröhlich, Ida. *'Time and Times and Half a Time': Historical Consciousness in the Jewish Literature of the Persian and Hellenistic Periods*. Sheffield: Sheffield Academic, 1996.

Frye, Richard N. *The Heritage of Persia*. London: Weidenfeld & Nicholson, 1962.

———. *The Heritage of Persia*. History of Civilisation. 2d ed. London: Cardinal, 1976.

———. *The History of Ancient Iran*. Munich: Beck, 1984.

———. "Iran and Israel in Antiquity." *JCama* 44 (1973): 71–75.

———. "Mithra in Iranian History." Pages 1:62–67 in Hinnells, ed., *Mithraic Studies*.

———. "The Political History of Iran Under the Sasanians." *CHI* 3.1:116–80.

———. "Religion in Fars Under the Achaemenids." Pages 171–78 in *Orientalia J. Duchesne-Guillemin Emerito Oblata*. Leiden: Brill, 1984.

Fuery, Kelli, and Patrick Fuery. "The Pharmakon of the Apocalypse." Pages 7–16 in Gutierrez and Schwartz, eds., *The End that Does*.

Gadd, C. J., and L. Legrain. *Ur Excavations: Texts*, vol. 1. London: British Museum, 1928.

Galambush, Julie. "Necessary Enemies: Nebuchadnezzar, YHWH, and Gog in Ezekiel 38–39." Pages 254–67 in Kelle and Moore, eds., *Israel's Prophets and Israel's Past*.

Gamkrelidze, Thomas V., and Vjačeslav V. Ivanov. *Indo-European and the Indo-Europeans: A Reconstruction and Historical Analysis of a Proto-Language and a Proto-Culture, Part 1:The Text*. Translated by Johanna Nichols. Berlin: de Gruyter, 1995.

Gammie, John G. "Spatial and Ethical Dualism in Jewish Wisdom and Apocalyptic Literature." *JBL* 93, no. 3 (1974): 356–85.

Gammie, John G., and Leo G. Perdue, eds. *The Sage in Israel and the Ancient Near East*. Winona Lake, Ind.: Eisenbrauns, 1990.

Garrison, Mark B. "A Persepolis Fortification Seal on the Tablet MDP 11 308 (Louvre Sb 13078)." *JNES* 55, no. 1 (1996): 15–35.

Garrison, Mark B., and Paul E. Dion. "The Seal of Ariyāramna in the Royal Ontario Museum, Toronto." *JNES* 58, no. 1 (1999): 1–17.

Garsoïan, Nina G. *The Epic Histories Attributed to P'awstos Buzand (Buzandaran Patmut'iwnk')*. Cambridge, Mass.: Harvard University Press, 1989.

Gaster, Theodor H. *Myth, Legend and Custom in the Old Testament: A Comparative Study with Chapters from Sir James G. Frazier's Folklore in the Old Testament*. London: Duckworth, 1969.

Genito, Bruno. "The Archaeology of the Median Period: An Outline and a Research Perspective." *Iranica Antiqua* 40 (2005): 315–40.

Gershevitch, Ilya. *The Avestan Hymn to Mithra: Introduction, Translation, and Commentary*. Cambridge: Cambridge University Press, 1959.

———. "Old Iranian Literature." Pages 1–31 in Gershevitch et al., eds., *Iranistik: Literatur*.

———. "Zoroaster's Own Contribution." *JNES* 23, no. 1 (1964): 12–38.

Gershevitch, Ilya et al., eds. *Iranistik: Literatur*. HO I.IV.2.1. Leiden: Brill, 1968.

Gesenius, D. Wilhelm. *Gesenius's Hebrew and Chaldee Lexicon to the Old Testament Scriptures*. Translated by Samuel P. Tregelles. London: Bagster & Sons, 1846.

Geyer, John B. "Desolation and Cosmos." *VT* 49, no. 1 (1999): 49–64.

Ghirshman, Roman. *Persia: From the Origins to Alexander the Great*. Translated by Stuart Gilbert and James Emmons. London: Thames & Hudson, 1964.

Gignoux, Philippe. "Bahman II: In the Pahlavi Texts." *EncIr* 3 (1989): 488.

———. *Glossaire des inscriptions Pehlevies et Parthes*. London: Lund Humphries, 1972.

———. "Monotheism or Polytheism in the Gathic Revelation?" Pages 65–71 in Shaked and Netzer, eds., *Irano-Judaica*, vol. 4.

Ginzberg, Louis. *Legends of the Jews*. Translated by Henrietta Szold. 7 vols. Baltimore, Md.: Johns Hopkins University Press, 1998.

Gitay, Yehoshua. "Deutero-Isaiah: Oral or Written?" *JBL* 99, no. 2 (1980): 185–97.

Glassner, Jean-Jacques. *Mesopotamian Chronicles*. Leiden: Brill, 2005.

Gnoli, Gherardo. "Avestan Geography." *EncIr* 3 (1989): 44–47.

———. "Babylonia II: Babylonian Influences on Iran." *EncIr* 3 (1989): 334–36.

———. "Bahrām I: In Old and Middle Iranian Texts." *EncIr* 3 (1989): 510–13.

———. "Bang I: In Ancient Iran." *EncIr* 3 (1989): 689–90.

Gnoli, Gherardo, and Antonio Panaino, eds. *Proceedings of the First European Con-ference of Iranian Studies (Turin, September 7–11, 1987)*, vol. 1. Rome: Istituto Italiano Per il Medio ed Estremo Oriente, 1990.

Goff, Matthew J. "Discerning Trajectories: 4QInstruction and the Sapiential Background of the Sayings Source Q." *JBL* 124, no. 4 (2005): 657–73.

―――. "Wisdom, Apocalypticism, and the Pedagogical Ethos of 4QInstruction." Pages 57–68 in Wright and Wills, eds., *Conflicted Boundaries*.

Goldingay, John. *The Message of Isaiah 40–55: A Literary-Theological Commentary*. London: T&T Clark, 2005.

Gonda, J. *Vedic Ritual: The Non-Solemn Rites*. HO 4.1. Leiden: Brill, 1980.

Goodell, Grace. "Bird Lore in Southwestern Iran." *AFS* 38, no. 2 (1979): 131–53.

Goodenough, Ward H. "Phylogenetically Related Cultural Traditions." *Cross-Cultural Research* 31, no. 1 (1997): 16–26.

Goody, Jack. *The Domestication of the Savage Mind*. Cambridge: Cambridge University Press, 1977.

―――. *The Interface Between the Written and the Oral*. Cambridge: Cambridge University Press, 1987.

―――. *The Power of the Written Tradition*. Washington, D.C.: Smithsonian, 2000.

Grabbe, Lester L. "Another Look at the *Gestalt* of Darius the Mede." *CBQ* 50 (1988): 198–213.

―――. "Archaeology and *archaiologias*: Relating excavations to History in Fourth-Century B.C.E. Palestine." Pages 125–35 in Lipschits, Knoppers, and Albertz, eds., *Judah and the Judeans*.

―――. *Ezra–Nehemiah*. London: Routledge, 1998.

―――. *A History of the Jews and Judaism in the Second Temple Period*. Vol. 1, *A History of the Persian Province of Yehud*. London: T&T Clark, 2004.

―――. "Introduction and Overview." Pages 2–43 in Grabbe and Haak, eds., *Knowing the End from the Beginning*.

―――. "Israel's Historical Reality After the Exile." Pages 9–32 in Becking and Korpel, eds., *The Crisis of Israelite Religion*.

―――. *Judaic Religion in the Second Temple Period: Belief and Practice from the Exile to Yavneh*. London: Routledge, 2000.

―――. *Judaism From Cyrus to Hadrian*. London: SCM, 1992.

―――, ed. *Leading Captivity Captive: "The Exile" as History and Ideology*. Sheffield: Sheffield Academic, 1998.

―――. "A Priest is Without Honor in His Own Prophet: Priests and Other Religious Specialists in the Latter Prophets." Pages 79–97 in Grabbe and Bellis, eds., *The Priests in the Prophets*.

―――. *Priests, Prophets, Diviners, Sages: A Socio-Historical Study of Religious Specialists in Ancient Israel*. Valley Forge, Pa.: Trinity Press International, 1995.

―――. "Prophetic and Apocalyptic: Time for New Definitions—and New Thinking." Pages 107–33 in Grabbe and Haak, eds., *Knowing the End from the Beginning*.

Grabbe, Lester L., and Alice Ogden Bellis, eds. *The Priests in the Prophets: The Por-trayal of Priests, Prophets and Other Religious Specialists in the Latter Prophets*. London: T&T Clark, 2004.

Grabbe, Lester L., and Robert D. Haak, eds. *Knowing the End from the Beginning: Prophecy, Apocalyptic, and Their Relationship*. London: T&T Clark, 2003.

Graf, David F. "Medism: The Origin and Significance of the Term." *JHS* 104 (1984): 15–30.

———. "The Persian Royal Road System." Pages 167–89 in *Achaemenid History VIII.* Edited by Heleen Sancisi-Weerdenburg, Amélie Kuhrt and Margaret Cool Root. Leiden: NINO, 1994.

Graf, Fritz. "Mythical Production: Aspects of Myth and Technology in Antiquity." Pages 317–28 in Buxton, ed., *From Myth to Reason?*

Graves, Robert, and Omar Ali-Shah. *The Rubaiyyat of Omar Khayaam: A New Translation with Critical Commentaries.* London: Cassell, 1967.

Gray, Louis H. "A List of the Divine and Demonic Epithets in the Avesta." *JAOS* 46 (1926): 97–153.

Green, Alberto R. W. *The Role of Human Sacrifice in the Ancient Near East.* Missoula, Mont.: Scholars Press, 1975.

Greenberg, Moshe. *Ezekiel 21–37.* New York: Doubleday, 1997.

Greene, John T. *The Role of the Messenger and Message in the Ancient Near East: Oral and Written Communication in the Ancient Near East and in the Hebrew Scriptures: Communicators and Communiqués in Context.* Atlanta: Scholars, 1989.

Greenfield, Jonas C. "Aramaic II: Iranian Loanwords in Early Aramaic." *EncIr* 2, no. 3 (1986): 256–59.

Greenfield, Jonas C., Bezalel Porten, and Ada Yardeni. *The Bisitun Inscription of Darius the Great: Aramaic Version.* London: Lund Humphries, 1982.

Greenfield, Jonas C., and Michael E. Stone. "The Enochic Pentateuch and the Date of the Similitudes." *HTR* 70 (1977): 51–65.

Grenet, Frantz. "Burial II: Remnants of Burial Practices in Ancient Iran." *EncIr* 4 (1990): 559–61.

Greppin, John. "Xvarənah as a Transfunctional Figure," *JIES* 1 (1973): 232–42.

Griffiths, J. Gwyn. "Archaeology and Hesiod's Five Ages." *Journal of the History of Ideas* 17, no. 1 (1956): 109–19.

———. *Plutarch's De Iside et Osiride: Introduction, Translation, and Commentary.* Swansea: University of Wales Press, 1970.

Gropp, Douglas M., et al. *Wadi Daliyeh II: The Samaria Papyri from Wadi Daliyeh and Qumran Cave 4 XXVIII.* DJD 28. Oxford: Clarendon, 2001.

Gross, Walter. "Lying Prophet and Disobedient Man of God in 1 Kings 13: Role Analysis as an Instrument of Theological Interpretation of an O.T. Narrative Text." *Semeia* 15 (1979): 97–135.

Gruber, Mayer. "Language(s) in Judaism." Pages 3:1535–50 in Neusner, Avery-Peck and Green, eds., *The Encyclopaedia of Judaism.*

Gruen, Erich S. "Hellenistic Judaism." Pages 77–134 in *Cultures of the Jews.* Edited by David Biale. New York: Schocken, 2002.

———. *Heritage and Hellenism; the Reinvention of Jewish Tradition.* Berkeley: University of California Press, 1998.

———. "Persia through the Jewish Looking-Glass." Pages 90–104 in *Cultural Borrowings and Ethnic Appropriations in Antiquity.* Edited by Erich S. Gruen. Stuttgart: Franz Steiner, 2005.

Gruenwald, Ithamar, Shaul Shaked and Gedaliahu G. Stroumsa, eds., *Messiah and Christos.* Tübingen: Mohr Siebeck, 1992.

Gunkel, Hermann. *Genesis.* Translated by Mark E. Biddle. Macon, Ga.: Mercer University Press, 1997.

————. *What Remains of the Old Testament and Other Essays*. London: Allen & Unwin, 1928.

Gutierrez, Cathy, and Hillel Schwartz, eds. *The End that Does: Art, Science, and Millennial Accomplishment*. London: Equinox, 2006.

Gutmann, Joseph, ed. *The Dura-Europos Synagogue: A Re-evaluation (1932–1992)*. Atlanta: Scholars, 1992.

Habel, Norman C. *The Book of Job: A Commentary*. Philadelphia: Westminster John Knox, 1985.

Hallock, Richard T. "New Light from Persepolis." *JNES* 9, no. 4 (1950): 237–52.

————. "Selected Fortification Texts." *Cahiers de la D. A. F. I.* 8 (1978): 109–36.

Hamilton, Malcolm, ed. *The Sociology of Religion*, vol. 5. London: Routledge, 2007.

Handley-Schachler, Morrison. "The *Lan* Ritual in the Persepolis Fortification Texts." Pages 195–204 in *Achaemenid History XI*. Edited by Maria Brosius and Amélie Kuhrt. Leiden: NINO, 1998.

Hanson, Paul D. "Apocalypse, Genre." Pages 27–28 in Crim, ed., *Interpreter's Dictionary of the Bible*.

————. "Apocalypticism." Pages 28–34 in Crim, ed., *Interpreter's Dictionary of the Bible*.

————. *The Dawn of Apocalyptic*. Philadelphia: Fortress, 1975.

————. "Jewish Apocalyptic Against Its Near Eastern Environment." *RB* 78 (1971): 31–58.

————. "Prolegomena to the Study of Jewish Apocalyptic." Pages 389–413 in Cross, Lemke and Miller, eds., *Magnalia Dei*.

————. "Rebellion in Heaven, Azazel, and Euhemeristic Heroes in 1 Enoch 6–11." *JBL* 96, no. 2 (1977): 195–233.

Harrington, Daniel J. "The Raz Nihyeh in a Qumran Wisdom Text." *Revue Qumran* 17, no. 1–4 (1996): 549–53.

————. *Wisdom Texts from Qumran*. London: Routledge, 1996.

Harrison, Simon. "Cultural Boundaries." *Anthropology Today* 15, no. 5 (1999): 10–13.

Harrison, Thomas. *Divinity and History: The Religion of Herodotus*. Oxford: Clarendon, 2002.

Hartman, Sven S. "Datierung der junavestischen Apokalyptik." Pages 61–76 in Hellholm, ed., *Apocalypticism in the Mediterranean World*.

Hartner, Willy. "Old Iranian Calendars." *CHI* 2:714–92.

Hasenfratz, Hans P. "Iran und der Dualismus." *Numen* 30, no. 1 (1983): 35–52.

Haug, Martin. *Essays on the Sacred Language, Writings, and Religion of the Parsis*. London: Routledge, 2000. First Published 1884.

————. "Über das Ardâî Vîrâf Nâmeh (die Visionen das alten Parsenpriester Ardâî Vîrâf) und seinen angeblichen Zusammenhang mit dem Christlichen Apocryphon, 'die Himmelfahrt des Jesaja' betitelt." *Sitzungsberichte der kgl.bayerischen Akademie der Wissenschaften* I, no. 3 (1870): 327–46.

Havelock, Eric A. "The Coming of Literate Communication to Western Civilization." *Journal of Communication* 30 (1980): 90–98.

————. *The Greek Concept of Justice: From Its Shadow in Homer to Its Substance in Plato*. Cambridge, Mass.: Harvard University Press, 1978.

Healey, John F. *The Targums of Proverbs*. Edinburgh: T. & T. Clark, 1991.

Heider, George C. *The Cult of Molek: A Reassessment*. Sheffield: JSOT, 1985.

Hellerman, Joseph. "Purity and Nationalism in Second Temple Literature: 1–2 Maccabees and Jubilees." *JETS* 46, no. 3 (2003): 401–21.

Hellholm, David, ed. *Apocalypticism in the Mediterranean World and the Near East: Proceedings of the International Colloquium on Apocalypticism, Uppsala, August 12–17, 1979.* Tübingen: J.C.B. Mohr, 1983.

———. "The Problem of Apocalyptic Genre and the Apocalypse of John." *Semeia* 36 (1986): 13–64.

Hendel, Ronald S. "The Nephilim Were on the Earth: Genesis 6:1–4 and Its Ancient Near Eastern Context." Pages 11–34 in Auffarth and Stuckenbruck, eds., *The Fall of the Angels.*

Hengel, Martin. *Judaism and Hellenism.* Translated by John Bowden. London: Xpress Reprints, 1996.

Hengel, Martin, Siegfried Mittmann and Anna M. Schwemer, eds. *La Cité de Dieu/Die Stadt Gottes.* Tübingen: Mohr Siebeck, 2000.

Henkelman, Wouter. *The Other Gods Who Are: Studies in Elamite-Iranian Acculturation Based on the Persepolis Fortification Texts.* Leiden: NINO, 2008.

Henkelman, Wouter, and Kristin Kleber. "Babylonian Workers in the Persian Heartland: Palace Building at Matannan in the Reign of Cambyses." Pages 163–76 in Tuplin, ed., *Persian Responses.*

Henkelman, Wouter, and Amélie Kuhrt, eds. *A Persian Perspective: Essays in Memory of Heleen Sancisi-Weerdenburg.* Leiden: NINO, 2003.

Henning, Walter B. "An Astronomical Chapter of the Bundahishn." *JRAS* (1942): 229–48.

———. "The Book of Giants." *BSOAS* 11, no. 1 (1943): 52–74.

———. *Selected Papers*, vol. 2. Leiden: Brill, 1977.

———. *Zoroaster: Politician or Witch-Doctor?* London: Oxford University Press, 1951.

Henze, Matthias. *The Madness of King Nebuchadnezzar: The Ancient Near Eastern Origins and Early History of Interpretation of Daniel 4.* Leiden: Brill, 1999.

Herman, Geoffrey. "Ahasuerus, the Former Stable-Master of Belshazzar, and the wicked Alexander of Macedon: Two Parallels Between the Babylonian Talmud and Persian Sources." *AJS Review* 29, no. 2 (2005): 283–97.

Herodotus. *The Persian Wars.* Translated by A. D. Godley. *The Persian Wars, Books III–IV.* LCL. Cambridge, Mass.: Harvard University Press, 2000.

———. *The Persian Wars.* Translated by A. D. Godley. *The Persian Wars, Books VIII–IX.* LCL. Cambridge, Mass.: Harvard University Press, 2001.

———. *The Persian Wars.* Translated by A. D. Godley. *The Persian Wars, Books I–II.* LCL. Cambridge, Mass.: Harvard University Press, 2002.

———. *The Persian Wars.* Translated by A. D. Godley. *The Persian Wars, Books V–VII.* LCL. Cambridge, Mass.: Harvard University Press, 2006.

Herzfeld, Ernst E. *Archaeological History of Iran.* London: Oxford University Press, 1935.

———. "The Traditional Date of Zoroaster." Pages 132–36 in Pavry, ed., *Oriental Studies.*

Heschel, Abraham J. *The Prophets.* New York: HarperCollins, 2001.

Hezser, C. *Jewish Literacy in Roman Palestine.* Tübingen: Mohr Siebeck, 2001.

Himmelfarb, Martha. "The Experience of the Visionary and Genre in the Ascension of Isaiah 6–11 and the Apocalypse of Paul." *Semeia* 36 (1986): 97–112.

———. *Tours of Hell: An Apocalyptic Form in Jewish and Christian Literature.* Philadelphia: University of Pennsylvania Press, 1983.

Hinnells, John R., ed. *Mithraic Studies: Proceedings of the First International Congress of Mithraic Studies.* 2 vols. Manchester: Manchester University Press, 1975.

———. "Reflections on the Lion-Headed Figure in Mithraism." Pages 333–70 in Duchesne-Guillemin, ed., *Monumentum H. S. Nyberg.*

———. *Zoroastrian and Parsi Studies: Selected Works of John R. Hinnells.* Aldershot: Ashgate, 2000.

———. "The Zoroastrian Doctrine of Salvation in the Roman World: A Study of the Oracle of Hystaspes." Pages 125–48 in *Man and His Salvation.* Edited by Eric J. Sharpe and John R. Hinnells. Manchester: Manchester University Press, 1973.

———. "Zoroastrian Influence on the Judeo-Christian Tradition." *JCama* 45 (1976): 1–23.

———. "Zoroastrian Saviour Imagery and Its Influence on the New Testament." *Numen* 16, no. 3 (1969): 161–85.

Hintze, Almut. "'Do ut des': Patterns of Exchange in Zoroastrianism." *JRAS* 14, no. 1 (2004): 27–45.

———. "Frašō.kərəti." *EncIr* 10 (2000): 190–92.

———. "On the Literary Structure of the Older Avesta." *BSOAS* 65, no. 1 (2002): 31–51.

———. "The Rise of the Saviour in the Avesta." Pages 77–97 in *Iran und Turfan.* Edited by Christiane Reck and Peter Zieme. Wiesbaden: Harrassowitz, 1995.

———. "The Saviour and the Dragon in Iranian and Jewish/Christian Eschatology." Pages 72–90 in Shaked and Netzer, eds., *Irano-Judaica*, vol. 4.

———. "Treasures in Heaven: A Theme in Comparative Religion." Pages 9–36 in Shaked and Netzer, eds., *Irano-Judaica*, vol. 4.

———. *Zamyād-Yašt: Edition, Übersetzung.* Kommentar. Wiesbaden: Reichert, 1994.

———. *A Zoroastrian Liturgy: The Worship in Seven Chapters (Yasna 35–41).* Wiesbaden: Harrassowitz, 2008.

Hirschberg, H. Z. J. W. "The Oriental Jewish Communities." Pages 119–225 in *Religion in the Middle East*, vol. 1. Edited Arthur J. Arbury. Cambridge: Cambridge University Press, 1969.

Hogeterp, Albert L. A. "Resurrection and Biblical Tradition: Pseudo-Ezekiel Reconsidered." *Biblica* 89, no. 1 (2008): 59–69.

Hoglund, Kenneth G. "The Achaemenid Context." Pages 54–72 in Davies, ed., *Second Temple Studies I.*

———. *Achaemenid Imperial Administration in Syra-Palestine and the Missions of Ezra and Nehemiah.* Atlanta: Scholars, 1992.

Holbek, Bengt. "What the Illiterate Think of Writing." Pages 183–96 in Schousboe and Larsen, eds., *Literacy and Society.*

Holden, Lynn. *Forms of Deformity.* Sheffield: Sheffield Academic, 1991.

Holladay, William L. *Jeremiah 1: A Commentary on the Book of the Prophet Jeremiah Chapters 1–25.* Minneapolis: Fortress, 1986.

———. *Jeremiah 2: A Commentary on the Book of the Prophet Jeremiah Chapters 26–52.* Minneapolis: Fortress, 1989.

Horsley, Richard. "The Origins of the Hebrew Scriptures in Imperial Relations." Pages 107 35 in Draper, ed., *Orality, Literacy, and Colonialism.*

————. "The Politics of Cultural Production in Second Temple Judea: Historical Context and Political-Religious Relations of the scribes Who Produced 1 Enoch, Sirach, and Daniel." Pages 123–48 in Wright and Wills, eds., *Conflicted Boundaries.*

————. "Religion and Other Products of Empire." *JAAR* 71, no. 1 (2003): 13–44.

Houtkamp, J. "Some Remarks on Fire Altars of the Achaemenid Period." Pages 23–48 in *La Religion iranienne a l'epoque achaemenide (Actes du collogne de Liege 11 decembre 1987).* Edited by Jean Kellens. Gent: Iranica Antiqua, 1991.

Huggins, Ronald V. "Noah and the Giants: A Response to John C. Reeves." *JBL* 114, no. 1 (1995): 103–10.

Hultgård, Anders. "Bahman Yasht: A Persian Apocalypse." Pages 114–34 in Collins and Charlesworth, eds., *Mysteries and Revelations.*

————. "The First Chapter of the Bundahišn. Remarks on the Text and Composition." Pages 167–90 in Gnoli and Panaino, eds., *Proceedings of the First European Conference of Iranian Studies.*

————. "Forms and Origins of Iranian Apocalypticism." Pages 387–412 in Hellholm, ed., *Apocalypticism in the Mediterranean World.*

————. "Das Judentum in der hellenistisch-römischen Zeit und die iranische Religion: ein religionsgeschichtliches Problem." *Principat* 19, no. 1 (1979): 512–90.

————. "Das Paradies: vom Park des Perserkönigs zum Ort der Seligen." Pages 1–43 in Hengel, Mittmann and Schwemer, eds., *La Cité de Dieu/Die Stadt Gottes.*

————. "Persian Apocalypticism." Pages 1:39–83 in Collins, ed., *The Encyclopedia of Apocalypticism.*

————. "Zoroastrian Myth in Bahman Yasht." Pages 15–27 in *The Middle East Viewed from the North: Papers from the First Nordic Conference on Middle Eastern Studies, Uppsala 26–29 January 1989.* Edited by B. Utas and K. Vikør. Bergen, 1992.

Humbach, Helmut. "Yama/Yima/Jamšēd, King of Paradise of the Iranians." *Jerusalem Studies in Arabic and Islam* 26 (2002): 68–77.

Humbach, H., Josef Elfenbein, and Prods Oktor Skjærvø. *The Gāthās of Zarathushtra and Other Old Avestan Texts.* 2 vols. Heidelberg: Carl Winter, 1991.

Humbach, Helmut, and Pallan R. Ichapora. *Zamyād Yasht, Yasht 19 of the Younger Avesta: Text, Translation, Commentary.* Wiesbaden: Harrassowitz, 1998.

Hüsing, G. "Gūgu (678–643)." *Orientalistische Literaturzeitung* 10 (1915): 299–303.

Huyse, P. "Noch einmal zu Parallelen zwischen Achaemeniden- und Sāsāniden-inschriften." *Archäologische Mitteilungen aus Iran* 23 (1990): 177–83.

Hyatt, J. Philip. "The Peril from the North in Jeremiah." *JBL* 59, no. 4 (1940): 499–513.

Ichapora, Pallan R. "The Legendary History of Iran in the religio-Historical Account of the Zamyād Yašt (Yt. 19)." Pages 106–10 in Shaked and Netzer, eds., *Irano-Judaica*, vol. 4.

Inostrantsev, K. A. "On the Ancient Iranian Burial Customs and Buildings." *JCama* 3 (1923): 1–28.

Insler, S. *The Gathas of Zarathustra.* Leiden: Brill, 1975.

Irwin, Brian P. "Molek Imagery and the Slaughter of Gog in Ezekiel 38 and 39." *JSOT* 65 (1995): 93–112.

Isaac, Ephraim. "1 (Ethiopic Apocalypse of) Enoch." *OTP* 1:5–89.

Jackson, A. V. Williams. "Zoroastrianism and the Resemblances Between It and Christianity." *Biblical World* 27, no. 5 (1906): 335–43.

Jackson, David R. *Enochic Judaism: Three Defining Paradigm Exemplars*. London: T&T Clark, 2004.

Jaffee, Martin S. *Torah in the Mouth: Writing and Oral Tradition in Palestinian Judaism 200 BCE–400 CE*. Oxford: Oxford University Press, 2001.

Jakobson, Roman. "The Slavic God Velesb." Pages 33–48 in *Selected Writings VII*. Edited by Stephen Rudy. Berlin: Mouton, 1985.

Jamasp Asa, Kaikhusroo M. *Aogəmadaēcā: A Zoroastrian Liturgy*. Vienna: Österreichischen Akademie Der Wissenschaften, 1982.

Jamzadeh, Parivash. "An Assyrian Motif in the Shāhnāma." *Iranica Antiqua* 38 (2003): 167–72.

———. "A Shahnama Passage in an Achaemenid Context." *Iranica Antiqua* 39 (2004): 383–88.

Janowski, Bernd. "Die Toten loben JHWH nicht: Psalm 88 und das alttestamentliche Todesverständnis." Pages 3–46 in *Auferstehung–Resurrection*. Edited by Friedrich Avemarie and Hermann Lichtenberger. Tübingen: Mohr Siebeck, 2004.

Jason, Heda. "Study of Israelite and Jewish Oral and Folk Literature: Problems and Issues." *AFS* 49, no. 1 (1990): 69–108.

Jastrow, Morris, Jr. *Babylonian-Assyrian Birth-Omens and Their Cultural Significance*. Giessen: Töpelmann, 1914.

Jeanrond, Werner G. "Hermeneutics." Pages 282–84 in Coggins and Houlden, eds., *A Dictionary of Biblical Interpretation*.

Jeremias, Jörg. *Theophanie: Die Geschichte einer alttestamentlichen Gattung*. 2d ed. Neukirchen: Neukirchener Verlag, 1977.

Jones, Elaine Marie. "An Examination of the Influence of Zoroastrianism on the Development of Belief in Resurrection of the Dead in Judaism." M.A. diss. University of Wales, 1989.

Jong, Albert de. "The Contribution of the Magi." Pages 85–99 in Curtis and Stewart, eds., *Birth of the Persian Empire*.

———. *Traditions of the Magi: Zoroastrianism in Greek and Latin Literature*. Leiden: Brill, 1997.

Josephus. *Jewish Antiquities*. Translated by H. St. J. Thackeray. *Jewish Antiquities I–III*. LCL. Cambridge, Mass.: Harvard University Press, 1998.

———. *The Jewish War*. Translated by H. St. J. Thackeray. *Josephus III: The Jewish War Books IV–VII*. LCL. London: Heinemann, 1928.

Kaminka, A. "Septuaginta und Targum zu Proverbia." *HUCA* 8–9 (1931–1932): 169–91.

Kanga, M. F. "Barsom." *EncIr* 3 (1989): 825–27.

Keall, Edward J. "Archaeology and the Fire Temple." Pages 15–22 in *Iranian Civilization and Culture*. Edited by Charles J. Adams. Montreal: McGill, 1972.

Keith, Chris. "'In My Own Hand': Grapho-Literacy and the Apostle Paul." *Biblica* 89, no. 1 (2008): 39–58.

Kelber, Werner H. "Orality and Biblical Studies: A Review Essay." *Review of Biblical Literature* 12 (2007): n.p. Online: http://www.bookreviews.org/pdf/2107_6748.pdf.

———. "Roman Imperialism and Early Christian Scribality." Pages 135–54 in Draper, ed., *Orality, Literacy, and Colonialism*.

Kelle, Brad E. "Ancient Israelite Prophets and Greek Political Orators: Analogies for the Prophets and Their Implications for Historical Reconstruction." Pages 57–84 in Kelle and Moore, eds., *Israel's Prophets and Israel's Past*.

Kelle, Brad E. and Megan Bishop Moore, eds. *Israel's Prophets and Israel's Past*. New York: T&T Clark, 2006.

Kellens, Jean. "Avesta." *EncIr* 3 (1989): 35–44.

———. *Essays on Zarathustra and Zoroastrianism*. Translated by Prods Oktor Skjærvø. Costa Mesa, Ca.: Mazda, 2000.

Kelly, Thomas. "Persian Propaganda: A Neglected Factor in Xerxes' Invasion of Greece and Herodotus." *Iranica Antiqua* 38 (2003): 173–219.

Kent, Roland Grubb. "The Name Ahuramazda." Pages 200–208 in Pavry, ed., *Oriental Studies*.

———. "The Name of Hystaspes." *Language* 21, no. 2 (1945): 55–58.

———. *Old Persian: Grammar, Texts, Lexicon*. 2d ed. New Haven, Conn.: American Oriental Society, 1961.

———. "The Oldest of the Old Persian Inscriptions." *JAOS* 66, no. 3 (1946): 206–12.

Khaleghi-Motlagh, Dj. "Aždahā II: In Persian Literature." *EncIr* 3 (1989): 199–203.

Khorenats'i, Moses. *History of the Armenians: Translation and Commentary*. Translated by Robert W. Thomson. Cambridge, Mass.: Harvard University Press, 1978.

Kierkegaard, Søren. *Either/Or*. 2 vols. Translated by Howard V. Hong and Edna H. Hong. Princeton, N.J.: Princeton University Press, 1987–1990.

———. *Philosophical Fragments: Johannes Climacus*. Translated by Howard V. Hong and Edna H. Hong. Princeton, N.J.: Princeton University Press, 1985.

Killingsworth, M. Jimmie. "Product and Process, Literacy and Orality: An Essay on Composition and Culture." *College Composition and Communication* 44, no. 1 (1993): 26–39.

Kingsley, Peter. "The Greek Origin of the Sixth-Century Dating of Zoroaster." *BSOAS* 53, no. 2 (1990): 245–65.

———. "Meetings with Magi: Iranian Themes Among the Greeks, from Xanthus of Lydia to Plato's Academy." *JRAS* 5, no. 2 (1995): 173–209.

Klein, Ralph W. *1 Chronicles: A Commentary*. Minneapolis: Fortress, 2006.

Knibb, Michael A. "Apocalyptic and Wisdom in 4 Ezra." *JSJ* 13, no. 1–2 (1982): 56–74.

———. "The Date of the Parables of Enoch: A Critical Review." *NTS* 25 (1979): 345–59.

———. *The Ethiopic Book of Enoch: A New Edition in the Light of the Aramaic Dead Sea Fragments*. 2 vols. Oxford: Clarendon, 1978.

———. "Interpreting the Book of Enoch: Reflections on a Recently Published Commentary." *JSJ* 33, no. 4 (2002): 437–50.

———. "Temple and Cult in Apocryphal and Pseudepigraphal Writings from before the Common Era." Pages 401–16 in Day, ed., *Temple and Worship in Biblical Israel*.

Knoppers, Gary N. *1 Chronicles 1–9: A New Translation with Introduction and Commentary*. New York: Doubleday, 2003.

Koch, Klaus. *Daniel 1. Teilband Dan 1–4*. Neukirchen–Vluyn: Neukirchener Verlag, 2005.

———. "Dereios, der Meder." Pages 287–99 in *The Word of the Lord Shall Go Forth*. Edited by Carol L. Meyers and M. O'Connor. Winona Lake, Ind.: Eisenbrauns, 1983.

———. *The Rediscovery of Apocalyptic*. Translated by Margaret Kohl. London: SCM, 1972.

Koenen, Ludwig. "Greece, the Near East, and Egypt: Cyclic Destruction in Hesiod and the Catalogue of Women." *TAPA* 124 (1994): 1–34.

Kohn, Risa Levitt. "Ezekiel at the Turn of the Century." *CBR* 2, no. 1 (2003): 9–31.

Kohut, Alexander. *Über die Jüdische Angelologie und Dämonologie in ihrer Abhängigkeit vom Parsismus*. Leipzig: Brockhaus, 1866.

Kotwal, Firoze M., and Almut Hintze. *The Khorda Avesta and Yašt Codex E1*. Wiesbaden: Harrassowitz, 2008.

Kraeling, Emil G. *The Brooklyn Museum Aramaic Papyri: New Documents of the Fifth Century B.C. from the Jewish Colony at Elephantine*. New Haven, Conn.: Yale University Press, 1953.

———. "The Meaning of the Ezekiel Panel in the Synagogue at Dura." *BASOR* 78 (1940): 12–18.

Kramer, Samuel Noah. *The Sumerians: Their History, Culture, and Character*. London: University of Chicago Press, 1970.

Krappe, Alexander H. "Albinos and Albinism in Iranian Tradition." *Folklore* 55, no. 4 (1944): 170–74.

Krasnowolska, Anna. "Some Heroes of Iranian Calendar Mythology." Pages 371–82 in Fragner et al., eds., *Proceedings of the Second European Conference*.

Kratz, Reinhard G. "Statthalter, Hohepriester und Schreiber im perserzeitlichen Juda." Pages 93–119 in *Das Judentum im Zeitalter des Zweiten Temples*. Edited by Reinhard G. Kratz. Tübingen: Mohr Siebeck, 2004.

Kraus, F. R. "Ein sentrales Problem des altmesopotamisehen Rechtes: Was ist der Codex Hammu-Rabi?" *Genava* 8 (1960): 283–96.

Kreyenbroek, G. *Sraoša in the Zoroastrian Tradition*. Leiden: Brill, 1985.

Kuhn, Thomas S. *The Structure of Scientific Revolutions*. 3d ed. Chicago: University of Chicago Press, 1996. First Published 1970.

Kuhrt, Amélie. "The Achaemenid Concept of Kingship." *Iran* 22 (1984): 156–60.

———. "The Achaemenid Persian Empire (c. 500–c. 330 BCE): Continuities, Adaptations, Transformations." Pages 93–124 in *Empires: Perspectives from Archaeology and History*. Edited by Suasan E. Alcock et al. Cambridge: Cambridge University Press, 2001.

———. "The Cyrus Cylinder and Achaemenid Imperial Policy." *JSOT* 25 (1983): 83–97.

———. "Making History: Sargon of Agade and Cyrus the Great of Persia." Pages 347–61 in Henkelman and Kuhrt, eds., *A Persian Perspective*.

———. "Nabonidus and the Babylonian Priesthood." Pages 117–56 in *Pagan Priests*. Edited by Mary Beard and John North. London: Duckworth, 1990.

———. *The Persian Empire: A Corpus of Sources from the Achaemenid Period*. London: Routledge, 2009. First Published 2007.

Kuhrt, Amélie, and Susan Sherwin-White. "Xerxes' Destruction of Babylonian Temples." Pages 69–78 in Sancisi-Weerdenburg and Kuhrt, eds, *Achaemenid History II*.

Kuiper, F. B. J. "Ahura Mazda 'Lord Wisdom'?" *Indo-Iranian Journal* 18 (1976): 25–42.

———. "Remarks on the Avestan Hymn to Mithra." *Indo-Iranian Journal* 5 (1961): 36–60.

Kvanvig, Helge S. "Origin and Identity of the Enoch Group." Pages 207–12 in Boccaccini, ed., *Henoch*.

———. *Roots of Apocalyptic: The Mesopotamian Background of the Enoch Figure and the Son of Man*. Neukirchen–Vluyn: Neukirchener Verlag, 1988.

———. "Throne Visions and Monsters: The Encounter Between Danielic and Enochic Traditions." *ZAW* 117, no. 2 (2005): 248–72.

LaCocque, André. *The Book of Daniel*. Translated by David Pellauer. London: SPCK, 1979.

LaCocque, André, and Paul Ricoeur. *Thinking Biblically: Exegetical and Hermeneutical Studies*. Translated by David Pellauer. Chicago: University of Chicago Press, 1998.

Lactantius, Caeculius. *Divine Institutes*. Translated by Anthony Bowen and Peter Garnsey. *The Divine Institutes of Lactantius*. Liverpool: Liverpool University Press, 2003.

Laertius, Diogenes. *Vitae Philosophorum*. Translated by R. D. Hicks. *Diogenes Laertius I*. LCL. Cambridge, Mass.: Harvard University Press, 1980.

Lambert, W. G. *The Background of Jewish Apocalyptic*. London: Athlone, 1978.

Landes, Richard. "Roosters Crow, Owls Hoot: On the Dynamics of Apocalyptic Millennialism." Pages 19–46 in O'Leary and McGhee, eds., *War in Heaven/Heaven on Earth*.

Lang, Bernhard. *Monotheism and the Prophetic Minority: An Essay in Biblical History and Sociology*. Sheffield: Almond, 1983.

———. "Street Theatre, Raising the Dead and the Zoroastrian Connection in Ezekiel's Prophecy." Pages 297–316 in *Ezekiel and His Book*. Edited by J. Lust. Leuven: Leuven Univerity Press, 1986.

Lange, Armin. "Literary Prophecy and Oracle Collection: A Comparison Between Judah and Greece in Persian Times." Pages 248–75 in Floyd and Haak, eds., *Prophets, Prophecy, and Prophetic Texts*.

Lange, Armin, Hermann Lichtenberger, and K. F. Diethard Römheld, eds. *Die Dämonen/ Demons: Die Dämonologie der israelitisch-jüdischen und frühchristlichen Literatur im Kontext ihrer Umwelt*. Tübingen: Mohr Siebeck, 2003.

Lapp, Paul W., and Nancy L. Lapp, eds. *Discoveries in the Wâdī Ed-Dâliyeh*. Cambridge, Mass.: ASOR, 1974.

Larson, Gerald J., C. Scott Littleton, and Jaan Puhvel, eds. *Myth in Indo-European Antiquity*. Berkeley: University of California Press, 1974.

Lemaire, Andre. "The Sage in School and Temple." Pages 165–84 in Gammie and Perdue, eds., *The Sage in Israel*.

Leopold, Anita M., and Jeppe S. Jensen, eds. *Syncretism in Religion: A Reader*. London: Equinox, 2004.

Lessa, William A. "'Discover-of-the-Sun': Mythology as a Reflection of Culture." *Journal of American Folklore* 79.311 (1966): 3–51.

Lesser, Alexander. "Social Fields and the Evolution of Society." *Southwestern Journal of Anthropology* 17, no. 1 (1961): 40–48.

Lester, Robert C. "Hinduism: Veda and Sacred Texts." Pages 126–47 in *The Holy Book in Comparative Perspective*. Edited by Frederick M. Denny and Rodney L. Taylor. Columbia: University of South Carolina Press, 1985.

Levine, Baruch A. *Numbers 1–20*. New York: Doubleday, 1993.

Levine, Lee I. *The Ancient Synagogue: The First Thousand Years*. New Haven, Conn.: Yale University Press, 2000.

———. *Judaism and Hellenism in Antiquity: Conflict or Confluence?* Seattle: University of Washington Press, 1998.

Levine, Louis D. "Prelude to Monarchy: Iran and the Neo-Assyrian Empire." Pages 39–46 in Adams, ed., *Iranian Civilization*.

Levine, Samuel J. "Looking Beyond the Mercy/Justice Dichotomy: Reflections on the Complementary Roles of Mercy and Justice in Jewish Law and Tradition." *Journal of Catholic Legal Studies* 45 (2006): 455–72.

Levy, Habib. *Comprehensive History of the Jews of Iran: The Outset of the Diaspora*. Translated by George W. Maschke. Costa Mesa, Ca.: Mazda Publishers, 1999.

Lewis, David M. "The Persepolis Tablets: Speech, Seal and Script." Pages 17–32 in Bowman and Woolf, eds., *Literacy and Power*.

Lewis, Jack P. "Noah and the Flood: In Jewish, Christian and Muslim Tradition." *BA* 47, no. 4 (1984): 224–39.

———. *A Study of the Interpretation of Noah and the Flood in Jewish and Christian Literature*. Leiden: Brill, 1978.

Lidzbarski, Mark. *Ephemeris für Semitische Epigraphik*. Vol. 1. Giessen: Töpelmann, 1902.

———. *Ephemeris für Semitische Epigraphik*. Vol. 3. Giessen: Töpelmann, 1915.

Light, Timothy. "Orthosyncretism: An Account of Melding in Religion." *Method and Theory in the Study of Religion* 12, no. 1 (2000): 162–85.

Lincoln, Bruce. "The Center of the World and the Origins of Life." *HR* 40, no. 4 (2001): 311–26.

———. "'The Earth Becomes Flat'—A Study of Apocalyptic Imagery." *Comparative Studies in Society and History* 25, no. 1 (1983): 136–53.

———. "The Indo-European Myth of Creation." *HR* 15, no. 2 (1975): 121–45.

———. "The Lord of the Dead." *HR* 20, no. 3 (1981): 224–41.

———. *Priests, Warriors, and Cattle: A Study in the Ecology of Religions*. Berkeley, Ca.: University of California Press, 1981.

———. *Religion, Empire and Torture: The Case of Achaemenian Persia with a Postscript on Abu Ghraib*. Chicago: University of Chicago Press, 2007.

———. "Review: Mitra, Mithra, Mithras: Problems of a Multiform Diety." *HR* 17, no. 2 (1977): 200–208.

Lindblom, J. *Prophecy in Ancient Israel*. Oxford: Blackwell, 1962.

Linville, James R. "The Day of Yahweh and the Mourning of the Priests in Joel." Pages 98–114 in Grabbe and Ogden, eds., *The Priests in the Prophets*.

Lipinski, E. "Western Semites in Persepolis." *Acta Antiqua Academiae Scientiarum Hungaricae* 25 (1977): 101–12.

Lipschits, Oded. "Achaemenid Imperial Policy, Settlement Processes in Palestine, and the Status of Jerusalem in the Middle of the Fifth Century B.C.E." Pages 19–52 in Lipschits and Oeming, eds., *Judah and the Judeans*.

Lipschits, Oded, Gary N. Knoppers, and Rainer Albertz, eds. *Judah and the Judeans in the Fourth Century B.C.E.* Winona Lake, Ind.: Eisenbrauns, 2007.

Lipschits, Oded, and Manfred Oeming, eds. *Judah and the Judeans in the Persian Period*. Winona Lake, Ind.: Eisenbrauns, 2006.

Lommel, Herman. *Die Religion Zarathustras nach dem Awesta dargestellt*. Tübingen: Mohr Siebeck, 1930.

Lord, Albert B. *The Singer of Tales*. 2d ed. Cambridge, Mass.: Harvard University Press, 2000. First Published 1960.

Loubser, J. A. "Bobby". "Moving Beyond Colonialist Discourse: Understanding Oral Theory and Cultural Difference in the Context of Media Analysis." Pages 65–82 in Draper, ed., *Orality, Literacy, and Colonialism*.

Lucas, Ernest C. "Daniel: Resolving the Enigma." *VT* 50, no. 1 (2000): 66–80.

———. "The Origin of Daniel's Four Empire Scheme Re-examined." *TynBul* 40, no. 2 (1989): 185–202.

Luria, Aleksandr R. *Cognitive Development: Its Cultural and Social Foundations.* Translated by Martin Lopez-Morillas and Lynn Solotaroff. Cambridge, Mass.: Harvard University Press, 1976.

Lyman, R. Lee, and Michael J. O'Brien. "Cultural Traits: Units of Analysis in Early Twentieth-Century Anthropology." *Journal of Anthropological Research* 59, no. 2 (2003): 225–50.

MacDonald, M. C. A. "Literacy in an Oral Environment." Pages 49–118 in Bienkowski, Mee and Slater, eds., *Writing and Ancient Near Eastern Society.*

MacKenzie, D. N. "Bundahišn." *EncIr* 4 (1990): 547–51.

———. *A Concise Pahlavi Dictionary.* London: Oxford University Press, 1971.

———. "Zoroastrian Astrology in the Bundahišn." *BASOR* 27 (1964): 513–29.

Magee, Peter et al. "The Achaemenid Empire in South Asia and Recent Excavations in Akra in Northwest Pakistan." *AJA* 109, no. 4 (2005): 711–41.

Malandra, William W. *The Fravaši Yašt: Introduction, Text, Translation and Commentary.* London: University Microfilms Intl, 1977. Ph.D. diss., University of Pennsylvania, 1971.

———. "Frawardīgān." *EncIr* 10 (2001): 199.

———. *An Introduction to Ancient Iranian Religion.* Minneapolis: University of Minnesota Press, 1983.

Mallory, James P. "Cosmology." Pages 130–31 in Mallory and Adams, eds., *Encyclopedia of Indo-European Culture.*

———. "A Short History of the Indo-European Problem." *JIES* 1 (1973): 21–65.

Mallory, James, and Charles J. Adams, eds. *Encyclopedia of Indo-European Culture.* London: Fitzroy Dearborn, 1997.

Mallowan, Max. "Cyrus the Great (558–529 BC)." *CHI* 2:392–419.

Manning, Gary T., Jr. *Echoes of a Prophet: The Use of Ezekiel in the Gospel of John and in the Literature of the Second Temple Period.* London: T&T Clark, 2004.

Manson, T. W. "Sadducee and Pharisee: The Origin and Significance of Names." *BJRL* 22 (1938): 144–59.

Martínez, F. García. "Apocalypticism in the Dead Sea Scrolls." Pages 1:162–92 in Collins, ed., *The Encyclopedia of Apocalypticism.*

———. "Apocalypticism in the Dead Sea Scrolls." Pages 195–226 in *Qumranica Minora I.*

———. "Is Jewish Apocalyptic the Mother of Christian Theology?" Pages 129–52 in *Qumranica Minora I.*

———. *Qumran and Apocalyptic: Studies on the Aramaic Texts from Qumran.* Leiden: Brill, 1992.

———. *Qumranica Minora I: Qumran Origins and Apocalypticism.* Edited by E. J. C. Tigchelaar. Leiden: Brill, 2007.

Martyr, Justin. *The First Apology.* Pages 159–87 in *The Apostolic Fathers with Justin Martyr and Irenæus.* Edited by A. Cleveland Coxe. ANF 1. Repr., American ed. Edinburgh: T. & T. Clark, 1996.

Mason, Steve. "Jews, Judaeans, Judaizing, Judaism: Problems of Categorization in Ancient History." *JSJ* 38, no. 4–5 (2007): 457–512.

Matassa, Lidia D., and Jason M. Silverman, eds. *Text, Theology, and Trowel: Recent Research into the Hebrew Bible.* Eugene, Ore.: Pickwick, 2011.

Mathieson, Ian, Elizabeth Bettles, and H. S. Smith. "A Stela of the Persian Period from Saqqara." *JEA* 81 (1995): 23–41.

Mayer, Rudolf. "Monotheismus in Israel und in der Religion Zarathustras." *Biblische Zeitschrift* 1 (1957): 23–58.

Maynard, John Albert. "Judaism and Mazdayasna: A Study in Dissimilarities." *JBL* 44, no. 1–2 (1925): 163–70.

———. "Studies in Religious Texts from Assur." *AJSL* 34, no. 1 (1917): 21–59.

McDonald, J. I. H. "The Hermeneutical Circle." Pages 281–82 in Coggins and Houlden, eds., *A Dictionary of Biblical Interpretation*.

McIver, Robert K., and Marie Carroll. "Experiments to Develop Criteria for Determining the Existence of Written Sources and Their Potential Implications for the Synoptic Problem." *JBL* 121, no. 4 (2002): 667–87.

McKeating, Henry. *Ezekiel*. Sheffield: Sheffield Academic, 1995.

McLuhan, Marshall. *The Gutenberg Galaxy*. Toronto: University of Toronto Press, 2002.

———. *Understanding Media*. London: Routledge, 2001.

Mearns, Christopher L. "Dating the Similitudes of Enoch." *NTS* 25 (1979): 360–69.

Meeks, Wayne A. "Apocalyptic Discourse and Strategies of Goodness." *JR* 80, no. 3 (2000): 461–75.

Meiggs, Russell, and David Lewis. *A Selection of Greek Historical Inscriptions to the End of the Fifth Century B.C.* Rev. ed. Oxford: Clarendon, 1989.

Milik, Józef T. *The Books of Enoch: Aramaic Fragments of Qumran Cave 4*. Oxford: Clarendon, 1976.

Millard, Alan R. "The Knowledge of Writing in Late Bronze Age Palestine." Pages 317–26 in *Languages and Cultures in Contact*. Edited by K. van Lerberghe and G. Voet. Leuven: Peeters, 1999.

———. "Oral Proclamation and Written Record: Spreading and Preserving Information in Ancient Israel." Pages 237–41 in *Michael: Historical, Epigraphical and Biblical Studies in Honor of Prof. Michael Heltzer*. Edited by Yitzhak Avishur and Robert Deutsch. Tel Aviv: Archaelogical Center Publications, 1999.

———. "The Practice of Writing in Ancient Israel." *BA* 35, no. 4 (1972): 97–111.

———. *Reading and Writing in the Time of Jesus*. Sheffield: Sheffield Academic, 2000.

Miller, J. Maxwell, and John H. Hayes. *A History of Ancient Israel and Judah*. 2d ed. London: SCM, 1999.

Miller, Patrick D. *The Divine Warrior in Early Israel*. Cambridge, Mass.: Harvard University Press, 1973.

Mills, Lawrence H. *Avesta Eschatology Compared with the Books of Daniel and Revelation*. Chicago: Open Court, 1908.

———. "Mr. Moulton's Zoroaster and Israel." *The Thinker* 1, no. 6 (1892): 508–14.

———. *Our Own Religion in Ancient Persia*. Chicago, 1913.

———. *Zarathuštra, Philo, the Achaemenids, and Israel*. Leipzig: Brockhaus, 1905–6.

Minorsky, Vladimir. *Iranica: Twenty Articles*. Hertford: Stephen Austin, 1964.

Molenberg, Corrie. "A Study of the Roles of Shemihaza and Asael in 1 Enoch 6–11." *JJS* 35, no. 2 (1984): 136–46.

Monette, Connell. "Heroes and Hells in *Beowulf*, the *Shahnameh*, and the *Táin Bó Cúailnge*." *JIES* 36, no. 1–2 (2008): 99–147.

Montgomery, James A. *A Critical and Exegetical Commentary on the Book of Daniel*. Edinburgh: T. & T. Clark, 1927.

Moorey, P. R. S. "Aspects of Worship and Ritual on Achaemenid Seals." Pages 218–26 in *Akten des VII International Kongress für Iran: Kunst und Archäologie (Munich, 1976)*. Berlin: Dietrich Reimer, 1979.

———. "The Persian Empire." In *Cambridge Ancient History*. Edited by John Boardman. Plates to vol. 4. Cambridge: Cambridge University Press, 1988.

Morrison, George. "Persian Literature (Belles-Lettres) from the Earliest Times to the Time of Jāmī." Pages 1–82 in *History of Persian Literature from the Beginning of the Islamic Period to the Present Day*. Edited by George Morrison. HO I.IV.2.2. Leiden: Brill, 1981.

Moulton, James H. *Early Zoroastrianism: The Origins, The Prophet, The Magi*. Amsterdam: Philo, 1972.

———. "Zoroaster and Israel I." *The Thinker* 1, no. 5 (1892): 401–8.

———. "Zoroaster and Israel II." *The Thinker* 2, no. 4 (1893): 308–15.

———. "Zoroaster and Israel III." *The Thinker* 2, no. 6 (1893): 490–501.

———. "Zoroaster and Israel—A Reply." *The Thinker* 2, no. 1 (1893): 16–18.

———. "Zoroastrian Influences on Judaism." *Expository Times* 9 (1898): 352–58.

Mowinckel, Sigmund. *He That Cometh*. Translated by G. W. Anderson. Grand Rapids: Eerdmans, 2005.

Muilenburg, James. "The Biblical View of Time." *HTR* 54, no. 4 (1961): 225–52.

Müller, Hans-Peter. "Magisch-Mantische Weisheit und die Gestalt Daniels." *Ugarit-Forschungen* 1 (1969): 79–94.

———. "Mantische Weisheit und Apokalyptik." Pages 268–93 in de Boer, ed., *Congress Volume: Uppsala 1971*.

———. *Ursprünge und Struckturen alttestamentlicher Eschatologie*. Berlin: Töpelmann, 1969.

Murphy, Frederick J. "Apocalypses and Apocalypticism: The State of the Question." *CBR* 2 (1994): 147–79.

Mustafavi, M. T. "The Achaemenid Royal Road: Post-Stations Between Susa and Persepolis." Pages 14:3008–10 in Pope and Ackerman, eds., *A Survey of Persian Art*.

Na'aman, Nadav. "Royal Vassals of Governors? On the Status of Sheshbazzar and Zerubbabel in the Persian Empire." *Henoch* 22, no. 1 (2000): 35–44.

Narten, Johanna. *Die Aməša Spəntas im Avesta*. Wiesbaden, 1982.

———. "Bahman I: In the Avesta." *EncIr* 3 (1989): 487–88.

———. *Der Yasna Haptaŋhaiti*. Wiesbaden: Reichert, 1986.

Neusner, Jacob. "Jews and Judaism Under Iranian Rule: Bibliographical Reflections." *HR* 8, no. 2 (1968): 159–77.

———. "The Rabbi and the Magus." Pages 78–86 in *Talmudic Judaism in Sasanian Babylonia*. Edited by Jacob Neusner. Leiden: Brill, 1976.

———. *The Theology of the Oral Torah: Revealing the Justice of God*. Montreal: McGill-Queen's University Press, 1999.

Neusner, Jacob, Alan J. Avery-Peck, and William Scott Green. *The Encyclopaedia of Judaism*. 2d ed. 4 vols. Leiden: Brill, 2005.

Newman, Hillel. *Proximity to Power and Jewish Sectarian Groups of the Ancient Period*. Leiden: Brill, 2006.

Newport, Kenneth G. C., and Crawford Gribben, eds. *Expecting the End: Millennialism in Social and Historical Context*. Waco, Tex.: Baylor University Press, 2006.

Newsom, Carol A. "The Development of 1 Enoch 6–19: Cosmology and Judgment." *CBQ* 42, no. 3 (1980): 310–29.

Nickelsburg, George W. E. *1 Enoch 1*. Hermeneia. Minneapolis: Fortress, 2001.

———. "Apocalyptic and Myth in 1 Enoch 6–11." *JBL* 96, no. 3 (1977): 383–405.

————. "Apocalyptic Judaism." Pages 1:68–84 in Neusner, Avery-Peck and Green, eds., *The Encyclopaedia of Judaism.*

————. "Early Jewish Eschatology." *ABD* 2:579–94.

————. "Enochic Wisdom." Pages 81–94 in Boccaccini and Collins, eds., *The Early Enoch Literature.*

————. "Patriarchs Who Worry About Their Wives: A Haggadic Tendency in the Genesis Apocryphon." Pages 137–58 in *Biblical Perspectives.* Edited by Michael E. Stone and Esther G. Chazon. Leiden: Brill, 1998.

————. *Resurrection, Immortality, and Eternal Life in Intertestamental Judaism.* Exp. ed. Cambridge, Mass.: Harvard University Press, 2006.

————. "Where Is the Place of Eschatological Blessing?" Pages 53–72 in Chazon, Satran and Clements, eds., *Things Revealed.*

————. "Wisdom and Apocalypticism in Early Judaism: Some Points for Discussion." Pages 17–38 in Wright and Wills, eds., *Conflicted Boundaries.*

Nickelsburg, George W. E., and James C. VanderKam. *1 Enoch: A New Translation Based on the Hermeneia Commentary.* Minneapolis: Fortress, 2004.

Niditch, Susan. *Oral World and Written Word: Ancient Israelite Literature.* Louisville, Ky.: Westminster John Knox, 1996.

————. *Underdogs and Tricksters: A Prelude to Biblical Folklore.* San Francisco: Harper & Row, 1987.

Nielsen, Eduard. *Oral Tradition: A Modern Problem in Old Testament Introduction.* London: SCM, 1954.

Nielsen, Katherine. "'*Hver tíðendi eru at segja frá um ragnarøkr?*': The Debate Over Christian Influences in Norse Indo-European Tradition." *JIES* 30, no. 1–2 (2002): 61–77.

Niskanen, Paul. *The Human and the Divine in History: Herodotus and the Book of Daniel.* London: T&T Clark, 2004.

Nissinen, Martti, "The Dubious Image of Prophecy." Pages 26–41 in Floyd and Haak, eds., *Prophets, Prophecy, and Prophetic Texts.*

————. *Prophecy in Its Ancient Near Eastern Context.* Atlanta: SBL, 2000.

————, ed. *Prophets and Prophecy in the Ancient Near East.* Atlanta: SBL, 2003.

Noll, K. L. "Deuteronomistic History or Deuteronomic Debate? (A Thought Experiment)." *JSOT* 31, no. 3 (2007): 311–45.

Noth, Martin. *A History of Pentateuchal Traditions.* Translated by Berhard W. Anderson. Englewood Cliffs, N.J.: Prentic Hall, 1972.

Nyberg, Henrik S. *A Manual of Pahlavi: Texts, Alphabets, Index, Paradigms, Notes and an Introduction.* Wiesbaden: Harrassowitz, 1964.

Nykolaishen, Douglas J. E. "The Sway of the Persian Sceptre: The Narrative Characterisation of the Persian Kings in Ezra–Nehemiah." Ph.D. diss. University of Edinburgh, 2007. Online: http://hdl.handle.net/1842/1732.

Nylander, Carl. "Achaemenid Imperial Art." Pages 345–60 in *Power and Propaganda.* Edited by Mogens Trolle Larsen. Copenhagen: Akademisk Forlag, 1979.

O'Brien, Steven. "Eschatology." Pages 180–83 in Mallory and Adams, eds., *Encyclopedia of Indo-European Culture.*

————. "Indo-European Eschatology: A Model." *JIES* 4 (1976): 295–320.

O'Connor, Neil. "'Take One, It's FREE!' The Story Behind the Worldwide Church of God and The Plain Truth Magazine." Pages 163–201 in Bowie and Deacy, eds., *The Coming Deliverer.*

O'Kane, Martin. "Isaiah: A Prophet in the Footsteps of Moses." *JSOT* 21, no. 69 (1996): 29–50.

Oded, B. "The Settlements of the Israelite and Judean Exiles in Mesopotamia in the 8th–6th Centuries BCE." Pages 91–103 in *Studies in Historical Geography and Biblical Historiography*. Edited by Gershon Galil and Moshe Weinfeld. Leiden: Brill, 2000.

Odell, Margaret S. "'You Are What You Eat': Ezekiel and the Scroll." *JBL* 117, no. 2 (1998): 229–48.

Oeming, Manfred. *Contemporary Biblical Hermeneutics: An Introduction*. Translated by Joachim F. Vette. Aldershot: Ashgate, 2006.

O'Kane, Martin. "Isaiah: A Prophet in the Footsteps of Moses." *JSOT* 21, no. 69 (1996): 29–50.

O'Leary, Stephen D., and Glen S. McGhee, eds. *War in Heaven/Heaven on Earth: Theories of the Apocalyptic*. London: Equinox, 2005.

Olmstead, A. T. *History of the Persian Empire: Achaemenid Period*. Chicago: University of Chicago Press, 1948.

Olyan, Saul M. "Purity Ideology in Ezra–Nehemiah as a Tool to Reconsitute the Community." *JSJ* 35, no. 1 (2004): 1–16.

Omidsalar, Mahmoud. "Rostam's Seven Trials and the Logic of Epic Narrative in the Shahnama." *AFS* 60, no. 2 (2001): 259–93.

Ong, Walter J. "A Comment on 'Arguing about Literacy'." *College English* 50, no. 6 (1988): 700–701.

———. *Interfaces of the Word*. London: Cornell University Press, 1977.

———. "Maranatha: Death and Life in the Text of the Book." *JAAR* 45, no. 4 (1977): 419–49.

———. *Orality and Literacy*. London: Routledge, 2004. First Published 1982.

———. "Orality, Literacy and Medieval Textualization." *New Literary History* 16, no. 1 (1984): 1–12.

———. *The Presence of the Word: Some Prolegomena for Cultural and Religious History*. London: Yale University Press, 1967.

Oppenheim, A. Leo. "The Babylonian Evidence of Achaemenian Rule in Mesopotamia." *CHI* 2:529–87.

———. "The Eyes of the Lord." *JAOS* 88, no. 1 (1968): 173–80.

Orlov, Andrei A. *The Enoch-Metatron Tradition*. Tübingen: Mohr Siebeck, 2005.

Overholt, Thomas W. *Channels of Prophecy: The Social Dynamics of Prophetic Activity*. Minneapolis: Fortress, 1989.

Ovid, Publius. *Metamorphoses.* Translated by Frank J. Miller. *Ovid III: Metamorphoses I.* LCL. 3d ed. Cambridge, Mass.: Harvard University Press, 1977.

Owen, Paul. "The Relationship of Eschatology to Esoteric Wisdom in the Jewish Pseudepigraphal Apocalypses." Pages 1:123–33 in Evans, ed., *Of Scribes and Sages*.

Oxtoby, William Gurdon. "Interpretations of Iranian Dualism." Pages 59–70 in Adams, ed., *Iranian Civilization*.

Panaino, Antonio. "Calendars I: Pre-Islamic Calendars." *EncIr* 4 (1990): 658–68.

———. *Tištrya I: The Avestan Hymn to Sirius*. Rome: Istituto Italiano Per il Medio ed Estremo Oriente, 1990.

Pardee, Dennis. *Ritual and Cult at Ugarit*. Atlanta: SBL, 2002.

Parke, H. W. *Sibyls and Sibylline Prophecy in Classical Antiquity*. Edited by Brian C. McGing. London: Routledge, 1988.

Parpola, Simo. "The Originality of the Teachings of Zarathustra in the Light of Yasna 44." Pages 373–83 in *Sefer Moshe*. Edited by Chaim Cohen, Avi Hurvitz and Shalom M. Paul. Winona Lake, Ind.: Eisenbrauns, 2004.

Parry, Milman. *The Making of Homeric Verse: The Collected Papers of Milman Parry*. Edited by Adam Parry. Oxford: Clarendon, 1971.

Pausanias. *Description of Greece*. Translated by W. H. S. Jones and H. A. Ormerod. *Description of Greece, Books III–V*. LCL. Cambridge, Mass.: Harvard University Press, 1977.

Pavry, Jal Dastur Cursetji, ed. *Oriental Studies in Honour of Cursetji Erachji Pavry*. London: Oxford University Press, 1933.

Peabody, Berkley. *The Winged Word: A Study in the Technique of Ancient Greek Oral Composition as Seen Principally through Hesiod's Works and Days*. Albany, N.Y.: SUNY Press, 1975.

Pearce, Laurie E. "New Evidence for Judeans in Babylonia." Pages 399–412 in Lipschits and Oeming, eds., *Judah and the Judeans*.

Pedersen, Olof. *Archives and Libraries in the Ancient Near East 1500–300 BC*. Bethesda, Md.: CDL, 1998.

Peiser, Felix E. "Miscellen." *ZAW* 17 (1897): 350.

Peters, John P. "The Cock." *JAOS* 33 (1913): 363–96.

Petersen, David L. "Defining Prophecy and Prophetic Literature." Pages 33–44 in Nissinen, ed., *Prophecy in Its Ancient Near Eastern Context*.

———. *The Roles of Israel's Prophets*. Sheffield: JSOT, 1981.

Phillips, E. D. "The Scythian Domination in Western Asia: Its Record in History, Scripture and Archaeology." *World Archaeology* 4, no. 2 (1972): 129–38.

Photius. *The Bibliotheca*. Translated by N. G. Wilson. *Photius: The Bibliotheca*. London: Duckworth, 1994.

Pines, Shlomo. "Wrath and Creature of Wrath in Pahlavi, Jewish and New Testament Sources." Pages 1:76–82 in Shaked and Netzer, eds., *Irano-Judaica*.

Pinker, Aron. "A Goat to Go to Azazel." *Journal of Hebrew Scriptures* 7 (2007): 1–23. Online: http://www.arts.ualberta.ca/JHS/Articles/article_69.pdf.

Pirart, Eric. "Le sacrifice humain: Réflections sur la Philosophie Religieuse Indo-Iranienne Ancienne." *JA* 284, no. 1 (1996): 1–36.

Plato. *Alcibiades I*. Translated by W. R. M. Lamb. *Carmides, Alcibiades I & II, Hipparchus, The Lovers, Theages, Minos, Epinomis*. LCL. Cambridge, Mass.: Harvard University Press, 1964.

———. *Laws*. Translated by R. G. Bury. *The Laws, Books I–VI*. LCL. Cambridge, Mass.: Harvard University Press, 1967.

———. *Phaedrus*. Translated by Harold North Fowler. Plato I: Euthyphro, Apology, Crito, Phaedo, Phaedrus. LCL. Cambridge, Mass.: Harvard University Press, 1982.

———. *Seventh Letter*. Translated by R. G. Bury. Pages 463–565 in *Plato IX: Timaeus, Critias, Cleitophon, Menexenus, Epistles*. Cambridge, Mass.: Harvard University Press, 1975.

Plöger, Otto. *Theocracy and Eschatology*. Translated by S. Rudman. Oxford: Blackwell, 1968.

Plutarch. *Artaxerxes*. Translated by Bernadotte Perrin. Pages 127–204 in *Plutarch Lives XI (Aratus, Artaxerxes, Galba, Otho)*. LCL. Cambridge, Mass.: Harvard University Press, 2002.

———. *Isis and Osiris*. Translated by F. C. Babbitt. Pages 1–191 in *Moralia V*. LCL. Cambridge, Mass.: Harvard University Press, 1935.

———. *Lysander*. Translated by Bernadotte Perrin. *Plutarch's Lives IV*. LCL. London: Heinemann, 1986.

Polaski, Donald C. "Mene, Mene, Tekel, Parsin: Writing and Resistance in Daniel 5 and 6." *JBL* 123, no. 4 (2004): 649–69.

Poole, Fitz John Porter. "Metaphors and Maps: Towards Comparison in the Anthropology of Religion." *JAAR* 54, no. 3 (1986): 411–57.

Pope, Arthur Upham, and Phyllis Ackerman, eds. *A Survey of Persian Art*. 16 vols. London: Oxford University Press, 1938–1960?.

Porten, Bezalel. *Archives from Elephantine: The Life of an Ancient Jewish Military Colony*. Berkeley, Ca.: University of California Press, 1968.

———. *The Elephantine Papyri in English: Three Millennia of Cross-Cultural Continuity and Change*. Leiden: Brill, 1996.

———. "The Jews in Egypt." *CHJ* 1:372–400.

———. "Persian Names in Aramaic Documents from Ancient Egypt." Pages 165–86 in Shaked and Netzer, eds., *Irano-Judaica*, vol. 5.

Potts, D. T. "Cyrus the Great and the Kingdom of Anshan." Pages 7–28 in Curtis and Stewart, eds., *Birth of the Persian Empire*.

Powell, Barry B. *Writing and the Origins of Greek Literature*. Cambridge: Cambridge University Press, 2002.

Price, James D. "Rosh: An Ancient Land Known to Ezekiel." *Grace Theological Journal* (1985): 67–89.

Pye, Michael. *Syncretism Versus Synthesis*. Cardiff: Open University, 1993.

Quirke, Stephen G. J. "Judgment of the Dead." Pages 173–77 in *The Ancient Gods Speak: A Guide to Egyptian Religion*. Edited by Donald B. Redford. Oxford: Oxford University Press, 2002.

Rae, Murray A. *History and Hermeneutics*. London: T&T Clark, 2005.

Ramat, Anna Giacalone, and Paolo Ramat. *The Indo-European* Languages. London: Routledge, 1998.

Ravid, Liora. "The Book of Jubilees and Its Calendar—A Reexamination." *DSD* 10, no. 3 (2003): 371–94.

Razmjou, Shahrokh. "The *Lan* Ceremony and Other Ritual Ceremonies in the Achaemenid Period: The Persepolis Fortification Tablets." *Iran* 42 (2004): 103–17.

Redditt, Paul L. "Recent Research on the Book of the Twelve as One Book." *CBR* 9 (2001): 47–80.

Reed, Annette Yoshiko. *Fallen Angels and the History of Judaism and Christianity: The Reception of Enochic Literature*. New York: Cambridge University Press, 2005.

———. "Heavenly Ascent, Angelic Descent, and the Transmission of Knowledge in 1 Enoch 6–16." Pages 47–66 in *Heavenly Realms and Earthly Realities in Late Antique Religions*. Edited by Ra'anan S. Boustan and Annette Yoshiko Reed. Cambridge: Cambridge University Press, 2004.

Reeves, John C. *Jewish Lore in Manichaean Cosmology: Studies in the Book of Giants Tradition*. Cincinnati, Ohio: Hebrew Union College, 1992.

Rennie, Bryan, "Zoroastrian Bibliography." Unpublished paper, 2006.

———. "Zoroastrianism: The Iranian Roots of Christianity?" Paper presented at North American Association for the Study of Religion, Washington, D.C.

Roberts, J. J. M. "Myth Versus History: Relaying the Comparative Foundations." *CBQ* 38, no. 1 (1976): 1–13.

Root, Margaret Cool. "From the Heart: Powerful Persianisms in the Art of the Western Empire." Pages 1–29 in *Achaemenid History VI*. Edited by Heleen Sancisi-Weerdenburg and Amélie Kuhrt. Leiden: NINO, 1991.

———. *The King and Kingship in Achaemenid Art: Essays on the Creation of an Iconography of Empire*. Leiden: Brill, 1979.

———. "Reading Persepolis in Greek: Gifts of the Yauna." Pages 177–224 in Tuplin, ed., *Persian Responses*.

Ross, Sir David. *Select Fragments*. Works of Aristotle 12. Oxford: Clarendon, 1952.

Rowland, Christopher. "Apocalyptic Literature." Pages 170–89 in *It is Written: Scripture Citing Scripture*. Edited by D. A. Carson and H. G. M. Williamson. Cambridge: Cambridge University Press, 1988.

———. *The Open Heaven: A Study of Apocalyptic in Judaism and Early Christianity*. London: SPCK, 1982.

Rowland, Christopher, and John Barton, eds. *Apocalyptic in History and Tradition*. London: Sheffield Academic, 2002.

Rowley, H. H. *Darius the Mede and the Four World Empires in the Book of Daniel*. Eugene, Ore.: Wipf & Stock, 2006.

Rudolph, Kurt. "Mitra, Mithra, Mithras." *Orientalistische Literaturzeitung* 74, no. 4 (1979): 309–20.

———. "Zarathuštra—Priester und Prophet: Neue Aspekte der Zarathuštra- bzw. Gatha-Forschung." *Numen* 8, no. 1 (1961): 81–116.

Rufus, Quintus Cutius. *History of Alexander*. Translated by John C. Rolfe. *Quintus Curtius I, Books I–V*. LCL. London: Heinemann, 1946.

———. *History of Alexander*. *Quintus Curtius II, Books VI–X*. LCL. London: Heinemann, 1946.

Russell, D. S. *The Method and Message of Jewish Apocalyptic: 200 B.C.–A.D. 100*. London: SCM, 1964.

Russell, James R. "Burial III: In Zoroastrianism." *EncIr* 4 (1990): 561–63.

———. "Early Armenian Civilization." Pages 23–40 in *The Armenians*. Edited by Edmund Herzig and Marina Kurkchiyan. London: Routledge, 2005.

———. "Ezekiel and Iran." Pages 1–15 in Shaked and Netzer, eds., *Irano-Judaica*, vol. 5.

———. "God is Good: On Tobit and Iran." *Iran and the Caucasus* 5 (2001): 1–6.

———. Review of Edwin M. Yamauchi, *Persia and the Bible*. *JQR* 83, no. 1/2 (1992): 256–61.

———. "Zoroastrian Elements in the Book of Esther." Pages 2:33–40 in Shaked and Netzer, eds., *Irano-Judaica*.

———. "Zoroastrian Notes." *Iran and the Caucasus* 6, no. 1/2 (2002): 1–10.

Sacchi, Paolo. *Jewish Apocalyptic and Its History*. Sheffield: Sheffield Academic, 1990.

Sæbø, M. "יום IV: Theological Usage." Pages 28–31 in *Theological Dictionary of the Old Testament*, vol. 4. Translated by David E. Green. Edited by G. Johannes Bottereck and Helmer Ringgren. Grand Rapids: Eerdmans, 1990.

Sancisi-Weerdenburg, Heleen. "Achaemenid History: From Hellenocentrism to Irano-centrism." Pages 253–59 in Gnoli and Panaino, eds., *Proceedings of the First European Conference of Iranian Studies*.

———. "Bāji." Pages 23–34 in *Studies in Persian History*. Edited by Maria Brosius and Amélie Kuhrt. Leiden: NINO, 1998.

———. "The Death of Cyrus: Xenophon's Cyropaedia as a Source for Iranian History." Pages 2:459–72 in Bailey et al., eds., *Papers in Honour of Professor Mary Boyce*.

———. "The Fifth Oriental Monarchy and Hellenocentrism." Pages 117–31 in Sancisi-Weerdenburg and Kuhrt, eds, *Achaemenid History II*.

———. "Nowruz in Persepolis." Pages 173–201 in *Achaemenid History VII*. Edited by Heleen Sancisi-Weerdenburg and Jan W. Drijvers. Leiden: NINO, 1991.

Sancisi-Weerdenburg, Heleen, and Amélie Kuhrt, eds. *Achaemenid History II*. Leiden: NINO, 1987.

———. *Achaemenid History III*. Leiden: NINO, 1988.

———. *Achaemenid History IV*. Leiden: NINO, 1990.

Sanders, E. P. "The Genre of Palestinian Jewish Apocalypses." Pages 447–59 in Hellholm, ed., *Apocalypticism in the Mediterranean World*.

Sanders, James A. "Hermeneutics in True and False Prophecy." Pages 21–41 in *Canon and Authority*. Edited by B. W. Coats and B. O. Long. Philadelphia: Fortress, 1977.

Sandmel, Samuel. "Parallelomania." *JBL* 81, no. 1 (1962): 1–13.

Sandy, D. Brent. *Plowshares and Pruning Hooks*. Downers Grove, Ill.: InterVarsity, 2002.

Sandy, D. Brent, and Daniel M. O'Hare. *Prophecy and Apocalyptic: An Annotated Bibliography*. Grand Rapids, Mich.: Baker, 2007.

Sarshar, Houman, ed. *Esther's Children: A Portrait of Iranian Jews*. Philadelphia: Jewish Publication Society, 2002.

Schams, Christine. *Jewish Scribes in the Second-Temple Period*. Sheffield: Sheffield Academic, 1998.

Schaper, Joachim. "The Death of the Prophet: The Transition from the Spoken to the Written Word of God in the Book of Ezekiel." Pages 63–79 in Floyd and Haak, eds., *Prophets, Prophecy, and Prophetic Texts*.

Scheftelowitz, I. "Die Mithra-Religion der Indoskythen und ihre Beziehung zum Saura- und Mithras-Kult." *Acta Orientalia* 11 (1933): 293–333.

Scheftelowitz, J. *Die altpersiche Religion und das Judentum: Unterschiede, Übereinstim-mungen, und gegenseitige Beeinflussungen*. Giessen: Töpelmann, 1920.

Schmidt, Erich F. *Persepolis I: Structures, Reliefs, Inscriptions*. Chicago: University of Chicago Press, 1953.

———. *Persepolis II: Contents of the Treasury and Other Discoveries*. Chicago: University of Chicago Press, 1957.

———. *Persepolis III: The Royal Tombs and Other Monuments*. Chicago: University of Chicago Press, 1970.

Schmidt, Lawrence K. *Understanding Hermeneutics*. Stocksfield: Acumen, 2006.

Schmitt, Rüdiger. "Artaxerxes." *EncIr* 2, no. 6 (1987): 654–55.

———. "Artaxerxes II." *EncIr* 2, no. 6 (1987): 656–58.

———. "Artaxerxes III." *EncIr* 2, no. 6 (1987): 658–59.

———. "Artaxerxes, Ardašīr und Verwandte." *Incontri Linguistici* 5 (1979): 61–72.

———. *The Bisitun Inscription of Darius the Great: Old Persian Text*. London: School of Oriental and African Studies, 1991.

———. "Darius i. The Name." *EncIr* 7 (1996): 40.

———. "Die theophoren Eigennamen mit altiranische Miθra-." Pages 395–456 in Duchesne-Guillemin, ed., *Étude Mithriaques*.

———. "Old Persian." Pages 76–100 in Woodard, ed., *The Ancient Languages of Asia and the Americas*.

———. "Thronnamen bei den achaimeniden." *Beiträge zur Namenforschung* 12, no. 4 (1977): 422–25.

Schniedewind, William M. *How the Bible Became a Book: The Textualization of Ancient Israel*. Cambridge: Cambridge University Press, 2004.

Scholes, Robert, Robert Kellogg, and James Phelan. *The Nature of Narrative*. Rev. and exp. ed. New York: Oxford University Press, 2006.

Schousboe, Karin, and Mogens Trolle Larsen, eds. *Literacy and Society*. Copenhagen: Akademisk Forlag, 1989.

Schultz, Richard L. *The Search for Quotation: Verbal Parallels in the Prophets*. Sheffield: Sheffield Academic, 1999.

Schwartz, Martin. "The Old Eastern Iranian World View According to the Avesta." *CHI* 2:640–63.

———. "The Religion of Achaemenian Iran." *CHI* 2:664–97.

Scott, James M., ed. *Exile: Old Testament, Jewish, and Christian Conceptions*. New York: Brill, 1997.

Scott, R. B. Y. *Proverbs, Ecclesiastes: Introduction, Translation, and Notes*. New York: Doubleday, 1965.

Scribner, Sylvia, and Michael Cole. *The Psychology of Literacy*. Cambridge, Mass.: Harvard University Press, 1981.

Seager, A. "The Synagogue at Sardis." Pages 178–84 in *Ancient Synagogues Revealed*. Edited by Lee I. Levine. Jerusalem: Israel Exploration Society, 1981.

Segal, Eliezer. "Justice, Mercy and a Bird's Nest." *JJS* 42, no. 2 (1991): 176–95.

Segal, J. B. "Intercalation and the Hebrew Calendar." *VT* 7, no. 3 (1957): 250–307.

Seneca. *Ad Lucilium Epistulae Morales*, vol. 1. Translated by Richard M. Gummere. LCL. London: Heinemann, 1961.

Setzer, Claudia. *Resurrection of the Body in Early Judaism and Early Christianity: Doctrine, Community, and Self-Definition*. Boston: Brill, 2004.

Shahbazi, A. Shapur. "An Achaemenid Symbol I: A Farewell to Fravahr and Ahura-mazda." *Archäologische Mitteilungen aus Iran* 7 (1974): 135–44.

———. "An Achaemenid Symbol: II Farnah (God Given) Fortune Symbolised." *Archäologische Mitteilungen aus Iran* 13 (1980): 119–47.

———. "Astōdān." *EncIr* 2, no. 8 (1987): 851–53.

———. "Darius' 'Haft Kišvar'." *Archäologische Mitteilungen aus Iran Supp 10* (1985): 239–46.

———. "Haft Kešvar." *EncIr* 11 (2003): 519–22.

———. "Hōšang." *EncIr* 12 (2004): 491–92.

———. "Iranian notes 1–6." Pages 2:497–510 in Bailey et al., eds., *Papers in Honour of Professor Mary Boyce*.

———. "The Irano-Lycian Monuments: The Principle Antiquities of Xanthos and Its Region as Evidence for Iranian Aspects of Achaemenid Lycia." Ph.D. diss., London University, 1973.

———. *Old Persian Inscriptions of the Persepolis Platform*. London: Lund Humphries, 1985.

———. "The Traditional Date of Zoroaster Explained." *BSOAS* 40, no. 1 (1977): 25–35.

———. "Zāl." *EncIr* (2004): n.p. Online: http://www.iranica.com/newsite/.

Shaked, Shaul. "Between Iranian and Aramaic: Iranian Words Concerning Food in Jewish Babylonian Aramaic, with Some Notes on the Aramaic Heterograms in Iranian." Pages 120–37 in Shaked and Netzer, eds., *Irano-Judaica*, vol. 5.

————. *Dualism in Transformation: Varieties of Religion in Sasanian Iran*. London: School of Oriental and African Studies, 1994.

————. "Eschatology I: In Zoroastrianism and Zoroastrian Influence." *EncIr* 8 (1998): 565–69.

————. *From Zoroastrian Iran to Islam: Collected Studies*. Aldershot: Variorium, 1995.

————. "Iranian Influence on Judaism: First Century B.C.E to Second Century C.E." CHJ 1:308–25.

————. "Mihr the Judge." Section IV in *From Zoroastrian Iran to Islam*. Aldershot: Variorium, 1995.

————. "The Myth of Zurvan: Cosmogony and Eschatology." Pages 219–36 in Gruenwald, Shaked and Stroumsa, eds., *Messiah and Christos*.

————. "The Notions *mēnog* and *gētīg* in the Pahlavi Texts and Their Relation to Eschatology." Section II in *From Zoroastrian Iran to Islam*. Aldershot: Variorium, 1995.

————. "Qumran and Iran: Further Considerations." *IOS* 2 (1972): 433–46.

————. "Two Judaeo-Iranian Contributions." Pages 1:292–322 in Shaked and Netzer, eds., *Irano-Judaica*.

Shaked, Shaul, and Amnon Netzer, eds. *Irano-Judaica: Studies Relating to Jewish Contacts with Persian Culture Throughout the Ages*. 3 vols. Jerusalem: Ben-Zvi Institute, 1982, 1990, 1994.

————, eds. *Irano-Judaica*, vol. 4. Jerusalem: Ben Zvi Institute, 1999.

————, eds. *Irano-Judaica*, vol. 5. Jerusalem: Ben Zvi Institute, 2003.

Shellenberg, Angeline. "Development of the Divine Warrior Motif in Apocalyptic." M.A. diss., Providence, R.I.: Providence College and Seminary, 1999.

Sicculus, Diodorus. *Library of History*. Translated by C. H. Oldfather. *Diodorus of Sicily IV, Books IX–XII*. LCL. London: Heinemann, 1946.

————. *Library of History*. Translated by Russel M. Geer. *Diodorus of Sicily IX*. LCL. London: Heinemann, 1947.

————. *Library of History*. Translated by C. H. Oldfather. *Diodorus of Sicily VI*. LCL. London: Heinemann, 1954.

————. *Library of History*. Translated by C. H. Oldfather. *Diodorus of Sicily I*. LCL. Cambridge, Mass.: Harvard University Press, 1989.

Silberman, Lou H., ed. *Orality, Aurality and Biblical Narrative: Semeia* 39 (1987).

Silverman, David P. "Divinity and Dieties in Ancient Egypt." Pages 7–87 in *Religion in Ancient Egypt*. Edited by Byron E. Shafer. London: Routledge, 1991.

Silverman, Jason M., ed. *A Land Like Your Own: Traditions of Israel and Their Reception*. Eugene, Ore.: Pickwick, 2010.

————. "Pseudepigraphy, Anonymity, and Auteur Theory." *Religion and the Arts* 15 (2011): 520–55.

Sims-Williams, N. "Baga II: In Old and Middle Iranian." *EncIr* 3 (1989): 404–5.

Skjærvø, Prods Oktor. "The Achaemenids and the Avesta." Pages 52–84 in Curtis and Stewart, eds., *Birth of the Persian Empire*.

————. "Ahura Mazdā and Ārmaiti, Heaven and Earth, in the Old Avesta." *JAOS* 122, no. 2 (2002): 399–410.

————. "The Antiquity of Old Avestan." *Nāme-ye Irān Bāstān* 3 (2003–4): 15–41.

————. "The Avesta as Source for the Early History of the Iranians." Pages 155–76 in *The Indo-Aryans of Ancient South Asia*. Edited by G. Erdosy. Berlin: de Gruyter, 1995.

———. "Avestan Quotations in Old Persian? Literary Sources of the Old Persian Inscriptions." Pages 1–64 in Shaked and Netzer, eds., *Irano-Judaica*, vol. 5.

———. "Aždahā I: In Old and Middle Iranian." *EncIr* 3 (1989): 191–99.

———. "The Importance of Orality for the Study of Old Iranian Literature and Myth." *Nāme-ye Irān Bāstān* 5, no. 1–2 (2005–2006): 9–31.

———. Review of Edwin M. Yamauchi, *Persia and the Bible*. *JAOS* 114, no. 3 (1994): 499–504.

———. "Royalty in Early Iranian Literature." Pages 99–108 in *Proceedings of the Third European Conference of Iranian Studies, Cambridge, 11–15 September 1995*, vol. 1. Edited by Nicholas Sims-Williams. Wiesbaden: Reichert, 1998.

———. "The State of Old Avestan Scholarship." *JAOS* 117, no. 1 (1997): 103–14.

Smith, Daniel L. *The Religion of the Landless*. Bloomington, Ind.: Meyer-Stone, 1989.

Smith, John M. P. "The Day of Yahweh." *AJT* 5, no. 3 (1901): 505–33.

Smith, Jonathan Z. *Imagining Religion: From Babylon to Jonestown*. Chicago: University of Chicago Press, 1982.

———. "Native Cults in the Hellenistic Period." *HR* 11, no. 2 (1971): 236–49.

———. "A Pearl of Great Price and a Cargo of Yams: A Study in Situational Incongruity." *HR* 16, no. 1 (1976): 1–19.

———. "Wisdom and Apocalyptic." Pages 131–56 in *Religious Syncretism in Antiquity*. Edited by Berger A. Pearson. Missoula, Mont.: Scholars, 1975.

Smith, Morton. "II Isaiah and the Persians." *JAOS* 83 (1963): 415–21.

———. "Bible II: Persian Elements in the Bible." *EncIr* 4 (1990): 200–203.

———. *Palestinian Parties and Politics that Shaped the Old Testament*. 2d ed. London: SCM, 1987.

Smith-Christopher, Daniel L., "Can We Speak of the Socio-Psychology of Exile in the Bible?" Paper presented at annual meeting of the Society of Biblical Literature, Boston, 24 November 2008.

Sokoloff, Michael. *A Dictionary of Jewish Babylonian Aramaic of the Talmudic and Geonic Periods*. Dictionaries of Talmud, Midrash and Targum III. Ramat-Gan, Israel: Bar Ilan University Press, 2002.

Speiser, E. A. "The Rivers of Paradise." Pages 175–82 in *I Studied Inscriptions From Before the Flood*. Edited by Richard S. Hess and David T. Tsumura. Winona Lake, Ind.: Eisenbrauns, 1994.

Spronk, Klaas. *Beatific Afterlife in Ancient Israel and in the Ancient Near East*. Neukirchen–Vluyn: Neukirchener Verlag, 1986.

Stausberg, Michael. "Persepolis, Zoroastrianopolis, Metropolis: Städte und Tempel in der zoroastrischen Religionsgeschichte. Eine Skizze." Pages 45–66 in Hengel, Mittmann and Schwemer, eds., *La Cité de Dieu/Die Stadt Gottes*.

Stave, E. *Über den Einfluss des Parsismus auf das Judentum*. Haarlem, 1989.

Steiner, Richard C. "The *mbqr* at Qumran, the *episkopos* in the Athenian Empire, and the Meaning of *lbqr'* in Ezra 7:14: On the Relation of Ezra's Mission to the Persian Legal Project." *JBL* 120, no. 4 (2001): 623–46.

Stern, Ephraim. "Achaemenian Tombs from Shechem." *Levant* 12 (1980): 90–111.

———. "Between Persia and Greece: Trade, Administration and Warfare in the Persian and Hellenistic Periods." Pages 432–45 in *The Archaeology of Society in the Holy Land*. Edited by Thomas E. Levy. London: Leicester University Press, 1995.

———. *Material Culture of the Land of the Bible in the Persian Period 538–332 B.C.* Translated by Essa Cindorf. Warminster: Aris & Philips, 1982.

————. "New Evidence on the Administrative Division of Palestine in the Persian Period." Pages 221–26 in Sancisi-Weerdenburg and Kuhrt, eds., *Achaemenid History IV*.

Stevens-Arroyo, Anthony M. "Syncretic Sociology: Towards a Cross-Disciplinary Study of Religion." *Sociology of Religion* 59, no. 3 (1998): 217–36.

Steward, Julian H. "Levels of Sociocultural Integration: An Operational Concept." *Journal of Anthropological Research* 42, no. 3 (1986): 337–53.

Stolper, Matthew W. "The Neo-Babylonian Text from the Persepolis Fortification." *JNES* 43, no. 4 (1984): 299–310.

Stolper, Matthew W., and Jan Tavernier. "An Old Persian Administrative Tablet from the Persepolis Fortification." *Achemenet: Arta* 5.1 (2007): 1–28. Online: http://www.achemenet.com/document/2007.2001–Stolper–Tavernier.pdf.

Stone, Michael E. *Fourth Ezra: A Commentary*. Minneapolis: Fortress, 1990.

————. "Lists of Revealed Things in the Apocalyptic Literature." Pages 414–52 in Cross, Lemke and Miller, eds., *Magnalia Dei*.

————. "On Reading an Apocalypse." Pages 65–78 in Collins and Charlesworth, eds., *Mysteries and Revelations*.

————. "A Reconsideration of Apocalyptic Visions." *HTR* 96, no. 2 (2003): 167–80.

Stott, Katherine M. *Why Did They Write This Way? Reflections on References to Written Documents in the Hebrew Bible and Ancient Literature*. New York: T&T Clark, 2008.

Strabo. *Geography*. Translated by Horace Leonard Jones. *The Geography of Strabo V*. LCL. London: Heinemann, 1928.

————. *Geography*. Translated by Horace Leonard Jones. *The Geography of Strabo VI*. LCL. London: Heinemann, 1929.

Strawn, Brent A. "'A World Under Control': Isaiah 60 and the Apadana Reliefs from Persepolis." Pages 85–116 in Berquist, ed., *Approaching Yehud*.

Ström, Åke V. "Indogermanisches in der Völuspá." *Numen* 14, no. 3 (1967): 167–208.

Stronach, David. "Anshan and Parsa: Early Achaemenid History, Art and Architecture on the Iranian Plateau." Pages 35–53 in *Mesopotamia and Iran in the Persian Period*. Edited by John E. Curtis. London: British Museum, 1997.

————. "Čahārbāg." *EncIr* 4 (1990): 624–25.

————. "Icons of Dominion: Review Scenes at Til Barip and Persepolis." *Iranica Antiqua* 37 (2002): 373–402.

————. "On the Evolution of the Early Iranian Fire Temple." Pages 2:605–27 in Bailey et al., eds., *Papers in Honour of Professor Mary Boyce*.

————. *Pasargadae: A Report on the Excavations*. Oxford: Clarendon, 1978.

————. "Tepe Nūsh-i Jān: The Median Settlement." *CHI* 2:832–36.

Strouve, V. V. "Religion of the Achaemenides and Zoroastrianism." *Cahiers d'Historie Mondiale* 5 (1959–60): 529–45.

Stuckenbruck, Loren T. *1 Enoch 91–108*. Berlin: de Gruyter, 2007.

————. *The Book of Giants from Qumran*. Tübingen: Mohr Siebeck, 1997.

————. "Genesis 6:1–4 as the Basis for Divergent Readings During the Second Temple Period." Pages 99–106 in Boccaccini, ed., *Henoch*.

————. "The Origin of Evil in Jewish Apocalyptic Tradition: The Interpretation of Gen 6:1–4 in the Second and Third Centuries B.C.E." Pages 87–118 in Auffarth and Stuckenbruck, eds., *The Fall of the Angels*.

Sulimirski, T., and T. Taylor. "The Scythians." Pages 547–90 in *Cambridge Ancient History*, vol. 3.2. Edited by John Boardman et al. 2d ed. Cambridge: Cambridge University Press, 1991.

Summers, Geoffrey D. "Archaeological Evidence for the Achaemenid Period in Eastern Turkey." *Anatolian Studies* 43 (1993): 85–108.

———. "Aspects of Material Culture at the Iron Age Capital on the Kerkenes Dağ in Central Anatolia." *Ancient Near Eastern Studies* 43 (2006): 164–202.

———. "The Median Empire Reconsidered: A View from Kerkenes Dağ." *Anatolian Studies* 50 (2000): 55–73.

Sumner, W. M. "Achaemenid Settlement in the Persepolis Plain." *AJA* 90, no. 1 (1986): 3–31.

Sundermann, Werner. "Bahman Yašt." *EncIr* 3 (1989): 492–93.

———. "Zoroastrian Motifs in non-Zoroastrian Traditions." *JRAS* 18, no. 2 (2008): 155–65.

Swadesh, Morris. "Diffusional Cumulation and Archaic Residue as Historical Explanations." *Southwestern Journal of Anthropology* 7, no. 1 (1951): 1–21.

Swain, J. W. "The Theory of the Four Monarchies." *Classical Philology* 35, no. 1 (1940): 1–21.

Swearingen, C. Jan. "Oral Hermeneutics During the Transition to Literacy: The Contemporary Debate." *Cultural Anthropology* 1, no. 2 (1986): 138–56.

Tadmor, Miryam. "Fragments from an Achaemenid Throne from Samaria." *IEJ* 24, no. 1 (1974): 37–43.

Talmon, Shemaryahu. "The 'Comparative Method' in Biblical Interpretation: Principles and Problems." Pages 320–56 in *Congress Volume, Göttingen 1977*. Edited P. A. H. de Boer. Leiden: Brill, 1978.

Talmon, Yonina. "Millenarian Movements." Pages 5:13–45 in Hamilton, ed., *The Sociology of Religion*.

———. "Millenarism." Pages 349–62 in *International Encyclopaedia of the Social Sciences*, vol. 10. New York: Macmillan, 1968.

Tannen, Deborah. "The Commingling of Orality and Literacy in Giving a Paper at a Scholarly Conference." *American Speech* 63, no. 1 (1988): 34–43.

Tanzer, Sarah J. "Response to George Nickelsburg, 'Wisdom and Apocalypticism in Early Judaism'." Pages 39–50 in Wright and Wills, eds., *Conflicted Boundaries*.

Taylor, Lily R. "The 'Proskynesis' and the Hellenistic Ruler Cult." *JHS* 47, no. 1 (1927): 53–62.

Teixidor, Javier. Review of Joseph A. Fitzmyer, *The Genesis Apocryphon of Qumran Cave I: A Commentary*. *JAOS* 87, no. 4 (1967): 633–36.

Teske, Raymond H. C. Jr., and Bardin H. Nelson. "Acculturation and Assimilation: A Clarification." *American Ethnologist* 1, no. 2 (1974): 351–67.

Thieme, Paul. "The 'Aryan' Gods of the Mitanni Treaties." *JAOS* 80 (1960): 301–17.

———. "The Concept of Mitra in Aryan Belief." Pages 21–39 in Hinnells, ed., *Mithraic Studies*.

———. "Mithra in the Avesta." Pages 501–11 in Duchesne-Guillemin, ed., *Étude Mithriaques*.

Thiselton, Anthony C. *New Horizons in Hermeneutics*. London: HarperCollins, 1992.

Thompson, Stith. *Motif-Index of Folk-Literature*. Rev. ed. 6 vols. Bloomington, Ind.: Indiana University Press, 1955–58.

Thucydides. *History of the Peloponnesian War.* Translated by C. Forster Smith. *Thucydides I.* LCL. Cambridge, Mass.: Harvard University Press, 1980.

Tierney, Kathleen J., and Joan Neff Gurney. "Relative Deprivation and Social Movements: A Critical Look at Twenty Years of Theory and Research." *Sociological Quarterly* 23, no. 1 (1982): 33–47.

Tigchelaar, Eibert J. C. *The Prophets of Old and the Day of the End: Zechariah, the Book of Watchers, and Apocalyptic.* Leiden: Brill, 1996.

———. "Some Remarks on the Book of the Watchers, the Priests, Enoch and Genesis, and 4Q208." Pages 143–45 in Boccaccini, ed., *Henoch.*

Tigchelaar, E. J. C., and F. Garcia Martinez. "4QAstronomical Enoch[a–b] ar." Pages 95–171 in *Qumran Cave 4: XXVI Cryptic Texts and Miscellanea Part I.* Edited by Emmanuel Tov. DJD 36. Oxford: Clarendon, 2000.

Tiller, Patrick A. *A Commentary on the Animal Apocalypse of 1 Enoch.* Atlanta: Scholars, 1993.

———. "Review: *1 Enoch 1.*" *JBL* 122, no. 3 (2003): 574–77.

Tillich, Paul. *A History of Christian Thought.* New York: Simon & Schuster, 1968.

Timus, Mihaela. "Stig Wikander: Les 'Haskell Lectures' University of Chicago, 1967." *Archaeus* 8, no. 1–4 (2004): 265–322.

Torrey, Charles C. "Armageddon." *HTR* 31, no. 3 (1938): 237–48.

Toy, C. H. *The Book of the Prophet Ezekiel.* Leipzig: Hinrichs'sche, 1899.

Tuell, Stephen Shawn. *The Law of the Temple in Ezekiel 40–48.* Atlanta: Scholars, 1992.

Tuplin, Christopher. *Achaemenid Studies.* Stuttgart: Franz Steiner, 1996.

———. "The Administration of the Achaemenid Empire." Pages 109–58 in *Coinage and Administration in the Athenian and Persian Empires: The Ninth Oxford Symposium on Coinage and Monetary History [held St. Hilda's College in April 1986].* Edited by Ian Carradice. Oxford: BAR, 1987.

———. "Darius' Accession in (the) Media." Pages 217–44 in Bienkowski, Mee and Slater, eds., *Writing and Ancient Near Eastern Society.*

———. "Persian Garrisons in Xenophon and Other Sources." Pages 67–70 in Kuhrt and Sancisi-Weerdenburg, eds., *Achaemenid History III.*

———, ed. *Persian Responses: Political and Cultural Interaction with(in) the Achaemenid Empire.* Swansea: Classical Press of Wales, 2007.

Tyler, Stephen A. "On Being Out of Words." *Cultural Anthropology* 1, no. 2 (1986): 131–37.

Uehlinger, C. "'Powerful Persianisms' in Glyptic Iconography of Persian Period Palestine." Pages 134–82 in Becking and Korpel, eds., *The Crisis of Israelite Religion.*

Vahman, Fereydun. *'Arda Wiraz Nama': The Iranian 'Divina Commedia'.* London: Curzon, 1986.

Van der Merwe, Jeanne. "Investigating Apparent Commonalities Between the Apocalyptic Traditions from Iran and Second-Temple Judaism." M.A. diss., University of Stellenbosch, 2008.

Van der Toorn, Karel. *Scribal Culture and the Making of the Hebrew Bible.* Cambridge, Mass.: Harvard University Press, 2007.

Vanderhooft, David. "Cyrus II, Liberator or Conqueror? Ancient Historiography Concerning Cyrus in Babylon." Pages 351–72 in Lipschits and Oeming, eds., *Judah and the Judeans.*

VanderKam, James C. "The Book of Parables Within the Enoch Tradition." Pages 81–99 in Boccaccini, ed., *Enoch and the Messiah Son of Man.*

————. "Biblical Interpretation in *1 Enoch* and *Jubilees*." Pages 96–125 in *The Pseude-pigrapha and Early Biblical Interpretation*. Edited by James H. Charlesworth and Craig A. Evans. Sheffield: JSOT, 1993.

————. *Enoch and the Growth of an Apocalyptic Tradition*. Washington, D.C.: Catholic Biblical Association, 1984.

————. "Putting Them in Their Place: Geography as an Evaluative Tool." Pages 476–99 in *From Revelation to Canon*.

————, ed. *Qumran Cave 4 XVII Parabiblical Texts 3*. DJD 22. Oxford: Clarendon, 1996.

————. "Recent Studies in 'Apocalyptic'." *Word and World: Theology for Christian Ministry* 4 (1984): 70–77.

————. *From Revelation to Canon: Studies in the Hebrew Bible and Second Temple Literature*. Leiden: Brill, 2000.

————. "Some Major Issues in the Contemporary Study of 1 Enoch." Pages 354–65 in *From Revelation to Canon*.

Vidal, Senén. "Resurrection in the Israelite Tradition." Pages 47–55 in *The Resurrection of the Dead*. Edited by Andrés T. Queiruga, Luiz C. Susin and Jon Sobrino. Concilium 2006/5. London: SCM, 2006.

Virgil. *Eclogues*. Translated by H. Rushton Fairclough. Pages 23–96 in *Virgil I: Eclogues, Georgics, Aeneid I–VI*. Edited by G. P. Goold. LCL. Cambridge, Mass.: Harvard University Press, 1999.

Vogelsang, W. J. *The Rise and Organization of the Achaemenid Empire: The Eastern Iranian Evidence*. Leiden: Brill, 1992.

Voigtlander, Elizabeth N. von. *The Bisitun Inscription of Darius the Great, Babylonian Version*. London: Lund Humphries, 1978.

Von Rad, Gerhard. *Old Testament Theology*. Translated by D. M. G. Stalker. Study ed. 2 vols. London: SCM, 1975.

————. "The Origin of the Concept of the Day of Yahweh." *JSS* 4, no. 2 (1959): 97–108.

————. *Wisdom in Israel*. Translated by J. D. Martin. Study ed. London: SCM, 1975.

Vroom, Hendrik M. "Syncretism and Dialogue: A Philosophical Analysis." Pages 103–12 in Leopold and Jensen, eds., *Syncretism in Religion*.

Wacholder, Ben Z. "Ezekiel and Ezekielianism as Progenitors of Essenianism." Pages 186–96 in *The Dead Sea Scrolls: Forty Years of Research*. Edited by Devorah Dimant and Uriel Rappaport. Leiden: Brill, 1992.

Wallace, Anthony F. C. "Revitalization Movements." *American Anthropologist* NS 58, no. 2 (1956): 264–81.

Wapnish, Paula, and Brian Hesse. "Pampered Pooches or Plain Pariahs? The Ashkelon Dog Burials." *BA* 56, no. 2 (1993): 55–80.

Warren, William F. "Babylonian and Pre-Babylonian Cosmology." *JAOS* 22 (1901): 138–44.

Wasson, R. Gordon. "The Soma of the Rig Veda: What Was It?" *JAOS* 91, no. 2 (1971): 169–87.

Waters, Matt. "Cyrus and the Achaemenids." *Iran* 42 (2004): 91–102.

Watkins, Calvert. *How to Kill a Dragon: Aspects of Indo-European Poetics*. New York: Oxford University Press, 1995.

Watson, Rebecca S. *Chaos Uncreated: A Reassessment of the Theme of "Chaos" in the Hebrew Bible*. Berlin: de Gruyter, 2005.

Watson, Wilfred G. E. *Classical Hebrew Poetry: A Guide to Its Techniques*. Sheffield: JSOT, 1984.

Watts, James W., ed. *Persia and Torah: The Theory of Imperial Authorization of the Pentateuch*. Atlanta: SBL, 2001.

Webb, Robert L. "'Apocalyptic': Observations on a Slippery Term." *JNES* 49, no. 2 (1990): 115–26.

Weber, Max. *The Sociology of Religion*. Translated by Ephraim Fischoff. Boston: Beacon, 1993.

Weiskopf, Michael. *The So-called "Great Satraps' Revolt", 366–360 B.C.: Concerning Local Instability in the Achaemenid Far West*. Stuttgart: Steiner, 1989.

Weiss, Meir. "The Origin of the 'Day of the Lord'—Reconsidered." *HUCA* 37 (1966): 29–60.

Welch, Kevin W. "An Interpersonal Influence Model of Traditional Religious Commitment." *Sociological Quarterly* 22, no. 1 (1981): 81–92.

Wellhausen, Julius. *Grundrisse zum alten Testament*. Edited by Rudolf Smend. Munich: Kaiser, 1965.

Wernberg-Møller, P. "A Reconsideration of the Two Spirits in the Rule of the Community (IQSerek III,13–IV,26)." *Revue de Qumran* 3 (1961): 413–41.

West, M. L. *Early Greek Philosophy and the Orient*. Oxford: Clarendon, 1971.

———. *The East Face of Helicon: West Asiatic Elements in Greek Poetry and Myth*. Oxford: Clarendon, 1997.

"Why Wars Happen." *The Economist*, 16 December 2008. Online: http://www. economist.com/daily/chartgallery/displayStory.cfm?story_id=12758508&source= features_box4.

Whybray, R. N. *The Book of Proverbs*. Cambridge: Cambridge University Press, 1972.

———. *The Making of the Pentateuch: A Methodological Study*. Sheffield: JSOT, 1987.

Widengren, Geo. "Iran and Israel in Parthian Times with Special Regard to the Ethiopic Book of Enoch." *Temenos* 2 (1966): 139–77.

———. *Iranisch-semitische Kulturbegegnung in parthischer Zeit*. Cologne: Westdeutscher Verlag, 1960.

———. "Leitende Ideen und Quellen des Iranischen Apokalyptic." Pages 77–162 in Hellholm, ed., *Apocalypticism in the Mediterranean World*.

———. "Stand und Aufgaben der iranischen Religionsgeschichte." *Numen* 1, no. 1–2 (1954–55): 16–83.

———. "Stand und Aufgaben der iranischen Religionsgeschichte II: Geschichte der iranischen Religionen und ihre Nachwirkung." *Numen* 2, no. 1–2 (1955): 47–134.

Wiesehöfer, Josef. "The Medes and the Idea of the Succession of Empires in Antiquity." Pages 391–96 in *Continuity of Empire (?): Assyria, Media, Persia*. Edited by Giovanni B. Lanfranchi, Michael Roaf and Robert Rollinger. Padova: S.a.r.g.o.n. Editrice e Libreria, 2003.

Wikander, Stig. *Vayu: Texte und Untersuchungen zur Indo-Iranischen Religionsgeschichte*, vol. 1. Uppsala: Lundequistska Bokhandeln, 1941.

Willey, Patricia Tull. *Remember the Former Things: The Recollection of Previous Texts in Isaiah 40–55*. Atlanta: SBL, 1997.

Williams, A. V. "Zoroastrian and Judaic Purity Laws. Reflections on the Viability of a Sociological Interpretation." Pages 3:72–89 in Shaked and Netzer, eds., *Irano-Judaica*.

Williamson, H. G. M. *Studies in Persian Period History and Historiography*. Tübingen: Mohr Siebeck, 2004.

Wilson, Robert R. *Prophecy and Society in Ancient Israel*. Philadelphia: Fortress, 1980.

Winfuhr, Gerot L. "Haoma/Soma: The Plant." Pages 2:699–726 in Bailey et al., eds., *Papers in Honour of Professor Mary Boyce*.

Winn Leith, Mary Joan. *Wadi Daliyeh I: The Wadi Daliyeh Seal Impressions*. DJD 24. Oxford: Clarendon, 1997.

Winston, David. "The Iranian Component in the Bible, Apocrypha, and Qumran: A Review of the Evidence." *HR* 5 (1966): 183–216.

Wold, Benjamin G. *Women, Men, and Angels: The Qumran Wisdom Document Musar leMevin and Its Allusions to Genesis Creation Traditions*. Tübingen: Mohr Siebeck, 2005.

Wolff, F. *Avesta: Die heiligen Bücher der Parsen, Übersetz auf der Grundlage von Chr. Bartholomae's Altiranishem Wörterbuch*. Berlin: de Gruyter, 1960.

Wood, Irving P. "Borrowing Between Religions." *JBL* 46, no. 1/2 (1927): 98–105.

Woodard, Roger D., ed. *The Ancient Languages of Asia and the Americas*. Cambridge: Cambridge University Press, 2008.

Woodbridge, Linda. "Add Context and Stir, or, the Sadness of Grendel: Thoughts on Early Modern Orality and Literacy." *Yearbook of English Studies* 25 (1995): 22–40.

Worsley, Peter. *The Trumpet Shall Sound: A Study of "Cargo" Cults in Melanesia*. 2d ed. London: Paladin, 1970.

Wright, Archie T. *The Origin of Evil Spirits: The Reception of Gen 6.1–4 in Early Jewish Literature*. Tübingen: Mohr Siebeck, 2005.

Wright, Benjamin G., III. "1 Enoch and Ben Sira: Wisdom and Apocalypticism in Relationship." Pages 159–76 in Boccaccini and Collins, eds., *The Early Enoch Literature*.

———. "Putting the Puzzle Together: Some Suggestions Concerning the Social Location of the Wisdom of Ben Sira." Pages 89–112 in Wright and Wills, eds., *Conflicted Boundaries*.

Wright, Benjamin G., III, and Lawrence M. Wills, eds. *Conflicted Boundaries in Wisdom and Apocalypticism*. Atlanta: SBL, 2005.

Wright, John W. "Remapping Yehud: The Borders of Yehud and the Genealogies of Chronicles." Pages 67–90 in Lipschits and Oeming, eds., *Judah and the Judeans*.

Xenophon. *Anabasis*. Translated by Carleton L. Brownson and John Dillery. *Anabasis*. LCL. Cambridge, Mass.: Harvard University Press, 2006.

———. *Cyropaedia*. Translated by Walter Miller. *Cyropaedia, Books V–VIII*. LCL. Cambridge, Mass.: Harvard University Press, 2000.

———. *Cyropaedia*. Translated by Walter Miller. *Cyropaedia, Books I–IV*. LCL. Cambridge, Mass.: Harvard University Press, 2001.

Yamamoto, Kumiko. *The Oral Background of Persian Epics: Storytelling and Poetry*. Leiden: Brill, 2003.

Yamauchi, Edwin M. *Persia and the Bible*. Grand Rapids, Mich.: Baker, 1996.

———. "The Scythians: Invading Hordes from the Russian Steppes." *BA* 46, no. 2 (1983): 90–99.

Yarbro Collins, Adela, ed. *Cosmology and Eschatology in Jewish and Christian Apocalypticism*. Leiden: Brill, 1996.

———. *Early Christian Apocalypticism: Genre and Social Setting*. Semeia 36 (1986).

———. "Introduction: Early Christian Apocalypticism." *Semeia* 36 (1986): 1–12.

Yarshater, Ehsan. "The Feared Child in Iranian Mythology." Pages 65–68 in *K. R. Cama Oriental Institute International Congress Proceedings (5–8 January 1989)*. Bombay: K. R. Cama Oriental Institute, 1991.

———. "Iranian Common Beliefs and Worldview." *CHI* 3.1:343–58.

———. "Iranian National History." *CHI* 3.1:359–480.

———. "Were the Sasanians Heirs to the Achaemenids?" Pages 517–33 in *Atti Del Convegno internazionale sul tempa La Persia nel Medioevo*. Rome: Accademia Nazionale dei Lincei, 1971.

Yates, Frances A. *The Art of Memory*. Chicago: University of Chicago Press, 1966.

Younger, K. Lawson, Jr. "The Deportations of the Israelites." *JBL* 117, no. 2 (1998): 201–27.

Zadok, Ran. "The Ethno-Linguistic Character of Northwestern Iran and Kurdistan in the Neo-Assyrian Period." *Iran* 40 (2002): 89–151.

———. "Iranians and Individuals Bearing Iranian Names in Achaemenid Babylonia." *IOS*7 (1977): 89–138.

———. *The Jews in Babylonia During the Chaldean and Achaemenian Periods*. Haifa: University of Haifa, 1979.

———. "Die nichthebräischen Namen der Israeliten vor dem Hellenistischen Zeitalter." *Ugarit-Forschungen* 17 (1986): 387–98.

———. "On Five Iranian Names in the Old Testament." *VT* 26, no. 2 (1976): 246–47.

———. "On the Connections Between Iran and Babylonia in the Sixth Century B.C." *Iran* 14 (1976): 61–78.

———. *On West Semites in Babylonia During the Chaldean and Achaemenian Periods: An Onomastic Study (Revised)*. Jerusalem: H. J. & Z. Wanaarta, 1978.

Zaehner, R. C. *The Dawn and Twilight of Zoroastrianism*. London: Phoenix, 2003. First published 1961.

———. *The Teachings of the Magi: A Compendium of Zoroastrian Beliefs*. London, 1956.

———. "A Zervanite Apocalypse I." *BSOAS* 10 (1940): 337–98.

———. "A Zervanite Apocalypse II." *BASOR* 10, no. 3 (1940): 606–31.

———. *Zurvan, a Zoroastrian Dilemma*. Oxford: Clarendon, 1955.

———. "Zurvanica I." *BSOAS* 9, no. 2 (1938): 303–20.

Zand, Michael. "Bukhara VII: Bukharan Jews." *EncIr* 4 (1990): 530–45.

Zimmerli, Walther. *Ezekiel 1: A Commentary on the Book of the Prophet Ezekiel, Chapters 1–24*. Translated by Ronald E. Clements. Philadelphia: Fortress, 1979.

———. *Ezekiel 2: A Commentary on the Book of the Prophet Ezekiel Chapters 25–48*. Translated by James D. Martin. Philadelphia: Fortress, 1983.

Zutterman, Christophe. "The Bow in the Ancient Near East: A Re-evaluation of Archery from the Late 2nd Millennium to the End of the Achaemenid Empire." *Iranica Antiqua* 38 (2003): 119–65.

INDEXES

INDEX OF REFERENCES

Index of Authors